# Mr. Tambourine Man

By

NICHOLSON

**Gotham Books**

30 N Gould St.
Ste. 20820, Sheridan, WY 82801
https://gothambooksinc.com/

Phone: 1 (307) 464-7800

© 2023 *Nicholson*. All rights reserved.

No part of this book may be reproduced, stored in a retrieval system, or transmitted by any means without the written permission of the author.

Published by Gotham Books (May 20, 2023)

ISBN: 979-8-88775-294-5 (P)
ISBN: 979-8-88775-295-2 (E)

Because of the dynamic nature of the Internet, any web addresses or links contained in this book may have changed since publication and may no longer be valid.

The views expressed in this work are solely those of the author and do not necessarily reflect the views of the publisher, and the publisher hereby disclaims any responsibility for them

# Contents

Chapter 1: First Base .................................................................. 7
Chapter 2: Going to the United States .................................... 11
Chapter 3: And Life Goes On .................................................. 15
Chapter 4: What Next? ............................................................. 19
Chapter 5: The Lonrho Years ................................................... 21
Chapter 6: Being a Dad ............................................................ 33
Chapter 7: After Lonrho .......................................................... 37
Chapter 8: Mr. Tambourine Man ............................................. 44

    Travels before the Gap Years ............................................. 47
    Gap Year Travels .................................................................. 49
    August 1999 Skiathos ........................................................... 50
    December 1999 Monaco ...................................................... 50
    April 2000 Paris .................................................................... 51
    August 2000 Zakinthos ........................................................ 52
    April 2001 Ile De Re ............................................................ 53
    August 2001 Skiathos ........................................................... 55
    April 2002 Vail. Colorado .................................................... 56
    August 2002 Zakynthos ....................................................... 57
    April 2003 Le Touquet ......................................................... 58
    July 2003 Sivota, Greece ...................................................... 58
    August 2003 Zakynthos ....................................................... 59
    May 2004 Hossegor, France ................................................ 60
    August 2004 Hossegor ......................................................... 61
    December 2004 Lanzarote ................................................... 62
    August 2005 Hossegor ......................................................... 64
    November 2005 Antigua ...................................................... 65
    July 2006 Crete ..................................................................... 68
    August 2007 Skiathos ........................................................... 69
    November 2007 Singapore, Malaysia, Thailand ................ 70

April 2008 Los Angeles, Mexico, New York ........................... 76
August 2008 Los Angeles, Mexico, New York ......................... 79
November 2008 Los Angeles, Mexico .................................. 82
March 2009 Los Angeles, Mexico ...................................... 84
Time for Decisions ....................................................... 86
July 2009 Los Angeles, Monument Valley ............................ 87
September 2009 Lemnos, Greece ...................................... 93
November 2009 Los Angeles. Palm Springs ......................... 95
February 2010 Los Angeles, Mexico .................................. 98
May 2010 Los Angeles .................................................. 102
July 2010 Los Angeles Yosemite ..................................... 104
November 2010 Los Angeles, Tucson, Santa Fe, Amarillo,
    Tulsa, St. Louis, Carmel ......................................... 108
February 2011 Los Angeles, Australia ............................... 114
July 2011 Marina del Cantonese, near Naples ..................... 127
August 2011 Los Angeles, Carmel, Eureka, Oregon Coast
    Trout Lake, Nspa ................................................. 129
November 2011 Rome .................................................. 136
December 2011 Paris ................................................... 138
March 2012 Los Angeles, Cook Islands .............................. 140
July 2012 Cornwall, Cognac ........................................... 147
September 2012 Venice, Pesaro ...................................... 150
November 2012 Miami, Key West, New Orleans,
    Los Angeles ........................................................ 153
February 2013 Grenada ................................................ 159
June 2013 Juan Les Pins ............................................... 163
August 2013 Padstow ................................................... 165
September 2013 Los Angeles, Carmel, Bodega Bay
    Lake Tahoe ......................................................... 166
November 2013 Naples ................................................. 170
December 2013 Los Angeles .......................................... 172
February 2014 Los Angeles, Hawaii .................................. 173
April 2004 Whitstable .................................................. 179
July 2014 Amsterdam .................................................. 180
August 2014 Sicily ...................................................... 181
November 2014 Hongkong, Vietnam ................................. 184
December 2014 New York, Queen Mary ............................ 192
March 2015 Portugal ................................................... 196
July 2015 Sicily .......................................................... 199

August 2015 France .................................................................. 202
October 2015 Portugal ............................................................. 205
November 2015 Miami .............................................................. 207
February 2016 St Lucia ............................................................. 213
April 2016 Los Angeles, Mexico ............................................... 217
June 2016 Sicily ......................................................................... 222
August 2016 Skiathos ................................................................ 228
September 2016 Rhodes ........................................................... 230
November 2016 Madeira ........................................................... 232
February 2017 Cruising the Carribean ..................................... 237
April 2017 Lisbon ...................................................................... 244
June 2017 Sicily ......................................................................... 246
September 2017 Sardinia ......................................................... 248
October 2017 Languedoc ......................................................... 250
November 2017 Seychelles ...................................................... 251
February 2018 Cuba .................................................................. 255
April 2018 Algarve .................................................................... 260
June 2018 Cardiff And Sicily .................................................... 261
August 2018 Los Angeles, Mexico ........................................... 266
September 2018 Calabria ......................................................... 270
November 2018 Marrakesh ...................................................... 271
January 2019 Langkawi ............................................................ 272
June 2019 Sicily ......................................................................... 279
August 2019 Scilly Isles ............................................................ 284
September 2019 Calabria ......................................................... 284
November 2019 Venice ............................................................ 285
January 2020 Singapore And Indonesia ................................. 288
March 2022 Cyprus ................................................................... 293
June 2022 Los Angeles ............................................................. 294
August 2022 Sicily ..................................................................... 297

Conclusion ...................................................................................... 304
Restaurants ..................................................................................... 308
Recipes ............................................................................................ 317
Movies ............................................................................................. 324
Books ............................................................................................... 335
About the Author ........................................................................... 347
About the Book .............................................................................. 348

# Chapter 1

# **First Base**

Our story starts in 1965. It is a time of change. All kids have been brought up in strict Victorian households, where they are not allowed to have any opinions. In fact, they are hardly allowed to speak.

When I was nearly twelve, my parents had a party to celebrate their fortieth birthdays, which were three days apart. My sister and I were sent to bed in our pajamas. Sometime during the evening, we were paraded in front of their friends but not allowed to say anything.

Many years later, when I turned fifty, I had a party in the garden with 120 people. David White, a great DJ from Radio Cornwall, played the music. My only daughter was nearly thirteen. I was delighted to have her there with a few friends and her similarly aged godbrothers, and we all danced the night away together. But the times they are a-changing, as Bob Dylan famously sang to us, and music will have a profound effect on everybody. It probably started with the Beatles and, to a lesser extent, the Rolling Stones. My bigoted mother hated 'Satisfaction' because she only heard the words, 'He can't be a man because he doesn't smoke,' and ignoring 'the same cigarettes as me.'

Pirate radio was our saviour, and Radio Caroline and Radio London were our lifelines to a new real world where we could be free. In 1965, the pirates played 'Mr. Tambourine Man' a lot. One day, I was walking in my local town and looked in the shop window of Greens, the local music store, and there displayed in its orange

CBS sleeve was the forty-five of 'Mr. Tambourine Man.' It just looked wonderful, and I wanted it, but no chance. In 1965, thirteen-year-olds had no money except perhaps from generous relatives at birthdays and Christmas. So it was not to be. Does anybody remember 'The Ten Ton Yellow Mustard Seed' on Radio Caroline or London? Every night around 7.15, they played three psychedelic music tracks. It was always 'Light My Fire' by the Doors, 'White Rabbit' from Jefferson Airplane, and one other really out of the way.

We will get to own the great song, and it will have very real impact at extraordinary times. But that is to follow.

We had no money in 1965 and could not see how we would ever have any money. So how did we get money? When you were fifteen, you could get a holiday job and earn a little. And it was a little; in the sixties, there was no minimum wage, so schoolkids were exploited. My first job was as a cashier in Golden Egg. The pay rate was supposed to be four shillings and six pence per hour for the eleven-to-four shift, five days per week, and free Golden Egg lunches. But somehow it became just four shillings per hour, or a hundred shillings per week (I think it is £5 in today's money). Of course, you had to pay the train fare to get there, but compared to some, I was probably rich. What did I learn from this? That I hated fried food every day - and to think that people paid for it - and God, work is even more boring than school.

In my next holiday job, I did learn a couple of things. I moved up to be a dogsbody in the Debenhams Food Hall. I came in early to unload the bread, stack the shelves, fill the freezer compartments, work on the bacon counter and, if really lucky, the hot pies. You could get a free one for lunch, which was probably stealing. The ultimate was to work the tills. At coffee and tea breaks, I learned something by spending time with the full-time employees. I could see I had to do something with my life to avoid being stuck in an endless life of boredom. If you talked to these people, you found out they had nothing to say of any interest whatsoever. I didn't want to be one of those.

Much more exciting was the girl on the Parker Pen counter. She was five years older and just finished teacher training college.

## Mr. Tambourine Man

We became very good friends after I met her at Mr. Mos Messenger's dance, which she attended to be with her married boyfriend, Mr. Mos, who obviously didn't take his wife to gigs.

I also met Jane Llewellyn, or Janie Loo, at the same dance hall and boasted about Leonard Cohen. She had his album, too: *Suzanne*, still one of the greatest records ever. My mum hated it when she came to pick me up in her Vauxhall Viva. At this time, I thought I had really made it.

Spooky Tooth, a great group, played at the same dance hall once. I still have two of their forty-fives: 'Sunshine Help Me' and 'Love Really Changed Me,' which I played the other day. You should really check them out. They were released on Island Records, the baby of Chris Blackwell, who championed a lot of great music and discovered Bob Marley. In 1988, I shared a taxi with him into Manhattan after getting off the Concorde. We had a great chat, and I got to pay the cab fare because he got out first. By this time, he had sold Island for hundreds of millions and got into hotels in the Caribbean. So how did we get to go on the Concorde? Our story will tell us.

The next great musical event happened in March 1969, before humans had even been to the moon. It was the annual school dance, and we had a band to play. It was Free, who were quite big then and became superstars later with 'All Right Now.' Paul Simon once played at the school Folk Club, but I missed it. 'Homeward Bound' is one to remember. It does not seem believable that these superstars were in the habit of visiting obscure schools, but they had to eat and pay the rent.

Here we met my first love, Katy. It only lasted six months or so, with me going to Spain for five weeks and her going to the United States for six weeks. She was the first and only girl to dump me, and about once a month, I still think of her fondly. She must be over sixty years old by now and is probably an uninteresting old woman.

I am now over sixty and don't look forward to the milestones at all. Sometime ago, Eric Clapton and Johnnie Walker the DJ turned sixty in the same week, and a one-hour show played their favourite music, and they chatted. One said when he was fifty, sixty seemed really old, and he wondered what it would be like to be seventy.

Well, Paul McCartney was seventy in June 2012, and his gig for the Queen's Diamond Jubilee was a pretty special set of four songs for millions of people. Going back to 1965, who would have predicted that the music would live on, still sound fantastic, and be part of the establishment? My favourite Beatles album is still *With the Beatles*.

# Chapter 2

# Going to the United States

Somehow, I got to eighteen without being chucked out of school. I took three A levels and an S level. I failed physics O level and somehow got to do maths for A level, which were pure maths, at which I was brilliant (100 per cent in the mocks), and applied maths, just like physics (10 per cent in the mocks). I cannot believe that we were never given proper advice about our subjects. It could have been so different.

The day after my birthday, on July 3, I boarded a British Caledonian Boeing 707 and went to New York. I had a job in an office for six weeks and then a Greyhound bus ticket to take me anywhere I wanted to go in the United States.

There were many good things about this. Mainly, for the first time ever, I was able to get away from the repressive home environment and could do what I wanted to do when I wanted (except, of course, when I had to go to work). Secondly, I was earning some money. I decided to live like a king in the United States, but to make sure I didn't run out of money, I had a budget of $10 per day (which was £4 at 1970 exchange rates). Lastly, the United States is a great place. After Essex, it is huge and the land of opportunity.

I believe my three months in the United States transformed my life. It enabled me to always see the bigger picture. I think if I had spent that holiday working in the Debenhams Food Hall, I would not have been able to achieve anything much in life. I would strongly advise all mums and dads to send their kids into the world as soon as possible to make them bigger people. My daughter went to Los Angeles for a year two days after her nineteenth birthday and stayed nearly six years. She came back a much more confident and worldly wise person.

So what did I do in New York? First of all, I stayed in the YMCA, but I did not like it. I found a cheap hotel just off Times Square; I liked it even less. I used to go to Howard Johnsons for the 'all-you-can-eat' chicken and fish on Wednesdays and Fridays. The waiter told me his neighbour was looking for a lodger. I went up to East Ninety-Sixth Street and did a deal for a room with bars on the windows (so I couldn't get out) and food, if I was there, for $10 per week. It suited me fine.

There were too many highlights to list, but surprise, surprise, I loved the city and still love it to this day. I spent New Year's Eve 2014 in New York with my godson and our wives. I paid the bill, which was expensive, and he later took us to Rafele, this amazing Italian restaurant in Greenwich Village. I thought it was pretty good so checked it out on Trip Advisor. Rafele is number eleven out of 8,800 restaurants in New York; everybody should go there. As we progress, I will talk about food quite a lot.

When I was in New York, I met this gorgeous girl from Boston. It was now time to get on the Greyhound, and I thought, why not Boston first, so I called her. She was so excited to hear from me, and we arranged to meet at the bus station on Saturday lunchtime. I arrived in Boston on a beautiful sunny August day. And there was this gorgeous blonde girl, so excited to see me. We went into the car park to her convertible Mustang. Heaven: I had only driven an 850cc Mini at home. We drove to the Cambridge area of Boston and pulled up outside a beautiful old Victorian house. I thought, *I am going to just stay here and go nowhere else; who needs America?* We went inside, and she introduced me to her boyfriend. He was very polite and played me both sides of *Sweet Baby James* by James Taylor (still one of my favourite records). When she reappeared, I made my excuses and left to meet some friends from the plane. I slept on their floor for a couple of nights, and then I went back to the bus station.

'Please, may I have a ticket from Boston to San Francisco?'
'Certainly, sir.'
'And how long will that take?'
'Seventy-two hours.'

The first night, I didn't sleep a wink and will always remember the middle of the night in Cleveland. The bus station was full of drug dealers and pimps; it was really quite scary. After that, I always went to sleep from dusk to dawn and found sleeping on the bus a good way of saving money.

And so to San Francisco, a lovely city. I ended up on honeymoon there ten years later.

After San Francisco, I took the Greyhound seventy miles south to Morgan Hill, to meet an old friend of the family, who was staying in this ten-bedroom, nine-bathroom house with three girlfriends and a load of kids. For the weekend, the husbands came down from Seattle, and I had a life-changing experience. On Saturday, an Italian woman Millie was brought in to cook us lunch. And what did she make? Pizza. I was eighteen years old and had never experienced the wonderfulness of a good pizza. That is what happens if you are brought up in the restricted atmosphere of Essex. I loved the pizza and still love a good pizza to this day.

It was now time to leave Morgan Hill. On a Sunday morning, I turned up at the bus station, but I misread the timetable, and there were fewer buses on Sunday. The next bus to Los Angeles was not for two hours, so I decided to hitch-hike. I got a lift in a beat-up old car with a strange guy who said he was a schoolteacher (but that was not really believable). We stopped because he wanted a beer; he didn't buy me one, as I was only eighteen, and you had to be twenty-one to drink in California. Then he wanted me to drive; to be honest, I failed with the stickshift. Hey, I had only driven a Mini. He was driving again and there was no conversation; just as we were approaching Salinas, he pulled off the freeway and said he had to take some prunes to his aunt. I thought this was the end, but he let me out, and I hot-footed it to the bus station and waited. I went back to Salinas many years later and visited the Steinbeck Museum. Everybody should go.

And everybody should go to the Grand Canyon. No helicopter sightseeing tours for poor old student me. I met a guy on the bus there, and we decided to walk down. We bought water, oranges, and bread and got to the bottom in about ninety minutes. There were about ten people there with food, wine, guitars, and dope; we had a wonderful evening and slept on a rock. With sunrise, we dipped our feet in the Colorado River and set off back. The temperature got to 100 degrees, and it took ten hours to get back to LA. But nevertheless, it was one of the great experiences ever. And had a Chinese meal in Flagstaff on the way back. Took my wife to the Grand Canyon many years later, and it was still the most spectacular place.

When I was in the United States, I rediscovered Van Morrison and his first solo album, *Blowin' Your Mind*, which had a number of great tracks, including 'Brown-Eyed Girl' and 'TB Sheets.' Shortly after, he made *Astral Weeks*, which still remains one of the greatest albums ever.

# Chapter 3

# **And Life Goes On**

While all this was happening, the A level results came, and I did all right. An A in Geography, and I passed the S level. I must be going to university. But wait, no, my father has decided that it would be much better for me to become a chartered accountant. After all, university is a waste of time and really too much fun. He got me hired by a chartered accountant, and I was sent to the City of London Polytechnic for a year to pass the Foundation exam.

It all seemed pretty boring, but I did enjoy Economics, and I passed. Auditing was a complete mystery.

The best thing that happened was the Rag Week Walk, London to Canterbury, setting off at midnight and getting there who-knows-when. My partner was a very fit girl who played hockey for Wales schoolgirls. We had a few drinks, and off we went down the A2. It all seemed quite tiring, and by 3 a.m., we had maybe done about ten miles; the relief transit van appeared and asked if anybody needed a lift. I did and decided to leave my partner and had an uncomfortable journey to University of Kent. She arrived at around four in the afternoon, having walked the whole way, and has not spoken to me to this day.

Another girl who no longer speaks to me is Nina Harris. We went out a few times and had fun, and then I heard Ian Dury's 'Billericay Dickie' (Billericay is where Chrissie comes from), with the immortal line 'Nina in the back of my Cortina.' Nina only came in the back of the Mini, which I guess was not as good as a Cortina.

During the Christmas holidays, I was a postman. I used to take my bag in the Mini in the early morning, deliver all the Christmas cards, and go straight back to work, where I got told off for being back to early; after that, I always had a coffee at home before going back. When I got my wage packet, I went off to the record shop to buy Neil Young's *After the Goldrush*, still one of my favourite albums (it comes up early on the i-Pod when you search albums), but my favourite Neil Young track will always be 'Cowgirl in the Sand,' especially if it is a twenty-minute live version.

And so to the chartered accountants. My first job was to go out on an audit, which was still a complete mystery. We went to the Otis Elevator Company, mostly in London, but we did have a couple of trips to Liverpool. Most notably, I was asked to audit the wages but had no idea what I was supposed to do. The wages man was very unhelpful and quite rude, so I had to go and see the audit manager. 'Don't worry,' he said. 'I'll do it.'

And he did and discovered the wages man was on the fiddle, something to do with rounding off some numbers, with the balance going to his bank account; he ended up in jail. He should have been nice to me, and I would have probably just ticked all the boxes; there were an awful lot of boxes to tick in auditing, which is I guess what makes it so exciting. Another box story was counting expensive equipment at a factory in Croydon. The things we were supposed to be counting were in a barrel covered in thick oil. As I was in my suit, I just accepted the count and ticked my box.

Life as an auditor was actually quite fun. I went to many exciting places, like Bethnal Green, Shepherds Bush, and Slough, but the most exciting was two six-week periods in Havant at Normand Electrical. SH Benson, the advertising agency, was also good fun. We used to go to the first Pizza Express by the British Museum for lunch. Still go to Pizza Express from time to time, and it's still surprisingly good.

What wasn't such fun was the pay. We were paid £800 per year or £16 per week, which came to £56 per month after tax and National Insurance. This meant I never had much money, just enough to go

## Mr. Tambourine Man

down to the pub from time to time. But in the summer of 1972, I did manage somehow to go to Corfu, Greece. The main memory was seeing girls sunbathing topless for the first time. Brilliant; it was so nice to see. I have seen thousands of topless girls, but the first ones were the best. The music was good too; that summer, 'School's Out' by Alice Cooper and 'Suffragette City' by David Bowie were played all the time.

I failed to get on the plane going home, as I hadn't confirmed my seat (too much drinking and watching topless girls). I've been in love with Greece ever since. I can't remember much about the food, except waiting a long time for chips; I went into the kitchen to observe an old lady slowly peeling the potatoes. The big question was, was I ever going to make any real money?

About this time, I was becoming increasingly frustrated with life in Essex; even today, I still hate going back. Easy solution: get married. I saw the error of my ways early enough to get out, and I got the ring back, but that's what you do.

Through all of this, I managed to pass the two finals so I could become a chartered accountant. It was quite good because you got six weeks' study leave before the exams and did twelve weeks of evening classes, so it was pretty hard work. Evening classes were a lot better than the Foulkes Lynch correspondence course, which I could never get the hang of. And I grew a beard.

But what to do next? Much to my surprise, I was actually a pretty damned good accountant, one of the best. The firm that hired me offered me a partnership in a couple of years. Quite tempting, really: the safe option and potential for loads of money. Maybe it was because I had been to America and saw the bigger picture, but somehow it all seemed a bit small.

Before we move on, I better talk about my love life. On 11 August 1973, when I was two-thirds of a chartered accountant, about five weeks after I turned twenty-one, I went to the Zero Six in Southend on a Saturday night. I had always had the girls queuing up, as I was very good looking. Across the room, I saw this gorgeous girl. What should I do? I guess I better chat her up.

I wandered over, and my first line was, 'I am fed up with talking to girls, so I thought I would come and talk to you.'

It sort of worked; we danced all night and arranged to meet the next night. When I went to pick her up, she was not ready, so I had to be nice to her mother. I have always been very good at this, and it is a good plan, as you can get away with murder.

When we got in the Mini, I put my glasses on to drive; she said, 'I didn't know you wore glasses.'

Good start.

But it got better, and seven years later, Chrissie and I got married in a church in Little Venice, London, and had a reception at Didier, a French restaurant, for thirty people. It was one of the greatest days of my life, and we're still going strong after thirty-six years.

# Chapter 4

# What Next?

I didn't want to be an accountant for the rest of my life and decided to go into business. It had to be more exciting. Actually, it wasn't because I went as assistant group accountant to a company where all the directors had the same name as the company. It was all so dull; the most exciting thing I did was go to meetings with a hangover. The salary was great, £3,000 per year, which was more than I had ever made.

Chrissie and I moved into flat in Golders Green in West Heath Road, overlooking Hampstead Heath. It was great, except the night she tried to cook moussaka for some friends, including the great John Smethwick of Irish brewery fame, who declared it the best ever (what a bullshitter). Luckily, over the years, her cooking has got a lot better.

The office was in Park Lane, and I often saw Tiny Rowland from Lonrho, who lived opposite. I read about him a lot and thought he was a great man. Every Thursday, I used to look in the *Financial Times* jobs for a new challenge, and one day, I saw an advertisement for a job, but there was no company name; for some reason, I thought it must be Lonrho. I phoned up the employment agent and got an interview. The best thing to do the night before an interview is have a dinner party, which we did, finishing the night with a couple of bottles of port. Disaster. I managed to wake up the next morning at 9.15 for a 9.30 interview. Rush, rush, rush, and got there at about 9.50.

Nevertheless, I was very relaxed (and still a bit pissed from the night before).

I had no cigarettes, and the interview took about two hours; afterwards, I bummed a cigarette from the interviewer, and then I was offered the job. This was actually the last job I ever applied for, and it seems obvious what the tactics should be. I really wanted this job, but instead of an early night to be on top form, we had the dinner party. I got the job, so the advice has to be if you really want a job, just get hammered the night before so you turn up relaxed and composed, and they just have to give you the job.

I handed in my notice and went off to Luz Bay in the Algarve, Portugal, for a two-week holiday before the new job. In the first week, I met the son of the chairman, and we had a good time.

He said, 'Dad's coming next week, so you must visit him.'

My partner and two of our friends (one of the girls looked like Joanna Lumley) went over for lunchtime drinks. We had white port, which was very nice, but we got pissed quite quickly. The chairman and his wife had two friends, and they were quite dull. When Mrs. Chairman said lunch was ready, we tried to make our exit. Mr. Chairman was obviously also bored with the company and insisted we stay for another drink. We did, and he told me off for leaving the company. Another lesson: If you want to get on in a company, just go to the chairman's villa in the sunshine with a couple of pretty girls and show him what he's missing, and you will get promoted.

Despite this, I did go to Lonrho on 1 October 1976, still an assistant group accountant but now earning £4,000 per year.

I was to stay there for years and finish as associate director, earning £95,000.

# Chapter 5

# The Lonrho Years

During my sixteen years at Lonrho, I became a businessman. To be honest, I am not sure how this came about, but I'll try to explain. I'm not sure that everyone who wants to be a businessman should necessarily follow my lead, but here goes.

For the first two years, I carried on as an assistant group accountant but somehow got noticed for my potential. I even had a trip to Malawi and South Africa, which was a lot better than Cheapside. And I have to mention one of my colleagues, who I will call Paul. I didn't talk about my schooldays much, but I never really fitted in. I hated the discipline and generally considered the masters inferior, and as already mentioned, I did all the wrong A levels. I never even made it to prefect. Paul had been deputy head prefect and the leader of the CCF (this is like ROTC in America, where you have to play soldiers and dress up in uniform once a week and march around and fire guns with blanks). When we left school, everybody would have said he is really going make it in the world, but poor old Paul was going nowhere. He got sacked for incompetence, and I went on, I think, to achieve great things.

After two years, because of my potential, I was promoted to executive (interesting job title). The job description was to work with a senior executive, monitoring company performance. There were about eight hundred companies in the group, in about thirty subdivisions. Additionally, we worked on acquisitions and disposals as necessary, from time to time. This was more like it, and I took to it like a duck to water. And I even got a company car.

So far in my life, I had only driven Minis. Sometime after I was twenty-one, I bought myself a white MG Midget convertible for £700 (one of my favourite cars to this day). After a few years, I upgraded to an MGB convertible and then a nearly new black MGB GT. And then I bought a Volkswagen Scirocco. But I had to sell the MGB GT. I put it into the Exchange and Mart, and the only call was from Cornwall. We agreed on a deal, and I agreed to take it down on the May bank holiday.

I drove the new Scirocco, and Chrissie followed in the MG. After driving for some time down the M5, I looked in my mirror, and she wasn't there. I pulled over to the hard shoulder. Eventually, she turned up and said there was a problem with the fuel. I followed her, and she stopped about four times before we got there (pretty late). I explained the problem, and as the car was still under warranty, so the deal went through.

On the way back, we got to the Lugger in Portloe just before closing time and had a lovely dinner of lobster with lots of champagne and wine. (I stayed there again in 2015; it was still a lovely hotel, although the food was a little touristy.)

One of the first things I did at Lonrho was develop a monthly sheet for each subdivision, detailing performance that month for turnover, gross margin, overheads, and net profit, compared to budget and to the previous year. This became a key tool for monitoring the performance of the businesses, and I have continued to use a version of it to this day. Later, we also developed a similar tool for cashflow and working capital, which was equally important. Profit is great, but cashflow is king.

In order to monitor the company performance, we were appointed to subsidiary boards and usually attended monthly board meetings. The first board I was appointed to was a new acquisition: Harrisons in High Wycombe. Harrisons printed stamps for the Royal Mail and had just started printing currency. I got in my new Scirocco and drove to High Wycombe, arriving in good time. The board meeting started, and I listened attentively, but I probably didn't say anything. The first meeting is always very hard; I've now attended thousands of board meetings; today, I probably say too much, but you have to start somewhere. But attending board meetings is nevertheless a great way to learn a business, and I have learnt so much over the years, sitting round the table, discussing performance and strategies.

Lonrho started in Africa in Rhodesia and grew over the years through international acquisitions. By the time I left, these were the principal businesses:

- agriculture: sugar estates, tea, cotton, and pigs in Africa
- mining: platinum in South Africa and gold in Ghana and Zimbabwe
- motors: Audi/Volkswagen in the UK, along with retail motor outlets; Toyota, Mercedes, Massey Ferguson in Africa
- hotels: Princess Hotels in Mexico, Bermuda, the Bahamas, and Arizona; Metropole Hotels in London, Birmingham, Brighton, and Blackpool; Norfolk Hotel in Nairobi, Mount Kenya Safari Club and other safari hotels
- manufacturing: Harrisons (printing), Brentford (nylons and steel processing), and others. Textiles, buses, CocaCola bottling, and others in Africa
- newspapers: *The Observer*, Scottish newspapers, and *The Standard* in Kenya
- other: insurance brokers, cotton trading, international trade finance, brewing

In all, there were around eight hundred companies, and there was never a dull day. At the same time, being involved in such a wide range of international firms was a great school for learning how to be a businessman.

'Never a dull day' meant that I got to travel an awful lot. Because I wasn't a director, I had to travel Business Class (although not even First Class had flat beds in those days, but the food and champagne were a lot better). I keep lists, which means I can now tell you where I went over the years:

Kenya (seventeen times), Zimbabwe (fourteen), United States (ten), Germany (ten), Belgium (nine), Zambia (eight), South Africa (five), Nigeria (four), Holland (three), Hungary (three), France (two), and Mexico, Australia, Bermuda, Malawi, Swaziland, Norway, Botswana, and Portugal (all once).

That is ninety-three overseas trips in my time at Lonrho. At the same time, I did a lot of travelling in the UK, with frequent trips to Newcastle, Manchester, Liverpool, Glasgow, and Edinburgh.

There were many highlights of my experiences; I will try to put them in some logical framework:

## Aeroplanes

I flew back from New York on the Concorde on a Saturday. The Concorde was just the best plane ever; I went to a dinner party and couldn't stop talking about it. Later, I paid twice to fly back from Barbados from my holidays. The second time, we were with my daughter Lauren, who was three years old at the time. Michael Winner and Jenny Seagrove were on the plane, showing off. I went to the loo with my daughter, and Jenny pushed in front of us. I was quite annoyed, but she came out after less than a minute.

I glared at her and said, 'You are very fast for a lady.'

The last time I took the Concorde to New York, I had a wonderful experience. I was waiting for a taxi, and another guy rolled up. We agreed to share when one came along. It did, and we got chatting. It was Chris Blackwell of Island Records fame; we had a good chat about Bob Marley. He got out first, so I had to pay for the cab. Bob Marley made some wonderful music; his best song has got to be 'Could You Be Loved?'

I once flew from Nairobi to Eldoret for a board meeting of the East Africa Tanning Extract Company, flying in a small six-seater twin-engine plane. We were returning, and it was the rainy season. We were in the Rift Valley, and the weather up front looked terrible. The pilot said we had to go back. Mark Newman, who was chief executive of Lonrho East Africa, and I agreed, but unfortunately, the other member of our party said we must go on. He was Mark Too, our fixer in Africa, who was also the illegitimate son of President Moi. The pilot carried on, and the forward weather got worse and worse. Eventually, Mark Too agreed to go back, but the weather behind was even worse.

The pilot said, 'Don't worry, we will go to Nanyuki,' but the weather had closed in that way too. 'Don't worry, we will go to Nakuru'; no way. Last chance: Lake Baringo. We landed on a dirt strip and walked a mile to the lodge in our suits, carrying our briefcases. Luckily, they had some rooms, and we had a very nice night (I still have the T shirt). I heard later that two planes had been lost that night in the rains.

Next up, we went to Nigeria. We owned 40 percent of a public company in Nigeria (which was all that was allowed under their law). Annual general meetings (AGMs) were held in Lagos; over three thousand people used to turn up and fight for the freebies. We decided to hold our AGMs in Abuja, where nobody would turn up, and I agreed to go. I was staying in the company flat, and my boy made me a light lunch, and then my minder turned up to take me to the airport (in Nigeria, you always needed a minder).

Anyway, we get on this old fifty-seater propeller plane with about ten other people and take off. They bring round a disgusting lunch, which I am about to decline, but my minder says to take it. He eats both lunches, and then the captain comes on the radio and says, 'We have a problem and are going back.' We slowly descended, and the jungle got closer and closer, and at last, we landed. We wandered over to a BAC1-11 on the tarmac, and my minder managed to get me on the plane. And then two more disgusting lunches, so my minder had now had four lunches and was very happy.

'Good afternoon, ladies and gentlemen, this is your captain speaking, and welcome to our flight today calling at Kano, Kaduna, and then onto Abuja.'

I told my minder that I was not happy, as it would take so long. He went up, knocked on the captain's door, and went in. Shortly after, he came back with a big smile.

'Good afternoon, ladies and gentlemen, this is your captain speaking again. Change of plan: We are going to Abuja first today.'

Abuja was built to be the federal capital of Nigeria, and it is very strange. It has ten-lane motorways, huge mosques, enormous hotels, and no people. I slept in the biggest bed ever in the Hilton. Fewer than ten people came to the AGM, which we deemed a success.

And now to South Africa, where amongst our many businesses we had the Lear Jet franchise. I accompanied Hector Sants of Phillips & Drew (who was later to become head of the Financial Services Authority) to southern Africa to look at our businesses. After a good trip through the gold mines of Zimbabwe, the sugar estates in Swaziland, and the platinum mine in South Africa, for the last day, we decided to take the Lear Jet demonstrator down to Cape Town to have a look at our businesses there. When we got there, the pilot decided to cruise Cape Town Bay at two hundred feet, at a very low speed. It was a truly great experience, which everybody should enjoy.

## Tiny Rowland

During my business career, I have been privileged to do business with very rich people, many of whom were well-known. You should not be mistaken: Very rich people are different from the rest of us. I am not sure why; maybe it's because of the time and effort required to become very rich, but they are different. Because I have dealt with many over the years, I have developed a way with these very rich people. Basically, always tell them that they are right, even if they are completely wrong, and then sort it out in your own way later. Tiny Rowland, in my view, was the cleverest and most talented of all the very rich people I have known.

Over sixteen years, I spent a reasonable amount of time with Tiny and will only recount a few instances here:

Tiny was in Mexico for his summer holidays in the late 1980s. Mexico had a financial crisis and decided to devalue the peso by 100 percent overnight. The Mexican managers went into meltdown, and Tiny decided that he needed a sensible person from London to sort it all out. I had a call from the deputy chairman at ten o'clock one night, and the next morning, I was on a plane to Acapulco via Houston. I was met at the airport by some Mexicans and taken at high speed to Tiny's villa. I was dressed for travelling in smart trousers, jacket, and tie. He opened the door, wearing just a pair of shorts and nothing else, for a man who was renowned for being smartly dressed and always attired in Saville Row suits (he privately owned the tailors Anderson & Shepherd).

He looked at me and said, 'I have been coming here for twentyfive years and never worn a tie.'

I immediately took my tie off and put it in my briefcase. The villa was beautiful and was set on a hilltop with stunning views of Acapulco Bay; he explained to me he would always have the views, as he owned all the land down to the beach (the very rich again).

Actually, the devaluation was great for us, and we made a load of money. Nearly all our customers in the Acapulco hotels were Americans. We just doubled the price of everything in pesos; to the Americans, it was still the same price, but our costs remained in pesos, which meant we made loads of money. It took about three days to persuade the Mexicans that this was the only way to go, but eventually, they came round.

Once I was in Lusaka, Zambia, at the same time as Tiny and was told he wanted to see me. I was escorted to the garden, where he was sitting in the only sunny place left that afternoon. He loved the sun, but it was eventually to kill him, as he died of skin cancer.

Tiny wanted to buy the House of Fraser and Harrods. He had acquired a 30 percent stake from Sir Hugh Fraser. Lonrho made a bid, which was referred to the Monopolies Commission, who found it was not in the public interest. Tiny was not amused, but after three years, we made another bid, which was again referred to the Monopolies Commission. This time, we were even more organised and amongst other things got an economics professor from Oxford to advise us. I went to Oxford for a meeting one afternoon, and it really is another world. It was getting close to the Monopolies Commission verdict.

Late one Friday afternoon, I was called into Tiny's office. I said that I was certain we would be successful at the Monopolies

Commission but had to admit that I couldn't guarantee it. He told us that he was working on a plan. He was going to sell the Lonrho stake to Mohamed Fayed. Fayed was in his view the worst possible person to own Harrods, and the government would be knocking on our door, begging us to buy Harrods. It didn't work out, and Fayed gained control of Harrods. In later years, this greatly distracted Tiny, and we had to spend long hours in the Fayed battle: 'From Hero to Zero,' and so on. This distraction was one of the reasons I was to eventually leave Lonrho, but more on that later.

The Monopolies Commission verdict came: Lonrho was clear to acquire House of Fraser and Harrods, but Fayed was now in control.

Despite this error, I can only describe Tiny as an inspirational leader who achieved so very much and taught me so much of what I know. I will always be grateful for the opportunities he gave me.

But if you are very rich, you don't have time to read the newspapers. One of my jobs was to get in early and read the newspapers: *Financial Times*, *Wall Street Journal*, *Sun*, and so on. Tiny would then call around nine o'clock, and I would tell him the important business and political stories. My colleagues were very jealous of my input and were always trying to find a story I missed (which was always possible).

I will always remember one summer evening. I was last in the office and picked the phone up. It was Tiny on his yacht, *Hansa*, in Antibes. He wanted to talk about business, business, and business. After a couple of hours, he most charmingly said, 'I must get home for my dinner.' Driving home, I thought about this and decided if I was very rich on my yacht in Antibes, I would not spend two hours talking to me. But I am not very rich, and I am not like Tiny, who was always totally dedicated to the business and spent every waking moment on the case. He once told me that when he saw the prospects for platinum, he spent a whole year living in a tent in the bush, buying mining rights when they became available. Platinum became Lonrho's most important asset; it just shows what dedication can achieve.

## Alan Bond

Tiny was on his boat in Antibes, as usual, and who should pull up next door but Alan Bond. Tiny had a moan to Alan, as you do, but Alan misread the signals. Next thing, he had borrowed a load of money from Merrill Lynch and bought a sizeable stake in Lonrho, declaring that he wanted to take over the company.

Tiny was furious and told us to destroy him. We got to work, analysed Alan Bond, and came to the conclusion that he was just a hall of mirrors. We produce a hundred-page document with the headline 'Alan Bond Is Technically Insolvent.' We sent the book to every bank in the world and government departments in the UK and Australia. We held press conferences in the UK and visited Australia, where we talked to everybody and appeared on television to talk about Bond's troubles. Our document had a white cover and became known as the 'White Book Defence.'

During our trip to Australia, we hooked up with the billionaire Robert Holmes A'Court, who hated Bond because he had screwed him a number of times. We had lovely lamb chops and the first wine from a new vintage from his own vineyard. But he was happy. He had just had the fuel tanks enlarged on his private Boeing 727 and could now fly from Perth to London nonstop. This is what makes you happy if you are very rich.

We were quite successful, and Alan Bond ended up going to jail; he certainly didn't take us over.

## Marriage

During my time at Lonrho, I got married to Chrissie; we had known each other for nearly eight years. I proposed in Lindos on Rhodes at the beginning of October, and she had me married by the end of November. We went to see the vicar and asked him to bless us. He asked which of us was divorced: neither. 'Okay, then, come and get married in my church,' he said, which we did in Little Venice, London, and then had a wonderful reception for thirty people in Didier's restaurant. For our honeymoon, we went to San Francisco, a glorious city. We hired a car, drove south, discovered Carmel, another glorious town; we have been back a few times since. We have always stayed in the Dolphin Inn, which has fireplaces and a nice swimming pool. For dinner, you have to go to Andre's Bouchee for fine food and an excellent wine list.

## Associate Director

After a time, I became a senior executive and was appointed to the Finance Committee. The Finance Committee was key to the company and controlled all the group finances through yearly budget meetings and approval of all acquisitions, disposals, and capital expenditures. And then later I was promoted to associate director. But I was an ambitious person and wanted to be a director, not just for the honour, but it also meant loads of money.

In the early 1990s, there was a bit of a recession going on, and Lonrho had a structural problem concerned with the Advanced Corporation Tax (ACT), which was payable on dividends and had to be written off every year, about £15 million; Lonrho had a large dividend. Tiny owned 92 million shares, or about 14 percent of the company, and would get dividends of about £13 million per year.

I sat down with some of my colleagues and we put together a master plan to help the company deal with the ACT problem. Tiny was getting on for eighty years old; he hated change and also hated our plan.

A small story about Ashraf Marwan. He had been head of security for President Nasser in Egypt but had an affair with one of his wives and left for London, where he became a celebrated businessman and a very good friend of Tiny. He bought two properties from us; I went to the completion meeting, where he was supposed to pay with banker's drafts. He smiled at me and said there were no banker's drafts but would a personal cheque be okay? I had about one second to reply - there were a lot of considerations - but said yes (with a lot of trepidation). Luckily, his lawyer then said that was no good, for tax reasons, and they would use a solicitor's cheque: job done.

Ashraf was eventually found dead below his penthouse on Jermyn Street. The coroner did not rule out foul play.

Tiny had a lot of very good friends and liked to help people who were down on their luck. Jim Slater had been everyone's business hero in the 1970s. He had this idea of buying old mansion blocks in London and selling off the flats one by one, so we had a joint venture, Strongmead. I went to a meeting in Wimbledon but never met him. The JV was a great success. I did meet Freddie Laker, who had the office next to mine. He didn't turn me on, and I was shocked that he got the tea ladies to cut his hair. We worked on suing British Airways and setting up Laker 2. The story was leaked to the newspapers, and after talking to our contacts with the *Observer*, we found out who had leaked it. He was shown the door and left with his briefcase and a pencil.

One of the most distressing stories was our chairman, Edward du Cann. He was an MP and quite greedy; he was paid around £400,000 per annum by Lonrho. One of my responsibilities was PJH Group, which sold kitchens and bathrooms. Edward came to my office one day and asked me to arrange for the MD to have a meeting with a friend of his. Me and Steve went off to a serviced office by Marble Arch, where we were met by Edward and Anthony Dobson, a strange man with bouffant grey hair and elevated shoes. He said that his company, called Homes Assured, arranged mortgages for people to buy their homes; they had this great idea of arranging a bigger mortgage so the homeowner could have a new kitchen and bathroom. He wanted a credit line from PJH.

As I had been taught to do, we said yes, yes, yes, and left. After getting back to the office, we checked Anthony Dobson with our friends at the *Observer*; they sent over an article detailing his fraudulent and criminal past. We called Edward into the office, showed him the article, and told him to reconsider his position. He went bright red, flew into a rage, and told us not to interfere in his business. Within a year, there was a criminal investigation of Homes Assured; Edward had to resign as Lonrho's chairman and faced ruin: a lesson to be very careful who you deal with.

It was getting near my fortieth birthday.

At the same time, I was approached to become finance director of a company in a corporate recovery situation. I was being offered a basic pay of £200,000 per annum plus performance-related bonuses.

It all sounded very interesting. I somehow managed to get myself into the Lonrho board for a discussion about the future. I made a great play to be appointed to the board, which I have already said was my ambition, knowing I had this new job opportunity in the background. A couple of days later, my appointment was rejected.

I had been with Lonrho for sixteen years and had a wonderful time. I started as a lowly assistant group accountant and now was an associate director. I had moved on from being just a good accountant to being a businessman with a huge experience of international finance. I didn't really want to go. I had a wife and three-year-old daughter to support, and there were risks in corporate recovery. But hey, you have to move on, and I decided to leave for the big pay pack

# Chapter 6

# **Being a Dad**

Whilst I was at Lonrho, I also became a dad. It was quite complicated. Chrissie and I discovered we could not have children, but we still wanted a family. Our doctor introduced us to the Phyllis Holman Adoption Society in Putney. It was a lovely society that had been started many years ago by a rich lady who found a newborn baby in a phone box and decided to try and help. They did lots of checks on us and found us to be okay.

We used to go for social Sunday lunches from time to time and met people with their new children. The waiting was hard.

On 11 August 1989, Chrissie had a call from the adoption agency, saying they had a kid for us. Great; it was a great way to celebrate our anniversary. On Saturday morning, we went to Mothercare to buy all the necessary supplies (we got a few odd looks, as she did not look pregnant). And then we were off to Queen Mary's in Roehampton to be introduced to this beautiful healthy girl called Lauren. We were told we could take her home the next day. We had a dinner party that night and told our friends, and then we went to bed.

Crash. A car had collided with four cars outside our house, but luckily not ours.

We picked up our beautiful daughter and took her home in a Moses basket. We got home, and I fell in love with my daughter and have loved her to this day. When we were going through the adoption, I sort of just went on with it, with no real paternal feelings.

But the moment I became a dad, it was truly wonderful; it must have been in there somewhere. I was always worried that her birth mother would change her mind; it was a huge relief the day we went to court, and it was all formalised for ever and ever.

I worked very hard and was never at home, but I made up for it in a few ways. Firstly, I used to tell her a story every night. The story went on for many years and was loosely based on *Star Trek*. The hero was Strakelov (in fact, a real Russian astronaut who I had met; he told me great stories about malfunctions and generals who wouldn't abort launches even when there were problems), Mister and Missus Poo, and a few others who had fantastic adventures in outer space. Next, every Saturday morning, I took her shopping, and she managed to acquire about a hundred Barbie dolls - lucky thing. And then I taught her to swim. By the time she was one year old, she could almost swim by herself.

It was time for our first summer holiday, but where should we go? We wanted sun but not too hot. In the end, we decided to go to Paxos in Greece for the last week of September and the first two weeks of October. Not a great journey, with plane and boat, but we arrived. When we got onto the beach, Lauren hated it. She hated the sand, and the sea was so big, not like the swimming pool. Luckily, she got used to it and loved the wonderful island of Paxos; we swam every day, except one day, she got ill on the beach, and we had to take her to a doctor. They suggested we give her rice water; I kept asking where I could buy it, until they explained you just boiled rice and took the water. To make sure she got better, he gave her a few suppositories - poor thing.

Paxos was so good; we were to have many holidays in Greece over the next eighteen years. My favourite place was Skiathos. It has wonderful beaches, particularly Vrolimnos, which also has the best beach taverna in Greece according to my friend Tony Kampanaos. The old town is beautiful, with lots of good places to eat. There were always plenty of topless girls too.

We're going to jump forward a little to 1998. I went to lunch in a fish restaurant in Old Amersham, Bucks, to decide what to do with our lives. By this time, we were quite rich, which I will explain later, but I had been working eighteen hours a day, seven days a week, and poor Lauren had dark circles under her eyes from waiting until past eleven every night for the next exciting instalment of the Strakelov story. Because the fish was terrible, we decided to move somewhere by the sea: Cornwall.

Lauren thought we must be joking, but we did go, and for the next ten years, I was able to be a proper dad, taking her to and from school, eating dinner together, and spending long days at the beach in summer. Lauren wanted to be a movie star; instead of A levels, she did a BITEC in Drama, which she passed with flying colours. She wanted to go to drama school in London, so we went to about thirty auditions. At last she got into the Academy of Live and Recorded Arts (ALRA) in Wandsworth, and she was in heaven. But when she came home at Christmas, she told us she hated it and wanted to go to movie school in Los Angeles. She agreed to try one more term and go to LA at Easter to check it out. We all agreed that she would go to LA in August.

Lauren's lucky number is 8. We were to set off on 8 August 2008, or 08.08.08. When we got in the rental car for our trip to LA, what was playing on the radio: 'Mr Tambourine Man' by the Byrds. It was just too much, for my favourite song ever to be playing on the radio just at that huge moment in our lives. Lauren was to stay in LA for six years, and I will write about it later.

There is one last thing we need to talk about with Lauren, and that is her birth mother. She was French, and while Lauren was in LA, she made contact with her and arranged to see her over New Year. She wanted Chrissie and me to go too, which of course we did. We all met in a small restaurant in Paris and got on really well. We then spent around three days with her, going up the Eiffel Tower and having dinner every night. On the last night, we had a wonderful New Year's Eve dinner in a lovely restaurant, like one happy family.

Lauren said after, 'I liked my birth mother but felt nothing for her; you will always be my mum and dad.'

I am so glad to be a dad; it is the best thing that could have ever happened. I have been very fortunate to make a lot of money, but life would never have been complete without being a dad.

In this context, it is interesting to look at my diary for 29 December 2003:

'Lauren is now skiing in Italy which means she has been away 2 out of 8 days so far - we both miss her - but as it is every time she goes away, I have to realise that she is growing up, and in probably 3½ years or less, she will be gone forever so to speak - no longer a little girl but a young woman who will probably live in London or go to Australia for a year; whatever, it will be different and a shame to lose her. I suppose as time goes by it will be marriage and maybe I will be a granddad. I quite like the idea of being granddad, and I hope I do a good job. At the moment I seem to have an ability to communicate with young people - I sort of enjoy the things they like and the innocence and enthusiasm of youngsters is to be savoured.'

Little did I know she would stay in Los Angeles for six years.

# Chapter 7

# After Lonrho

I more than doubled my salary, with the potential for big bonuses, and at long last, I began to feel quite rich. But there were two major problems: Firstly, all the directors had the same name (and one was even a lord). Secondly, there was a lot of debt, over £500 million, and no profits. We negotiate a standstill agreement with the banks, which was a very long and detailed document which said what we could and couldn't do. It basically gave us three years to sort out the problems. We had a bankers' meeting, and I had to stand in front of more than a hundred bankers and present our proposals. My right leg shook all through it, but they approved.

I was now finance director of a company, with responsibility of paying the banks back £500 million. I did it for three years and had great fun.

I didn't travel so much, but I did two trips to Brazil; I only went to Sao Paulo and stayed three nights each time. Brazilian girls are absolutely gorgeous, and I am sure that if I had gone there as a young man, I would never have come back. If you are young and single, just go to Brazil.

I did six trips to Australia, including four in eight weeks when we doing the prospectus for a flotation of our Australian and Far East food businesses. It was not so bad now, as I was travelling First Class, although in the 1990s, they still didn't have flat beds, not even in First Class (now you get it in Business). The highlight used to be Qantas out of Sydney to London (only twenty-four hours), where you got caviar and chateaubriand for dinner, with some fine Australian wine.

My worst experience was a lost weekend. One Saturday, I had dinner at home and then was off to Heathrow; on the plane to Bangkok, I slept for twelve hours. I got off the plane in Bangkok for a few cigarettes, had a quick bite, and was off to sleep again for another eight hours; I arrived in Sydney at 6 a.m. on Monday morning, ready to go to work. Where did the weekend go? I spent most of my time in Sydney with Rothschild bankers and thought it was a great place. On my return as a tourist (which I will write about later), I had a different view.

I also had a trip to New Zealand (I never let the secretary book my trips). I had to go to Wellington to meet the New Zealand bankers. Route 1 was to go Air New Zealand via Los Angeles and Auckland; you departed at midday Monday and got to Wellington midday Wednesday. I found Route 2, which was to leave at 11 a.m. Monday, fly to Sydney, have a night in the hotel, and get on a plane to Wellington, arriving 1 p.m. Wednesday. There is always a better way to travel.

Anyway, we were quite successful. I got some small bonuses (£20,000) and then I got a big bonus of £650,000. It was time to repay the mortgage of about £120,000. From humble beginnings, when I didn't even have enough money to buy a 6-shilling record, I was now forty-three years old and lived in an £800,000 house, mortgage free, and had loads of money in the bank. But it was time to move on again. I had earned around £1.4 million in three years.

But as the finance director, I didn't exactly live up to appearances. One evening, we were having a meeting with Charterhouse bankers. I was going to see Pink Floyd at Earls Court and changed into my jeans and a very old leather jacket. I went back into the boardroom to say good night and got various comments, to the effect that I was really just an ageing hippy. We had some wonderful seats at the side of the stage, right at the front, with huge speakers by our ears; it was one of the best concerts ever. Pink Floyd have made some wonderful music over the years, from one of their first songs, 'Astronomy Domine' (which David Gilmour is still playing live), 'Set the Controls for the Heart of the Sun,' and my favourite album of all, which is a bit obscure: *Obscured by Clouds*, which includes music from the movie *La Vallee*. This has so many great tracks, from 'When You're In' to 'Absolutely Curtains.'

I took the summer off; there were quite a few traditional job offers, but nothing felt quite right. In my Lonrho days, I had been sent to the opening of a new golf course at Wentworth. We had a very good lunch from Willy Bauer at the Savoy, and then the Duke of Edinburgh was asked to speak. He started by saying he thought he had already made his speech and then talked off the cuff for an hour and was very amusing (but not politically correct). Here I had first met a property entrepreneur worth about £300 million. I had looked at a couple of deals with him, including a warehouse in Paris and a housebuilder. We got on well but never did any deals.

He asked me to help some friends who had got in financial trouble; he had invested in a number of businesses in Russia but it was a mess. He asked me if I would like to take over and try to build a venture capital fund. The salary was £260,000 per annum, with performance-related bonuses.

It all sounded quite interesting; we got some offices in Mayfair and went off to work. The investments were not very good, but no matter. I met some lottery people and decided this would be the way forward.

At the same time, we sold half the company to Nina Wang from Hong Kong. She was sixty years old and wore pigtails and a mini skirt; she was the richest woman in Hong Kong, worth about $5 billion.

Two stories about Nina: After I left, her ninety-year-old father-in-law had challenged her husband's will, which left all the money to her. Her husband had been kidnapped by the Triads, and she paid a $10 million ransom. He came back but a year later was kidnapped again; this time, the price was £25 million. She paid it, but he was never returned, and it took a number of years for him to be declared dead. When his father contested the will, she lost the first round; the father-in-law was a very rich man, as the will was deemed a forgery by the courts. Of course, she appealed and managed to win the appeal.

As an aside, when she died shortly thereafter, her soothsayer claimed he was the sole heir, but he is now in jail for fraud.

Secondly, she asked me to fly to Toronto with her for the weekend. We had just bought a 30 percent shareholding in Playdium, an upmarket theme park in Toronto, which she wanted to check out. All I wanted to do was get back to my family for another short weekend and made my excuses. Lauren insists I should have gone.

Back to lotteries. We signed up with the People's Committee for Peace to run the Russian National Lottery. Strakelov, who was the hero of Lauren's nighttime stories, was a real as astronaut, and he was the president of People's Committee; we had many amazing conversations with the help of a translator. We celebrated in Moscow with a lot of vodka. We decided not to use our money on this risky project.

For the money raising, we appointed Sir John Morgan, a retired diplomat, as chairman. One day, he invited me to lunch at his club in St James. It was all very strange, as the waiter was not allowed to write down the order, which Sir John had to do; even more bizarre, everybody was eating Dover sole and drinking Chablis Premier Cru. He told me the story of the day his great friend Ian Fleming, the creator of James Bond, asked him to come for afternoon tea. Cubby Broccoli, the producer, was bringing over Sean Connery, who was to play James Bond, to introduce him to Fleming. They had a very pleasant tea, and everybody was polite, and then Tubby and Sean left. Fleming was distraught and told Sir John that Connery was completely wrong. *Dr No* remains one of my favourite movies of all time, and Sean Connery was the best James Bond ever (Daniel Craig is not bad, either). Lauren is now working with a film production company who are trying to get Craig for a movie, at a cost of £1.5 million for eight days' work.

However, we did meet some people who wanted to run keno in the UK. Keno is an online lottery that runs every five minutes and was described by Donald Trump as 'more addictive than crack cocaine.' We decided to put about £40 million into this and signed up two thousand pubs, employing a bunch of Americans from the Massachusetts State Lottery, who had successfully run keno in the

United States. On launch day, it didn't work, and nobody wanted to play, not like their American cousins.

We left it for a couple of weeks, but it got worse. Nobody was playing. One Sunday night, I had a conference call with my owners, who were in Brazil and New York, and we decided to sack everybody. But we didn't have anybody to run it. 'Easy,' they said. 'You can do it, Paul.'

On Monday morning, I went into the office and sacked everybody, and now I had two jobs, which meant I had to work eighteen hours a day, seven days a week.

We set about sorting out keno. I did some market research and recruited Alex Bernstein, who had helped launch Camelot, another lottery in the UK. He had become the scapegoat and been sacked as part of the Richard Branson toilet drama surrounding the Camelot bid. He thought keno was a surefire winner, and we relaunched it, but it didn't work.

In between the lotteries, we did some interesting things. As I have already said, we invested in a theme park in Toronto. We also invested in light-emitting polymers with Lord Young, Mrs Thatcher's favourite businessman. I went to seven or eight board meetings in Cambridge, but to this day, I still don't really know what they are. We eventually sold out at a profit.

And then there was telephones. Kevin Maxwell, with his famous father, came to us and said we could buy the Russian equivalent of BT for $10 million. It was Russia's old military communications system, which covered the whole country. I had no visa and was forced to travel to Moscow via Hamburg and St Petersburg. Not a great day, as nobody met me at St Petersburg to help with the visa, which doubled in price, and then a scary transfer from the international to domestic terminal. And then I was put in Economy Class, with a seat number that didn't exist. I was not too happy with the proposal and got STET, the Italian BT, to advise me. We went to meet three generals in a Nissan hut in Moscow. They were pretty scary, so I just said yes, yes, yes. STET rightly advised that the technology was completely obsolete and needed billions of investment.

Kevin called me to his office late one Friday evening for a tactics session. I walked in and commented that he looked tired. He told me he was in court next week and had spent the whole week being trained to act the part. He did get away with it, so I guess that is what you have to do.

I was in Russia without a proper visa and decided to call Alexander Badran, my contact on the lottery project. He was ex-KGB, along with most of the Russians with whom we did business.

'Hi, Alexander,' I said. 'I am back in Moscow unexpectedly and thought I would give you a call to see how things are going.'

His response was, 'I wondered when you were going to call.'

I hate to think how he knew I was in Moscow illegally.

As keno was not working, we decided to sell it to the Russians. At the same time, we decided venture capital was no fun anymore and we should sell all the investments and call it a day. At this point, I had earned £2.2 million in the last six years.

For the three years I was in venture capital, it was always challenging and never boring, but I was worn out. The best part was that because I was earning so much, I treated myself to two midnight-blue Porsche 911s. I have always loved driving, and the 911 is just such a great car.

During this period, I travelled as follows: Russia (ten times), Sweden (eight), the United States (four), and Canada, Ireland, Malaysia, and Hong Kong (once each).

And so back to the fish restaurant in Old Amersham. I had a number of very good job offers but decided it really was time to be a dad.

During all these years, we had been quite good at property. When we got married, we bought a two-bedroom Victorian conversion flat in Rosary Gardens, South Kensington, for £43,000, selling it five years later for £86,000. We then moved to Chenies in Buckinghamshire, in a beautiful location on the edge of the Chilterns, and bought a three-bedroom Victorian house for £98,000. We sold this for about £130,000 and bought Grooms Farm in Ley Hill for around £380,000. This house was wonderful and had been built in the 1600s; it had five bedrooms, three bathrooms, and five acres of land. We improved the house quite a lot and put a tennis court in the garden and probably spent around £120,000. After five years, it was worth £800,000.

We went off to Cornwall in October 1998 and stayed in Watergate Bay Hotel; it was very much old school and not the wonderful beachside boutique hotel that it is today. We employed County Homesearch to find us our home. After a couple of disappointments, we came across Carclew Grange, about six miles from the cathedral city of Truro, a wonderful Victorian house which had not had much done to it for fifty years. It had five bedrooms, two bathrooms, a one-bedroom cottage, and a coach house, but only three acres of land. We decided to downsize and bought the house for just under £400,000 (the sellers had got married on the same day as Chrissie and I)

# Chapter 8

# Mr Tambourine Man

It was time to take stock. I started off with no money and did not even have six shillings to buy that record I so much wanted.

Now I had a net worth of £1.7 million, with £700,000 in the bank. It was actually all in Guernsey, to get the interest gross and pay the tax later, which I always did. I decided that my days of work were behind me. When we moved to Cornwall, the first thing we had to was plan. We had a high net worth and quite a lot of money in the bank, but we had to have a budget and live a little less in the fast lane.

The first thing to do was to sell the Porsche. It had been so great to have such a fantastic car for six years, but hey, you need to cut back somewhere. In our motor poverty, we were left with two relatively new BMWs: a 328i convertible for fun and a 328i for the long journeys with lots of luggage: the sensible car.

The second thing to do was to have a budget for living. I sat down and carefully considered all our day-to-day costs. The total budget came in at around £46,000. This included £16,000 for food, wine and cigarettes; £6,500 for holidays (as you have to get away sometime); and £3,000 for entertainment, as life has to be fun and you need to go to the cinema and eat out from time to time. However much or little money you have, budgeting is really important. Without a budget, you risk losing direction, and if like me you are not working, you risk running out of money and losing your lifestyle.

I have not earned any money for eighteen years but still have a great lifestyle. I believe that strong budgeting was key to achieving this objective. At the end of every month, I analyse all the expenditures for that month and compare it against budget; whenever it seems necessary, I put in cutbacks. It may seem like a business, but at the end of the day, if you choose to treat your life as a business and put in the controls and all the checks and balances, you will find that you can survive very well without any income.

When I was planning the future, I expected to earn a reasonable amount of interest on the cash balances. Unfortunately, interest rates have been stuck at 0.5 percent, but we have still survived and are in good shape.

I decided to call my time off a gap year, as I considered myself too young to retire. I am now in my eighteenth gap year, which is probably a record, but it does show a different way of looking at the world. There are two basic rules: Firstly, never drink at lunchtime or indeed before six o'clock; otherwise, you really risk the slippery slope. Secondly and probably more importantly, make sure that you are occupied. We will discuss this at length later, but I have managed to be occupied and maybe even useful (whilst not earning any money).

At Grooms Farm, we used to have two gardeners, but for twelve years, I looked after the three acres all by myself. Generally, it was fun, except clearing up the leaves from the many trees in the autumn and the constant attack on the knotweed (the bugbear of Cornish gardens). The best bit was the vegetable patch, which I started from scratch with a rotivator. I tried to concentrate on higher value items and grew wonderful asparagus, artichokes, and raspberries, along with lots of other things. As a real foodie, picking your own produce and taking it straight to your table is simply wonderful.

Next, I got involved with the Prince's Trust and became a business mentor to young kids who had been given loans to start businesses. I took on and cared for ten kids; I would have done more, but the Prince's Trust became too politically correct, and I lost a little interest (although I am still helping three of them). I became the treasurer of the Truro Lawn Tennis Club for four years and then moved on to be chairman, where I stayed for nine years. Our goal was to be the best club in Cornwall and to promote the interests of the kids. I think we were successful in our objectives, and I was particularly pleased that three youngsters were good enough to move to full-time training in London. In later years, I have become a nonexecutive director of Jamie Oliver's Fifteen Cornwall, which has been great for a foodie who loves kids.

Before we continue, I am going to write about two of my great loves: food and tennis.

Around 1995, when I got my £650,000 bonus, we went off for a night at the Manoir aux Quatre Saisons to celebrate. Before dinner, chef Raymond Blanc came into the bar to say a brief hello to everyone. We were delighted to say hello and went on to have a wonderful dinner. After dinner, we went back to the bar for coffee, armagnac, and ciggies; Raymond came and sat with us and talked for half an hour. He is just such a nice man, and his food is great too. We have eaten there seven or eight times and stayed twice; we even took Lauren for lunch. They have a special kids menu, which was perfect, and Lauren sat with us for three hours and got a certificate for good behaviour. With its wonderful kitchen garden, superb food, and wonderful rooms, this just has to be one of the best places.

Again around 1995, I was invited by Rothschild Bank to go to Wimbledon to see my favourite game. I was always getting invited to these sorts of things, particularly rugby at Twickenham, and always declined due to lack of interest; in my view, corporate hospitality can really spoil sport, with the spectators not interested in anything except the bar. I have been to Wimbledon many times, but this was only the second time in the Debenture Lounge. We had a light lunch at noon and were in our seats by one. Apart from a short break for a cup of tea, we sat in our seats with our hosts until around eight o'clock and saw some wonderful tennis. When it was time to go, we thanked our hosts for a great day.

'No,' they said, 'thank you; it has been such a pleasure to be with people who really enjoyed the tennis.'

## Travels before the Gap Years

I was always a great traveller before the gap years. Family holidays started with a trip to Ostend, Belgium, when I was seven years old. After that, we went on quite a lot of holidays to Spain and Italy. I learnt to swim and eat pasta in Rimini, Italy. When I was a little older, we went to the Costa Brava. There were two sisters. The younger looked like Twiggy and was gorgeous, and she had an older less glamorous sister. I used to spend all day hanging around Twiggy, but she had boyfriends for the night time, and I had to take the older sister to the nightclub; we danced to Frank Sinatra's 'Strangers in the Night' (still a great record).

When I was nineteen, I went on a club holiday to Dubrovnik. Loads of girls and not too many guys, so it was great fun. I hooked up with a lovely Danish girl I met on the beach. I went to a nudist beach with a doctor friend, and I had to lay on my front. Next year, I think it was camping in Cornwall (not a great fan, and I have avoided camping as much as possible over the years). And then I met Chrissie.

Our first trip away together was Russia in January: not a great fan, as it was too cold and a bit dull. The highlights were Charlie, our friend, being caught with dope (he was given it back and immediately flushed it away), Uri Gagarin's spacecraft from the first flight to outer space (it seemed so small), and a very long train ride from St. Petersburg to Moscow. Having been quite a few times on business since, I don't think I will ever return to Russia.

But we did like Greece and went there many times over the years. The Greek islands are beautiful, and the people are really nice and great with kids.

Our first trip was to Spetses, a special place. The thing I remember most was that there were very few tourists; we met up with a group of about twelve. There were about five restaurants, and every night, we used to negotiate the best deal and usually got a free bottle of ouzo or Metaxa. One night, we were in a restaurant and a new girl from the sailing boats joined us. She sat next to me and told me she wanted my body. This was awkward, as I was with Chrissie; I gently suggested she try Roger. After dinner, we started dancing, but Roger had disappeared. Sometime later, he returned to the dance floor with a big smile and dusty knees.

We then discovered Lindos on Rhodes, where we were to go many times. It is perfect, with two splendid sandy beaches, some really nice restaurants, and a couple of discos. One of our favourite records to dance was 'Bobby Brown Goes Down' by Frank Zappa, which has an infectious beat and out-of-this-world lyrics to sing along to. Chrissie and I eventually ended up getting engaged in the restaurant Manot's. We also used to drink pina coladas all night long and played backgammon before it was time to party.

We've been to other islands too. The best was probably Mykonos. We had to take a night flight to Athens on Dan Air and then a boat from Piraeus. We arrived at a beautiful cottage just outside the town, with marvellous seaviews with its outside kitchen and bathroom and a sleeping area up a very steep ladder. We took the mattress down to the living room floor and had a quick nap before dinner, only to wake up rather hungry at breakfast time. And so off to Paradise Beach, where nobody had any clothes. It was a great sense of freedom. Our favourite beach, however, was Elia, a short bus ride away.

Other islands included Skiathos, Andros, Crete, Cepholonia, Poros (probably the least favourite), and Paxos for Lauren's first overseas holiday. In their own way, they were all lovely and well worth a visit.

We went to Gambia once, which was Chrissie's only trip to black Africa. We used to go to the beach every day; we'd have lunch in the beach bar and leave a small tip for the waiter. When we were leaving, he said he was so grateful for the tips because it meant he could go home on the bus rather than sleeping in the bar. And by the way, he was getting married soon and could we send him some shoes? We got a piece of paper and traced his feet. At home, we went to Marks and Spencer for cheap black shoes and filled them with odd bits of currency we had from various worldwide places. A few weeks later, we received a wonderful letter of thanks. It felt good to help, but we were glad he never showed up at our door because that would have been just too much.

As we got richer, we started to go farther. Barbados became our favourite, and we went there four times, the last with Lauren when she was three and a half. The first three times, we stayed at Treasure Beach, right on the sea, with lovely rooms and great food. We were having dinner one night, and Gary Sobers, the cricketer, came in with Ted Dexter. The staff were very excited. Gary Sobers was the nicest guy and was so sweet to everybody, which was so good to see.

I learnt to waterski, and it has become a passion. I even got so good that I could mono ski. Wherever I am in the world today, I always look for the waterski boats in the hope that I can have a go.

The third time, we came back on the Concorde just before Christmas for a very low premium. I have flown on the Concorde four times; it was always a great experience and so much better than a long overnight flight home. The last time, we were with Lauren; I sat next to her and ate her caviar, as she was too young to appreciate it (although she does like it today). Michael Winner was on the plane with Jenny Seagrove. She pushed in front of us when we were waiting for the loo but came out very quickly.

I looked at her and said, 'You are very fast for a lady.'

Another trip was to Florida and New York. Disney World was okay, and we then went to the beach and then onto New York. We decided to go ice skating in Central Park, but it had melted quite a lot. I clung onto the edge without knowing what to do. A gay man came and took my hand and glided me round until I could be rescued by Chrissie and Lauren. Hey, New York is a great city and always fun.

## Gap Year Travels

When Lauren was ten years old, I suggested we all keep a diary. She stopped after two days, but I have carried on for eighteen years. I am now going to recount my travelling from those diaries:

## August 1999

We went to Skiathos again. It was very hot, with temperatures around 97 degrees. We had great lunches every day in the Vrolimnos beach bar; our favourites were *gavros* (small fried fish) and stuffed tomatoes. Food Report said that the dinners are generally quite good, with a lot of fried aubergines and courgettes and *zatsiki*. If you have lobster, dinner costs around £50. Stamatis was the best authentic Greek restaurant in the town. Platanas and the Windmill had stunning views and okay food.

James Fox, the actor, was there with his family, and I went water skiing with his sons. Laurence will later become quite famous, marrying Billie Piper and starring in 'Lewis.' Jack, the youngest, is a little older than Lauren, who fights every day with her first boyfriend, William, for her attention (it was nice to have a beautiful daughter). Other sports included tennis, volleyball, and windsurfing. But my diary records 'Time seems to move very slowly here, unlike Cornwall, where it dashes by.'

Skiathos is a lovely island, and we know it quite well, having been there nine times in total.

## December 1999

It was Chrissie's fiftieth birthday. We had a brilliant dinner at Rick Stein's on the big day: fish soup and monkfish vindaloo for me and crab bouillon and sea bass for Chrissie, but Lauren had the best dish: mussels in black bean sauce. This all cost around £130.

When I asked Chrissie what she wanted for her birthday, she said helicopter flying lessons. Thinking outside the box, we flew to Nice and then took the helicopter both ways to Monte Carlo.

We stayed in the Hermitage Hotel, with a wonderful view of the harbour and some burnt-out remains of a building opposite. It turned out that it was the result of the death of a very rich banker, Edmond Safra, who died in a fire, allegedly started by his nurse but as in cases such as this, there were many stories, from the Russian mafia onwards.

Monaco was okay but it was somehow claustrophobic, in the same way as Hong Kong. And I didn't like the people much, which is described below.

We liked the aquarium and the tourist train ride and thought the classic cars were very good but found the zoo depressing and the doll museum to be just for girls.

Our favourite restaurant was the Cafe de Paris, where we had dinner and lunch. For dinner, I had chevre in pastry and foie de veau (I have always loved calves liver) and apricot tart. Chrissie had leek and broccoli terrine and gamba kebab, and Lauren had langoustine, which they peeled, and lamb kebab; with two kir royales and a very good bottle of Bandol, it was £130. For lunch, I had foie de veau again and Chrissie a wonderful rabbit stew, with a hamburger for Lauren and some very fine pattiserie to follow; with a couple of glasses of red wine, it cost £60. A truly nice French restaurant in a great central location.

For another dinner, we looked in the guidebooks and chose Rambolis, an Italian restaurant. We were first in. Chrissie and I both had tortelloni with white truffle sauce, except the truffle was notably absent, and then I had lobster and Chrissie duck a la orange. Lauren had prawn cocktail and pasta; with a bottle of Sancerre *rouge*, it all came to £140 but only scored 4 out of 10. But the floorshow was great.

Gradually, people started to come in, and every couple was an old grey-haired man with a blonde trophy wife. They came to tables of four and sat down opposite each other, without really speaking. Shortly after, an identical couple would come to the table and sit down, but the man ignored the other guy's trophy wife and just talked to the other guy, probably about business. All the tables in the restaurant seemed to be set up this way. As someone who has always loved the ladies, it just seemed all so wrong.

## April 2000

We were in France again, this time in Paris. We went to Euro Disney, which seems to suffer from the problem of lowest common denominator (LCD). A major strategic plus was that we only bought a one-day ticket, so we didn't have to go back. The major problems were too many people, too many queues, and crap food. We spent most of the time on Space Mountain, holding my glasses; I couldn't see how scary it was (if indeed it was scary). Florida's Disney World, where we had been before, seemed so much better.

It was a poor hotel with no *pains au chocolat* for breakfast and no restaurants nearby. We did find Penang, the Malaysian restaurant, which was pretty good, with wonderful dim sum and a few prawn dishes, all for around £40, with a good bottle of Cote de Rhone.

We had a great lunch in Paris overlooking the Seine: white asparagus and skate for me, pate and omelette for Chrissie, and chicken and chips for Lauren (which was not on the menu). With a half-bottle of Brouilly, it was around £60, which was not cheap.

We did a lot of galleries and shopped in Paris. Musee D'Orsay was the best, with Manet, Monet, Renoir, and Degas. Almost too many pictures but saw *Whistler's Mother*, which is a great painting. The Louvre was busy as ever, but *Mona Lisa* and *Venus de Milo* were great, and we saw some excellent Rembrandt sketches.

We had lots more to eat, including Penang again; it was all pretty good but still spending around £50 for dinner and a little less for lunch. Eating in France was normally a pleasure and, I guess, one of the reasons we keep going back.

## August 2000

We were back in Greece again, in Zakynthos. We visited Club Peligoni with our old friends and their three boys, around Lauren's age.

The whole point of Peligoni is sailing and windsurfing. For the first week, we stayed in a tacky apartment, but the second week, we went for an upmarket villa, the Olive Press.

For a typical day, I had an early waterski, then windsurfed for a couple of hours and then had lunch and relaxed and read a book. Except one day, I decided to become a sailor. Did the dry land lesson and then got in a Pico with Chrissie. I capsized the boat three times and needed some help to get it back. I have never sailed myself since that day, and there wasn't even much wind.

They also had a tennis tournament, but I didn't do too well. However, I did get to umpire the finals.

The food was all a bit Greek. It normally cost around £30; the club had BBQs and dish suppers, which were all very nice but not haute cuisine.

At the end of the holiday, we had a party, and I got a prize for my beginner's windsurfing.

We all decided Zakynthos was not our favourite Greek island, but we had a good active holiday, and I became a little hooked on windsurfing.

# April 2001

We were in France again, on the Ile de Re. We took the boat from Plymouth to Roscoff and then drove the three hundred miles. We had a nice apartment with two bathrooms in the centre of the main town, St Martin.

There was lots to do here, with a swimming pool, the gym, and bike rides. Cycling was fun and easy, as it was very flat. And we went horse riding. I had not been for many years, and the very pretty French lady told me my horse was *tres gentile*, except when we were in the woods, and she said to gallop, which is actually canter, and I had to hang on for my life. Chrissie and Lauren went again, but I laid on the grass, reading my book, until a man upset his stallion, which reared and looked as if it was going to knock me out.

The food was pretty good. My best dinner was *soupe de poissons,* followed by St. Pierre (John Dory) with a foie gras sauce and very thinly sliced parsnips, all for about £50. We also ate in a really nice Chinese restaurant, because that's what kids like. At the same time, we ate a lot of langoustines, which are a regional speciality, but steered clear of the oysters. The best lunch was in La Flotte overlooking the harbour; we ate langoustines with mayonnaise and chips, all for £30.

In the middle, we went for a day trip of 330 miles to see my cousin in the Dordogne. A small house with two *gites* and not much land, but we did have a very nice lunch and wine.

Most of the time, it was warm and sunny for so early in the year, but on the last day, it rained a lot. As fitness freaks, we still went for a bike ride but got very wet indeed.

On the way back, we stopped in Brittany for a couple of nights. It was a complete disaster, as the hotel was full of English golfers, who talked in very loud posh voices about their rounds, which was so boring. But there was a pinball table and pool, which kept us amused.

We once went on a road trip to Venice with some very good friends. Two things happened of note: Firstly, on the recommendation of Fodor, we went to El Grotto, a folk club where they played authentic music; we should have known. We ordered an expensive bottle of wine, and all these tourists came in, and they started to play '*E Viva Espana.*'

It was time to leave, but the waitress demanded the price of two bottles, as that was the policy. We asked for a bottle of champagne, which we got and drank very fast. We then retired to a proper bar and drank grappa.

Secondly, on the way back, we arrived in France and stayed in a hotel overlooking Mont Blanc and went to the local bar. We didn't have many francs and had to decide between pinball and more drinks. As great pinball fans, we played pinball and stayed thirsty. We had a good dinner with lobster canneloni (but wrapped in cabbage, not pasta, which was not quite right) and quail stuffed with foie gras. We visited Port Aven, which was quite nice, with a very good museum devoted to Gaugin and his mates. We also went to Le Poulbot, which was on the seaside.

My diary recorded that I was a little homesick and looking forward to getting home; the more I thought about it, I was glad I was not living in the Dordogne, like my cousin. Was I really such a good traveller?

## August 2001

But I was travelling again, and just for a change, we were in Skiathos again. Before we left, I bought Prince's *Greatest Hits* and Burt Bacharach's *Love Songs* to listen to on the beach. Prince is one of the greatest; my favourite songs are '1999' and 'When Doves Cry.' Burt Bacharach is a legend, and I have to give special mention to 'Twenty-Four Hours from Tulsa,' 'What the World Needs Now Is Love,' and 'Do You Know the Way to San Jose?' although there are too many more great songs to list. We started with a great lunch at the Vrolimnos beach bar: fried shrimp, sardines, and *sadsiki*, all for £16.

There was lots of activity as ever, with water skiing, windsurfing, volleyball, and tennis. And for the first time, I tried wake boarding, but as a mono skier, I think I will stick to that.

On the way back from dinner, I could see Lauren holding William's hand. I was going to have to adjust to my daughter growing up and size up all her boyfriends, which is I guess what fathers have to do, but I didn't have any experience in this department. I needed to learn as I went along.

On the next night at dinner, William had his arm around her, and they went off alone to the beach. William's father went off to sort them out (I had no idea what to do) and told them they had to come and choose their ice creams. I mentioned it on the way back to Lauren, who said it was okay because she had done it with Peter too. However, when William left before us, Lauren didn't seem too tearful, which may be a good sign. As an aside, I think I can confidently say that all her boyfriends have been a disaster, but I don't have enough time to recount the reasons why, one by one. William and Jack Fox were still fighting over Lauren. The Fox family were all delightful, and James was always particularly charming.

Another problem was that the TV in the room had only one English channel. In my working years, I spent many nights in my hotel room eating room service (I never socialised, as this was what the saddest people did), and my only friend was the TV. As a result, I have always banned bedroom TVs in our houses. The highlight of the TV was the Milosovic trial live from the Hague on BBC World, which felt like watching real history.

I was forty-nine years old and seemed to keep talking to people about getting old. I decided that 'Old-Aged Pensioner' is out of date; I am going to be a Young Aged Pensioner.

We had some nice dinners at Stamatis and the Windmill again and discovered Anemos, a new place with a lovely terrace overlooking the harbour. They did a wonderful meze and then Anemos prawns, cooked with Grand Marnier and lemon, a truly great dish which everybody should try. Dinner was normally £50 or £60. But to be honest, we were in Greece, and the lunches were probably better; the gavros and stuffed tomatoes from Vrolimnos were very hard to beat.

Skiathos was as wonderful as ever, but I felt that we needed to get out more and find some new places.

## April 2002

We were off somewhere more exciting. Sometime ago, we had gone to Val D'Isere in France for Christmas, and I had tried to learn to ski. I was so bad that I got demoted from the beginners class to sub-beginners. This was full of Japanese who were even worse than me, and after a day, I got promoted back to beginners. Even after a week, I wasn't very good. But then we decided to go to Vail in the Colorado Rockies.

We stayed in Denver two nights, and I went to Ralph Lauren and bought some shirts. On the second evening, we had dinner in a bank vault at the Broker and ate delicious Gulf shrimp and terrible duck with my old friends, Tom and Paul. I met them during my Lonrho years, when we had discovered fraud at our amethyst mine in Zambia. The fraudulent sales agent had spent three months each year skiing in Aspen, so we had jurisdiction in the Colorado courts, and I went there four or five times for the case. Good to see them again.

This time, no beginners course but private ski lessons, which cost $411 (or £300) for three hours. I fell over getting off the ski lift the first time but was helped up by a very pretty girl. Otherwise, it all seemed to go quite well, with the snow plough mastered and turning well and standing up nicely, and at the end, I even asked to go faster. It was money well spent.

The first night, we went to Russell's, a nice restaurant, and ate sirloin teriyaki, but it did cost $157.

The skiing got better, and we started to do green runs and even consider the blue runs. In the afternoons, we went to the top of the mountain, where there was a long, wide, and gentle two-mile run with fantastic views. We also did the Eagle's Nest run in forty-two minutes, which was great. The Meadows and Lion's Way were also within our capabilities. It was getting near the end of the season, and the lift pass went down from $483 per week to $99.

The food was okay but not brilliant; probably the best was Southern fried chicken in the American Bar for $110 (with lots to drink).

So the spring skiing was great. It was a lot warmer, and we did really well, spending all that money on a private coach. We progressed really well; Colorado was fantastic if a little expensive. My diary says 'Did I enjoy skiing? Yes, a lot.' It mentions our next trip, but we haven't been back again.

Before the next trip, two things happened: I traded in the blue BMW convertible for a red Audi TT 225 Roadster; it was a great car that I loved for six years. And I turned fifty years old. To celebrate, we put a marquee in the garden, which we did up with palm trees and beach shacks, and had 120 people for champagne, supper, and dancing. The DJ was David White from Radio Cornwall, and he kept us all dancing until the late hours. Instead of presents, people made donations to the Sunrise Appeal; we raised £500, and I got to appear with David on the radio. I quite liked being fifty, and the day after, all my friends went to the Porthminster Beach Cafe in St Ives. I had tempura lemon sole and wonderful rosewater and pistachio ice cream.

## August 2002

We were back to Peligoni on Zakynthos again.

We spent our time windsurfing, playing tennis, and water skiing. The weather was lovely, as always.

Eating was pretty Greek; we ate a lot of stuffed tomatoes and suvlaki, for around £10 per head. We ate at the club a lot, which always seemed to serve chicken curry.

And then it was party night. Lauren was now thirteen years old, and we danced together in the disco. We danced to 'School's Out' by Alice Cooper. The lyrics, attitude, and beat were fantastic, and I remembered dancing to this the first time I came to Greece in 1972, and here we were, thirty years later, just after my fiftieth birthday, doing exactly the same thing, but now with my teenage daughter.

## April 2003

We were in France again, this time in Le Touquet for two nights.

The first night's dinner was at Diamont Rose. Big problem: the golfers again. There were twenty-four of them at three separate tables, and they were the pits. We had asparagus, black cod with a cream sauce, and very good warm tarte Normande (apple, custard, and calvados), all washed down with Sancerre rouge and costing around £65 for the three of us. The second night was a different restaurant without the golfers; we ate fish soup, skate with olive oil and raspberry vinaigrette, and *tarte Tatin*, all for around £50.

Two nights was enough in Le Touquet, and we didn't seem to do too much except eat and drink; no exciting sporting activities to report.

## July 2003

We were up at 1 a.m. to drive to Gatwick and catch another plane to Greece. This time, we were going on a Nielsen activity holiday to the Retreat at Sivota.

First impressions were good, with a nice room and a great view, but there were too many eight-year-olds. But we were later to discover the adults-only beach, which meant we didn't have to see them.

It was interesting here, because it was basically full board, except you go out to dinner a couple of nights a week. Breakfasts were great, with fruit and smoothies, and of course, you get stuffed tomatoes for lunch. Dinners were generally okay, but the baklava kept running out. The best night was Italian night, with good antipasto and very good gnocchi. They also did a Mexican night, which was good fun. When we went out to dinner, we ate normal Greek food, and it cost around £10 per head. The best dinner was crayfish spaghetti.

But the whole point of this holiday is activity. My diary records that in the first week my activity was tennis (eight times), windsurf (seven), waterski (three), volleyball (two), and lots of swimming. Another important activity is the disco; we went every night until around 2 a.m. Activity in the second week seems to be around the same as the first week.

We went on this holiday with two thirteen-year-old girls, and it was a great success. Lots of friends for everybody and lots of good activity. The sports were very good and most of all fun. Generally, the food was good (if not Michelin class). It was difficult not to have a good time here.

## August 2003

One month on, and we were back to Peligoni on Zakynthos again, but only for a week.

It was much the same as ever, with plenty of activity: windsurfing, waterskiing, tennis, and swimming.

On party night, there was a problem, as they lost 'School's Out,' which meant we couldn't relive our memories.

The food was much the same as ever, with the best food probably at the club. One night, it was garlic king prawns and sirloin steak with horseradish and mustard sauce.

The bill for a week was E1,000, which included five dinners and four waterskis, but it seemed quite expensive here.

We cannot decide which we liked the best: Sivota or Pelegoni. They were both the same, with plenty of activity, but also different. All we can say is that we liked them both.

# May 2004

It seemed a long time since we went away. Lauren decided that she wanted to surf with her dad, so at the age of over fifty, I was going to have to learn some new tricks.

We were in Hossegor near Biarritz, in southwest France.

Firstly, we had to meet our surf instructor, Clare, who was very pretty and very nice; a good start. After a chat, we all went off surfing. The first lesson went quite well. The sea didn't seem too cold, although I was in the long wet suit. I caught the waves okay but really couldn't seem to stand up. Clare said that I was trying to get up too late, so tomorrow I must be quicker on the draw. The second day, surf progress seemed a little slow, but I now had the record of standing up for five seconds. By day three, it was all getting so much better, and I could stand up for eight seconds, but my feet always seemed to be in the wrong place.

On the last day, I improved again and managed to stand up for around fifteen seconds. I was a lot better than the first day, but I would have liked to have done so much better. It seemed to be difficult to learn new tricks.

We liked this area a lot: good sea, good restaurants, nearly always good weather, and a great feel to it. It was different from the Cote d'Azur in a nice way: No low life and very French, with hardly any English (which is always a good thing). It was a place to come again.

And the food. We ate one night at Bidant La Tantina de la Playa in St Jean de Luz and had soupe de poissons and grilled whole sea bass with a Provence rosé at a table with a seaview a bit like Fistral Beach at Newquay; the meal cost E100. Another night, we ate at La Cottage in Hossegor. We had ate de foie gras, confit de canard (crispy), fromages, and tarte aux fraises with two bottles of the most expensive rosé; it was E143 for four, as we were treating friends. A fine restaurant, to which we shall return in the future.

The best night was when we met the Hamiltons. Christine Hamilton is now quite old but played tennis for England in the Wightman Cup; she once beat the great and almost unbeatable Billy Jean King. We went to a local restaurant and ate the E10 menu with deep-fried camembert and lotte, with coquillages for me and many jugs of vin rosé. Christine was wonderful company and a tremendous storyteller.

We were to come here again for more surfing stories.

# August 2004

We went back to Hossegor. The last time, we drove, but this time, we flew Easy Jet. We were Easy Jet virgins; Chrissie was just out of hospital, and they gave us priority boarding, which was very welcome. We flew into Bilbao and had to drive through the poor roads of Spain; there were an awful lot of crashed cars at the side of the road.

The next day, I was surfing again, but I recorded that I still didn't seem to be very good. Clare was as nice as ever and tried to encourage me. The following day, we started at nine o'clock, which was a bit early; by the time I woke up, I did four or five good runs, which was a big improvement on yesterday and proved to me that I was not just a one-off. But the next day, it got worse; I blamed the sea, which was difficult, with lots of cross waves (or maybe it was just me). In the afternoon, we watched the *Rip Curl Masters*, and I could see what I was trying to do.

The next day started much better, with my best surf ever, but it then went downhill. I got tired and couldn't control the waves. On my last surf, I was doing quite well and got beyond the break. But disaster: I got hit by a large wave and lost my glasses (I was blind for the rest of the afternoon). I do like surfing but was not very good; I guess you would say my surfing was like my French.

Eating was as good as ever. The first night, we went to Chez Mimies and had serrano ham and *moules*. It cost E89 for five, which was good for such a nice restaurant. Better than the second night, when we had tapas and pizza for E88 in a dive. The next night was better at Le Bistro: crab tarte, cheese in brioche, and fillet steak with a mushroom sauce. The restaurant had a nice atmosphere with a great waitress and a bill to match, at E149 for five.

Next was Chez Albert, which had just been written about in the *Sunday Times*. Everybody said you had to queue, even if you've booked a table. We didn't but got a really nice table on the terrace. We had langoustines and coquilles St Jacques, with a nice rosé; it cost E103 for two, which was expensive but a great location and service and somewhere to remember. And then a Vietnamese restaurant for some Asian goodies. And then to Ducamp, which was expensive and disappointing. We had crevette cassoulet and turbot au beurre blanc, not really up to it and E153 for four. For the last night, we went back to Chez Mimies for good gambas, sardines, and moules.

# December 2004

And so to a new place for us: Lanzarote. I think the strategy was to get a bit of winter sun (which we did; it was around 70 degrees every day) and do a bit of surfing, which was my new favourite pastime. Before we left, we were surfing at Fistral in 55 degree water. In summary, I would not recommend going to Lanzarote, as it has so little to offer. We left a few days before Christmas and felt really sorry for the people getting off the plane, who were going to have to spend their holiday there.

The food was generally terrible. On the first night, we walked from our hotel and found six Chinese restaurants all very close together. We were looking in one, and a conman came up and told us this one was very good, so we went in. We ate average dumplings, seaweed, and prawn toast, followed by orange duck and sweet and sour chicken; with a bottle of Rioja, it came to E66, which seemed a lot for average.

For the next night, we went to a French restaurant, Montmartre, which had been recommended by a friend who had a house in Lanzarote. We were put off by the Spanish guy pretending to be French and the really annoying music. And the food wasn't much better. We had prawns in garlic (the prawns were a little small and tasteless) and calves liver with a green pepper sauce, which was creamy and overpowering. And this all cost E72 for three.

We did better at lunch the next day in Golfe; we had a great fish lunch with grilled sole, dorado, and Lanzarote with two great chilli and mint/garlic dips. And it only cost E37. The next night's dinner was also better at Era, a nice restaurant with a series of small private dining rooms; I had fish soup and prawns, and Chrissie had chicken stuffed with crab and rolled in sesame. It cost E81 for three.

But then it went downhill again. We went to a trattoria that was full of men wearing grey shoes, which is never a good sign. We started off with serrano ham, which was okay, but hey, it's not difficult. Then we had grilled hake, which was excessively overcooked and almost too hard to eat. Rule number one is that you should never overcook fish; it is delicate and beautiful and needs to be treated with respect. And this all cost E50.

It got better. Next, we went to El Asadero, which was a bit out of the way, but a find at last. To start, we were the only customers, so no grey shoes; later, a Spanish family joined us, adding to the atmosphere. We started with some mussels tapas, and I ate a really nice canary soup and T-bone steak cooked correctly: medium rare. With a Lanzarote red, it all came to E60. The tourists will never find this place, and they don't know what they are missing, but I guess if it was full of tourists, it would have got spoilt.

But the next night, we went for a poor curry, which costs E77, which was ludicrous. For our last night, we went to La Finca for potato and leek soup and grilled sole; it was just about okay and cost E70. The conclusion had to be, if you want to eat well, go to France and give Lanzarote a miss.

What was there to do in Lanzarote? Not much. We had a few swims in the sea, but it was quite cool. And we went to Famora for some surfing. It was windy and not as pretty as Hossegor or Fistral Beach. I did a few good runs and was starting to get my feet better positioned, but somehow, it wasn't great fun, which about summed up Lanzarote. I don't think we'll be coming here again. I have never been to Tenerife but suspect I would have the same reaction.

# August 2005

It was ages since we went away, and we returned to Hossegor with four kids, which was important, as you will discover later. We flew to Bordeaux and picked up a big hire car, which was supposed to be a Renault Espace but turned into a Kia SUV, which already had lots of dents and was a nightmare to drive. It's difficult to believe that anybody would buy such a rubbish car.

The surfing was definitely improving; I managed to stand up a lot and do some really good runs. One day, the surf was difficult, with on-shore winds. I did six good early runs in the first twenty minutes and then only two in the next ninety minutes; tired, I guess. But one day, I had to show off. A film crew from the Discovery Channel in Los Angeles turned up. They were making a five-minute film of alternative family holidays. We had to pretend that we were a family of six, having a great time in SW France. We met at 8.30 in the morning and spent the whole day until 11.30 at night, filming our activities. I was filmed surfing and losing a pair of glasses, just to make it really exciting.

At the end of the day, they wanted me to do a one-on-one interview; I had to take off my glasses and have makeup, as my forehead was too shiny. We all went to the local hot spot, Dick's Bar, and drank Sex on the Beach whilst being filmed; the locals must have thought we were megastars. They shot fifteen hours of film for five minutes; it seemed excessive, and despite my best efforts, I have never seen the finished product, so who knows how I come over on the big screen?

Because we were in France, we were now going to have some good food. The first night, we went to a restaurant on the lake and had the E16 menu. We had pate, pepper omelette, confit de canard, and wonderful warm apple tart, and it only cost E127 for seven. The next night, we went back to Le Bistro for a nice atmosphere and good food. We had crab and cote de bouef with a nice red wine at E82 for three.

We then discovered a lovely hotel restaurant, Villa Stings in Saubusse, with lovely river views, and we got the best table. We ate prawns, artichokes, mushrooms, *rognons*, couer de veau, and rabbit. And for dessert, a red fruit gazpacho with lemon sorbet, all washed down with a bottle of Sancerre rosé. A bargain at E103 for two.

In the middle of the holiday, we decided to visit the mountains for the weekend to get away from the kids. We were going to St Peter Port in France. But first, we travelled through Spain to get some cheap cigarettes and then on to lunch; to my horror, *le menu* was all in Basque. We had no idea what anything was but managed to order *omlettes Espanol,* which were quite nice. We had a nice drive in the mountains and went back to France, which somehow seemed much better than Spain.

St Peter Port was very crowded and touristy. We chose an expensive room at E160 and somehow managed to park outside. After a swim in the outdoor pool (not indoor, as per Rough Guide), we sat down for dinner. We ate from the E50 menu: monkfish with fennel in a light curry sauce and fillet of lamb with haricot beans. And the breakfast cost E15, which made our hotel bill E333, which seemed a bit excessive for a corporate outing.

One night, we left the kids at Dick's Bar, with a taxi booked for 2.15. The taxi failed to appear, and Lauren, bless her heart, negotiated a lift home in a police car for the four of them. This girl was going places.

And so it was nearly the end of summer. France was great again, with fine food and surfing and so much better than Lanzarote.

# November 2005

Chrissie and I had been married twenty-five years. We were at Gatwick, checking in early for our British Airways Business Class flights, and got the front row, as there was no First Class on this route. We were going to Antigua for the first time. We flew over Cornwall and saw the snow, glad we were going somewhere warm.

We stayed at Chez Pascal, which is a gourmet French restaurant with four rooms. We had a nice first dinner with soupe de poissons and steamed grouper with a very good beurre blanc sauce. Starters were around £8 and mains £18.

After a really nice breakfast of juice, fresh fruit, freshly baked croissants, and coffee, it was time to explore. First, we walked past Giorgio Armani's winter house and strolled into an all-inclusive beach hotel. It was very strange, as all the guests were drinking rum punches and were already pissed at 10 a.m., and we couldn't buy a drink, as they didn't do cash. We walked on a bit, and all we found was a nudist beach; the sea was too rough for waterskiing. We got a taxi and went to Darkwood Beach. After this trip, we decided we really needed a car, so we ordered one.

The second dinner was also very good, with chicken liver parfait and shrimp saffron.

The car arrived. On the first day, we drove fifty miles, but it felt like five hundred, as the roads were not very good. We were looking for the perfect beach with great Caribbean food and waterskiing. We tried the St James Club, a nonsense all-inclusive, where the waterskiing stopped at 11.30. We came home via Tunes Beach, which would not be on our return list.

Chez Pascal closed some nights, and we went to Castaways in Jolly Harbour. It was not jolly and looked like a Berni Inn, with a lot of fried food. I ate a fairly terrible chicken curry.

More exploring to Dickensian Bay, Millers Beach, and the Royal Antigua Hotel, with eight hundred rooms and no guests. No waterskiing, either. We had a couple of nice swims in the Caribbean and then the hotel pool. We had dinner at Millers Beach with really good conch chowder and okay red snapper with Creole sauce for £43.

It was the big day of our anniversary, and we decided to go to Carlisle Bay, a wonderful hotel with a fabulous beach and great food. We had a glass of champagne and then an amazing lunch; I would have gladly eaten everything on the menu. We ordered king prawn roti with four lovely sauces. This all cost £63. And then later, we had an amazing afternoon tea with artichoke bread, pastrami pizza, and scones with cream and jam, for around £8 each.

And the dinner was even better back at Chez Pascal. We had kir royales (on the house), gazpacho, and lobster thermidor, followed by tarte Tatin with ice cream, flaming calvados, and a special message to the two of us. And then we had rum punches. It was a great evening to celebrate such a historic event.

With a good hangover, I went to Jolly Beach for the first waterski; I got up the first time and didn't fall over. I had so much fun; it was one of the great pleasures of life.

We didn't stay at Jolly Beach, as it was too touristy, and retired to the pleasures of Darkwood, which was to become our go-to beach. We were encouraged to go to a roadside stall for lunch. We ordered goat and rice, which was served in large white polystene trays. It all came with about eight different things; it was an experience we decided not to try again, but there were no after-effects, so it must have been very clean.

We had another great dinner at Chez Pascal, with shrimp salad with avocado and grapefruit and tenderloin from New York with *beurre maitre d'*. To follow, we had a glass of twenty-year-old rum, which smelled and tasted just like cognac.

It was now Chrissie's birthday, so we caught a boat and had a picnic on Green Island, which is a small paradise where everyone should go. We had kir royales and lobster thermidor for dinner again.

We took an interesting trip to St Johns with our waitress, Neva, and her four-year-old daughter. The strangest thing was when we visited the port, where there were no cruise ships, but we still got charged £40 for four drinks at a bar. I was glad I was not a cruiser, getting ripped off everywhere.

We had a wonderful dinner for the last night, with gazpacho and *carre d'agneau* and, of course, the twenty-year-old rum, which had become a staple.

I ended up going waterskiing four times and doing a lot of delicious Caribbean swimming. We had previously been to Barbados four times, and it was always brilliant. I think I might have liked Antigua better, as it was more laid back, but what really made this trip was the fantastic food at Chez Pascal. Pascal trained in Lyons, and every dish was near-perfect classic French cuisine; you couldn't ask for much more. We experienced all the joys of the Caribbean and dined as if we were in one of the best restaurants in France; what could be better?

## July 2006

We went for a family holiday to Crete. Lauren went to Malia, where it was young and lively, and we went thirty miles down the road to the much more sedate Agios Nicholios, where we spent a Greek Easter many years ago. It was very fine, and every night we danced to 'Stayin' Alive' by the Bee Gees from *Saturday Night Fever*. It was all okay, except for the boat trip to Spinalonga, when we got hit by a storm and nearly drowned. Then we took a bike ride to the twelve-kilometre beach, and the tyre shredded halfway back. It looked like we were all going to have some adventures.

We arrived at midnight and drank pinot noir on the balcony, overlooking the sea and watching the full moon; such a nice way to start a holiday. The hotel had left beer, water, and bottles of Coke, but we brought our own wine. I was to drink the Coke bottles later, and it tasted so much better than the cans or plastic bottles we got at home; Coke should only really come in glass bottles.

We went into town for dinner on the first night. It was very touristy, and all the restaurants were hassling you to go in. We finally went to a fish restaurant and had sardines, tzaziki, and shrimp risotto, but it was all very expensive at E69, which was ridiculous for a simple Greek dinner.

There was a really good tavern on the beach, where we went most days for fresh rolls, Greek omelettes with feta and potatoes, and wonderful fennel cake.

For the second night, we had a really good dinner at Gargadons, near the hotel. We had good shrimp and black bream with lemon and caper sauce, and it only cost E54: better food and far more reasonable. Another night, we ate here and had fantastic grilled vegetables (yes, they were particularly good, especially the onions) and moussaka, which was rated as the best ever. A few nights, we ate at the hotel. The owner was a wonderful host and cooked the most delicious whole lamb, but more about this later.

Later, we discover a sort of Greek tapas bar called George's, where we ate a number of nights. Chrissie was very excited because the maitre d' was very handsome and went into the garden to pick vegetables especially for her. We eat salad, butter beans, *stifado*, aubergine croquettes, rabbit, and many other good things, and with a lot of house wine, it only cost around E15 per head.

Unfortunately, the sea was a bit rough; every day, I promised myself I would go waterskiing, but I never did. The only activity was two or three swims a day in the beautiful Mediterranean.

And now it was time to leave, and the nice Greek owner gave me my bill. I gave him my credit card; he said I could pay for the room on the credit card but had to pay him cash for the food and drink: E311. I told him that I had no cash. He said, 'Don't worry, we'll get in my car and go to the bank.'

So we did, and I had to go to two banks to get enough cash. I was obviously helping the Greek to avoid taxes, and it was all a bit boring. Anyway, Crete was nice, and we had good food and good times, but I suspect Lauren had more fun in Malia. And this was our only trip away that year.

# August 2007

It was a year since we went away, but we returned to our favourite Greek island: Skiathos.

We were staying in a really nice three-bed, two-bath villa with lots of outside space and terraces with great seaviews.

Most days, we had lunch at the Vrolimnos beach bar, which was as good as ever. Gavros, shrimp, stuffed tomatoes, and tzaziki (or a combination) was the norm. For dinner on the first night, we went back to Stamatis, and they remembered us (they even recalled that we liked to drink Grand Reserve). It was so nice to be back. Dinner for four, with curried lobster for me, cost E93. We ate here quite often. We also returned to Anemos for the amazing shrimp. Other nights, we ate at local places: Skilithri and the Kanapitsa beach bar, which were very Greek and enchanting, but somehow, there was not too much to say about the food. On other nights, we went to the Lemon Tree or Alexandros and had good shrimp souvlaki.

The weather was better here, so I managed a few waterskis, which was good, and lots and lots of swimming and a little beach volleyball.

But there was excitement. There were signs in the town saying they want extras for the filming of *Mama Mia*. On Friday, we got up early and went to town to see if we could get the girls parts in the movie. They had everybody they wanted, so we went to a bar for a drink. There was a Greek lady with the biggest camera I had ever seen, and we asked her what she was doing.

She said, 'I am trying to take pictures of Colin Firth and Pierce Brosnan, who are on that boat out there,' which we could just about see.

A lot later, the boat came into port, and we wandered down to the pier to take a closer look. We saw a man with socks and sandals, and Chrissie said, 'That cannot be my hero Colin, as he would never wear such an ensemble.'

And she was right, as we found out from a man on the pier; because it was long shots, it was not Colin or Pierce but their doubles. The boat was old and beautiful, and we were told it was built in Hong Kong by Naval Intelligence and used to spy on the Japanese in the Second World War. *Mama Mia* was to become one of the girls' favourite films.

It was time to go home. We have been to Skiathos around ten times, and it always feels like a home away from home.

# November 2007

On my many trips to Australia, we always stopped off in Singapore or Bangkok, but I never visited either. Our next holiday started in Singapore and ended up in Bangkok. In the old days, I used to travel First Class, but now we had been demoted to World Traveller Plus. The leg room seemed quite small but not too bad. The food was economy with smoked mackerel salad and sweet and sour pork. Sleep was not easy, and you woke up quite often, even after the more than plentiful booze.

The Amoy was our hotel, a nice boutique hotel centrally situated so we can ride the metro, which was very clean; we had a nice dinner there: cold crab salad with sake and a prawn wasabi, foie gras, Peking duck, fillet perch, bean crumbs and soya sauce, rack of lamb with Chinese honey, fried rice with seafood, and platinum bean sprouts - quite a feast.

On our first day, we took a river cruise, visited the Asian Civilisations Museum, and had lunch on Long Quay: dumpling prawn soup, chicken satay, and prawn cakes. For our aperitif, we went to Raffles. I would hate to stay there, with so many tourists. Singapore slings were S$47 for two. We had a hamburger in the Raffles deli, which was not the best; the Heinz ketchup tasted of Asia.

The next day, we slept late and missed breakfast. We went up to the shopping area, Orchard Road, and couldn't find anywhere for breakfast so had a sort of brunch later; we were not doing so well at eating here.

But it got better. After a trip on the Night Safari, we went to Food Street in Chinatown for dinner and picked a white-tablecloth restaurant with a smoking corner. We ate really well with steamed and grilled dumplings, prawns with oats, sweet and sour fish and Tibetan lamb. We then saw the last two dishes being made on TV on a programme which featured our restaurant for the night.

Singapore seemed a bit soulless, sort of like Monaco. We were really here for the Singapore sling, which in itself was a bit disappointing, but we did have two good dinners, and we had many adventures to follow.

Our adventures started as we boarded the train in Singapore Station to take us to Kuala Lumpur in Malaysia. It took eight hours twenty minutes rather than seven hours. But the train ride was wonderful, a great experience, and it made you feel like a real traveller. At the first stop in Malaysia, an oldish man and woman and we presumed their daughter got on the train. Somewhere on the way, the train stopped for some time, and we all got off to have a smoke. He introduced himself, and the older woman, who was his sister, and the other girl was his fiancée. He went on to tell us that he was in the military and had been in Guantanamo Bay for a number of years; it was very lonely and he got engaged to a cleaning girl to pass the time.

We arrived at Traders Hotel and had a good room with a big bed, a big sitting room, two plasma TVs, and a large bathroom with good views of the Petronas Towers. It was all so soulless, with 571 rooms of corporate dullness. We ate in the restaurant and enjoyed a Malaysian gourmet night for around £30 per head: tomatoes, gazpacho, tomato tart, and tomatoes with goat cheese, which was very nice.

We also had tagliatelle with octopus and asparagus, tenderloin Australian beef with mushroom ragout, and roasted vegetables and pulses.

It was a good dining experience but no way was it Malaysian, which was a pity; the whole place seemed to be full of people you would not really want to spend time with.

For our one day in K-L, we had a private city tour for about £60 with a nice interesting chap, who knew a lot about Malaysia and also showed us that K-L did not have a lot to offer. We also went on a visit to the Concord Hotel, where I stayed on my business trip but the pool bar was closed; we could not have the prawns and spinach, which was one of the best dishes ever.

But our last-night dinner was good. There were traffic jams everywhere, so we walked for about twenty minutes to the Food Market. Dinner here was an experience not to be missed. There was lots of life; we found a place with four or five kitchens and wandered around, ordering from each of them, and then sat at a great white table. It was mostly delicious; we ate BBQ squid (a bit chewy), bean sprouts with salt fish (great), grilled leatherjacket with curry paste and chilli sauce (even better), fried prawns with chilli sauce, and two fried noodles and washed it down with Tiger beer. And the total cost was only around £16.

The next day, we caught a plane to Phuket; we went to Thailand. We took a one-hour cab ride to Khao Lak and the Orchid Beach Resort, which was featured in the 2012 tsunami disaster movie *The Impossible*. The hotel took the full force of the tsunami; the hotel's map showed lodges in the gardens which were no longer there. The hotel had a problem in that it was full of holidaymakers from northern Europe on cheap package tours, who killed all the atmosphere; they didn't even come for the half-price sundowner cocktails. Most nights, there were just the two of us.

We ate at the hotel restaurant on the first night; it was only average and cost £30. Again, it was completely lacking in any atmosphere, so we decided to go downtown from then on. At breakfast, you had to produce an entitlement slip; again, it was all quite average.

Every night, there is a pickup, which we take, and some other riders tell us to go to Kungs, which we did and had a truly great dinner: roast duck, sweet and sour (almost the best sweet and sour ever; the pieces of lime with the duck were divine), steamed prawns with soy sauce, steamed snapper with lemon sauce, and steamed rice, with a couple of beers and a couple of glasses of wine. The cost was only £13 for a memorable dinner.

The next night, we decide to go upmarket and headed off to the Sarojin for the beach buffet dinner. We ate prawn soup in a clear chilli broth, lobster, river prawns, snapper, noodles and veg, and banana fritters with ice cream; we drank an expensive bottle of Chilean Sunshine merlot, and it all came to £105 (or around six times the price of Kungs and actually not so enjoyable).

We ended up going to Kungs three more times and always had a great dinner for around £15 (because we drink a little more).

For lunch most days, we took a long walk along the white deserted beach for maybe two miles to go to a little beach bar we found. The best dish was fried rice with shrimp paste, omelette, pork, chilli, onion, and green beans for a magic dish. With beer to drink, lunch for two normally cost around £7. The beach bar had a BBQ on our last night; we ate very well, with chicken and red snapper with a wonderful tamarind sauce and a bottle of Two Oceans red from South Africa, which was half the cost of dinner, at £35.

We did a lot of swimming in the pool and the sea, which was always a little rough and felt a bit dangerous; we also had two adventures.

First we went on an elephant ride. We were looked after so well and were helped up on our elephants and spent about forty-five minutes going up and down a very steep gradient, to be followed by pineapple and water. Next, we got into a canoe and for nearly an hour did a slow punt down a beautiful river, with a few scary rapids on the way. We felt it was a perfect morning, and all for £20 for the two of us.

The second was more poignant: We went to the Tsunami Museum. It was a major catastrophe for the town; eight thousand people died, including twenty-five hundred tourists. By the museum was the police boat, which the waves had taken over one mile inland, to where it was now resting. Despite this, everything seemed to have been rebuilt, and life went on as normal.

We liked Khao Lak a lot; the beaches and the food were wonderful, and it was all quite cheap.

We went back to Phuket, but instead of flying to Ko Samui, we decided to take a car and boat instead. We had a thirty-two-year-old lady driver in a Nissan, and we took a spectacular three-mile drive over the mountains in the interior of Thailand. We were back to being real travellers again; it was so much better than flying. And then we took a ninety-minute boat ride to Ko Samui.

We stayed in the Pavilion, which was very classy; we were upgraded to a superior junior suite, which apart from the big bed gave us a Jacuzzi all to ourselves. The breakfasts were much better here, with freshly squeezed orange juice, fresh croissants, and good coffee, and pancakes if you wanted them, which I didn't.

For our first day, we went to a Thai cookery class with just Chrissie and me and two chefs. We were given the ingredients for three dishes to chop up: lemongrass, ganga, kaffir, lime leaves, and chillis. We made prawn soup (I was told I put in too much lime, but it tasted great to me), chicken soup with coconut (and no chilli), and lastly prawns with fresh rice noodles and a very complicated tamarind sauce. And then we ate it all with a couple of beers. It was a nice way to spend a morning.

Quite a few nights, we ate in the hotel, which had a really nice beachside restaurant. The spring rolls were very good, as was the crab with yellow curry; we had a special dinner for our anniversary: salmon carpaccio and Phuket lobster thermidor; it was *tres bon,* and with a bottle of Bin 451, it all came to around £65.

Another night, we went to Sua Yuan, the fish market, and had prawn rolls and red snapper with Thai sauce and quite a lot of wine for £11. About three hundred yards from our hotel was the local food centre, with around seven restaurants set in a dirt car park. We ate chicken broth with small veg and chicken with rice, and pork with crackling and rice; with a couple of beers, the bill was £2.27 for a really delicious atmospheric dinner. I gave them a 45p tip, and they couldn't believe my generosity. Somehow finding places like this is what travel should be all about. To find such nice food at such cheap prices and to have a great time is what makes travel special - whole dinner for less than fish and chips for one back home.

Our activity here was mostly swimming, which we did three or four times a day, and beach walking, which was always a pleasure.

The last night here, it all went wrong. We had met some German Swiss on the beach: Simone and her boyfriend Philippe, who spoke no English, and her brother Felix. One night, we went for a lazy sundowner with them and decided for the last night, we would have dinner together. We all went off to the Happy Hour Bar and had three pina coladas and went off for a shower. They carried on drinking. We decided to go to Jah Peace, a restaurant just down the beach, where we had taken a few nice lunches. It was an okay dinner with masaman prawn curry and a couple of beers, and it all came to £4.50 per head. As it was our last night, we were given free sambucas by Leon, the owner.

As we were leaving, they started to play the Beach Boys: classics like 'Help Me Rhonda' and 'California Girls' (the Beach Boys are one of the greatest groups ever and particularly good for dancing on the beach). We danced on the beach and had a few more sambucas. Philippe disappeared, and we went back to the bar to pay and have a chat, as you do.

Felix then pulled the monkey, and about twenty people appeared from nowhere, all demanding a drink. Felix had no money, so I offered to pay but was not allowed. Philippe came back and knocked over Leon's Thai fiancée and started a fight with Simone. And the twenty people all got nasty and threatened Simone; Chrissie got in the middle and tried to calm down a man who said he had already killed two people, and Leon said he was calling the police. Somehow, we left and then heard the twenty people shout, 'Let's get them,' so we ran very fast back to the hotel (which luckily was not too far). We never saw or heard from the three of them again, and the moral of the story is don't hang out with German Swiss who cannot hold their liquor.

We were hungover and took a Bangkok Airways Boeing 717, which must have been at least forty years old, to Bangkok. And it was the king's birthday; there were a lot of fireworks. We took the hotel shuttle, a three-wheeler, past lots of beggars to the Skytrain. We went to the State Tower's fifty-second-storey restaurant with obligatory smart casual dresswear. We sat on a breezy terrace and ordered too much: vegetable dim sum, wasabi prawns, steamed white Pacific cod, and roast duck with pak choi, which is all quite nice. It cost £100, and I drank one beer. With less breeze and less hangover, it could have been great, but still the king's fireworks carried on.

And the next day, we discovered Bangkok, which is a very exciting city. We went for two rides on the river, firstly private, for around £25, which was a bit dull, and then we went with everybody else, 50 pence each, which was far more fun.

We hired a *Chut Chut*, which took us all round the city; we visited temples, where we had to dress up, and jewellery shops, where we bought a sapphire ring, and it all cost £1. I am glad I visited Bangkok; it was frantic, not scary, and all the people seemed so nice, but I do not think I will be rushing back.

The whole Far East experience was great; it felt like we have had some real travel experiences, but we were not backpackers (more flashpackers, I guess).

# April 2008

I haven't written about Lauren and drama school yet. Instead of A levels, she went to college and did a BITEC in Performing Arts. Her lifelong ambition was to go to drama school in London, so in 2006-07, I took her to London for about twenty auditions. She was finally offered a place in the Academy of Live and Recorded Arts (ALRA) in Wandsworth, and she was in heaven. Except when she came home at Christmas and said she hated it, but it was okay because she now wanted to go to film school in Los Angeles instead. We did a deal that she would do one more term at ALRA, and at Easter, we would go to Los Angeles and check it out.

So here we were in Premium Economy again, relatively comfortable with eighteen people in a cabin for thirty on our way to LA.

In LA, we stayed in a very nice, modern apartment owned by our friend Janet in San Pedro, about thirty minutes from downtown LA on the freeway.

We ate a nice dinner (prawn with chilli mustard and sand dabs) for around £31.

On day one, we explored LA in our rental car. It is such a big city, but we discovered Shuttles on the beach in Santa Monica. We had an excellent lunch, with crab Louis salad, and £31 again. We are to return here many times over the next few years.

On day two, we pitched up at the New York Film Academy (NYFA) for Lauren's interview. We met a nice lady in the equipment room who told many good stories. And then a pretty girl showed us round the site and took us on a private tour of Universal Studios. We saw the set for *Jaws* and a lot of other movies, and it was all fun. NYFA said if we wanted to come, we would be welcome, which seemed very straightforward.

For the rest of our time in LA, we spent time looking at property because Lauren might be living here. We also sent to Sunset, which was uplifting, and the Getty Museum, which was free (apart from $8 for the car park) and full of amazing stuff and such a beautiful location after the train ride up the hill.

We had some nice food; I had a brilliant pork chop in Le Bistro, which was to become a favourite but has now become a Thai restaurant.

After LA, we travelled to Mexico, taking the four-hour flight to Cancun. We stayed in Akumal, a large beachside village about one-hour drive south from the airport. We had a good time here, with a lot of swimming in the glorious sea. Attached to our condo was a really nice restaurant, La Lunita, which is still number six out of thirty-five restaurants in Akumal, according to Trip Advisor. Dinner here normally costs around £60 for three; we ate here a number of times, with jumbo shrimp, grilled fish, and lots of margaritas and Mexican cabernet.

One day, we took a taxi ride to the ruins at Tulum. Apparently, three million Mexicans lived here from AD 400 to 1800, when the Spanish came and screwed it up. It was all very pleasant, but at the end of the day, a ruin is a ruin. We liked Mexico with the weather, the people, and the food and drink all good, and it didn't seem too expensive.

Next stop was New York, where we checked out some more film schools, in particular the NYFA New York. We arrived there, and they were not expecting us, but we got shown around by a nice Chinese girl and then went off to Soho, where the acting takes place. We did an acting for TV class with Bob Goodman, and there was so much energy, I wanted to sign up there and then. I have a friend who is a judge in Manhattan, and his daughter is a musician in the city, so we arranged for Lauren to spend an evening with her to find out about the town.

Apart from all this, we had some fun in New York. I love this city and was here for six weeks when I was eighteen, so it is very dear to my heart. We went to the Metropolitan Museum, which is always a joy, and saw some amazing vases from 700 BC and lots of modern art from Picasso, Keel, Dali, and one special Chagall. It is such a nice museum, you could easily spend a lot of time there. Another day, we went to the Waldorf Astoria for lunch. We were glad we weren't staying here, as it was full of suits with name tags, but we had a very good lobster salad in the Bull and Bear, a sort of steakhouse, for £46.

We had some nice low-key Manhattan dinners, but the best and most expensive was in Ruby Foo's, where we ate dim sum and Peking duck with pancakes and drank mai tais, all for about £150 for four of us. But of course we also went to the Oyster Bar in Grand Central Station one night and ate New England clam chowder, cold Maine lobster, and banana ice cream with Bloody Marys and merlot for around £90 for three. Oyster Bar was probably the best meal of this whole trip.

The trip went back downhill when the monkey trailer trash toilet cleaners got upgraded from Economy to the seats next to us. I was going to have to work out a way to at least fly Business in the future.

After all the excitement of LA and New York, Lauren made her decision. She was going to NYFA in LA starting in September.

# August 2008

Lauren's lucky number is 8. It was 08.08.08, and we were getting in the car to start Lauren's journey to LA; I switched on the engine, and what was playing on the radio: 'Mr Tambourine Man' by the Byrds. It was too much.

On the plane, Chrissie and Lauren got upgraded to Club but I had to remain in World Traveller Plus. I swapped seats with Lauren for afternoon tea.

The first job was to find Lauren somewhere to live. First, we looked at an apartment by the Kodak Theatre, which is a dreadful tourist spot, and then a couple of others in rundown areas, but then we found the perfect apartment in Maplewood, which is by Paramount Studios. It was delightful with two bedrooms, two bathrooms, two terraces, granite worktops, a pool and fitness centre, and secure parking (sharing with the delightful Gay Ross), and only costing $1,150 per month, against a budget of $1,200. But we had to buy beds, mattresses, shower curtains, and quite a few other things.

Next, we needed a car. We ended up going to Santa Ana Mini and found a nice Black Mini Cooper convertible, with a price of $23,999. After a little negotiation, we got it down to $23,526. And then we had to get insurance, which cost $1,563, and Lauren needed to take the California driving test, as she could not use her UK licence.

With the fees for NYFA, this was a very expensive adventure, but I was so happy to be able to help and support my daughter.

We stayed in the apartment in San Pedro again, and we often went to Le Bistro for dinner and had pork chops, fish ruffi, and calamari couscous; it normally cost around £60, and we got free chocolate ravioli, which were truly delicious, and port to wash it down with. One night, they had live music from Laura Cramer, who was great and gave us a free CD of her music. There was also a really good Italian restaurant, Louis, in Larchmont (near Lauren's new apartment), and we had lunch one day sitting next to Kevin Bacon. They did a very good eggplant Parmigiana, and it only cost around £21 for lunch.

After all the excitement of getting Lauren settled, it was time for a road trip. On the first day, we got as far as Malibu for lunch. Malibu seemed strange, but we had a nice outside lunch at the Beachcomber on the pier. Next stop was Santa Barbara; we stayed in the Sandpiper Inn, which was miles from anywhere, but we had a large room with two bedrooms for $139 per night. For dinner, we drove to the Santa Barbara Shellfish Company on the pier, for lovely views of the sunset. We drank Santa Barbara Blonde beer and ate clam chowder and lobster tacos; it was a very fine evening for £35.

We next took the scenic drive up Highway 1. We had lunch at the Harbour Hut in Moro Bay, where we stayed for one night on our honeymoon: shrimp, crab, and avacado salad for me, with lemonade to drink, all for about £26, and such fond memories. Then to Hearst Castle, where it was too late to go in, and on to Big Sur, which I found overrated, so we carried on to Carmel, where we had spent a few nights on our honeymoon; it was such a romantic day. We stayed in the Pines Hotel, which was very nice, at $179 for two rooms.

There was only one place to go for dinner in Carmel (maybe or maybe not). It had been our favourite local restaurant in 1980, the Hog's Breath, then owned by Clint Eastwood. The dinner was not very good, partly because of the suits making a lot of noise, and I had to send back my fillet mignon, which was overcooked; with a bottle of Lockwood Marley pinot noir at $37, it all came to $151, the most expensive yet. I don't think we'll ever go back.

The girls went shopping, as they do, and I went down to the beach and had a really long walk and a paddle in the cold Pacific; there is a cold current in California, which comes down from the Arctic. It makes swimming in the sea very rare. Carmel was so pretty. And we took pictures outside the Dolphin Inn, where we had stayed on our honeymoon.

We did the seventeen-mile drive round Pebble Beach, which was nothing to write home about, and headed to Santa Cruz via Monterey, which was a pretty cool town. It sounded great but it really wasn't. We stayed in the Edgewater Beach Motel, which had nice views of the Pacific but was expensive; our room was $189 for two nights and then $289 for Friday night, and we had to pay $129 for a pretty small room for Lauren. There was not much to do in Santa Cruz except sit around and swim in the pool, so we decide to go to San Francisco.

This wasn't great either, as we drove the wrong way down a one-way street, failed to find anywhere to park, and ended up going to the expensive parking on Fisherman's Wharf. It was all so touristy and had no atmosphere. When we stayed here in 1980 on our honeymoon, we took a streetcar down to the wharf and ate dinner on a pier, which was somehow magical, but being there in the day with all the tourists was most certainly not. The best part of the day was the drive over Golden Gate Bridge; everybody should do it sometime.

We ate okay in Santa Cruz; it wasn't too expensive, costing around $60 for the three of us. The best was Riva, which Trip Advisor had as number three out of 228 restaurants in Santa Cruz, and Aqua Blue was also not too bad. We were glad to leave Santa Cruz; it was full of low-class people.

The drive back along Highway 5 was fascinating, with hundreds of miles of just dry grassland, and I learnt how to go faster by undertaking, which is what everybody does out here. Back in LA, we ate in the Bistro again; the waitress, Maria from Puerto Rico, was gorgeous and is still in love with me. We asked Laura to play us 'Hungry Heart,' by Bruce Springsteen, which was our honeymoon song. The next time we were there, she played it; we danced and got a name check; such a great song and such a wonderful singer. Then we discovered P F Chang's, which was a good Chinese place with excellent steamed shrimp dumpling, honey shrimp, and hot kung pau chicken.

It was time to plan road trip two. I always wanted to stay in the Del Coronado in San Diego, which was featured in *Some Like It Hot* with Marilyn Monroe, Tony Curtis, and Jack Lemon (I own an authenticated signed self-portrait by Lemon, which I got in a charity auction for Children with Leukaemia). Trip Advisor put me off: long check-in queues and six hundred rooms, so not our sort of place; we went next door to the Glenatta Bay Inn, with a bay view room for $199. We visit Del Coronado and were so glad we were not staying there, a real tourist trap, but I did take a rare swim in the sea and pretended I was starring in *Some Like It Hot* (although they no longer have the famous changing cabins). We also visited Sea World, which is truly great if you like queuing, as it took over thirty minutes just to get in. The killer whale show was just about all right, but a lot of splashing water; if you give this a miss, you will not have missed much.

We had some nice dinners at the Boathouse, Chez Loma, and Tartines. The latter only because we took an evening boat ride into San Diego for dinner, but the port area was devoid of nice restaurants, so we hot-footed it back. Tartines did a wonderful handmade herb gnocchi with pomodoro sauce and shaved Parmesan.

On the way back, we took the long way through Palm Springs. It was very hot here, at 111 degrees. We went up the cable car to get some cool air and did two nice hikes on the Desert View trail in 72 degrees. We had a really nice dinner at Copley's, with rack of lamb with truffle and white bean sauce and a bottle of $50 Genesis merlot, all for $135. And a not-so-good dinner at Wang's where we didn't understand the menu, but it only cost $67.

We were in America for thirty-two days (the garden back home was going to be a real mess). But it was time to say goodbye to Lauren. It was very hard; I was going to miss her so much. We now had Skype, which made it a little easier, as it was almost like she was in the room. Only one thing to do, and that was to increase her allowance so she could have a really good time.

## November 2008

We were back in Premium Economy on our way to LA. It would be so good to see Lauren again. The temperature was around 90 degrees, which was great. Lauren had lots of friends, and we all went to dinner in a steakhouse near NYFA; the food was terrible. The next night, we went to dinner with Esa and Raquel at P F Chang's, which was much better.

But after two days, we were off to Manzanillo in Mexico. We stayed in the Dolphin Hotel next door to Los Holos, which was where Dudley Moore and Bo Derek filmed *Ten*. Our hotel gave us a pass to the Los Holos private beach, which was very fine. We were glad we're not staying, as the hotel seemed to be full of ancient Yanks who all had hip replacements and walked with canes. We had a nice room with a terrace and glorious seaviews. And one morning at breakfast, we saw dolphins swimming in the sea.

There weather here was great, but there was not much to do except lay on the beach and go swimming in the warm and delightful Pacific. One day, we took a bus ride for $2 into Manzanillo; a drunken Mexican fisherman helped us get the right buses. Manzanillo is suburban Mexico and not touristy, with a really nice plaza but no bars to get a drink.

We ate in the hotel a couple of nights, which was cheap at around $35 but with no atmosphere; most nights, we got a cheap taxi for a few dollars and ventured out. Our favourite restaurant was Toscana. Here, we ate gazpacho, shrimp and fish tempura, and tarte Tatin, for example, and normally around $80, with lots of margaritas and wine. There was lots of atmosphere and a really nice staff, and they always gave us a free coconut liqueur at the end. Another favourite was Chipotle in a Mexican neighbourhood where you ate tacos and baby lobster, for which you got three for $20.

Manzanillo was great. We had fine weather, there was lots of nice food, and we enjoyed the Mexican people, who were so friendly and welcoming, but it was time to go back to LA.

It was Thanksgiving. We were invited by Esa's mother, Winnie Hervey, to their house in Hancock Park for Thanksgiving dinner. The turkey was amazing and so was Winnie. She wrote and produced *The Prince of Bel-Air* and discovered Will Smith; she seemed to know just about everybody in Hollywood. We will meet her many times over the years.

During this trip, we also had a great dinner at Gordon Ramsay's at the London Hotel. Cauliflower puree, foie gras with apple, and Maine lobster all made it a dinner to remember.

Another day, we went to see John, who owned the San Pedro apartment with Janet. He had a five-litre V8 1988 Mustang and asked if I would like a drive. Sure, and I did about three miles at 30 MPH in third gear, but oh, so such a great experience.

Time for another road trip, so we took off in the lesser powered hired Mustang convertible and drove three hundred miles to the Stovepipe in Death Valley, for a $96 room. The temperature was mid-70s rather than 120 degrees in the summer. We drove about a hundred miles through the valley; it was truly awesome. There were hardly any people; Zabriskie Point was the highlight, and Badwater was very good too. The whole place was amazing, so peaceful and beautiful; I think everybody should try to get there sometime. On the way back, we got stopped doing 82 MPH in a 50 limit, but with our English charm (or whatever), we get off.

And Lauren's car needed fixing, and it would cost $4,600, which was not good news.

At the weekend, we took a 190-mile roundtrip to Carlsbad to meet an old friend, Gee. He was at Morgan Hill for the weekend when I was eighteen and had pizza for the first time. We were both wearing jeans and T shirts. We both thought that after thirty-eight years, we should have grown up and be wearing tweed jackets and ties for Saturday lunch, which was how we were brought up and observed our parents acting. It was interesting to reflect on this because our parental generation were very staid, but we somehow avoided all of that and learned to live more naturally without being dominated by convention.

## March 2009

We missed our daughter, so we went back to Los Angeles and stayed in the London Hotel, which was our favourite because of the double showers, smoking on the balcony, and Gordon Ramsay's restaurant. I was behind him once in LA immigration and got my bags at the same time; we made eye contact, and I told him how much I enjoyed his TV series. I got a big smile in return.

But the first night, we went to Petit Four on Sunset, which was a great French bistro; I ate artichoke vinaigrette and calves liver and got dinner for two for around $100. For the second night, we were back in San Pedro and eating at the Bistro, with the gorgeous Maria, who pretended she missed me so much.

We didn't stay too long in LA, and so it was off to Mexico again. This time, we explored Zihuatenejo on the Pacific coast. We stayed in Villas Miramar, a really nice hotel; they squeeze the oranges for breakfast, and it's right on the beach. Raphael made great margaritas, and we asked him where to go to dinner. He recommended Los Braceros, and we have to ask loads of people where it is, but after we found it, we sat down to a great dinner of *medula*, which is a marrow soup, and shrimp tacos, with more margaritas and lots of red wine, and it all cost around £25. Another night, we went to Rufo's Grill and had lots of great food, including red snapper and lots of wine, again for £25. To be really expensive, we went to Elvira Casa and ate lobster, and still the bill was only £34. We went there a number of times.

The weather was sunny, around 85 degrees, and we spent all day on the beach, with lots of swimming in the luxurious Pacific. And we had great lunches on the beach, which normally cost around £5 for lovely ceviche and a couple of beers.

We then met two charming ladies from America and Canada and went on a boat trip with them to Playa Gatas; we watched a cruise boat take four hours to get the punters onshore. I am sure cruising is not for me. I don't want to go somewhere for a couple of hours with lots of hassles; it's so much better to live somewhere and explore and find the great restaurants and just hang out.

One night, we went to Athenas, a Mexican restaurant with plastic tablecloths; it was established in 1975. We had chicken soup, chicken with beans, and guacamole and drink beer, and it all came to £7. After, we went to Jimmy's Bar to dance salsa; all the ladies agreed that I was not very good. But hey, it was such a difficult dance. Another dancing place was Bandiros Saba, which had a fantastic band and okay disco, but after trying for many hours, the girls still don't think I am good enough. They prefer to dance with others. And another night, there was a bar celebrating its ninth year, which was loud and fun.

But it was time to go back to LA. We really liked this place: 85 degrees and sunny every day, good OJ for breakfast, great beaches with good swimming, and we ate lots of really good cheap food and had plenty of fun dancing. I would really recommend it, but as yet, we have not been back.

It was good to be back in LA and see Lauren again. We hung out in her condo and watched *The Poseidon Adventure,* probably the worst disaster movie ever.

We celebrated Easter with a gang of kids and had a real feast, starting with Heidsick Red Label champagne and Cadbury cream eggs, shrimp, ham, devilled eggs, and mustard potatoes, and finishing with Raquel's very impressive pineapple upside-down cake. Then we played Charades, but everybody really wanted to play Beer Pong, which just has to be one of the world's greatest games; it really should be an Olympic sport, but there aren't any rules, so it could be a little difficult. We met a guy called Eric who Lauren seemed to quite like. We'll hear more of him later.

And so ended the second trip to LA. It was a city I liked; it always had good weather with lots of sunshine. We found some nice restaurants, and Lauren was happy, with lots of friends.

## Time for Decisions

It seemed obvious that we were going to go to LA a lot. I had not earned any money for a number of years but still had a reasonable amount in the bank; however, we lived in a five-bedroom house with a cottage and unconverted coach house and three acres of land, for which I am the sole gardener; it gets in a real mess, particularly when we go away in the summer. Our costs on the house, including all the refurbishments, are around £600,000, but its value was £1.2 million. So we put it on the market and started looking for somewhere new. We looked at a couple of places by the sea and found a wonderful art deco house near Newquay. But then we went for a walk around and saw the horrible tourists who kept invading. We looked in Portloe, which was nicer, with a good restaurant at the Lugger and a nice pub, but can't find the right house. We also looked in Falmouth, but it seemed a little downmarket, and again we failed to find the right house. One afternoon, we did Location, Location and started off in a Georgian townhouse in Truro, which we loved, and then saw a converted barn near the cattle market in Truro, which we hated, and then looked at a house in Wadebridge, with stunning views of the Camel but horrid kitchen, plastic windows, and too much space upstairs.

After a lot of backwards and forwards, we finally agreed to buy the Georgian townhouse in Truro for £640,000. It was a wonderful house which had just been done up. It had four bedrooms, five bathrooms, and a cloakroom (making six loos in all). There was a wonderful drawing room through to dining room with original wood floors, a downstairs den, a study, and a great kitchen with Aga and lots and lots of glass, as well as a utility room. Outside, we had a small walled garden and parking for four cars. The garden would soon have asparagus, artichokes, and a variety of seasonal vegetables (but not too a lot of flowers).

In all, we had about the same square footage as Carclew, but we had an extra £500,000 in the bank, which would keep us solvent for some time. In some ways, it was not like downsizing at all, and we would continue to live very happily in our Georgian splendour. It seemed that over the years, we had done very well from property and used our profits to support our lifestyle; we were very lucky to live mortgage-free in such a great house and still have so much money in the bank. We moved in a week before Christmas and had the whole family to stay for a very enjoyable time.

## July 2009

And now it was time for our fifth trip to LA. We now bought Premium Economy and used our miles to upgrade to Business, which was a better way to travel. After my later business years of travelling First Class everywhere, it is quite difficult to downgrade. But the plane was six hours late, and we didn't get to LA until 4.30 a.m. UK time, which was a bit of a drag. It was so nice to see Lauren again; I did miss her so. She came along to meet us with Eric, who seemed like a nice boy, but we would find out differently later on. We rented a white Mustang convertible from National, which set us up nicely for the trip.

This time, the San Pedro apartment was not available, so we started off in a hotel in Hermosa Beach, which was just about okay for $179; it had a nice seaview but a poor breakfast. On the first day, we took a walk to Manhattan Beach, which took around thirty minutes, and later had a $20 dinner from Panda Express.

The next night, we met Eric's mum, sister, and her boyfriend, who all seemed quite nice, and we ate in an Italian at Toluca Lake.

We finally got back to the apartment in San Pedro; we really feel at home here. It also meant that we can go to the Bistro for dinner and see Maria. San Pedro had a very old movie house, the Warner Grand, and for $20, we went to a champagne reception and watched *Paris 36* from the front row of the balcony, sipping our champagne and eating peanuts.

There was a major problem: We played beach volleyball, and I got so covered in sand that I went for a swim. It would be my first swim in the California Pacific; it was supposed to be 70 degrees, but it felt colder. But the weather was nice, and it was sunny as always in LA; the temperature was around 90 degrees.

But it was now time for a road trip, and our main purpose this time was to go on Route 66. But first, we had to take the 11, 91, 15, and 40 before we got onto Route 66 at Kingsman. In the car, we had a CD of the Rolling Stones' first album; track 1 is '(Get Your Kicks on) Route 66,' which we put on as soon as we were on the road. We loved 66, as there was not too much traffic; it was pretty straight, and you could drive fast. We drove through Williams, which looked like an interesting town, and had lunch in Ludlow, with rough waitresses and a not-very-good tuna sandwich. At Needles, it was 114 degrees. And we arrived in Flagstaff for the first time in thirty-nine years; when I was last here, I ate Chinese on my way back from the amazing Grand Canyon trip. We stayed in the old Connoly Hotel, which was lovely and old and was built in 1926, after the community raised two

## Mr. Tambourine Man

hundred thousand dollars to build it. Paul McCartney stayed here; I hope he liked it as much as we did, with even a rocking chair in the bedroom.

We had a great dinner in the Cottage Place: excellent tomato soup, spinach salad, rack of lamb with roast potatoes, lovely local vegetables, and English mint sauce. We drank wine by the glass, as the list was expensive, and spent $111 plus tip for a truly great dinner. The trains woke us up during the night, but after wandering around, we decided we liked Flagstaff.

We now had a five-hour drive of 220 miles through Monument Valley to the Recapture Inn in Bluff, which was 4,300 feet above sea level and seemed nice and friendly, with lots of restaurants within walking distance. After a couple of swims, which seemed like hard work with the altitude, we went to the San Juan Grill for artichoke dip, catfish, and smoked pork shoulder; with some wine and beers, it all costs $75, including tip.

The next day, we went to Monument Valley with the roof down. Monument Valley is quite breathtaking; a lot of movies have been made here. John Ford was always here, and they made *The Eiger Sanction, Thelma and Louise, Mission Impossible 2, Back to the Future 3* here, just to name a few. It was quite touristy, and you had to be careful not to get ripped off. We paid $65 each for a ninety-minute trip in a twelve-seater open pick-up, but there were only five people, so it was quite comfortable. We had a Navajo guide, who was a joy, and had a really nice drive, looking at the amazing rocks. The best bit was the last, when we stopped at Eagle Eye. This was the cave where the famous snake scene in *Raiders of the Lost Ark* was filmed. Our Navajo got out a flute, a bit like a recorder, and played beautiful Native music; the acoustics of the cave were just fantastic. It was a lovely day out.

Dinner was at the Cottonwood Steakhouse: salad, BBQ chicken, and catfish and drinking beer for $53.

The next day, we toured around the area and ended up at Four Corners, where Utah, Colorado, Arizona, and New Mexico all meet; it's the only place in America where four states touch. We had dinner again at San Juan Grill with good tomato stuffed with polenta and vegetables, and only $56 this time.

The new day, I revisited the Grand Canyon, possibly one of my favourite places in the world; I had such fond memories of sleeping at the bottom and the long, long walk back up. We drove the 250 miles in about four hours and arrived at midday. First, we had a very nice lunch on the terrace at El Tovar: wild shrimp cocktail and bruschetta with artichoke, olive, and tomato, all for $29 with a couple of lemonades.

The Grand Canyon was truly wonderful, being five thousand feet deep with just the most amazing views. We found the trail I walked up and walked down it a little and then get a three-mile bus trip to find the trail I went down. We started descending, and I wanted to go all the way down again but didn't. Then we watched the California condors, which were great to see. I can only say that if you are in the area, just go because it is such an unforgettable place.

From here, we were off to A Shooting Star Inn, which is miles from anywhere; it's about twenty miles from Flagstaff, at seven thousand feet, and quite difficult to find. The power is solar, and they bring the water in by truck.

Shooting Star is a magical place if you are in the right mood. It's all about the sky. Before dinner, we used the telescope to look at Saturn and the moon; Saturn's rings were so interesting to see. For dinner, we ate steak, broccoli, and chips and drank homebrewed beer and listened to Tom Taylor, who played three songs. We went back to the telescope to see lots more, including Jupiter and Mars. Everybody seemed to see shooting stars except me. Shooting Star just added to the great experiences of this trip and was truly memorable.

It was an eight-hour trip back to LA, making the road trip 1,836 miles. We did another 150 miles on Route 66, driving about half each; Chrissie was overtaken by one car and overtook nothing, and I did much better, overtaking one car. Route 66 is a delight; if only all roads could be like this. We stopped at Amboy at 3.30, and the temperature was 120 degrees in the shade, my hottest ever, and it is truly hot hot.

We were back home in San Pedro for a few days. We just hung around and went to the Bistro for really good stuffed pork chops, P F Chang's, and an Italian place, and saw *The Hurt Locker* with Eric whilst Chrissie and Lauren went to see *Harry Potter*. I would take *The Hurt Locker* any day.

But it was time for another road trip, and this time, we were off to Napa Valley. On the way, we revisited Morgan Hill. This trip was turning into real nostalgia, with the third revisit after thirty-nine years. The memories came flooding back, and we walked around the thirty-two acres. It only had eight bedrooms and four bathrooms (rather than the ten bedrooms and nine bathrooms I remembered), and the wine cellar was gone, but they still had the piano, which I spent many hours playing to the kids back in 1970. It was great to be back, but we had to go on. I thought Napa would be small, but it's not; our hotel was around two miles from the centre.

For dinner, we drove into town and found a great restaurant with smoking, but there were no waitresses; eventually, we found Zuzu's Tapas and Wine Bar. We had a lovely dinner: bruschetta with anchovy and egg; salad with artichoke, mushroom, and St Jorge cheese; prawns with chilli; a Tunisian pasty with tuna eggs and peppers; and to follow a peach pastry; two Amber ales and two Napa merlots, and all for $73, and the eggs were so good. A real find.

The first thing to do in Napa was go on Silverado, the wine train, which costs $99 for two. It takes three hours, and you can't smoke, but it's a lovely slow trip through the vineyards. The waitresses gave us a great commentary, and we saw Robin Williams's house. We had to have a couple of glasses of vintage champagne (well, actually, it's only sparkling wine) at $12 per shot, and we ate mushroom soup with three sorts of bread, and it all cost $72, including service. Although it all seemed quite expensive, somehow it was not a rip-off and a really nice way to spend three hours.

That night, we went for an Indian and spent $39 on bhajis, tandoori lamb, and pea and potato curry, all of which were delicious, and we washed it down with four glasses of pinot noir and Syrah, which cost $60.

On the tourist trail, we visited Castilago and found a nice town museum dedicated to Robert Louis Stevenson, and then we lunched in St Helena. We had a great lunch in Tra Vigre: mitto fritto with prawns, calamari asparagus, and squash with a brilliant chilli mayonnaise, and then squash blossoms stuffed with cheese and tomatoes. With a couple of lemonades, it was only $32 plus tip.

It was time to go to a winery. After much deliberation, we went for Terra Valentine up in the hills, for a tour with only ten people. The other people were on their fourth winery of the day and of course had a chauffeur-driven car. We tasted a Spring Mountain 2005, which was 95 percent cabernet, a pinot noir, and two more cabs, which were all brilliant. And then we bought Lauren a couple of bottles of rosé, and it was all free. What a great afternoon out; the vineyard was so pretty, set in the hills. For dinner, we took a $10 taxi ride to Uva; we drank an Oberon Napa merlot 2006 at $38 and ate boring veal; there was no atmosphere, and it all came to $93 plus tip.

It was time to leave, but we went back to the honeymoon in Carmel. On the way, we stop in Morgan Hill again for lunch. Bad news: All the estate agents were closed down, which meant we were unable to investigate the property prices. On our revisiting theme, we next stopped in Salinas and went to the Steinbeck Museum. John Steinbeck is probably one of my favourite authors, and *The Grapes of Wrath* is my favourite book ever. I read it about every three years; the descriptions of poverty and despair are out of this world. From my current position of affluence and well-being, it makes me realise how very lucky I have become. The museum is a really interesting history of Salinas and Steinbeck country, and we sat in a model T Ford truck, which Chrissie particularly loved. In the gift shop, we bought books we had never heard of, a T shirt, and a martini glass for Lauren. I would completely recommend a visit to this place.

We were back in the Dolphin Inn, where we spent our honeymoon, with glorious views of the Pacific through the trees and a nice warm pool to swim. I can see why I fell in love with this place twenty-nine years ago. We were only here for one night, and there were so many choices for dinner. We eventually decided on Brochette and had an excellent dinner. We shared lobster salad and foie gras with apple, and I had John Dory with tagliatelle, which was all excellent. But the John Dory came from New Zealand (what is all that about?). We drank a Monterey merlot, Villa Christina 2006, and it all came to $155 plus tip, but altogether a lovely evening in a lovely place which was so special to us.

The next day, we set off in the fog along Highway 1 for Morro Bay, which we also visited on our honeymoon. We revisited our favourite restaurant and had clam chowder and lemonade, all for $15 for two. And then back to the London Hotel, which has wonderful rooms and great service. It was Lauren's twentieth birthday, and we all went off to Sunset Marquis with a load of her friends. We ate prawn tempura, lobster sausage, and sticky toffee pudding and drank quite a lot; it all cost $724. But hey, I love being a dad, and it's so nice to have enough money to give special treats from time to time.

And dinner the next night was just as expensive. We entertained eight at Gordon Ramsay's in the London. We eat a mousseline of foie gras and smoked mushroom, excellent skate, lobster, and halibut and drank Santa Barbara Syrah and Sancerre rosé, and it all came to $720, including service. Winnie was one of our guests, and we talked about Quincy Jones, who is her favourite person.

It was August 8, and we had been here for twenty-five days; it was time to go home. This trip had been great, and the nostalgia was brilliant. Revisiting Flagstaff, the Grand Canyon, and Morgan Hill after thirty-nine years was a joy. When I first visited them, I was an innocent eighteen-year-old who had only known the very limited confines of Essex, but I liked them all, and here I was returning a man of the world, with many experiences, but I could still enjoy them and had a good time. And it was so nice to stay in the honeymoon hotel again; Carmel was truly a special place and will remain in my heart for ever.

# September 2009

After four weeks, we were off again, this time to Lemnos in Greece. My nephew George was working there with Neilsen for the summer, and we set off at 4 a.m. for Gatwick with my sister, her husband, and four friends. We were going to have a ball.

Lemnos was 80 degrees and very windy. The island is not at all pretty and must be pretty low in the charts of beautiful Greek islands; I had seen so much better.

At Neilsen, you get mostly full board except a couple of nights when you go out, and to start, it was all very average. Lamb, butter beans, and asparagus for dinner and spinach pie and tzaziki for lunch were pretty normal fare.

The wind was a problem, and water skiing was cancelled; my wind surfing was totally dreadful because I just could not get it. Tennis was better, and I was in the top group; one of the players was Ella, who was fifth in the UK under fourteen, who knew some of the good girls at our club in Truro. I was expecting to have some really enjoyable tennis with her over the next week. But on the second day, it rained, and we only got forty minutes; it's just not supposed to rain in Greece in early September, and the temperature was only 65 degrees.

The first night out, we went to a restaurant with blue tables at the end of the pier and ate fried courgettes and aubergines and sea bream (which was overcooked), and it all cost E24 per head.

The weather got better, and I got my first water ski. It was quite rough, but I got up the first time and just about managed to hold it together and didn't fall over.

But we had another rainy day, and the tennis tournament managed to last just over one hour. At the last dinner, I won player of the week.

It was nice to see George, but Greece was not much fun in the rain. I only got one waterski, and the windsurfing was terrible, and the tennis kept getting rained off. The flight home on Thomas Cook was as bad as ever, with no room and terrible food. I cannot believe the CEO would allow such a disgusting beef chilli to be served; maybe they just don't care and are only concerned with the bottom line, which in my experience is totally the wrong way to approach business because in the end, you lose out with more unhappy customers who will just seek a better product.

Back in England, it was 70 degrees with lovely sunshine, so what was the point of going to Greece?

On 21 October, my father passed away at eighty-five years old; he had dementia and lived in a nursing home for a couple of years. I was concerned that I would also get dementia, as three of my cousins on my father's side also have it. The home was so depressing, with no spirit, just a lot of old people waiting to die. I made a deal with Chrissie that I would never be subjected to a home, but we would get two gorgeous Thai girls to look after me to ensure that my last days were happy ones.

## November 2009

We started this trip in London, with an early dinner party for twelve at Foxtrot Oscar's to celebrate Chrissie's big sixtieth birthday. We all drank a lot, and the food was a bit limited; although crab and sticky toffee were good, the fish pie seemed dull. I made a big speech but forgot what I said, and everybody I asked couldn't remember either; it all cost £840 for the twelve of us.

We went on our sixth trip to LA, flying Premium Economy, which is not too bad; I enjoyed a Bloody Mary, Grolsch, and chicken tikka Masala and watched Woody Allen's *Whatever Works*, which was pretty good. There was not much headwind, so it only took ten hours, but it still seemed forever without a cigarette. Flying was so much more fun when there were smoking seats.

We rented a grey Mustang convertible and drove to the loft in San Pedro. On the first night, we had to go to the Bistro; it was so nice to see Maria.

We went to see the movie *2012*, which was supposed to be serious, but all we could do is giggle. With the impending sale of Carclew, we were considering investing in LA property. Lauren had this idea of building a new house; we looked at a very steep piece of land, with great views in the Hollywood Hills. We looked at a few houses; the worst was a Korean short sale, where the apartment just felt so claustrophobic.

We went to Target to get things for Thanksgiving, and I ended up buying lots of CDs: Norah Jones, Ben Johnson, and Bob Dylan's Christmas album, and then we went to Whole Foods and bought a large turkey breast. Thanksgiving Day was beautiful, sunshine and 82 degrees, and we went for a long walk on Cabrillo Beach and ate a panini picnic. Thanksgiving dinner was great; we started off with Heidsick Red Label champagne and smoked salmon canapés, globe artichokes, and a wonderful turkey with roast potatoes (not mashed, which is the American tradition), asparagus, broccoli, corn stuffing, mashed sweet potato, and of course cranberry sauce, all followed by chocolate brownies and lemon meringue pie. It was a feast to fit the occasion; we had now celebrated Thanksgiving two years running.

We made turkey sandwiches and set off for Palm Springs, which should have taken around one hour but took over three because of the traffic. We arrived in two cars at a really nice house with pool but had to phone the owner to find out how to heat the pool. We got it up to 93 degrees in the afternoon, which was very pleasant, but it went down to 84 degrees by morning, so we had to fire it up again. The pool was very private and looked like it could be good for some fun.

Chrissie and I went exploring and found Miro's, the number one restaurant in Palm Springs, according to Trip Advisor, and we booked a table, but instead, we went to the Margarita Bar, which was not as good as we remembered.

We found that there were free tennis courts for anybody to play, and we hot-footed it to the sports store and bought two rackets, shoes and socks, and tennis balls, all for $72.

The next night, we had an expensive ($300) dinner at Copley's, where we ate before. Champagne to start and an Oregon pinot noir to follow; we ate very good tomato soup and lobster with prawns, peas, leeks, button onions, and a pastry top. The atmosphere was great, and it was a real treat for everybody.

Sunday was our twenty-ninth wedding anniversary. Lauren and Eric had to go back to LA; as soon as they left, we went skinny-dipping, and the feeling was just so wonderful. We could still be naughty after all these years. I went off on my own to buy Chrissie's big sixtieth birthday present. I found a likely looking jeweller, and they had pendants made from old car parts. I bought one for her, which she still adores to this day, which just goes to show the obvious is not always best. For her fortieth, I bought her diamond stud earrings, which she has worn just about every day since.

For the anniversary night, we went to see *Precious,* an amazing movie which was going to score quite low until the last scene, where the mother gave an Oscar performance, telling her daughter why she was such a shit, and the daughter then just walked away, saying, 'I never, ever want to see you again.' This was followed by dinner at P F Chang's: not memorable, but the skinny-dipping was.

On the last night, we went to see *The Maid,* which didn't seem to deserve to be a prizewinner at various festivals. For dinner, we went to Peppers Thai Restaurant, which opened in Palm Springs in 1989. The chicken satay was good, the honey roast duck with cabbage and sweet basil was excellent, and the prawn green curry only okay; it only cost $53 plus tip. Palm Springs seemed even better than in the summer, when it is so hot, and it had a good air, which made it worth visiting.

Back to LA and back to our favourite: the London Hotel. On the first night, we had dinner at Petit Four; I ate artichoke and calves liver, as always, and it cost $93 plus tip. It was Chrissie's big sixtieth; she liked her present and went off with Lauren to the beauty salon. For lunch, we went to the Ivy for the second year running and drank Veuve Clicquot and ate lobster risotto, salad, and tarte Tatin, and it all came to $203 plus tip. There was major excitement with the paparazzi, who could not stop taking pictures of this twenty-year-old girl. As I am very nosy, I went and chatted with them and found out that the object of their attention was George Clooney's girlfriend.

Next, it was time for the big birthday dinner; seven of us met up at Gordon Ramsay's at the London, including John (who owns the San Pedro loft) and my old friend Winnie and her daughter Esa. Dinner cost $988, which meant we did not quite break a grand. We all started with Laurent Perrier champagne at $24 a pop and later drank a Napa merlot at $75 a bottle. Chrissie and I both had smoked salmon to start, and I followed with roast partridge with foie gras, which was simply delicious; Chrissie ate John Dory. It was an expensive evening, but it was worth celebrating.

The next night, we went to see *A Serious Man* and had a cheaper $60 dinner at Petit Four, eating chicken tandoori and drinking beer and glasses of merlot.

During the day, we met an architect, who advised a geological survey on the land to make sure we can take the mountain out to build a house; we looked at three disappointing places for sale and think maybe the land is the front-runner. There is a lot to think about. After thinking about it, we offer $50,000, which is totally rejected, so we increase the offer to $70,000.

We were quite busy and we saw George Clooney in *Up in the Air* at 11.15 p.m., which we loved, but it didn't end until 1.15 a.m., which made us see how the young live. We also went off to Laguna to meet Ingrid from my 1970 trip to Morgan Hill, which was fun, but we had have a poor lunch with terrible service. And it got cloudy and was only 60 degrees; this was not the LA I had come to know and love. But it was time to go home.

When we got home, we only had a few days to get ready to move, but we managed it, and on 18 December, we moved into our new Georgian house. My diary records that I don't miss the gardens, and next year's diary was ready to record how it went. First impressions were good, and with the house having three thousand square feet, there was lots of space.

## February 2010

We liked it there, but after ten weeks, we were back to LA for the seventh time, flying Business and drinking champagne and eating lobster, but it's still a long flight.

This time, we were staying at the Safari Inn in Burbank, which was a great trendy motel, for $80 per night with a clean, biggish room and an okay bed.

We started off by looking at about eight houses and condos, but none of them seemed quite right. But we did find a great Realtor, Jackie, who told us about Angelino's, this great Italian place. We went there and ate the best cheese ravioli with a great tomato sauce and drank lemonade, as they had no licence.

But then we did find a nice house with loads of potential, called Chiquita, and we submitted an offer of $408,000. Our offer was rejected; the agent said there was another offer, but we didn't believe her. We went off and looked at another eight properties but didn't like any of them.

We then discovered Prosecco, another upmarket Italian place in Toluca Lake. We ate bruschetta with tomatoes, basil, and garlic, followed by osso buco and drink merlot and Peroni, and it only cost $83 plus tip. After, we watched New Orleans win the Super Bowl, 30-17, with a great interception at the end, but I don't think I'll get addicted to this game; soccer is much better, and I did play it for many years.

Next, we headed off to Mexico again; this time, we went to Mazatlan. We stayed in a really nice hotel, Casa Lucila Boutique. The restaurant was nice, but the pool was too small, and you had to take a twenty-minute walk and catch a boat to a decent beach on Stone Island.

But then we had a bad, bad experience. While we were walking to catch the boat to go to the beach, we bought a beach bag and sat down on a wall to smoke a cigarette. I noticed a guy walking by in an Abercrombie T shirt. He snatched the bag and ran off. Chrissie went running after him, but he got on the back of a motorbike and sped off. Nobody was hurt, and we met a nice taxi driver who took us to the local police station. There were about eight guys hanging around with machine guns, and of course they did not speak English. After a while, we understood that we had to go to the Tourist Police, which was miles away. We reported the theft and headed back, looking through the bushes on the motorbike route but finding nothing. Chrissie was very upset; I bought her a £2 hairbrush, but it didn't seem to do the trick. We are very good travellers, and the first thing we did when we arrived at our hotel was put the passports, credit cards, and money into the room safe (or failing that, give it to reception for safekeeping). Our bag only contained a camera, a couple of pairs of glasses, a cheap phone, and Chrissie's hairbrush, lipstick, and address book. So I guess we were lucky, but it really spoiled our mood and sort of put us off Mexico forever.

We stayed in the hotel and ate in the restaurant and drank margaritas; we had avocado and shrimp, tomato bruschetta, chicken satay, and fresh fish, which with a bottle of Mexican Malbec all cost around £55.

In all the excitement, we increased the bid on the house to $425,000. But they came back and wanted $498,000, so we seemed to be quite far apart.

And the weather was not very good; it was mostly cloudy and around 75 degrees (but felt colder in the wind). And the Mazatlan Fiesta was starting, with fences around our hotel and very loud music and the streets full of many people drinking beer. We were still suffering from the bag snatch, which made us feel low, and all this activity just made you so wary. We ate dinner at ChevaLea, and it all cost £10 for two margaritas, two pina coladas, and spicy shrimp and grilled chicken, with nice rice broccoli.

We went for a trip to the old town and sat in the cathedral, which is very Mexican and nice, and then we spent $2 watching divers from forty-five feet; it didn't seem like that much fun here, but the weather improved and it was a sunny 80 degrees. We went off to Stone Island and had a good time.

And it was carnival time. The hotel did a buffet for £25 each, which was quite expensive, and then we went onto the balcony to watch the fireworks. We had to hang around until 10.40, and then we got forty minutes of only okay fireworks, which all seemed a bit of a drag.

It was Valentine's Day, and we went to dinner at Lucy's Ta Amour, where the food and drink were very good, with particularly good rabbit and lamb; the margaritas were great. We didn't have enough cash to pay the bill, but they said no worries, just come back tomorrow and pay us the rest.

But then the disaster hit. We got a phone call from Lauren at 2 a.m. to tell us that the kennels had just called; they had to take Maudie, our beautiful fifteen-year-old black Labrador, to the vets. There was another call at 3 a.m. to say that she couldn't walk and her organs were deteriorating; they had to put her to sleep. Maudie was my first dog, and she was delightful; it was so sad to see her go. I get a lump in my throat just thinking about it, and we weren't even there to say goodbye.

The hotel recommended a small local restaurant just round the corner, Casa Azel; we went, but there was no alcohol, so we had to drink tonic water. There were only four tables, and nobody spoke any English; we had to share a table with a Mexican couple and communicated with the help of pen and paper. We managed to eat *pollo a la playa* and small tortillas with beef, chilli, tomato, and carrot, and it all cost around £12. The Mexicans asked us to their apartment; were we going to get rolled again? But it was okay, as he was a secondary school science teacher, and she was an artist; we went to their apartment, which was full of pictures and sculptures, and drank wine in a most sociable way. The corridors seemed full of people and children playing; it was so different.

The next day, we were standing on the terrace, looking at the pool and the sea, and we met a nice couple from Laguna Beach (just down the road from LA). Bob and Jamie were to become great friends, as we shall see as the story goes on, but first we went out together for supper. We went to Tapelo, a new restaurant, and had to wait ages for a table, so we drank two margaritas each and then walked over what seemed like cat litter to our table. None of us can understand the menu, so we all ate pork shank with mashed potatoes, but as we were all a bit wrecked, I have no idea if it was good or bad.

And the next night, we went to Casa Azel again and had some drinks in the bar first. They were out of chicken, so we had to eat Doritos and enchiladas with nice flavours of who knows what, but it only cost £11 for four; we went onto Lucy's for dessert and spent £60 with some very nice tequila to go with the fried plantain and mango ice cream.

But it was time to go, and we have not been back there since.

It was good to be back in LA, which felt like home (or a home away from home, at the very least). We went to see an immigration lawyer with Lauren, who reported that her chances of getting a visa were nil, and if she wanted to stay, she would have to go back to school, which was the only way of staying, but we found another solution (to be described later).

We spent a bit of time looking at houses, but we were not impressed. Chiquitta had an open day at the weekend, which could work to our advantage. We went to the open day, but it was not open; however, we knew how to get the keys and had another look around and decided this could be the house at the right price.

In the meantime, we went to see *Shutter Island*, a really intriguing movie, and we spent hours in the restaurant discussing it. We decided we shall never know the truth. A few years later, I saw the movie on TV with a different ending, where it was all explained; the only way to see this movie is the original cinema version, which had a simply brilliant ending.

And we ate well. We had lunch at M&S on Rodeo Drive, and I had really good Dungeness crab from Oregon with mango and avocado; we went to Prosecco in Toluca Lake, and I ate a really good ravioli with chicken and zucchini, and with wine and a couple of Peroni, it only cost $54; good food and a good value. The reason we were in Rodeo Drive was to buy a new bag for Chrissie to replace her stolen Armani bag; we failed in Rodeo Drive and went to Riverside, where we eventually found a new Coach bag for $320, which made her very happy.

But it was time to go home again; we really missed Lauren.

## May 2010

We were back in Club on BA for our eighth trip to LA; the real reason was to see the new house. We had bought a really nice 1930s two-bedroom bungalow in Toluca Lake (which is quite close to Universal Studios and very close to Warner Bros.), with a swimming pool of decent size and orange trees in the garden, for $515,000. And the house was once owned by the famous rock star Toto, who used to have orgies in the swimming pool. From overseas, I had negotiated with a contractor to put in a second bathroom and do some other works for $26,417, a very precise amount.

We arrived at the house, and it was truly nice, with a great feel. I slept well for jet lag, and although I woke at 3 and 6, I still slept to 9 (which was 5 p.m. UK time).

## Mr. Tambourine Man

It was 84 degrees and sunny, which was wonderful; we really enjoyed the new house, and it felt like after so many years, I now had a holiday home. I liked this house; it felt very different visiting, as with our house, we rather belong here. But we did go to an Irish bar on Ventura for lunch to see Tottenham versus Manchester City: a new experience and quite fun. And we set about decorating the new bathroom, which had a terrific shower. We got the pool guy to come and clean, and we could then go swimming, which was so nice.

Prosecco was just round the corner; we ate very good bruschetta and ravioli with mushroom and sun-dried tomato and drank excellent organic Italian red wine. Next, we discovered Angelino's, another neighbourhood Italian place where you had to drink lemonade, as they had no licence, but they did this fantastic cheese ravioli with a tomato sauce to die for, and it only cost around $15 per head for some of the greatest food ever.

We started painting the rest of the house, which had a large reception area, dining room, and utility room, so it was quite roomy and felt like lots of space. Meanwhile, after five days of wrangling, David Cameron became our prime minister with stupid Nick Clegg as his deputy; I felt quite smug that I now had some money invested in prime US real estate, which would give us a hedge against those people.

We went to see *Iron Man 2,* which was not really a great movie, but we caught two glimpses of Eric, for which he worked a number of sixteen-hour days, all for $500, but it's good to see movies with somebody you know. And after a few false starts, we found the perfect colour for the drawing room: white jasmine, which was truly delicious; as always, I got a lot of paint on me when I did the business.

We met a guy called Mark at tennis, and he was playing a gig in the Smokehouse. Chrissie and I had a great time dancing to 'Do You Wanna Dance,' 'All Right Now,' and a fantastic ten-minute version of 'Mustang Sally.' Another time, we went off to Paradise Cove in Malibu, where you only had to pay $3 for parking (with validation), instead of $25, and I ate a very nice Maine lobster pasta for $29, but it was only about 64 degrees and foggy, so it was difficult to tell if this was truly paradise.

We ate quite often at Angelino's, drinking lemonade and having really great pappardelle with tomatoes and mushrooms. And we went again to Petit Four on Sunset and enjoyed the calves liver.

It was nearly time to go home. We just about finished all the painting, planned a new kitchen, and found a great place for cheap granite worktops. I was pretty active too, with fourteen games of tennis, ten swims in our wonderful new pool, and four visits to the gym. It was sunny and hot for nineteen out of twenty-one days, and we felt at home. The house looked great, and I was sure it would be a winner. We were saving so much on Lauren's rent and living somewhere really nice, and Chrissie and I had a holiday home for the first time.

We reviewed Lauren's future and found a great two-year course at UCLA for only $6,500, which will give her visa security and at least another two years in this great place.

## July 2010

It was now time for our ninth trip to LA. This time, it was really exciting, as Lauren was going to get married, and three days later, she would turn twenty-one years old. We booked Premium Economy but got upgraded to Club, and I watched *Dr No*, which is one of the greatest films ever.

We arrived in LA, and it was 104 degrees; the house was looking so good, and it felt really comfortable. The new kitchen looked pretty good; I had forgotten how much I liked it. In this weather, it was so great to have a pool.

I spent the first week painting the outside walls, and Chrissie spent her time being the wedding planner. Then I hired a Mustang convertible, and we headed off to Yosemite, which is three hundred miles (around five hours) away. We stayed in the mall town of Maraposa, which was forty-three miles from the park. The hotel was small and quaint. The first night, we ate at Savoury's, which was number two on Trip Advisor in the town. We had red pepper hummus, shrimp and enchilada soup, and jambalaya, and drank

Sierra Nevada beer and a nice bottle of Mariposa 2005 merlot, all for $75 plus tip.

We headed into Yosemite, which was at four thousand feet, and paid $20 to park. We went to the visitor centre and bought sandwiches and took a bus to Mirror Lake, where we had a picnic by the water. It was all very pretty, and we took loads of pictures. After a nice long walk back to the bus, we went on a field trip with a ranger. It's actually a ninety-minute walk through some pretty cool meadows, and then we looked at the waterfall. The waterfall was 2,425 feet high, the fifth biggest in the world after falls in Venezuela, South Africa, and two in Norway (Niagara and Victoria Falls are not even in the top ten). In reality it was not really that impressive, as you would think looking at the fifth biggest in the world should have some wow factor, but it didn't, really. There was a lot of traffic, and it took well over an hour to get back.

We went for dinner at the Butterfly Cafe, which was the Trip Advisor number one, but it was hard to tell why. The menu was boring, and so was the food. I ate onion soup and lemon chicken with rosemary potatoes, but the Maraposa merlot was as nice as ever. It cost around $71 plus tip.

The next day, we went back to Yosemite and took a long walk to see the giant sequoias (which don't seem all that giant). Our thoughts on Yosemite were that it was all very beautiful but not as great as everybody says; all it really does is to do what it says on the tin. There were no surprises. In our trips to Death Valley, Monument Valley, and the Grand Canyon, there was always something unexpected to excite; here, not even the fifth biggest waterfall in the world was really inspiring.

For our last night, we went to the Charles St Diner and spent $123 on a much better dinner in a terrific atmosphere: portobello mushrooms with Gruyere, New Zealand lamb chops (which you get nine), and apple pie with Silver Fox Mariposa merlot. It was a nice way to end our stay here before we went back for the wedding.

It was only one day to go, so what did we do? Played tennis and went to the movies to see *The Kids Are All Right*; we also went to the best diner ever, Patty's in Toluca Lake, and had corned beef hash with fried eggs over easy. And we practised blackjack for going to Vegas.

I got married in a church in Maida Vale, London, on a snowy November day and then went to Didier's French restaurant for a great lunch in what turned out to be the best day of my life. We weren't originally going to get married in a church, but we went to see the vicar to ask for a blessing. After establishing that neither of us was divorced, he said he would love to marry us in the church, even if we didn't really believe in God, so that was how we ended up in church.

Lauren was going to get married at the house by the pool. It was a beautiful sunny day, around 85 degrees. With a lump in my throat, I walked her down the aisle with loads of flowers and rose petals and Bach playing. There were twelve people in total, and the pool setting was perfect; it was a truly happy event.

They opened their presents, and we all piled into a fourteen-seater Lincoln stretch limo, drinking champagne, and went to Il Cielo for our wedding breakfast. Il Cielo looked simply splendid. We had a fantastic four-course dinner, with lobster the highlight, and drank more champagne and some very good wine; it all took about four hours, and they opened the roof so that we could stargaze. At the end, we all piled back into the limo and headed for the London Hotel, where we had more drinks on the roof terrace. It was a very special day, and I think maybe it was the second-best day of my life. Somehow, I didn't think that my lovely daughter, who would be twenty-one in three days' time and I always loved to bits, was lost. Eric and Lauren stayed in the London for their honeymoon night, and we headed back to the house.

The honeymoon was going to be in Las Vegas, and we were going too (we had already booked to celebrate Lauren's twenty-first birthday). Here in Las Vegas for the first time, and the first impressions were not too great. We stayed at the Wynn, one of the more upmarket and expensive hotels. We got no help getting out of the car and had to queue for ages to check in and then lug our bags through the casino to the elevator to get to the room, which for $300 can only be described as okay. On the second day, I noticed a dirty patch on the carpet and despite two calls to room service, it never got dealt with; it looked like maid service never bothered to hoover the room, which kind of summed up Vegas. The service in the hotel is non-existent; you had to queue for breakfast, and despite temperatures of 107 degrees, the water at the pool ran out and did not get replenished, so we were all thirsty and dry, which was terrible. We found out that last week, the hotel sacked three hundred employees, but that was no excuse for not looking after the customers; the day would come when the golden goose is dead. There was not much to do here except sit round the pool, but most of the seating area lost the sun at 1.30, so again, not very good. My only gambling was to play the five-cent slots; I lost about $20 over the whole time we are here. After Lauren turned twenty-one, she played blackjack and won the first two hands; she thought she had it tapped but then lost the next ten and gave up. Lonrho owned casinos, and I had seen the returns: The house always wins, so you are better off not playing, but I guess in such a boring place, people found it difficult to find any other amusement.

The first night, we went to the Eiffel Tower for dinner. The menu was dreadful; I didn't want to eat there but ended up with two starters and not much to drink, and it cost $100 per head, which was just stupid for a little to eat and drink in quite an unpleasant atmosphere. If you're ever in Vegas, do not go here on any count.

For Lauren's twenty-first birthday, we booked to go to the French restaurant in the Hotel Alex, which was excellent and turned out to be about the only thing in Vegas that I could possibly recommend. We were given the choice of a private dining room or the chef's table overlooking the kitchen. We chose the chef's table, which was great. We started off with amuse bouche, including lobster and tuna tartare, and I go on to eat lobster risotto and Wagyu beef, which was all excellent. We had a birthday cake and drank $165 merlot, which was glorious, and the whole dinner costs $2,000 for eight, but I have only one daughter who will only be twenty-one once. I really hoped she had a great day. Then it got stupid, as we were supposed to have VIP entry to the nightclub, but some jobsworth tried to make us queue with all the plonkers. We got straight in anyway and bopped a bit, but at the end of the day, it was all a bit dull, just like Vegas.

For our last night, we went to Stratosphere, a revolving restaurant up high where the steaks are $50, so I had two starters again and not much to drink. Eric's dad chose this and Eiffel Tower, so he must be lacking in taste. It was good to get out of there and back to Cornwall.

## November 2010

It was now time for the tenth trip to LA. I was getting wise and managed to get us Club both ways for £900 each: buying Premium Economy and upgrading to Club, which costs over £3,000 each. I used to travel First Class in my later business life, but I guess I can put up with Club if I have to pay.

We travelled a lot in 2010 and at the end of the year had been away for 122 days, but there were some exciting times to come.

It was 73 degrees and very pleasant, and we got back to our nice new holiday home. On the first day, I went for a swim in the pool, but it was quite cold.

There was not much going on, but we saw a couple of movies: *Morning Glory* with Harrison Ford and Diane Keaton, which was not much, and *Pursuit of Happyness* with Will Smith, which was much better. Then Jamie and Bob, our new friends from Mazatlan, came over, and we went to Prosecco. I ate Parma ham with artichoke ravioli with a vodka sauce, which was very nice indeed. Prosecco was a great neighbourhood restaurant. Jamie did Iron Man Triathlons, which is a 2.4-mile swim, a 115-mile bike ride, followed by a marathon; she must be very fit but still drank like a fish and knew how to have fun. The next night, we went to Angelino's again, and I ate great penne with seafood ragout and one langoustine, and drinking lemonade, it only cost $64 plus tip.

But it was time to get the Mustang convertible and head off on another road trip.

Our first stop was Tucson; we drove 532 miles in around eight hours, driving pretty fast on virtually empty roads, and arrived at a B&B in the desert at Alta Vista. The B&B had a four-acre garden and was very pleasant, with a nice breakfast. Tucson was very laid back and attracted a lot of famous people. The story goes that Linda

McCartney came here to die, and Diana Ross and Arnie Naess had houses here. All the houses seemed big with extensive grounds.

On the first day, we went to the Cactus Desert and took a long drive around, but the desert seemed too clean. Next, we went to the Air and Space Museum, which was great fun; my favourite plane was the SR71 Blackbird, which is the fastest plane in the world and does 2,100 MPH. Then we went off to some movie studios where lots of westerns were shot; that was a lot of fun too.

Eating was not great in Tucson; we ate in Joe's Crab Shack and the Bamboo Club, which were both 'never again.'

It was time to move on, and we drove another 501 miles to Santa Fe, where it was a lot cooler, only around 60 degrees. We stayed in an expensive hotel with a really nice room, but we had trouble getting into the bed because the sheets were shortened. Santa Fe seemed pretty hip, and we booked dinner at Geronimo. According to *The London Times*, 'The prettiest restaurant in town also happens to serve some of the finest food in the United States. *The New York Times* says its food presentation is an art form.'

We were really looking forward to this dinner, but my impression after we finished was that I did not quite agree. We both started with good (which was just good, but not outstanding) quail and crab bisque, and I had Colorado rack of lamb with red potatoes, broccoli, onion, and a mint jus which was only okay, and Chrissie had chicken with Dauphinoise potatoes, which again was only okay. The bill was $201 plus tip, and it was not a dinner to remember, which with all the hype, it should have been nearer. The service was very nice, though.

We wanted to try the tourist train, but it stops at the end of October, so instead, we went on a historic walk. It was all very interesting, and we found out that New Mexico was founded in about 1600 and sold by Mexico in 1846 for $15 million; in 1912, it became the forty-seventh state of the Union.

For our last night, we went to Cafe Pasqual's, recommended by the hotel. It was a nice homely place with great staff, and we ate very well: roasted golden beets and roasted scallops with bacon, and smoked salmon and a squash dish for Chrissie, and with a $57 bottle of merlot, it all cost $157 plus tip.

Next stop was Amarillo, which was another 305 miles, of which we did about half on Route 66 (and in all that distance, I overtook two cars and got passed by none); I am sure you all know the song. We were going downmarket again and staying in another B&B. The lady was very nice and told us it didn't get dark until 6 p.m., so we went for a walk. We were really in the Bible belt; there were just so many churches, including some very large churches. But there was nowhere to have dinner, as all the restaurants (of which there are only about three in the whole of downtown) were closed because it was Sunday. Our friendly B&B lady made a few phone calls and discovered Dyers BBQ in a shopping mall was open, so off we went. It was great, as we could smoke and watch American football. I drank Lone Star beer and ate ribs, potato salad, coleslaw, beans, onion rings, and toast, and Chrissie had a burger and merlot. It was all really nice and only cost $22 plus tip.

It was a nice sunny day, around 65 degrees, and we took a seventeen-mile drive to a famous canyon, which was a small version of the Grand Canyon but still pretty impressive. We had a hot dog for lunch and set off on a long walk, which was very nice (and we didn't meet any rattlers). Then we went to Canyon to a museum, which had some good old cars, oil drilling rigs, and pictures by a famous American artist, Georgia O'Keeffe. The dinosaurs were good too.

In Amarillo, you can buy a three-bedroom, two-bathroom house with 2,300 square feet for $169,000 (negotiable), but I could never live here, and downtown doesn't really exist. We went to see Russell Crowe in *The Next Three Days* and left quite late and can't understand why the cinema was full of young kids. It was because they had the midnight premier of *Harry Potter*.

We had dinner at Mexican Jo's, which was very nice, with seafood and artichoke pasta and chicken Florentine, all for about $45, sitting inside but feeling like you were outside.

We were now 'Twenty-Four Hours from Tulsa,' one of the greatest songs ever from Gene Pitney, and drove the 373 miles in about four hundred minutes, with 110 miles on Route 66. Just into Oklahoma, and we bought gas in Erick; the girls were just so pretty, and we found as we went along that all the people in this state were just the nicest ever.

We stayed in the Ambassador Hotel, which was empty for about twenty years but had now been refurbished; we had a lovely large room with great views of the river and don't have to pay too much money. If you are ever in Tulsa, this is the place to stay. We took a walk around the town, which had some fine older buildings, and checked in at reception to find where to have dinner. We rejected the Irish pub and settled on the Palace. We got in the hotel limo, which was a large smart SUV, and were pleased to have the best dinner of our trip so far. I started with a Marshall's beer and then a Washington State merlot; the food was brilliant. I had lobster corn dog served with ketchup and grain mustard, followed by fettucine with spinach and pesto, which was completely delicious. Chrissie had squash soup and chevre lollipops, and we shared a banana crème brûlée with a large caramel star. This was really funky food and all so delicious, and it only cost $111 plus tip. Just a great, great restaurant.

The purpose of this trip was to get to St Louis, which is where Eric came from; they were going to get married again in front of the St Louis crowd. It was a long way to come to do something I thought we had already done. It was another 411 miles here, and it brought our trip to 2,360 miles, which I guess is a proper road trip. We did some more on Route 66, but Missouri was not much fun, with lots of curves and narrow bits and too many towns. We had done around eleven hundred miles on Route 66 on this trip, and it was a real pleasure in California, Arizona, and New Mexico; everybody who likes driving should have a go in these states. I was glad to have done such an amazing trip; we saw local America and went to new places and had new experiences. Tulsa was the highlight, and the whole of Oklahoma just had a really good vibe.

First of all, we were here for Thanksgiving, and we all went off to Eric's aunty's house. We ate turkey with all the trimmings, and then we played games; the best was Boxers and Briefs. A nice family affair.

Back to property. Eric's dad lives in a six-bedroom house with a cellar and a third of an acre, which he bought seventeen years ago for $172,000 and which was now worth around $300,000. Nice-looking house in a good neighbourhood, but it was cheap.

Eric took us on a tour of St Louis, but there was not a lot to see. We went to the Gateway Arch, which is 625 feet tall, and we gazed at the Mississippi River, both of which were quite (but only quite) impressive. We went to Forest Park and looked at the outside of the zoo and the Art Museum, and then we went into the History Museum. The best bit was Charles Lindbergh's original *Spirit of St. Louis*. It made the first transatlantic flight from New York to Paris in 1927. It took thirty-four hours, and he used 425 gallons of fuel and ate five sandwiches (two ham, two corned beef, and one egg). And the plane was not much bigger than a car.

It was time for the second wedding. For some reason, Eric's mum made us go to the venue ninety minutes early, and we had to hide in a small back room. It was all a bit flat, which was a real shame, as the first wedding on 2 August was so great. This time, I paid another 50 percent for something I thought I had already paid for. We went to a local Italian restaurant for the second wedding breakfast, which was only okay; we danced a little, and I made a speech and then left at 10.30.

For the life of me, I don't know why anyone would want to live in St Louis. It has cold and dreary winters and hot and humid summers, and there seems to be no life and not a lot to do, and it was full of the Midwest ethos. But we were getting away.

The next stop was Carmel again, where we were going to celebrate our thirtieth wedding anniversary where we went on our honeymoon. First, we went on the world's worst airline, US Airways, which really sucked. I looked at the ZAGAT ratings in *USA Today*, and US Airways had the lowest rating of any American airline for Premier Class, at only 14.04. We were travelling Business; the website said breakfast was served on both legs of our journey, first to Phoenix and then San Francisco. We ignored Dunkin Donuts in the airport and got on the plane, to be served coffee and a stale biscuit. No matter; we would get breakfast in the lounge at the Phoenix airport, but they wouldn't let us in, so we had to go and queue at Starbucks to get a late breakfast.

Back to the Dolphin in Carmel, where we spent some honeymoon nights; it was as lovely and romantic as ever. We played Bruce Springsteen's 'Hungry Heart' in the car, which was our honeymoon song. On the first night, we revisited Andre's Bouchee and ate mushroom soup with truffle oil and French onion soup and *magret de canard* with raspberry sauce and confit of duck with a parsley/garlic sauce and white asparagus and thin potatoes, followed by divine petit fours. We got a free glass of champagne and drank merlot, and it all cost around $100 plus tip.

The big day was beautiful and sunny, with temperatures around 60 degrees, which was fine for 29 November. Chrissie bought me some very nice gold cufflinks, and the day before in Carmel, I bought her some antique pearl earrings, which looked great on her. We went off for a romantic breakfast at Carmel Belle and then took a walk along the beautiful beach and took a couple of selfies. We had a nice lunch in a Greek restaurant, and I took a long swim in the nicely heated pool. For dinner, it was back to our favourite, Andre's Bouchee.

The night before, we told the maitre d' we wanted a special bottle of wine (but not to exceed $100, including tax). He chose a Martin Alfaro Grays Vineyard St. Lucia Highlands 2007 for around $85. We ate foie gras with apples, cured salmon, lobster salad and halibut, and tarte aux pommes. With our free glass of champagne to start, it all came to $173 plus tip, and it was a night to remember. Tulsa still seemed better somehow, but it beat Geronimo easily.

We went to the Andrew Molera State Park and took a spectacular three-mile walk to the ocean. Dinner at the Greek place was slightly disappointing.

We went back to LA; there seemed to be a lot of cops on the road, but I didn't get stopped, which meant that we drove around three thousand miles without getting a ticket. At the end of the day and after all the places, California was still my favourite state. The weather was great, and there was a lot of diversity to keep you amused for a very long time.

It was Chrissie's birthday again. She went off to see *Harry Potter* with Lauren, and I went alone to see *127 Hours*; I don't get nightmares, but it was pretty scary when he had to saw off his arm to get away. We had dinner at one of our favourites, Prosecco: bruschetta and mushroom risotto, and Chrissie got a candle in her panna cotta to celebrate the big day. It cost $155 for the four of us in a really good neighbourhood restaurant. The next night, it was back to Patty's for corned beef hash with fried eggs over easy. Burning Bonzai, a good Asian place, was just down the road; we always ate well there: hot and sour soup, shrimp tempura, leek dumplings, and sweet and sour chicken, to name a few.

We went to Pasadena to the Laemelle cinema, which was special, and saw *Inside Job,* which is all about Lehman Bros. and Salomon Bros. and the credit rating agencies. The corruption was fun to watch. The weather was great, at around 73 degrees, and we picked oranges from the garden and squeezed them for breakfast.

But it was time to go home again. This was a great trip, with really great experiences, celebrating thirty years in such a romantic way (although we did not really enjoy Lauren's second wedding). I found that Amarillo and Missouri were places I just couldn't live, even if you could buy a nice house for peanuts.

## February 2011

It was now time for our eleventh trip to LA, but this time, we added something different: We flew Club in the upgrade from Premium Economy; the plane was late due to three missing passengers. Colin Firth was on the plane, going to collect his Oscar for *The King's Speech*; in London, there were four or five photographers, but in LA, there were hundreds; it was a complete and utter scramble.

We spent $24,000 getting Craig to update the pool to salt water with solar heating. It looked great but was only 58 degrees, too cold to swim, which would have been nice, considering all the money. But it was good to be back; I like the house a lot.

It was only around 60 degrees, but we got the pool up to 72 degrees, and I went for a swim. We ate a good dinner at Burning

Bonzai just up the road, with hot and sour soup, shrimp tempura, and very good chicken with broccoli and shrimp chow mein.

And it rained, which was not much fun in LA, so we went to see *Hall Pass*, which was not that funny (except for the shit scene). And the weather got worse, with over an inch of rain; as described by *The LA Times*, 'there was hail, ice pellets, and a frozen variety of precipitation known as graupel that certainly looked like real snow.'

After we watched the Oscars, we got ready for our trip Down Under. Lauren said she needed a quiet word, and we sat down to talk. She said she did not want us to stay in the house. This was not very nice, and it made me quite annoyed, as I really liked this place. It required some deep thought. We found out much later that it wasn't Lauren who didn't want us to stay in the house but Eric. He lived here for nothing but felt we disturbed his precious routine, which was insulting and nonsense. It was typical of the man, and Lauren soon found out he was not her ideal man. They divorced in 2013.

For the first time in her life of sixty-one years, Chrissie was south of the Equator; we were on our way to Australia on Virgin Australia Upper Class. It didn't start too well, as we had to go in the Alaska Airways lounge, which was rubbish. There were two and three seats in a row, but we are in a row with two, which was comfortable, and we started with a glass of champagne.

Dinner took a long time, but it was marginally better than BA: carrot and ginger soup, smoked salmon, rack of lamb, and Haagen Dazs vanilla ice cream, with some nice Shiraz to drink. They give us some Virgin pyjamas, and after about five hours, we were woken by turbulence; eventually, we landed in Sydney at 6.05 a.m. (no flights are allowed to land before 6 a.m.). Overall, the flight seemed okay, but it was quite expensive. And we crossed the International Date Line and so lost a day.

We got to our hotel at 7.10 a.m., but the room was not ready, so we had to go exploring. It was around 70 degrees and cloudy; we headed towards the bridge and the Opera House and got some really nice views. There was a jazz concert at the Opera House on Sunday night, and we bought two tickets for $155. On the way back, we walked round some gardens and had a bacon roll for lunch; after walking around five miles, we got to our hotel room but don't really know what to do for the next five hours before dinner (due to a bit of jet lag).

Out first night, we walked just up the road to the French Bistro, which only had sixteen seats and only took cash. We ate potage Lucifer, a speciality, and chicken liver and pork pate, followed by chicken tarragon for Chrissie and fillet steak with Béarnaise sauce for me, and drank a nice bottle of $39 pinot noir. The bill came to $158, which seemed very expensive for a simple bistro meal, but as we found, Australia was a pretty expensive place to go.

The next day, it was sunny and 78 degrees, and we headed off exploring again. We bought four tourist passes and saved about $80. The first stop was the Sydney Tower; the views from the top were really fantastic, and from way up there, you really got a feel of the city. The next stop was the aquarium, where we saw some sharks and rays, but I have to say I have seen better and had more fun in other aquariums. Then we went to a wildlife centre, where we saw a very large croc and some kangaroos; the general impression was that it could have been better. We walked to the Rocks and found a great place for lunch. I had kingfish ceviche, soft shell crab, with Asian salad and Barramondi, which was excellent at $19.95, but I drank a Lord Nelson Pale Ale, which was brewed just up the road, and was charged $8.90 (they must be joking).

We walked another five miles, and the highlight must be going up the Sydney Tower.

We went to Challis Street to find an Italian place, which was quite difficult, as there were six restaurants next door to each other. We spent £140 on a Sicilian beer, a bottle of Chianti Classico, two glasses of wine (whilst smoking outside later), and calamari risotto and scampi pompadour at $59. It was all very nice but outrageously expensive.

In my business days, I had gone to Manley one night for dinner and thought it was wonderful. So, we got on a ferry to return. Somehow, it didn't shape up and seemed to lack any magic; we returned to Sydney for lunch.

Cafe Sydney was number one on Trip Advisor, and we just about managed to get a table without a reservation. The prices were again extraordinary, so we opted for small crab cakes, nice chips, and a couple of beers, but it still cost around $90 (or £60) for a modest lunch. There was a great view of the bridge. And then we went to Bondi Beach, the great icon. We had to walk two miles from the train station, but it was pretty impressive; we celebrated with lots of pictures, had an ice cream, and took a bus back to the train station. For dinner, we went just up the road to the South India Curry House and had a really good dinner: *doria* with potatoes (which is a sort of pancake), cauliflower and potatoes, hot prawns for six, and a wonderful butter chicken. We drank two beers and two glasses of merlot, and it was almost reasonable (for here) at £60. It would probably have only cost £40 back home.

So if it's Saturday, it must be Belgium, but in our case, it was the Blue Mountains, which were now crossed off our list of must-dos and put on the list of never-to-return. The journey was terrible, as there was line maintenance, and we had to take a one-hour bus ride in the middle. There was a nice soup for lunch: zucchini and bean and even better pumpkin and sweet potato, but with a beer and Earl Grey tea, it still cost £18. There was a very good view at Echo, but not much else to write home about; the whole tortuous journey did not seem worth the effort.

We celebrated our return by going to see Matt Damon in *The Adjustment Bureau* in a very nice VMax cinema on George Street, but it still cost £11 for a senior rate ticket. We returned to the Italian, but it was closed on a Saturday night (which was pretty odd) and ended up in the Lotus next door for fusion food. We ate tempura Japanese mushrooms, crab with asparagus and ginger, pork belly with water melon, and steamed barramundi, washed down with a Western Australian merlot, which was all very nice and exciting, and it only cost £85 (well, it was Australia).

We had a funny last day in Sydney. We went to a market which seemed full of Chinese fat fish stalls and got creative at the Museum of Contemporary Art, which was rubbish. Later, we went to the New South Wales Art Museum, which was much better, with some

nice pictures from Reynolds, Gainsborough, Degas, and Rodin (but the Manet, Pissarro, and Cezanne were disappointing).
Another £50 lunch for a steak sandwich, chicken liver parfait, and two Lord Nelsons.

But then we had our magic night at the Sydney Opera House: Veuve Clicquot at £16 a glass or cava at £5 a glass. Well, this was special, so it had to be the Verve. We had high central seats with a pretty good view; I got told off by security for taking a photograph, and that was before the performance even started (strange place). We came to see Jack DeJohnette, who was Miles Davis' drummer, perform *Miles Davis: A Tribute to Jack Johnson*. I have the vinyl at home, and it is one of my favourites.

We had a ninety-minute nonstop jazz evening with drums, bass, guitar, sax, and of course trumpet, playing the movie's music as the movie showed in the background. This was all followed by a long-improvised encore with a happy-looking band and an audience who have had just such a wonderful experience. It was one of the best concerts ever, and in such an iconic place.

To finish the evening, we went to the harbour and sat right by the water, eating bream fillets and chips with a glass of merlot each, and it cost £65. A great end to a truly memorable evening.

It was time to go to Queensland, for the first time to Cairns. And it had been raining there, with eight inches on Sunday night and still raining, and all the roads were flooded; it took ninety minutes to get to the hotel from the airport, instead of thirty. We stayed in the most expensive hotel of our trip, Kewarra Beach Resort, with rooms at over £200 per night; it somehow didn't seem like our kind of place, as it was a long way out and felt a bit like being in prison. We were glad we're only staying here three nights. The first dinner was only just about okay, with shrimp tempura, nowhere as good as the Trip Advisor write-up, followed by barramundi with mash and asparagus, and all washed down with a bottle of Chain of Fire merlot. And it all cost over £100. But we found someone had taken our umbrella, and the hotel had to send us back to our room in the buggy in the pouring rain.

We went on the bus to a waterski place, where you sort of get pulled round this circuit on a high-level rope. I paid £24, and on the first go, I fell off after five yards but then got the hang of it. Not as much fun as being behind a boat on the ocean. But here, you can't go in the ocean. At this time of year, the sea was infested with poisonous jellyfish and you had to swim in netted areas (but these had all been blown away by a recent cyclone and not yet replaced). You could only swim in the pool, which was a bit dull, to say the least.

Our second dinner was not much better, with coconut and sweet potato soup and a pretty boring version of chicken piri piri and the Chain of Fire again, and this only cost £90. The last night, we had tempura shrimp again, spring rolls, spaghettini with bugs (which are like small lobsters), and barramundi again, with the same bottle of merlot and a dull tarte Tatin, for over £110.

We decamped to the Waterfront Terraces for five nights in downtown Cairns, and they let us in at 11 a.m., a good start. We picked a first-floor room with a balcony overlooking the esplanade; there was a reasonable bedroom and bathroom and a nice kitchen with laundry room, and it only cost £80 per night; the view is much better too.

The lagoon looked nice, but again, you couldn't swim, as the nets had not been repaired. We sat round the pool, and it was so hot, sweat dripped into my eyes; I couldn't read and so had to sit in the shade. We went exploring downtown and discovered a couple of movie houses, and we booked a table at Trip Advisor's number one restaurant, Piccolo Cucina. We ate fried sardines and potato gnocchi with a rich tomato sauce and drank a South Australian pinot noir, which was all very nice, but it cost over £100. It was about a thirty-minute walk, so I guess about two miles there and back.

We went to the movies to see *No Strings Attached,* which was fun but my ticket cost £11, and the Maltesers were £4. Dinner was at Bellacolle, which was Trip Advisor's number five; we ate fried whitebait and osso buco, with two bones each, and drank a cabernet Shiraz merlot from the specials at £22, and it all came to over £70 for something that would cost around £45 back home, but the atmosphere was very good.

Cairns was all a bit boring; the weather was supposed to be six hours of sunshine a day and nineteen days of rain in the month. We seemed to get about one hour of sunshine, and it rained and rained every day. I would suggest you don't come here in March. Another thing that was wrong with Cairns was that it was full of Aborigines, who seemed to have nothing to do except get drunk and cause trouble. After our first night walking home, we got a taxi for the two-mile trip, as the atmosphere was a little threatening.

Trying to save money, we went on a short walk to the Bayleaf, a Balinese restaurant. We had nice chicken satay but couldn't have duck curry, so we had duck parcels, which was pretty boring, and a nameless grilled fish in banana leaf, washed down with Wild Oats Shiraz, and it all came to £60. The next night, we went to Splash. Chrissie had mahi mahi fish and chips, and I had a slightly disappointing Red Spot Emperor with soya and shallots; we got free drinks, and it only cost £36 for good value with nice service. As we had a kitchen, we decided to have dinner at home, and for £30, we managed to buy a pretend champagne, Yellowglen Yellow, flavoured with melon, pineapple, and citrus, sugar-cured smoked sea trout, two Moretta Bay bugs, and a half-kilo of tiger prawns.

We went and saw another movie (Australian this time), *Wasted on the Young*, which was all about drugs and guns; it's all quite fun.

It was nearly time to move on to Mission Beach. We had planned to take the train, but the tracks were washed away by all the rain. We investigated hiring a car, but again it was so expensive, we opted for the Greyhound bus, which only cost £28. The bus ride was quite an adventure. There was a mixture of backpacking girls, dodgy Australian blokes, and a couple of Aborigines. We set off following the railway line and looking at sugar cane and mountains. Scott the driver said that due to flooding of the roads, the bus would probably have to turn back to Cairns at Tully, which was before Mission Beach. After a few false starts, somehow we got to Mission Beach ten minutes late, at 3.15.

We went to the Tahitian, which was very remote but in a very nice position on an amazing long sandy beach; the swimming nets were washed away again, and our swimming pool was on the small side. We were opposite Dunk Island, which had been wiped out by the cyclone and completely closed; to be honest, a lot of Mission Beach also looked fairly wiped out. As we were so remote, we hired a Hyundai Getz for £33 per day and risked the insurance. It was not a Mustang convertible, but it would get us around.

We started off with a good dinner at Bellaude, and we shared slow-baked ricotta with roast pepper and chilli oil, followed by veal escalope for me and gnocchi for Chrissie, with a bottle of cabernet merlot, for about £70. The next night, we went to Scott's for rump steak and chips for me and fish and chips for Chrissie, with a couple of pale ales and two glasses of Shiraz. About ten of us ended up dancing to the jukebox, and I mistook a lady traveller from Norwich for a bloke. It all cost around £40 and was a jolly good evening. And we went to Scott's again on St Patrick's Day and ate roast pork with all the trimmings and drank the same; this time, it was only £33 (but there was no dancing).

There was not a lot to do here, so I swam in the small pool, and we went for a glorious three-mile walk along the beach. The next day, we went exploring in the Getz. We started off at Flying Fish Point, which was very pretty; there was a capsized boat from the destruction of the cyclone. Next, we went to a crocodile farm, which was quite good fun. Then we joined a group of dumb Americans, who all seemed chicken. The largest crocs were five metres long and weighed five hundred kilos. I did get to hold a small one, but on balance, I think crocs are quite scary (although Chrissie seemed to like them). We fed the kangaroos, patted some dingos, and had a feel of a carpet python.

Some of the restaurants here were closed because of the cyclone, but a restaurant called Blarney's was open for a couple of nights. On the first night, we ate very good tempura prawn and roast orange duck for me, and seafood crepes for Chrissie, just drinking beer and glasses of wine. On our second night, I ate nice slow-cooked pork belly with Asian salad and grilled herbal Barramundi, with our usual limited drinks. Both times, it cost around £70. Another night, we went to the Spicy Thai Hut and had some excellent satay with spring rolls and some chicken, prawn, and noodles, with glasses of wine and

Tiger beer, for £48. And then there was a place called Castaways. Trip Advisor said housekeeping was rubbish, which I could imagine, with very young and slightly stupid waitresses. The bruschetta was made with veg rather than tomatoes, which was a bit odd, but I did have a very nice Silkwood sirloin with mushrooms and Béarnaise and with a beer and a couple of glasses of wine; it all costs £60.

Mission Beach was pretty dull, but we had four days of sunshine out of six; there didn't seem too much to do but go for long walks down the beach, swim in the small pool, and reflect that maybe it was better before the cyclone. Roll on, Magnetic Island.

And then we were on Magnetic Island, staying at Robyn's Magnetic Island B&B; the shock was there was no en suite, which meant we had to share. However, there were lovely homemade cookies and lovely carrot cake for afternoon tea. Getting there was an experience; nearly four hours on a bus, which didn't go to the ferry. It took ages to find a local bus to the ferry. Eventually, we found a bus which took us on a long circuit of Townsville, which did not seem to have much to recommend. We arrived at the ferry with six minutes to spare and had a nice, sunny, and windy ride here.

It seemed better here. There were two stinger nets, which meant you could swim in the sea; we booked a Barrier Reef cruise for Friday, which depended on the weather, so we needed to check (at a cost of £120 for me and £85 for Chrissie, as she was not going in the water). The restaurant had a jazz night again on Friday, and we took a Saturday evening cruise with champagne. We also booked a crap car, a Daihatsu Charade, for £50 per day, with an $800 excess (which was probably more than the car was worth: a total rip-off ).

For the first night, we got a lift to Horseshoe Bay, which was not too far, and we ended up walking back. The choice was Noonies for Mexican or the pub, and we opted for Noonies. We ate guacamole and some other dips and chips, and I had paella, and Chrissie a burrito, and we had a margarita and three glasses of red wine, and it all cost £60, which for a pretty dull Mexican was too much.

We got the crap car and drove back to Horseshoe Bay, and I got to do a lovely long swim in the sea for about one kilometre round and round; we had a light lunch, but it still cost £20. We ended the day with dinner at Barefoot, and it was really nice. We shared scallops with asparagus, mushroom, and soy, and I had rack of lamb with ratatouille, and Chrissie barramundi with a mayo salsa, but the highlight was a Margaret River merlot at £30 (they only make eight hundred cases); it still only cost £60 for an excellent dinner, which puts Noonies to shame.

But now it was the big day. We got to the quay at 7.15 and got on the boat for a two-hour ride to the reef at Lodestone, with twenty-one other nice people. There was a little light rain, and we all put on wetsuits, flippers, and masks; a brilliant thing happened: They had prescription lenses for the masks, so I was able to see. Into the water, and I spent around thirty minutes looking at fish; in reality, the reef itself was beautiful and far more interesting to look at than the fish. We had an average lunch (with no beer, as this was serious) and then back in the water to look at the reef again, which was truly wonderful. We were in about six metres of water, but in some places, you could stand on the reef. We got out and took pictures. The sea was very blue, but there were black patches where the reef was near the surface. It was a magical day; I guess we experienced one of the wonders of the world. The snorkelling was absolutely fantastic and has to be put down as one of my great life experiences. What an amazing day; I will always remember this special day. Even Chrissie, who didn't swim, had a wonderful time, and it got even better when she was allowed to drive the boat back for nearly an hour; they let us smoke on the forward deck, as the captain was himself addicted.

After such a day, the jazz night at Barefoot felt a bit of a let-down, but we drank a lot, and I ate a kangaroo burger, and it all cost around £70.

We tried Picnic Bay but it was a bit of a let down too, with no stinger nets, and the beach was terrible for sitting, so we returned to Horseshoe to swim. At 3.30, we went on the four-kilometre Fort Walk with some really great views, and I got to pat a koala, which was great to see in the wild.

For dinner, we went to Battleship with our hosts and had an enjoyable family evening, eating salt and pepper calamari, scallops, and reef fish, and drinking lots of wine.

We went back to Horseshoe, but the weather was not great, so we left around lunchtime, as there was something important to do. It was the start of the Grand Prix season, and I watched the Melbourne race live; it would have been night in the UK and would have watched later. We went for dinner at Banister's for fish and chips, and I had excellent Coral Sea trout, and it was only £24, but that was without drinks, as we had to bring our own bottle of £10 merlot.

The weather was still not good, and Robyn's husband Phil took us in his four-wheeler for a really nice drive to West Point. This was a magical, out-of-the-way place, and the vegetation was superb. For our last night, we had dinner at home with our hosts. Pat and Mary from Minnesota, who were also staying at the B&B, joined us, and we had a delicious dinner of roast beef, chicken, loads of veg, and chocolate sponge pudding. This was a real B&B experience.

It was time to leave, but we had a disaster with the Daihatsu: The car would not start; we wrote 'Not fit for purpose' and left a note, demanding our money back, which of course we never saw. Robyn drove us to the ferry for the JET flight back to Sydney. It was nice to be back there for a couple of days, as Sydney had a totally different atmosphere to Queensland; I guess it was more my sort of place.

It was time to read *The Australian,* the *Times* of Australia, and long at about a hundred pages. There were pages and pages of carbon credit news and then a lot of boring local stuff, and then on page 98, the real story of the moment: There was a tsunami in Japan and a nuclear power plant is on the brink of meltdown; its positioning sort of sums up Australia.

As you see from the narrative, it was really, really expensive here, and everything you did seemed to cost so much. The visit to the Opera House and the Great Barrier Reef would be treasured memories for a long, long time, and the Sydney Tower was pretty good. We did not really have a memorable meal, despite going to the best restaurants in Sydney and Cairns, and we were nowhere near discovering the culinary masterpiece we had expected. The $59 scampi was probably the highlight. Cairns and Mission Beach were overall pretty boring, but Magnetic Island was nice in a laid-back way. The Australians were generally friendly, but we didn't like the aborigines in Cairns.

Robyn and Phil really went the extra mile. Otherwise, they were a little unsophisticated, but their heads seemed in the right place. I had thirty-two swims and got a good tan, despite quite a lot of rain. We were really glad that we experienced Australia, but we were a little disappointed overall; somehow, it could have been much better. In 1994, I made five jet-lagged trips to Australia in ten weeks, when we were doing an IPO for Angliss Pacific, but I was always hanging out with the Rothschild guys; it seemed much more sophisticated.

We flew back to Los Angeles on Virgin Australia Premium Economy for a thirteen-hour flight, leaving Sydney at midday and arriving 9 a.m. LA time. After champagne, Bloody Mary, and three glasses of red wine, sleep eluded me, and I watched endless movies: *Who's Afraid of Virginia Wolfe* (for which Elizabeth Taylor got an Oscar, but Richard Burton was somehow better), and *Singular Man* with Michael Douglas and *Stone* with Robert de Niro, which were both about okay.

At National Car Rental, they had six Sebrings but no Mustangs. However, a very nice girl managed to find me a silver Mustang.

But my heart was still broken. After a nice lunch at P F Chang's, Lauren asked what time we were leaving the next day. We had nowhere to go, and I paid all this money and thought I had a happy holiday house in the sunshine. So we now had to book three nights in Santa Monica, which cost another $800. I wished I was not so pissed off, but I did paint the walls and fences in the sunshine. Downtown LA had the hottest last day of March ever, at 92 degrees, beating the record of 90 degrees set in 1966. Dinner at Angelino's cheered me up a little, with the superb cheese ravioli and tomato sauce, and drinking lemonade, only $38 for two.

But we were exiled to Santa Monica. It was not too bad, with four movie houses within 250 metres, an English shop that sold Maltesers for the movies, and a nice boardwalk on the beach. We ate a nice dinner at Ocean Avenue Seafood; I had clam chowder and a one-and-a-half-pound lobster and drank a very nice $80 merlot, and it all cost $139 plus tip. I tried to book a surf lesson, but they want $80 for 90 minutes so I gave it a miss.

We saw *Barney's Version*, which was quite thought provoking, and met our friends Jamie and Bob from Mazatlan. We started with vodka martinis in the Georgian Hotel bar and then went fifty yards away to the BOA Steakhouse. I ate foie gras, followed by bone-in ribeye cooked to perfection, with béarnaise sauce, chips, and spinach. We drank a $60 merlot, which was very pinot, and some after-dinner wine and cognac, and the bill was $478 plus tip for four, which was a lot of money for steak and chips (but luckily we split the bill). We retired to the English Pub to drink Guinness at $6 per pint. Chrissie can hardly get into bed, but amazingly, no headache and only a glimmer of a hangover. We should have fab evenings like this more often.

Next, we hired bikes, which cost $6 for one hour, and we cycled the three to four miles to Venice Beach and then back. It was all quite magical, and I thoroughly enjoyed. It was English Mother's Day, and Lauren phoned (what is going on here?) and joined us for lunch at Coast at Shutters on the beach; we got the best table, and I ate a really nice corned beef hash, with eggs Benedict for Chrissie and egg and chips for Lauren: a delightful experience.

We went farther for dinner, this time 150 yards, to the Ivy. I started with a chilli martini and then had very good artichoke and soft shell crab, followed by Santa Barbara cod with mushrooms and sherry, but poor Chrissie was given the biggest plate of fish, shrimp, scallop, and calamari ever, which she can only manage around one-eighth, which kind of spoilt it, and it cost $161 plus tip.

We were 'allowed' back to the house; the pool was 78 degrees, and I swam a lot. I finished the outside painting and paid the property tax ($7,300) and insurance ($1,300). I felt that I really did not want to come back here, as I simply could not stand the atmosphere, which was a real travesty. We went to see a couple of movies: *Jane Eyre*, which was first-rate, and *Win Win*, which was okay but not funny as expected. We went back to Angelino's and ate polenta with mushrooms and a fourteen-inch pizza, which we can only manage half, and with the lemonade, only $35: a real bargain. And then we returned to Burning Bonzai and had a great $41 dinner with hot and sour soup, shrimp tempura, and sweet and sour chicken, drinking Sapporo beer and merlot; a real bargain for really nice food.

And then it was time to go home after a very long trip of about seven weeks.

# July 2011

It was time to go off again. We were in Bristol Airport, flying Thomson, and the 757 took off at 1.13 (against the scheduled 1.15), and after two hours, we were in Naples. We stayed at Hotel La Certosa in Marina del Cantone, which was right on the beach; they sent a car, and it took ninety minutes to get to Cantone. It was quite cheap and what we expected for the price, but we did have a side view of the sea; later, Chrissie thought the bed was too hard, but it seemed fine to me. As we were quite late, we ate in the hotel restaurant and had bruschetta, spaghetti with courgette, and good grilled fish, and a very nice E15 bottle of local wine; it cost E63 all up, which was pretty good. The OJ at breakfast was indifferent but was improved with great fresh fruit: watermelon, cherries, apricots, strawberries, and great croissants and wonderful coffee. Jamie and Bob, who were doing a tour of Italy, turned up.

We had a couple of Camparis on the beach and went to the hotel again for dinner. I ate cannelloni and grilled fish again, and we drank a bottle of local wine and a 2000 Borde at E40 (which was a very lovely wine), and the bill was only E113 for the four of us. We found a bar and had a couple of grappas until gone midnight, and no hangover again. After a morning swim, at midday, we set off on a private boat to Capri (or is it Crapi, as I preferred our village). It cost E150 but would have cost E120 on the crowded tourist boats. After we arrived, we were not sure what to do but decided to spend E1.60 and took the funicular to the top and wandered around. We found a nice-looking restaurant, Villa Verde, and I had some tasty scampi and a Peroni.

We wandered back down to get the boat back. It was only okay here and not the special place you'd expect. There was a Michelin restaurant next door, Taverna del Capitano, which Jamie and Bob adored but I found a little disappointing. I started with a fried courgette flan, which was a little heavy, and followed with stone fish wrapped in spaghetti, and potato with tomatoes, celery, and onion soup, which was all a bit odd. We drank two bottles of E45 red wine, and somehow the bill came to E360, which seemed quite a lot. We met the forty-year-old chef, who took us into his eleven-thousand-bottle wine cellar, and I bashed my head, spilling much blood. It was really great spending time with Jamie and Bob, but they left at 5 a.m. to catch their plane home.

We were alone, so we spent a nice day on the beach and went to Maria Grazia for dinner, where we had nice antipasto followed by pappardelle with courgettes and clams; we drank the house red, which was cold, and it all cost E60 for what was a very nice dinner. And the next night, we returned to the hotel and ate bruschetta and spaghetti with seafood ragout and local wine, and it only cost E53 for a really good dinner.

For our next dinner, we went Michelin again. Good town, this, for such a small place to have two Michelin restaurants. The restaurant was Quattro Passi, which means 'four steps.' We got to the square and spotted the courtesy car, but there was no driver, and we started walking, but after a while, he came by, and we flagged him down. We got there for a nice large Campari accompanied by slightly too heavy buns and cheese. I ordered pearl of scampi, and Chrissie red mullet. The scampi came with a nice small soup and clams, but the scampi left me cold. Chrissie liked the mullet. Next, I had lamb with garden potatoes. It was pretty, but no sign of potatoes, and two sorts of lamb, with part of it being the smallest rack ever. Chrissie had tempura fried fish, but we liked the Ivy just too much. We didn't order pudding but were given a very nice peach jelly. We drank an excellent 1997 Tourasi, and it cost E213 plus tip. This was all very expensive and not at all world-class. You could eat much better in Cornwall or even at our hotel for one-quarter of the price.

There was a problem: Our village did not have an ATM, and we were running short of cash. We took a fifty-minute bus ride to Sorrento and managed to get some cash there. We bought Lauren a E390 Emporio Armani handbag (discounted 40 percent to only E243). We then took the E6 thirty-minute train trip round town (they even had the commentary in Russian, which seemed weird).

Back to normality with dinner at the hotel: prosciutto and lasagne, which we had seen them making while we had breakfast, followed by strawberries and the local wine, and all for E54. I haven't mentioned Mary's, which was a delightful beach bar just by the hotel, where we went every night for Campari and backgammon before dinner and quite often for lunch for their excellent red prawns. We went down to the beach for dinner, and the non-frozen prawns tasted frozen. But we returned to the hotel and had spinach and ricotta pancakes, scampi, and spaghetti and some delicious frozen limoncello. And the next night, it was Parma ham and melon, followed by baked fresh local fish; all very delicious, and it felt like home.

Speaking of home, it was time to go back. We loved this town, the beach, and dining at the hotel; somehow, we are sure we'll be back, if only for Mary's Camparis.

# August 2011

And here we were on trip number twelve to Los Angeles. For some reason, we have switched from National to Dollar, which had no Mustangs, so we had to take a horrible SUV for the first night and returned the next day for a Mustang. But the weather was great, with temperatures well into the 90s. In order to overcome the staying problem, we converted the garage into a grandpa flat, but it was not quite finished. And Lauren has made contact with her birth mother, who was nearly forty-two but looked much younger; Lauren has a half-brother.

On the first night, we had dinner at P F Chang's. The temperature went over 100 degrees, and I had a really nice swim in the pool. We saw *Final Destination 5* in the afternoon and went to Angelino's for dinner. They now had a licence, so we drank beer and Chianti with our favourite cheese ravioli, and it still only cost $37 plus tip; it had become a very nice proper Italian restaurant.

But it was time to go on another road trip.

Our first stop was Carmel; we drove with the roof down in the sunshine and could see the fog in the valley just before we got there. The temperature was only 62 degrees. It's about 350 miles and took seven hours. We had dinner at Andre's. A free glass of champagne, and I ate lobster and artichoke salad, followed by rack of lamb, and drank an excellent $42 Camel Valley merlot. It all cost $137 plus tip and seemed so much better than the Michelins in Italy; the food was better, and it was not nearly as expensive.

We drove to Big Sur, which seemed as dull as ever, and continued onto Julia Pfeiffer Burns State Park, which had a waterfall but was also dull. We had a good clam chowder lunch at Rocky Point. We went to a tapas place, Mandake, for dinner. The food was great, with duck pate, fried squash flowers, shrimps and clams, and cauliflower with horseradish (and of course potatoes bravas). Drinking the house wine, it was only $69 for a great dinner, with really nice service. It was number four out of 108 restaurants in Carmel, according to Trip Advisor. For our last night, we had a very good dinner at the Flying Fish. We shared artichoke and tempura prawns to start, and I had black Alaska cod, and Chrissie almond-crusted sea bass, and with the Flying Fish merlot, it was only $103 plus tip.

But it was time to get back in the car. We drove over Golden Gate Bridge, which was always special, and stopped at Muir Woods. The parking was terrible, but we got inside, and the 252-foot redwoods were magnificent. There were a lot of people, but somehow, it all seemed very tranquil. Unfortunately, our next stop was Eureka. Not much was going on this place, and it didn't do anything for us. The temperature was only 68 degrees, and we were told this was the hottest it ever gets. The town was full of vagrants, and there wasn't much to do.

We went to dinner at 301. We had an amuse bouche of smoked tuna on a cracker and followed it with foie gras with a plum, apple, and strawberry sauce, followed by steelhead trout with ratatouille; we drank an Envy merlot at $45, and it all came to $178 plus tip, which seemed terribly expensive for such a hick town.

The next day, we went on a seventy-five-minute boat trip and saw seals, porpoises, herons, egrets, and lot of other birds. What struck us most was how industry seemed to have all gone somewhere else.

The following night, we went to the Minor Theatre in Arcota, which was built in 1912; we sat in the front row of the balcony and watched a Woody Allen movie, *Midnight in Paris*, a truly wonderful experience. And we went to dinner at the Lost Coast Brewery and ate very good steak and chips (for me) and fish and chips (for Chrissie) and drank the local beer. The atmosphere was fantastic, and it only cost $40, which was a quarter of the 301, and oh, so much better.

Luckily, it was time to leave; our advice to you would be leave Eureka well alone.

We drove three hundred miles into Oregon and had a nice clam chowder lunch in Brandon, by the sea, and did the last hundred miles with the roof off, in temperatures of around 69 degrees. We stayed in the delightful town of Yachats, and our resting place was the Deane's Oceanfront Lodge, which was built in the 1940s, as evidenced by our kitchen (which we did not use, except for the fridge). The seaview from our room was simply wonderful. We drove the two miles into town and had a great dinner at Heidi's Italian. We ate Dungeness crab on toast with a béchamel sauce and Italian sausage lasagne, flavoured with herbs and fennel. Drinking a couple of Peronis and a couple of glasses of Chianti, the bill was only $52 for such a nice dinner.

We had clear blue skies but a little cold at 64 degrees, and we went for a three-mile barefoot walk along the almost-deserted beach. In the afternoon, we drove to Cape Perpetua, and at 805 feet, we had great views of the ocean. We then did Captain Cook's Trail and the Geyser, which were all very good. We had a nice dinner at Luna: shrimp cocktail, followed by halibut, salmon, and tuna with chips, and drinking local beer and pinot.

Our last day was another amazing long barefoot walk along the beach, clam chowder lunch, and a visit to a dull local museum. Dinner again at Heidi's, which was just as good, with crab tart, followed by southern Italian pork with pasta for me, and drinking local beer, as you had to drive anywhere here. This time, we managed to spend $86, but it was a wonderful dinner. After Eureka, this was a very good place: fantastic beach, relaxing, and great food.

You'll remember much earlier that I went to Morgan Hill, California, when I was eighteen and stayed in a house with some ladies and their kids (where I was introduced to pizza). I was still in touch with Ingrid, who invited me there; she now lived in Portland but had a house in Trout Lake, which was our next stop.

Trout Lake was about a hundred miles east of Portland; the location was really really wonderful, with an amazing view of Mount Adams. There were no curtains in our nearly en-suite bedroom, and you woke up at 6.30 in the morning with an amazing view of the snow-capped mountain, which was to die for. We went for a long walk in the valley, around five miles, and had a nice home-cooked dinner with flank steak, roast potatoes, stir-fried local veg, and lots of red wine. And for dessert, we had a first: huckleberry pie. It was difficult to believe that I had never eaten huckleberries, but then, maybe not too many people have.

After a nice breakfast, we got in the car to go somewhere special: Timberline Lodge, where Ingrid's husband, Dick, was president of the trustees. It was built in 1937 but came to fame when it was featured in *The Shining*, Stanley Kubrick's movie starring Jack Nicholson. Dick showed us lots of the detail of the building, along with some great works of art (Durrell, an Austrian, was best in my view). Being there felt very special; it was a truly amazing place. We had a nice picnic and stopped for huckleberry milkshakes on the way back: another first. We had a nice salmon BBQ for supper and drank a Napa cabernet that we brought along. Ingrid and Dick were great hosts with great food, and the whole place was just really nice (even if Trout Lake itself was a bit of a let-down). Timberline was so special.

But it was time to move on.

We had a very pleasant drive along the Columbia River with the roof down and then got onto the 5, and after 270 miles, we were in Roseburg: a godforsaken place. We stayed in the Rose Motel, which was cheap at $52 a night, but the room was so dark, and we had to drive for dinner. We go to McMenaries, by the railway station, and managed to drive the wrong way up a one-way street. It was a micro brewery, and we had a couple of beers each and fish and chips, and it only cost $31.

## Mr. Tambourine Man

The next day, we drove another 440 miles to Napa and decide to stay for a couple of nights. We stayed in St Helena, which we liked when we came on our last visit. One of the reasons was the great lunch we had in Tri Vigna, so we were going there for dinner. But it was all a bit of a disappointment. We ordered a bruschetta with mozzarella, peppers, sea salt, and extra virgin oil to start, but we got around a pound of mozzarella and forty peppers; it was just all way too much and rather off-putting. I followed with risotto with duck leg, which was only okay and nothing special, and Chrissie had an okay pasta but just too big again. Drinking $50 2007 Swanson Oakwood merlot, the bill came to $143 plus tip for a mediocre meal with too big portions.

We had a really nice day in St Helena, going round the shops and swimming in the pool. We ate dinner at Brassicon. We sat outside and had green gazpacho, really light fried eggplant, and courgette flowers, followed by spicy garlic shrimp, sardines, and potatoes bravas, all washed down with a Zinfandel from Frogs Leap; we talked with Cindy, the charming chef/owner, who owned a few restaurants and spent her fiftieth birthday at the Lizard, near us. All up, it was $110 plus tip for a good dinner.

We were now back in Los Angeles after a road trip of 2,574 miles; quite a long way and without a speeding ticket. It was really good to have the time to do these road trips, but sometimes, the road can be too much; the extra night in Napa was absolutely right. Yachats and Trout Lake were a delight, after three visits in two years, Carmel was a little déjà vu, and Napa was always an enjoyable place (but whatever you do, don't go to Eureka).

We stayed in the new pool house. It was really nice, with a fiftyone-inch TV, amazing shower, and great view of the palm tree from the bed; Lauren seemed to be very welcoming in the new regime but didn't get it when I made a late-night joke about moving back into the house. As usual, we had dinner at P F Chang's; spring roll and spicy shrimp were fine, and it all cost $101 for four.

We spent $29 a seat going to the Gold Cinema; you got free popcorn and a comfortable seat, but the movie, *Warrior*, was dreadful, with a really bad performance from Nick Nolte and a terrible script.

We had dinner before at Louise, which has a place in West Hollywood where we once sat next to Kevin Bacon. I ate okay pappardelle with spicy Italian sausage and drank beer, and it only cost $52 for four. The next day, we went shopping to Bloomingdale's, where I bought blue Ralph Lauren chinos for the bargain price of $20, and IKEA to spend another $150 on things for the house (which didn't please me too much).

Lauren's next-door neighbour was an actor called Sam Anderson, who was famous for *Lost* but was in lots of other things, including *Friends*. He got us tickets for a fringe play he was appearing in, *Blackbird*: a story about child abuse and love. It was a small forty-four-seat theatre, and we were very close; it was in the afternoon, and the play was set at night, and I noticed Sam's watch was set ahead: a true professional. There were only two actors, with a small part for a child at the end, and the whole thing was a joy.

It was the ten-year anniversary of 9/11, and like many security forces, we were a bit worried that another attack could happen, but luckily nothing did. We went to see a couple of movies: *The Help*, which was 150 minutes of $60 million drivel, which I hated, and *Crazy Stupid Love*, which was fun, and of course we had a great dinner at Angelino's, with the normal cheese ravioli and Peroni, and only about $40 for two. And we went to Burning Bonzai, which was as good as ever.

Then we went to see *The Debt*, which was a really good movie with a great story. And we had a nice dinner at Patty's Diner, with the normal corned beef hash and fried eggs over easy. We also saw *The Drive*, which was pretty good, and had another dinner at Angelino's. Going to the movies and eating in my favourite local restaurants suits me fine.

We managed to get a room at the Tides Inn at Laguna Beach and arranged to meet Jamie and Bob for dinner. We met at 6.15 at the 230 Restaurant for a 6.30 table, which was all we could get. I started with a pear martini and then had a grapefruit martini, which were both very good. We shared shrimp and clams, and then I had a half-rib, which was still pretty big, and we drank two bottles of 2007 Sanctuary pinot noir, which was a boutique wine, with only 29,600 bottles produced. We then went to a bar with live music and drank Pacifico beer and did a lot of shots and a lot of dancing. I woke up with a real Laguna Beach hangover.

On the road again, but only as far as Mission Beach. It didn't really seem our sort of place, but at least the hotel was cheap. I tried to go waterskiing on the lake but failed and looked at surf lessons, but it all seemed so expensive. We had a decent Italian dinner at Caffe Bella, but I only had one beer due to the hangover.

It did seem dreary here, but I managed to spend $100 on a surf lesson, which was a bit tiring for the first time in four years, but the instructor did push me, so I didn't have to do too much.

We had a couple of reasonable dinners: first, the Fat Fish Cantina Grill, where they had the world-famous lobster salad for $13.95 and a good atmosphere. Then Bareback, where we sat at the bar and drank Bareback amber ale and Stone pale ale and ate very good medium-rare hamburgers. And they cost $63 and $49 plus tip. But we had enough of Mission Beach and felt good that it was time to go back to LA.

Back in LA, we swam in the pool, played a little tennis, and ate BBQ. We went to see *Straw Dogs*, which had good suspense from the word go and then a lot of scenes which you seem to remember from the original. It was movie time, and we saw *Killer Elite* with Jason Statham and Robert de Niro, which was not too bad, and *Moneyball*, which was pretty good but quite long, although it was an interesting subject matter. More swimming and more tennis. It was quite relaxing in our holiday home, and it was sunny every day. We had a great dinner at Angelino's, with magical broccoli soup and the famous ravioli, with two drinks each, for $59 plus tip. We often had lunch at Le Pain on Ventura, which had wonderful gazpacho, great sandwiches, and organic lemonade: a perfect lunchtime treat. Another night, we had another BBQ and watched a DVD of *The Shining*; it was great to watch, having just been there.

We were away about five weeks, and it was time to go home. I was bored at home and started playing old 45s by Spooky Tooth - and then I started writing this book.

## November 2011

It was our thirty-first wedding anniversary, and we were celebrating with our first visit to Rome. We stayed in the Hotel Artemide, which was pretty central, with nice breakfasts and an upgraded room (which still felt quite small). We came Business courtesy of Avios and enjoyed our champagne and clotted cream tea and the fixed-price E40 taxi ride into the city. On our first night, we found a neighbourhood trattoria, Bellerisi, and ate scampi/linguine and courgette flowers, followed by rigatoni with smoked cheese and lamb and potatoes, drinking a nice Lazio wine. It all cost E72, and we felt very Italian.

The next day, we went for two hours on an open-top bus in the 66 degree sunshine; the Coliseum was the best. We ended up at the Spanish Steps, which were only pretty good, and found lunch at Otella all Concordu. It was nice, nice, nice, and we ate artichoke, Roman style, fettucini and Bolognese, and ravioli with a meat ragu, all for E40. Then we went to the Audrey Hepburn exhibition, who spent a lot of time here. Lots of photos, clothes, and stories of one of our heroes. For Lauren's eighteenth birthday, all the ladies came as Audrey Hepburn, so it meant something to us. We then went to the Vatican and plodded around for nearly two hours; it was not really that great, and even the Sistine Chapel somehow lacked magic. But we went to St Peter's Square, which was much better and had a great atmosphere, and we got into the church, which was fantastic, with the most amazing ceilings. We went everywhere on the open-top bus.

For our anniversary, we went to a smart restaurant with views of the Coliseum. It was in a hotel which had changed its name, and it took ages for the taxi to find it. We had a Campari to start and chose the seven-course taster menu at E120 each; this was how it rated:

- asparagus with quail egg, truffle (very little) and leek gratinee: 7/10
- cheese flan with avocado: 6/10
- Sicilian twisty pasta with tuna: 7/10
- ragout with oxtail: 8/10

- red snapper with red onion and asparagus: 7/10
- veal tenderloin with veg: 6/10
- cherry and cream and biscuit: boring, so 5/10

We drank the second-most-expensive of five Lazio wines at E75 (Lazio Mater Mutata), and the whole bill came to E377 with tip. There was no atmosphere; the view was great, but the food was only average at best. This seemed an awful lot of money, but we should have known from our experiences earlier in the year.

The next day, we went back to the Coliseum as tourists, walking from the hotel, which was not too far away. We paid E5 each for the guided tour; we learned it was built in AD 700 and had a capacity of 75,000, and there was a lot of killing, which went on about a hundred days per year. The whole place held us in awe; it had to be one of the most magnificent places we've been. We then went to the Capitali Museum and saw some Michelangelo pictures; *Cleopatra* and *Leda* were superb, and some Leonardo da Vinci, which was mostly technical drawing.

For dinner, we went to another neighbourhood trattoria, Cabonara, a wonderful local place established in 1906. Chrissie had grilled artichoke, which unlike all the Italians in the trattoria, she cannot eat. I had spaghetti with peppers, cheese, and oxtail, and Chrissie rigatoni with artichoke again, and we had a very nice bottle of Lazio wine. And it only cost E55 (or about one-sixth of the price of last night), for great food in a great atmosphere. We were learning.

My legs were tired, as we walked to the Parthenon and then onto the Spanish Steps and then to a shopping street which the concierge recommended. The Parthenon was very impressive, built in 432 BC; this was where Raphael was buried. We had another nice lunch in Otella, with spinach and cheese ravioli, fried fish, and more courgette flowers, and drinking a glass of wine and beer, it only cost E30 all up, which was not bad for such a nice place. For dinner, we went to the Piazza Novona to the Three Arches. We had a wonderful dinner with pappardelle with a hare sauce to start, calves liver for me, osso buco for Chrissie, and followed by chocolate tart; drinking a great bottle of 2005 Petit Vendon Nero, it only cost E53 plus tip. We were still learning, and the dinner was just so good.

It was Chrissie's birthday, and the hotel gave her a cake for breakfast with a candle; such a nice touch. And I took her shopping in the street by our hotel; she bought a black Italian coat with bright green lining for only about E100. It was a real bargain, and she looked great in it. To celebrate, we returned to Carbonara and had another great dinner. We started with tempura vegetables, frittata, followed by pasta with tomato and basil, followed by nice pink lamb for me and veal for Chrissie, and drinking Lazio Emmo 2008 at E26, the total bill was still only E65 for another great dinner. We had finally learnt to avoid the expensive places and ate well in a good atmosphere in just a simple trattoria.

But it was time to go. We just loved Rome; it was such a great city.

## December 2011

Now this was interesting: We went to Paris just after Christmas to meet Agnes, Lauren's birth mother. This was something which not too many people experience. We were in a small hotel with good breakfasts and a view of the Eiffel Tower just from our room. We walked there in five minutes, but there were a million people queuing to go up, so we gave it a miss.

We met Agnes in a local brasserie in Rue Hoffman with her son (and Lauren's half-brother), Jeremy. It was very quiet to start; we looked at Lauren's picture book, which Chrissie put together for her twenty-first. We ordered a bottle of Cotes de Bourg, and I started to speak my *petit francais*. We ate a little entrecôte with Lyonaisse potatoes and pear and apple tarte Tatin, and then we all went outside for a smoke. Somehow, it seemed like we were old friends meeting up for dinner, and it was all smiles and laughter: very difficult to describe. Agnes was delightful but not at all like Lauren to look at or in her demeanour. We met her again for afternoon hot chocolate and just talked and talked; she was just a delight.

## Mr. Tambourine Man

We all went off to dinner to a very famous restaurant, La Chartier in Rue du Faubourg in Montmartre, where you just had to queue to get in. I ate an excellent duck foie gras followed by *pot au feu*, which was basically meat, potatoes, carrots, and cabbage with no gravy, which was interesting if not great. We drank a Buvet Traditionalle, and the bill for six was only E85, which was a pretty good value. Then we all went bowling but had to play pool first, as it was very busy. It was a really friendly night.

The next day, we all went to the Louvre. The *Mona Lisa*, *Venus de Milo*, and the Sphinx were as good as ever, but this was not really my museum. But the Museum D'Isay was, with all the impressionists; Cezanne, Degas, Monet, Manet, and van Gogh just make it a great museum. And then at six o'clock, we went back to the Eiffel Tower. We got in, but it was raining and very cloudy. Getting very wet, we walked to the top, but we couldn't see anything. And we had to walk down in the rain; by now, it was ten o'clock, so we just went and got a pizza before bed. My legs were really tired again. And the day after, which was New Year's Eve, I walked to the Pompidou Centre and looked in four galleries. My favourite was *The Ten Lizzies* by Andy Warhol, but I also enjoyed some good Picassos and Matisses. There was a lot of culture in this city. And because it was New Year's Eve, the metro was free.

Agnes treated us to dinner at the LR Restaurant, and we ate very well, with carpaccio of coquilles St Jacques, homard, and fromage. I bought the drinks, and with some very good St Emilion Grand Cru, it was E133. We danced a lot and left around 3 a.m. But *merde*, our metro did not stop at our stop. We had to walk back across the Seine, but everybody in Paris was delightful; they were all merry and happy, and nobody was really drunk. I was glad I was in Paris, as London somehow would have been much more aggressive.

This was an interesting trip, and I think we have a new friend in Agnes. We had a lot of fun together and were able to share our mutual love. Lauren said she liked Agnes, but we were her mum and dad and would always be her mum and dad. My heart was melting.

We had visited two of the must-sees in a month: Rome and Paris. Which did I prefer? It was very close, but I must go for Rome for the Coliseum and the food, and it was sunnier and warmer, but it was very close because they were both great cities. I will write more about New York later on, and I have to say that it still remains my favourite city in the world, with Rome a close second and Paris not too far away in third.

## March 2012

We were back on British Airways for our thirteenth trip to Los Angeles. It was warm and sunny, and it was great to see my lovely daughter again. We couldn't stay in the house, as we now rented out the pool house to earn income; I noted that Eric had turned our room into his playhouse; he didn't really appreciate what he had. We stayed in the Tangerine, which was a fine hotel a few blocks away. It was fine, but I did not pay $525,000 to stay in a hotel. I used to love my holiday home.

We revisited Angelino's and enjoyed the supreme ravioli and a share of dessert from the lady at the next table; drinking our Chianti and a couple of Peronis, it was still only $55 plus tip. We went to see *A Separation,* which won the Oscar for best foreign film; it was a pretty good insight into life in Iran. I also played a bit of tennis. And I had the corned beef hash with two fried eggs over easy at Patty's. But we were only here for a couple of days because we were going on a big adventure.

Air New Zealand flies once a week from LA to Auckland via Raratonga in the Cook Islands, which was our destination. A girl at our tennis club went round the world during her gap year. I was now in gap year thirteen, and I asked her what her favourite place was, to which she replied the Cook Islands, which was why we were now here rather than, say, Tahiti. Air NZ Business Class does not have flat beds, and the food and wine got a verdict of 'not too bad.'

But we arrived in good spirits. We were given Polynesian flowers to put round our neck and seemed to get out of the airport in about five minutes, despite having too many cigarettes. John and Rachel were our hosts in their bed and breakfast. We had a really nice room with a partial seaview and about a thirty-yard walk to a beautiful sandy beach on a lovely lagoon, with the breakers on a coral reef some way out. I went for a swim and cut my feet on the rocks, but it was still glorious.

Our first night's dinner was terrible in Little Polynesia, just down the road. It took ninety minutes to get the fish of the day, which was tasteless grey tuna, and we drank Barefoot cabernet sauvignon, and it cost over £60. I hoped the dining was going to get better. The breakfast was great, though, and it was a delight sitting on the terrace.

The Internet didn't work, so we bought ten bus tickets for $25 (which is about £12) and headed into town and visited an Internet cafe. John and Rachel also owned a lunch place, the Moorings. We got back on the bus and had a great mahi mahi sandwich, which was one of the best sandwiches ever, and drank ginger beer, as they had no licence. And then we went back to the beach again to do more damage to my feet on the rocks.

Dinner at Viama was a lot better. We phoned them, and they sent a car to get us. I ate excellent smoked marlin, followed by very good hot tuna curry, and we drank the Barefoot again, but it only cost $30 (unlike Little Polynesia, where it was $45), and the whole bill was just over £50. Things were looking up on the dinner front.

It was a lovely day, around 82 degrees and sunny all day, with lots of swimming, no hurt feet, and I saw a royal blue starfish, which was something to behold. John and Rachel took us for a nice three-hour exploratory drive. We learned than Captain Cook discovered this place in around 1780, and what a place. We visit a museum and art gallery and had a nice lunch at the Saltwater Cafe just up the road. We felt adventurous and got on the bus to go to town for dinner. There seemed to be only two places open, and we ended up in Trader Jack's. I drank Cook's draught beer and ate shrimp and lobster ravioli, which was all very fine, and with Chrissie's smoked marlin fish cakes and wine, it only cost $72. We got the 9 p.m. bus back and felt like we had an adventure.

The next day was pretty laid back; we swam and then went to the Moorings for lunch, where I changed my sandwich to hot and spicy tuna, and went to Viama for dinner again. Chrissie had chicken delight, and I had a very good beef tenderloin with sauce Béarnaise and followed with Key lime pie.

But the next night, dinner got worse again at the Point, which seemed to have no point. There was no soul, and the food was awful. The special garlic gnocchi became potato cake, the chicken satay never arrived, and the catch of the day, yellow fin tuna encrusted in garlic, had not a whiff of garlic. We drank an Oyster Bay merlot, and it all came to $91, which seemed a lot of money.

We went back to Raratonga Airport and arrived at about 2.40 for a 3.30 flight; the check-in man said, 'You must be the Taylors, as you are the last foreigners.' Then our cases were put through a hole in the wall, with no labels or luggage tickets, and we got on the plane with no security or anyone worrying about liquids. We had a nice forty-five-minute flight on a small plane, which gave us great views of the island, Samede.

Samede was different; a population of only three thousand and a little rundown, but we were in a small hotel right on the beach. You could swim about thirty strokes and get to a very large sand bar and wander around, without a care in the world. Dinner was free, and we ate a good seafood chowder and very nice tuna coconut curry, and you could drink red or white wine, which was just about okay. We met some nice people.

The weather was around 84 degrees and mostly sunny. On the first morning, we took out a couple of kayaks, which was fun, but they leaked a bit. We went for a walk and discovered a brilliant small restaurant, Karo. I had a great bacon and tomato toastie but couldn't get a beer because it is Sunday, so I drank orange and mango. It was BBQ night, and we ate average chicken and potato salad, and our lights were out by 10.15, which meant a very good night's sleep.

We made some really good new friends, Charlie and Fiona, with their three daughters, Clara, Amy, and Grace, who were aged eleven, nine, and seven. I so like young people. They rented a house next door, and we went for dinner and enjoyed rum and tonic followed by guacamole, marinated raw fish, BBQ tuna salad, and fried bananas with loads of red wine.

## Mr. Tambourine Man

We all agreed to take a trip together round the lagoon, which was about twenty miles by twenty miles and oh, so beautiful. We were picked up at 9 a.m. and taken on a short drive to the Kia Orana. The first stop was One Foot Island, which was uninhabited, and we had a lovely snorkel. Then we went onto similarly uninhabited Honeymoon Island and then to Suntan Island. Our lunch could only be described as Michelin star. We had a smoked parrot fish, which was sublime, delicious breadfruit (which was a first time for me), bananas with tapioca and coconut, guava, watermelon, doughnuts, and bread and butter. We ate off banana leaves in the shade on a paradise beach, and it just had to be one of the greatest lunches ever. It was followed by a fantastic snorkel, where I saw a very large fish whose name I didn't get. It was a truly great day which I will remember for a long time.

The next day, we hired a car for about £36 plus gas and drove round the whole island, which was only about thirty miles. We rejected a couple of places for lunch and returned to Karo for another bacon toastie, chocolate cake, and iced coffee (since I was driving). In truth, there was not a lot to see, but we did spend an hour walking to the island's peak to get some good views, but the lagoon was the place to be. I didn't bother with a driving licence, although you were supposed to go to the police station and get one. We just turned up at the car rental place, gave them £36 cash, and drove off. It was like that here.

We had a nice dinner in the Boat Shed with our new family friends, and I ate nice Thai noodles with shrimp and drank pinot noir and played a good game of UNO, which was all great fun. The next day was a bit laid back, with a long one-hour kayak, plenty of swimming, and a very nice dinner at the hotel: spring rolls and butter chicken curry.

The next night, we all went off in a minivan to the local show. It started off with three guys dancing, which was okay, but then we got four beautiful Polynesian girls in coconut bras, who did a very sexy dance; at the end, they shook and wiggled their bums, which was like nothing I had ever seen. It can only be described as spectacular.

The next day, it was off for our second lagoon cruise on a larger boat, with about thirty people. This boat was slower, which made it somehow more enjoyable. We started off at Timber Island (where Channel 4 had a five-month survival programme) and snorkeled in the beautiful sea. We visited Heaven, which really was (for the first time) and then went back to One Foot, where we had a very nice lunch (but not quite up to Kia Orana standards). I did some more snorkelling to finish another perfect day in the lagoon.

Ned, the wine barman, and I decided to have a game of tennis. There were only three courts on the island, and the one we played was quite strange, with yellow and white lines and basketball markings. After some difficulty, we managed to find a couple of old balls, and I won the first set 6-2. But he won the second, 6-0. I explained that we had to play a ten-point tiebreaker, which he failed to understand; I won 10-6, so a victory for England. We had a nice lunch again at Karo, and I ate penne Neapolitan and chocolate cake and got a beer this time. For dinner in the hotel, it was a homely dinner of spring rolls and garlic prawns; the bar was very full, and we drank and danced a lot and didn't get to bed until midnight, which was very late for here.

We spent the next day on the beach, starting with a thirty-minute kayak and then lots of swimming. We went to Karo for lunch; it was Sunday again, so I had to drink a banana milkshake, but it went very well with the bacon toastie and toasted banana loaf with butter. Dinner was spring rolls again and pan-fried tuna, which was again homely rather than exciting, but Chrissie had a really good seafood omelette.

The weather was gloriously sunny and around 85 degrees; we went on our third lagoon cruise on the big boat, *Bishops,* and sat on the sundeck and did all the same things, but it was just as good. Here, you just needed to be on the lagoon.

On our last night, we celebrated with spring rolls again and prawn coconut curry and lots of beer and red wine. We had a fantastic eight nights here, and it could only be described as awesome. The lagoon was just one of the fabbest places I have ever been; the pace was great, and maybe a slightly posher hotel would make it perfect, but who needs posh hotels? We ate homely food and had great lunches at Kora, and don't forget the Michelin experience on Suntan Island.

It was a nice flight back to Raratonga, but I was told off for moving my seat in the plane to take photographs. Rachel met us at the airport and was as nice as ever, but we were put in a room farther back, which was not so nice, with no seaview. Rachel lent us a car, which made us mobile, and we drove to the Moorings for a very nice lunch. We returned to Viama for the third time and drank pina coladas and Wolf Bass cabernet sauvignon and ate smoked marlin, which was excellent, and tuna for me and beef Wellington for Chrissie, and it cost $137. Breakfast the next day was as good as ever, and I got to taste dragon fruit for the first time, which was delicious. For the next night, we went to Hidden Spirit, which was only open a couple of nights a week, and ate chicken with ginger and basil, which was very good, and porterhouse steak for me and mahi mahi for Chrissie. We drank a $52 bottle of Bluegrass, which impressed the owner, who chatted at length with us while we had our after-dinner ciggies.

We then decided to go into town with Michael and Janice, who we just met, to go to the Staircase for their Polynesian evening. For $35, you got dinner (which was chicken, shrimp, and interesting salads) and a floor show. There were only five guests, but around forty happy people gave us a great show of dancing and fun, which was really enjoyable and made us smile a lot. It was a really good time, for not much money.

On our last day, we met a lady from the Cook Islands called Lovely, who really was lovely in every way. We had a really good dinner at Viama with orange lamb and amazing mint potato.

This was a great place, and we were so glad we came, and there were no other English people visiting. Would we come back? Maybe; there were a lot of other places to go, so we shall see, but it will always be high on our list of favourite places.

We flew back to LA on Air New Zealand, and it only took eight and a half hours, so we only got about five hours sleep with no flat beds. The food and drink were adequate, but it seemed an expensive way to travel (but what the heck?). I had a convertible Mustang, and we stayed in the London, which was one of my favourites. We were not allowed to stay at our house; why, when we go out, did I always have to pay for everything?

We had dinner at Petit Four with artichoke and calves liver, which was as good as ever, with a great atmosphere. We walked to the Beverly Centre and bought Ralph Lauren jeans for me and Diesel jeans for Chrissie; we had a good hot dog at Johnny Rockets but got lost on the way back. And we went back to Petit Four with Winnie, Isa, Lauren, and Eric, and I ate the same. We talked about George Clooney, who Winnie met when he was an aspiring actor, and she told us what a great time she had at the Barcelona Olympics, when she was a guest of NBC; she had the best seats in the house. She moved in the best crowds but told us her favourite famous person was Quincy Jones.

Back in the London pool, I was approached by a gorgeous girl, with a phone call for me from Lauren. 'How did you find me?' I asked.

She said, 'I was just looking for a handsome guy wearing glasses.'

We went to Patty's a couple of times, and I had a great waffle for lunch and corned beef hash with two fried eggs over easy for dinner; we met old friends, Stuart and Janet, for lunch at Olive & Thyme. We moved out of the London to the Tangerine, which was a lot cheaper. We had dinner at Angelino's, with the ravioli pomodoro (as good as ever) and had an excellent dinner at Prosecco with osso buco.

Next, we were off to Dana Point to see our friends Jamie and Bobby. We stayed in the Blue Lantern, which was expensive, at $280 per night. But they had free bikes, and I set off, but there were no brakes: You just stopped pedalling. I had to push the bike up the hill. We had dinner at the Renaissance Cafe, which was very loud, and we drank martinis and red wine and ate mahi mahi teriyaki and danced a lot. An attractive girl tried to pick me up (we should come here more often). We took a long walk around the marina and then went to Jamie and Bob's house. They had a nice pool area with rocks, but it was too small to swim. Bob had a wine cellar which was very impressive, with a 2003 Smith Haut Lafitte (back to the old Lonrho days). We went to dinner at Luciano's, which was supposed to be one of the top thousand Italian restaurants in the United States. I had tomato soup and fettucini with shrimp, but I preferred Angelino's and Prosecco.

On 2 April, we had been away for just over one month. It was time to head back.

## July 2012

This time, we stayed in Cornwall to celebrate my sixtieth birthday, which was on 2 July. As I was now a director of Fifteen Cornwall, I decided to have a dinner for seventeen on the big day, which included Lauren, who came home (luckily, without Eric). To make it different, I asked everybody to get a good appetite by taking a two-day walk from Padstow to Watergate Bay. I arranged transport with a local company to make this all possible. On 30 June, we decamped to the ship in Padstow. On Sunday, 1 July, I met some of my Cornish friends on the quay in Padstow, and we walked a long way to get picked up and returned to Padstow. The walk was truly spectacular, taking in Trevose Head, Constantine Bay, and Portcothan Bay.

In Padstow, we met all our friends from London and had a riotous evening, promising to meet in the morning to continue the walk. But on the big day, it was raining, and everybody declined, so I got in my transport and went all alone. I finished on Sunday. I walked alone, and it was very wet but still great. We all met at Scarlett's for lunch, but I had to call and ask for dry socks and shorts, as I was soaked. We had a very nice lunch, and the sun came out, but I had to walk alone. This part of the walk was just as good with no people, and the best bit was probably Bedruthan Steps. Late in the afternoon, I got to Watergate Bay and stayed in a lovely room in Watergate Bay Hotel. They had a lovely new indoor swimming pool.

We drank some champagne, and everybody gave me presents; I guess the best was an i-Pad from Lauren. Chrissie bought me a really nice Raymond Weil chronograph watch, which went with my Rolex and Delphi watches from the 1950s.

And then, we went onto Fifteen and had a great dinner; here is the menu:

- Fiori di zucchini in pastella con fregola sarda
- Prosciutto di San Daniele with several farm broad beans, walnut dressing, and pea shoots
- Insalata of mozzarella di bufala, juicy Sicilian melon, mint, funky leaves, and aged balsamic
- Aged carnaroli risotto of Italian white peach, prosecco, and mint
- Ravioli di sol with Amalfi lemon butter sauce and crispy pancetta
- Line-caught fillet of Cornish sea bass with potato al forno, artichoke, olives, and tarragon aioli
- Crispy fillet of John Dory with lenticchie di Castellucio, mixed greens, and salmoriglio
- Char-grilled aged Angus beef fillet with borlotti beans, Newlinas wet garlic, rosemary, and anchovy dressing
- Gooseberry semi freddo with elderflower and gooseberry compote, black pepper, and sesame seed tuille
- Amedei No. 9 chocolate salted caramel tart with strawberry balsamic ice cream, Buttervillas strawberries, and brandy snap
- Fromaggi: White Lake, Ogle Shield, and Exmoor Jersey Blue, rosemary crackers, with apple and pear chutney
- Caffe e Cioccolatina: coffee with white chocolate raspberry truffles and cantuccini

This was just some dinner; I had a fantastic meal with my greatest of friends in one of the world's great restaurants, with seaviews to die for. It only cost £60 per head plus wine, of which there was a lot, but hey, as a director, I got a 30 percent discount.

We then went on the ferry going to Roscoff, after leaving the Fifteen board meeting early. We ate fairly rubbish food in the canteen, which was cheaper than the restaurant. We breakfasted nicely in Roscoff and set off and found a place called Penestin, where we had *jambon* baguettes. I went to the beach and swam and then saw a lot of jellyfish on the shore. We went for a night to La Roche Bernard and stayed in the Auberges Breton, where we may have stayed twenty-three years ago.

We had an interesting dinner. We went for the E45 menu. We each had a kir and the amuse bouche. I had an oyster baked in the shell with dough outside (the *garcon* had to show me how to eat it) and then *carre d'agneau,* which was just lamb chops with soggy couscous, and lemon tart to finish. On the waiter's advice, we had a nice E36 Samur from the Loire. After dinner, I had a 1984 Calvados, at E20 a pop.

It took us six hours to do the two hundred miles to Cognac, where we were going to meet Jamie and Bob again. There was a lot of traffic. Cognac did not seem to have many restaurants, but we found La Chine, which was not Chinese but looked okay and met Jamie and Bob. The dinner was very nice; we drank kir, Sancerre rouge, and E18 Martell cognacs. I ate foie gras de canard and *rognons de veau* with a mustard sauce; we all shared four desserts, of which the strawberry soup was exceptional. The bill was E326, but I paid, as they often treat us.

Next came the highlight of the evening: The Stranglers were playing a free concert in the park. We left the restaurant, and as we walked down, the Stranglers were playing one of their great songs, 'Golden Brown': a really surreal experience. We got close to the band, drank cognac with ice, and listened for ages to such great songs as 'Peaches,' 'No More Heroes,' and 'Hanging Around.'

We went for lunch at Oasis, which had very nice moules frites, and as everything else seemed closed, we came here for dinner too. It was 80 degrees and sunny, so we decided to go to the outdoor swimming pool. There were big picture signs saying 'No board shorts.' We sunbathed for a while, and when the lifeguard was not looking, I slipped into the pool and started swimming. A shrill whistle sounded, and the lifeguard indicated for me to get out. I did, and we had an interesting conversation, where I *non comprende*. But eventually, I had to go to the changing room and borrow a pair of speedos (which may or may not have been hygienic). I had a lovely swim in the fifty-metre pool.

Dinner at Oasis was great; we had the E19 dinner for four courses and a quarter-bottle of wine: avocado/crevettes, gigot d'agneau avec haricots blancs, a truly great brie, and tarte aux pommes. With two kirs and an extra carafe of vin rouge, it was all E49, a bargain.

We went to Cherbourg and stayed in an okay hotel right on the harbour but declined the extra E30 for a harbour view. We had a really nice dinner from the E36 menu: langoustines followed by St Pierre baked on a hot stove with lovely vegetables (carrots, peas, and mange-toots), followed by fraises. We finished with twenty-year-old armagnac for a fine evening. And then we took a nice short ride home on the fast ferry to Poole.

## September 2012

We took a not-too-bad Ryanair flight to Treviso, near Venice (it's much better to pay a small premium for priority boarding, which nobody else does; you get on the plane first and choose an aisle and middle seat, and nobody can be bothered to climb over to get the window). The hotel was nice, and the town was very Italian. We ate at Trattoria de Tomaso, a restaurant next door to the hotel, and shared scallops. I then had seafood risotto and calves liver with onions and polenta. We drank prosecco and Valpollicello Supreme and got a free after-dinner drink, all for E99.

It was 85 degrees and sunny, and the next morning, we took the local train to Venice; we were on a mission. Michael Winner, writing in the *Sunday Times*, had recommended Locanda Cipriano, on the outlying island of Torcello. The boat trip required two boats and took over an hour. We found the place, but it seemed closed; eventually, we found someone who took us into the most delightful garden ever, set with tables for lunch. And we had such a good lunch: courgette flowers stuffed with king prawns and rosemary on a courgette puree, followed by *taglioni* (small flat spaghetti) with a fresh tomato and basil sauce, which was really sweet and delicious. Chrissie had a crab and rosemary risotto, which was equally delicious. We drank Prosecco and beer, and it all cost E100. The setting and the food made this a lunch to die for. We had a nice dinner again at de Tomaso, with Parma ham and tagliatelle with small scampi. We didn't get a free drink, and it cost E94 but could not compare.

The next day, we were back on the local train, but about two miles from Venice, it stopped, and it stopped for ages. All the Italians were talking excitedly on their phones, and the guard turned up and said we had to walk. We got off the train and had a lovely two-mile walk along the tracks to Venice, noticing that the power lines had come down somehow. We walked to the Rialto Bridge and took a little time to find Trattoria Madonna, which we had fallen in love with thirty years ago. We had a wonderful lunch of artichoke hearts and fried scampi, with ravioli for Chrissie, and it all cost E52 with service: a great, great experience after so many years.

We took a E7 vaparetto ride to St Mark's Square, which was touristy. We got back on the vaparetto to the train station, and it was still pandemonium, with a lot of pushing and shoving, but somehow we got back to Treviso. We had dinner again at de Tomaso, and we argued about the table and only got a decent one with the help of the maitre d', eating scallops and a very good linguine with clams and drinking Valpolicello Supreme and getting a free drink; it was only E84 this time.

It was nice to revisit Venice. Treviso was nice, and we had two great lunches, three pretty good dinners, and the train track experience: a good stopover in a special city.

It was time to move on, and luckily, the trains were running properly again, with our three trains to Pesaro all running on time to the minute. It was difficult to find a decent lunch in the Bologna station, which seemed weird for Italy. We arrived in Pesaro, having paid about E100 each for the train ride, which seemed to be the cheapest and most efficient way of getting there. We had a nice balcony overlooking the beautiful Adriatic; it was all very Italian, with lots of beautiful girls to admire and a good joie de vivre, but there were about ten thousand beach umbrellas and chairs, and it cost E15 per day for two loungers and some shade.

For our first night, we went to L'Angelo, with a nice position right on the sea, and I ate small sardines on sticks and gnocchi with prawn and courgette, but the food seemed a bit corporate (the hotel receptionist described it as 'regular'), but it was quite cheap, at only E55. It was nice and sunny and hot, so we hit the beach. They had free beach tennis; our record was thirteen consecutive hits, which was good fun, and we swam a lot in the beautiful sea and ate nice baguettes for lunch.

Andy Murray won the US Open, but we could only follow it on the i-Pad, as Sky Italia did not show it. We tried Il Castigliane for dinner, which was an old castle with a lovely garden. I ate gnocchi with moules and scampi and creme caramel and drank a nice local wine, all for E72. After more time on the beach, we ventured the next night to Bristolino. It was a different experience, as there was no menu; we had been warned to watch the cost. We started with a scampi and prawn salad and followed with roasted scallops and turbot with potatoes and tomatoes and had four desserts and two dessert wines, along with some very nice local wine, all for E86: a real deal.

But it started to rain. We caught the train to Riccione. I visited here when I was seven years old and twice went to a restaurant where I had one of the best meals ever of sardines, scampi, and strawberries and cream. I could remember it in my mind's eye, but we couldn't find it. We went onto Rimini, where I learnt to swim fifty-three years ago. But the weather was so bad, we got no farther than the station and ended up at Burger King for lunch. Dinner was not much better at Rossini, made particularly bad by loud Newcastle people at the next table. And the weather was still dull, so we took a four-mile walk to the port and back. You need nice weather by the beach, and the sea was too rough to swim.

We returned to Rimini, and I stood in the sea where I learnt to swim, but it was too rough to show off my skills. We had a very nice lunch at the Milton Beach restaurant, sitting in the sunshine, which had returned. The gnocchi with scampi and lemon was excellent. Our receptionist recommended Bronaccio for dinner. It was all very nice but only average for tomato bruschetta, gnocchi, and lamb chops, with a 14.5 percent marche wine, but it only cost E59. We were still looking for that elusive great dinner.

The restaurants were all too near the main drag, so we consulted Trip Advisor and came up with De Sante, a trattoria in the old town. This was nearly the great dinner. The menu was only in Italian. We started with marinated sardines, which seem like anchovies, followed by spaghetti with clams and fried fish, which turned out to be squid and prawns. We drank the chilled one-litre bottle of red wine and were given free desserts and a bottle of frozen limoncello. And it only cost E44: a real bargain.

The next night, we went again and had a similar dinner for E44 again, but with taglione with clams and tomatoes this time for the second course. De Sante was closed, so we ventured to the local Chinese, where we had a dreadful dinner with terrible food and service for E37. But we did manage our last dinner at De Sante, who ran out of house red, so we had to buy quarter-bottles, which pushed the bill to E50. We ate nearly the same food but drank a lot of limoncello, and it all seemed very nice indeed.

Pesaro was not really our kind of place. It was too big, and the beach was too crowded, and it took us more than a week to find a decent restaurant. Beach tennis and the Italian people were truly great, but we looked forward to our next trip to Italy being somewhere else.

## November 2012

And then, we were in Miami Beach, flying only Premium Economy, which was okay. Miami had lots of energy and really nice people. We stayed in the Circa 39 Hotel, which was very nice. On the first night, we just had burgers and Bloody Marys in the hotel restaurant.

On the first day, we went for a long walk on the boardwalk to South Beach and had a nice sandwich for lunch. It was maybe five miles there and back, but it was great to be on the boardwalk. I had a quick swim in the pool. Our first proper dinner was at Ciceros in Soho House Hotel (formerly the London Hotel). We shared an excellent gorgonzola gnocchi, and I had spaghetti with Maine lobster, and Chrissie had cuttlefish gratinee with a butternut squash risotto, which was excellent again. We drank a $72 bottle of Italian wine, and it all came to $173, which seemed fine for such a nice place.

The hotel had chairs on the beach, so the next day, we headed there; I had a sort of swim in quite a difficult ocean. We retired to the pool for some proper swimming and had a nice spinach soup at the hotel for lunch. We took a taxi to see *Silver Linings Playbook* at the Regal Moviehouse in South Beach. Despite Bradley Cooper and Robert de Niro, it was not really that good. We dined at the nearby Provence Grill. It was French, but somehow, it was American. I ate vichyssoise and *moules mariniere* with French fries but no mayonnaise, and Chrissie has foie gras and branzino fish and shared a tarte Tatin. Drinking a $36 bottle of Bordeaux, it all cost $142. It was very nice but just seemed too much.

We just hung out for our last day and had a pretty average dinner just down the road at Amalfi, which cost $125, which was too much for an average dinner with no atmosphere.

We went back to the airport but only to get the Mustang convertible. We set off for the 160-mile drive to Key West. It was a bit cloudy, and somehow the scenery did not really excite. Many people think this is one of the great drives, but we only had the roof down for the last twenty miles. However, we did have a great lunch at Key Fisheries in Marathon: a fried mahi sandwich for Chrissie and Florida Keys lobster roll for me, and drinking lemonade, it was only $30 for a great restaurant, which we heartily recommend. We arrived in Key West, but there was nowhere at the hotel to park the car; I drove around forever to find a space which was miles away. The next morning, we hired bikes and didn't get in the car again until we left. I guess that's what you had to do in Key West.

We went to the Alonzo Oyster Bar and had a great dinner: Bloody Marys to start, followed by shared shell on prawns, stone crab for me (which was delicious), and dolphin for Chrissie. We had two glasses of merlot and two Key West ales, which was dark but nice, and it all came to $111 plus a $25 tip for a great waitress.

## Mr. Tambourine Man

We got on our bikes and went to the beach. We sat on our towels because we didn't want to pay $20 for the chairs. There was a food trailer, and we got hot dogs, cheese sandwiches, and banana smoothies for $14. The sea was warm, at 76 degrees, and it was shallow and smooth, unlike Miami, so we had a lot of fun in the water. Joy: There was an art movie house only a short walk from the hotel, and we went to see *The Sessions,* which was pretty good. We enjoyed our first twenty-four hours in Key West loads. We went for dinner at New York Pasta Company. Trip Advisor said to only order one main course, as it was very large. We ordered artichoke fritters and bruschetta and lasagne. The starters were okay, but the lasagne was a disgrace, with meat and tomato not mixed. We had a nice bottle of Berringer merlot for $27. The best thing you can say is that it only cost $78, including tip.

We got back on the bikes to the beach again, for some more nice swimming. For lunch, we had two hot dogs and two lemonades for $8 from the trailer. It was Thanksgiving, and we went to the Sunset Bar to watch the sun go down. I had a very nice Key West Sunset ale. To celebrate, we went to A&B Lobster House and had a truly memorable dinner. A Bellini martini and Hemingway Hammer (Blue Curacao, vodka, and lime juice) was a good way to start. We then had clam chowder and lobster bisque, followed by one of the best turkey dinners ever, with all the trimmings, all followed by pumpkin pie. And drinking a good $50 bottle of merlot (Provenance), it all cost $206 with tip for a great night out, and we were allowed to go and smoke cigarettes in the Cigar Lounge to make it perfect.

The next day was a beach repeat, and Alonzo's again, except we got a bad table and worse service. We had two Key West ales, two merlots, a half-pound of chilled shrimp with spicy sauce, seven-ounce lobster tail, and fish and chips, for $92 plus tip.

The weather here was great; it was around 78 degrees and very sunny. We went to the beach on the bikes again, and then we saw a very harrowing movie, *Trade of Innocents,* about child prostitution in Cambodia: a really terrible situation but a moving movie. We had a nice dinner at Marquesa, with a very nice Incognito wine at $48. We started with hummus and bread, and we both had butternut squash soup. I had lobster (again) with shrimp, pak choi, and rice, which seemed to have a bit too much going on, and Chrissie had gnocchi with duck and sherry. It was not cheap, at $126 plus tip, but pretty good.

The next day, guess what? We got on the bikes and went to the same beach again and had the same $8 hot dogs and lemonade and enjoyed the sea. We went to Santiago's Bodega, a tapas bar, for dinner and had a great meal. We ate bruschetta with olive tapenade and tomato, croquettes of prosciutto and cheese, duck and sweet potato hash, grouper with herb crust, and tenderloin. Drinking merlot and a local beer times two, it all came to $92. The atmosphere and the food were great for a really outstanding restaurant.

For our last night, we went to 2 Cents, which was very hip. We drank cabernet sauvignon and shared stone crab and both had the fisherman's stew with shrimps, clams, mussels, fish, and a hot tomato broth. We had a pumpkin-flavoured crème brûlée for dessert. It cost $123 plus tip, so not so cheap, but pretty good.

The weather there was perfect, and we had fun on the bikes (except when Chrissie fell off) and probably cycled around forty miles. Key West was a nice place with great beaches, a good moviehouse, and lots of interesting restaurants; we had such a memorable Thanksgiving dinner. It was supposed to be gay here, but we didn't notice.

It was time to find the car, which was still in the same place after a week, and we took the four-hour trip back to Miami Airport. On the recommendation of Trip Advisor, we stopped at Harriet's in Key Largo. The place had no style, and the corned beef hash was only okay. I would not bother again.

We headed to Gate D32 to catch our plane to New Orleans. We arrived and were driven to our B&B by a cab driver who was a total lunatic. We stayed in a wonderful old house with fourteen-foot ceilings, just outside the French Quarter. Someone recommended Adolfo's, an Italian Creole restaurant round the corner, and we just managed to get a table. We started with cannelloni with sausage and spinach, which was simply fantastic, with the lightest pasta ever, and then had grouper with shrimps and clams. We drank three merlot and a beer, and it only cost $68: a lovely dinner. We then retired to the Spotted Cat for some great jazz and booze, and you could smoke too.

We spent $3 for our transit tickets and rode around the city a little. We found the Movie Tour; a lot of movies are made in New Orleans, partly because of the tax breaks. The Movie Tour was great; we sat in a comfortable van with movie screens showing clips of movies, and then we'd pull up to where they were shot. We saw Benjamin Button's house and places where they shot *The Pelican Brief*. It was all very interesting and a great way to spend an afternoon.

Coop's was the place for dinner, but you couldn't book, so we queued up outside and got in after only five minutes. We ordered a beer and a bottle of wine but got a glass, which Chrissie drank. She asked again for a bottle and got a magnum, which was all they served. We tried hard but didn't quite manage to finish every last drop. We had good fried crawfish to start and both followed with chicken, rabbit, and sausage jambalaya and coleslaw. It was all very wonderful and only cost $68, including so much wine. We retired to the Spotted Cat again for more great jazz (but we only smoked because we had had too much wine).

It was a beautiful day in New Orleans, 74 degrees and sunshine. We took a tram ride and then had a long walk along the Mississippi and watched a paddle steamer leave the mooring. We had delicious catfish po-boy and pink lemonade for lunch, another local special. But it was wedding anniversary number thirty-two. We were told to go to Antoine's near Bourbon Street, which we didn't like much, as too touristico. We had to book the table to make sure I didn't need a jacket, since I didn't have one, but it was all okay. There was an important football game on, and we were shown into the back restaurant, which was nearly empty. Our starters arrived, and we were left alone in a sixty-seat space, so we asked to be moved to the front restaurant, which was still pretty empty. We drank average martinis and a good bottle of $65 Ferrari cabernet; in the back room, we started with crab gratinee for Chrissie and a classic dish, crevettes remoulade, for me. Moving into the front room, we shared a chateaubriand. The food was all very nice, but as described, the atmosphere was terrible. It cost $224, but we didn't leave a tip. To cheer ourselves up, we returned to the Spotted Cat for some more wine, great music, and a little dancing.

New Orleans was a fantastic city. We had two great dinners, three great trips to the Spotted Cat, and a brilliant movie tour; we just enjoyed hanging out in the city. But now it was time to get back to Los Angeles again to see our lovely daughter. We failed to get a Mustang and had to settle for a yellow Camaro convertible, which may be faster but was also a lot gayer.

It was as laid back as ever in LA. I played tennis at the Toluca Lake club, swam in Lauren's pool, and ate at P F Chang's and Olive & Thyme, a good local deli. We had a good dinner for Chrissie's birthday at the Sushi Yuza on Riverside, along with Esa and a friend. We took Lauren's very expensive dog for a nice hike towards the Hollywood sign, but we nearly lost the dog and so came right back. We went to see *Hitchcock* at the Arclight. It was a great movie, and we learnt that he didn't want the music for the shower scene in *Psycho* but was persuaded; that music became iconic.

It was nice to have sunshine and 72 degrees in December. We returned to Prosecco and ate good bruschetta with mozzarella, osso buco, and ravioli with artichoke and sun-dried tomato. We went shopping at Ralph Lauren and found I was now size 30 waist measurement; they have changed the sizes or I got thinner. Anyway, there were a lot better buys here because the prices were around half those in the UK. We returned to Angelino's and again ate the ravioli pomodoro, which was as good as ever, and with one Perni and a water for Chrissie, it was only $31. I played a bit more tennis and continued to swim in Lauren's pool. Back to Angelino's again, and this time I ate $26 spaghetti with Maine lobster, which was better than Miami and half the price. We also went and saw a few more movies: *Life of Pi*, *Hyde Park Hudson*, and *Rust and Bone*.

This was an interesting trip. Key West and New Orleans were both great firsts, and it was so good to have sunshine and warmth in late November/early December. This was trip number fourteen to Los Angeles, which we were getting to know well. We were away for ninety-one days this year, and it was now time to go home.

# February 2013

We were off to a new place: Grenada in the Caribbean, where lots of friends had gone and said it was wonderful. We carefully chose the Hotel Cabier, an eco resort with a Michelin restaurant, not charging Michelin prices (or so said Trip Advisor).

We got off the plane and took a forty-five-minute taxi ride for EC$110 (or about £30). Sometimes when you go househunting, you know straight away whether it is for you; well, I guess hotels are the same, and I knew immediately that this was not our sort of place. The room seemed dirty, no towels, no chairs, and worst of all, no curtains, but hey, maybe dinner would be good. It was not; the Trip Advisor Michelin posts must have been fake. We started with a papaya salad, boring, and then got some chicken with noodles and vegetables, with coconut crème caramel with sorrel for dessert. The only good thing was a nice Chilean Rothschild red.

I woke up on the first morning, and the first thing I said to Chrissie was that we were not going to stay here for eighteen days; she was so relieved. We had paid a 30 percent deposit, so about five days, but we needed to get out of there soon. I got onto the Internet and found a room at Grooms Beach Hotel, near the action, and booked a room for the rest of our stay. We had an okay breakfast and chicken roti for lunch. The beach was terrible; it was so dirty, and the swimming was very rough on the north coast. Dinner was terrible again, with lentil spiced soup and kingfish with the same things as the chicken the night before, followed by cheesecake, which I hated. I forgot to mention, there was no menu; you just ate what you were given. We told the patron we were leaving and asked for a taxi after breakfast in the morning.

I now have to write about the charges. When we left the hotel, they charged me for our food and drinks, and I unhappily paid the US$230 with my credit card. When I received the credit card statement, they had charged me for the whole eighteen days. After an exchange of emails, they told me that their booking conditions were that you were responsible for the whole lot, fourteen days prior to arrival. I checked my email booking, which made no mention of this condition, just demanding the 30 percent deposit. All this was sent to the credit card company, who agreed I had never been informed of the booking condition, and I got my money back. I travel a lot but am now very careful about booking conditions because as we saw here you can hate the place you have booked and need to go somewhere else and not pay for your mistake.

The Grooms Beach Hotel was close to a really nice beach with great swimming and two nice-looking restaurants within walking distance. We had a nice hamburger lunch in the Beach House Restaurant with great bread rolls, and it cost about £25. And we returned for an excellent dinner. We shared a gnocchi and both had the local lobster and drank a bottle of the Baron Rothschild Chilean red. It was all pretty good but not cheap, at US$168 plus tip.

We had a nice day on the beach with good swimming and a nice lunch at the Beach House, with spinach soup and a shared chickpea and potato roti, all very good and only about £20. And dinner again at the Beach House, with delicious tuna tartare followed by baby ribs, and drinking a cheaper Cotes de Rhone, it was only US$138. We were liking it there a lot.

The next day, we took a £10 taxi ride to Grand Anse Beach, which was one of the world's great beaches, and it sure was nice. I had my first waterski for about two years and just about get up and go round the bay two times. We had a very nice lunch in Umbrellas, with grilled fish in ciabatta and beers, only costing £15 for two. We took a nice walk back to the hotel. We went to LaLuna next door for dinner. We started with happy hour cocktails, and I ate gazpacho and calves liver, which was my favourite dinner, and Chrissie had lobster soup and risotto. We drank an expensive bottle of Italian Veneto merlot at EC$110, and the whole bill was over £100. But it was a good dinner in nice surroundings, with lots of atmosphere.

The waterski man didn't come to our beach, so we had a normal swimming day and had nice soup at the Beach House for lunch. We went back to LaLuna again for dinner. We shared tempura vegetables, and I had lobster ravioli, and Chrissie had snapper with a pineapple salsa; with a very nice bottle of EC$104 wine, it was over £100 again. But it was great there.

## Mr. Tambourine Man

We returned to Grand Anse, but the water was not great for waterskiing, so we just swam. We had lunch again at Umbrellas; the falafel was a bit dull, but it only cost £15. We took the forty-minute walk back to the hotel. Dinner in the Beach House was as enjoyable as ever. Chrissie had a rum punch, and I drank pina colada. We shared crab woantons, which were very good, and Chrissie had chicken, and I had lobster again; with the house merlot, it was just under £100 this time.

The weather was great, around 85 degrees and very sunny; we had another laid-back day on the beach but did have an expensive £25 lunch with crab wontons and shrimp. We went back to LaLuna for dinner, with gazpacho again, followed by fettucine ragu for me and special goat cheese and ravioli for Chrissie; with a couple of cocktails and a nice Italian wine, it was around £100 again. It seemed that dinner will always cost £100 here. We talked to Lauren, and it was raining in LA.

It was time to explore the island. Our driver, Wayne, picked us up at 9 a.m., and we headed off to the Concord, which was very pretty. Then we went to the Spice Centre, which was very interesting, and we spend EC$25 on mace, nutmeg, bay leaves, and cinnamon. We passed the fishing village of Gouyare and headed onto the Grand Etang Lake, which was a volcanic crater full of water. We stopped for a cheese sandwich and beer. We stopped again at nineteen hundred feet to get a wonderful vista and a great view of Grand Anse Beach. Wayne talked a lot about the history of the island and Maurice Bishop and the US invasion. St Georges, the capital, was old and pretty. Grenada seemed very nice and a good trip, for around £70 (or less than dinner). But we did manage an £80 dinner in the Beach House, with beef satay and dull swordfish for me and soup and conch curry for Chrissie, with the Cotes de Rhone. And the next night, we returned for a £102 dinner with shrimp, gnocchi, crème brûlée, and a nice Italian merlot.

We went back to Grand Anse, and I got my second waterski. We had a nice lunch at Umbrellas, with good shrimp and fries for me and a fish sandwich for Chrissie, and only £15. Dinner at LaLuna was as good as ever, with bresola (cured beef), seafood spaghetti for me, and pork tenderloin for Chrissie; with a good bottle of Linguine wine from Italy, it was just under £100. I got knocked over by a wave coming back, and my shoes were soaked. But we returned the next night and found the secret path away from the waves. We had live music and cocktails before dinner, and I had excellent chickpea soup and calves liver, and Chrissie had pappardelle with mushrooms and sausage; with a nice bottle of Italian red, we got out for only £90.

We walked to the aquarium, which was famous for Sunday lunch, but we didn't like the atmosphere. We returned through the all-inclusive Rex, which didn't look like our kind of place, and retired to the Beach House for a lovely pumpkin soup. Dinner at the Beach House was shared crab wontons, lobster for me, and chicken for Chrissie, which with Baron Rothschild was again around £100.

The sea got a bit rough, so we had to swim in the hotel pool, but it was still gloriously sunny. We had been there two weeks and so celebrated with pumpkin soup again. We had a nice dinner at LaLuna, with gazpacho and a ricotta and callaloo ravioli, with good Italian red wine, for just under £100.

Even though it was a bit rough, we walked to the BBC beach and went to Moulin Rouge. The sea was very calm there, and we ate tuna sandwiches for lunch. We had another nice dinner at the Beach House: tuna tartare and conch curry for me, and lobster soup and smoked salmon penne for Chrissie. With the Cotes de Rhone, it was just under £100.

We went back to swimming in the pool and had a nice roti for lunch. We had a great dinner at LaLuna; the antipasto Italiano had the freshest cut ham ever, and then we shared asparagus risotto and lobster ravioli. Drinking the nice Italian red wine, it was £100 again.

It was our last day, so we returned to Grand Anse, but it was too rough for waterskiing, so I just swam. We had a nice lunch at Umbrellas and our last dinner at the Beach House. I had my favourites (tuna tartare and lobster) and Chrissie had scallops and the smoked salmon penne. We started with rum punch and pina colada, and with a bottle of Baron Rothschild, it was all about £110. They were so sorry to see us go and gave us a large bottle of rum punch and a Grenada cookbook.

On leaving, our thoughts were, this is a great island. The people were so gentle, the beaches were great, and the food was pretty good. I only managed two waterskis but had thirty-five swims. The start was nearly a disaster, but we were so glad we came here; it was a joy.

# June 2013

We got up at 5.30 to catch the 7.40 to Nice, and we were in Juan les Pins again for the first time in twenty-five years. We had to walk to the car hire in Nice Airport, as the shuttle bus did not seem to be working, and then queued for a long time at Europcar, and then queued again to get out. It took us two and a half hours from landing to the hotel, but the Hotel des Mimosas was very nice. It had a good pool, friendly staff, and great breakfasts and was only a short walk to the beach.

Since we were early, we went to the beach. The sea was a little chilly, but we swam a bit and had a nice salad for lunch, with prawns, pineapple, and palm hearts, and with a couple of sunbeds, it was E97 for the four of us (Lauren and Eric were with us). For dinner, we went to Cap Riviera, which Trip Advisor said was the best in town. We shared crayfish and salmon starters, and I had a very nice cassoulet of lobster. We drank kirs and Sancerre rouge, and it all came to E246, so not so cheap.

The next night, we went to Capitole, a nice French bistro. We drank kirs and carafes of the local red. I had delicious fish soup and duck leg au sud-est, and it was only E110 for a really great dinner.

But then I turned sixty-one years old. I got lots of nice presents, had a great breakfast, and went off for my third waterski of the year. It was a little rough, but my instructor said I had a good style. We then took off for the very famous Eden Roc Hotel. We ate an excellent salmon tartare for me, courgette risotto for Chrissie, and sushi and spaghetti for the kids. With only beer and water, it was still E189, but a nice place to be. We then asked, as we were lunch guests, if we could swim in the lovely pool. Sure, but it would be E70 each. We were told off for sitting on a lounger to have a cigarette.

It was a nice experience, but oh, so shallow, and I would not really like to stay there. We found a nice beach and had a good swim on the way back. Before dinner, we went for the first time to St Paul de Vence, a nice town with lots of art galleries. We sauntered into La Colombe D'Or Hotel for a kir royale but were told we couldn't view the pictures. On leaving, we turned right instead of left and viewed the pictures: some great pictures given by poor artists who didn't have enough money to pay their way, in the good old days. I thought maybe Eric would buy me a birthday drink, but some hope; I paid again.

Dinner had to be Cap Riviera, and I had a good meal of foie gras and lobster and drank another kir and a Rose Premier Cru. Lauren had organised a birthday cake with two candles, and it was only E213 this time. I had a really, really nice day.

It was time to go to St Tropez, but it didn't really work. It took ninety minutes to get to St Maxime, and there were so many cars, and the GPS said it was another forty-five minutes. We gave up, walked around St Maxime, and went to a pizzeria and spent E66. We went on to Cannes, with an awful lot of traffic, and walked La Croisette and looked at the Carlton Hotel. Somehow, it didn't really grab me, but at least we showed Lauren and Eric a little bit of the South of France.

Back to Capitole for the two of us, and we had kir, a carafe of house rosé, smoked salmon, and gambas flambé at a proper French restaurant, and only E69.

We enjoyed the pink beach, swimming, and a couple of games of tennis on the clay courts and went back to Cap Riviera for our last night. we spent E245 on a half-homard and entrecôte for me, which was all delicious, in a good atmosphere, with the usual nice kirs and a bottle of Red Provence. It seemed expensive with no dessert or digestive, but we liked this place a lot and plan to come back one day.

The plane was full of kids, and a particularly nasty one kept kicking the back of my seat; it took nearly six hours back through awful traffic, particularly at Stonehenge.

# August 2013

It was time to celebrate Chrissie and I knowing each other for forty years; we were going to celebrate in Padstow. I had a haircut to look smart, and on the way, we stopped at Trevone for a swim. Then we went to the Old Ship Inn, where we stayed before. It was right in the centre of town and had a decent car park and nice cosy rooms.

For the first night, we went to Rick Stein's Seafood School for an Indian night. It started at seven, and we arrived a little early, like everybody else, and were given a nice glass of wine. On the dot of seven, Rick wandered in with his own glass of wine and proceeded to entertain us in the most pleasurable way for over two hours.

He cooked, and then we ate: breakfast bhaji, Madras fish curry with monkfish, tomato and tamarind, and Mr Singh's slow-cooked lamb curry with cloves and cardamom. The first two were the favourites. We had a friendly chat with Rick at the end; he was just so nice. I had a pint of Sharps back at the Old Ship before bed.

The next morning, we took the ferry to Rock. It still seemed like a dump, which we didn't really get, and so back to Padstow for a crab sandwich. We waited for ten minutes to get into Rick Stein's Fish 'n' Chips but had excellent tiger prawns, cod, haddock (for Chrissie), mushy peas, and chips, with Chalky's Bite and a glass of merlot, for £34.

We spent £14 on a couple of bikes and set off on the Camel Trail. We rode about twenty miles nearly to Bodmin, with a good lunch at the Camel Valley Tea Room. Dinner in Rick Stein's Cafe was very good, with moules mariniere and a rib-eye steak for me and tomato soup and sole goujons for Chrissie, and with a nice bottle of merlot, it was all £72, but very nice indeed.

The big four-oh arrived, and we went for a swim at Trevone, followed by antipasto lunch at Fifteen, with double world-class courgette flowers, prosciutto, melon, arancini, and a glass each of Prosecco, all for £34. We had to make a short visit to the tournament at the tennis club for coffee cake and tea.

But then it was time for the big dinner: a really good dinner, if a little expensive, at £172 plus tip. We started with a glass of champagne and a Bellini and then shared delicious prawn fritters and John Dory with a soft-boiled egg and leeks. For a main course, we both had lobster thermidor, which was as good as ever. We drank a chilled bottle of 2009 Samur Champigny, which was a fine wine and excellent with the food. It was a marvellous way to celebrate forty years together.

Our long Rick Stein weekend was interesting and great fun, and we sure ate well.

## September 2013

We were ready for trip number fifteen to LA. It was a quick flight of only ten hours, ten minutes (sometimes, it takes over eleven hours); Iceland and Greenland still had snow. The weather in LA was beautifully hot, at 98 degrees, and after quite a lot of discussion, National Car Rental got us a red Mustang convertible from Alamo.

On our first night, we had dinner alone with Lauren at Gundi Thai, and she told us something serious: It was not working with Eric, and they were getting divorced. This felt like good news. He had banned us from our house, where he lived free and paid no rent or costs, always taking and giving nothing back. We felt sorry for Lauren that it hadn't worked, but at least she got her Green Card.

With the fantastic weather, we swam in the pool a lot and ate very well. On the first day, we had waffles and blueberries for lunch at Patty's, followed by ravioli pomodoro at the famous Angelino's and a good sandwich at Olive & Thyme the next day.

Lauren met an interesting couple: an older guy, Stephen Maitland-Lewis (a Lazards financier turned author who gave me signed copies of his books), and his delightful wife, Jodi, a retired dancer whose best mate was Tippi Hedren (who had a hard time from Hitchcock in *The Birds*). We were invited to their very nice house in the Hollywood Hills and drank champagne and smoked looking at the amazing views. They took us to dinner at Bauchon, and we drank gin martinis and ate excellent onion soup and rib-eye, all in a great atmosphere.

We played a little tennis, went swimming, saw Woody Allen's *Blue Jasmine* (with the superb Cate Blanchette), and ate hamburgers, as you do in the United States.

It was time for another road trip, and we set off for the six-hour, 340-mile trip to our favourite place: Carmel. We booked dinner at Andre's, where we always got a free glass of champagne. We had a great dinner, with lobster salad, followed by quail stuffed with truffle, and drinking a local $66 pinot noir, it only cost $172 plus $25 tip. The next morning, we had to go on our Carmel beach walk, which was more wonderful than ever because we saw about a dozen dolphins in the water, which was pure magic. We had a good lunch at A W Shucks and Rose: clam chowder and amber beer from San Francisco, and only $29 for two. We had a good dinner at Vesuvius, with artichoke followed by black ink spaghetti with clams, and drinking a $48 bottle of wine, it was only $119 plus tip. It was nice to revisit the honeymoon site again, but then we went to the land of *The Birds*.

We went over the Golden Gate Bridge again, but somehow, it was always a joy, and after two hundred miles, we were in Bodega Bay. We had good corned beef hash in Stimson Beach on the way. Our hotel was Inn at the Tides, with a large room and a view of the sea. We stayed on a dinner B&B basis, so we had to eat the set menu: Bodega Bay fish chowder (which is more like minestrone with a bit of fish included) and fettucine seafood with three scallops, three prawns, and some white fish, which was actually not too bad.

The weather here was not so great, with a lot of mist and only around 60 degrees. I had to swim in the pool in the damp. Bodega Bay was great, however. We saw the church and schoolhouse and then drove on Bay Cliff Road, which was where they shot the famous scene with Tippi Hedren driving an Aston Martin. We went onto Bodega Head past the house (which was no longer there, but we had a very nice walk). We went to Spinal Point Crab Co. for an excellent $28 lunch of clam chowder, followed by a shared crab sandwich. In the afternoon, we headed to Sebastopol and went to see *The Butler* at the movies.

We had to wait for a table for dinner, and the dinner was forgettable. It was a great place of movie historic interest, but it was time to move on.

We had a great $17 lunch at Forester in Carmino, eating kiddy portions of tuna melt and crab melt with avocado, coleslaw, and lemonade on the side.

We were now in 'Las Vegas on Sea' (or Lake Tahoe, as it is known), and we were on the California side. We tried hard to get into it, but it was nice and sunny and 77 degrees. Trip Advisor recommended Black Olive Bistro, but it was now a burger bar. We dropped into a record store and bought CDs for the road trip: Grateful Dead, Clash, and Charlie Parker. Our first dinner was at Boathouse on the Pier, which was very nice, with clam chowder and lobster tail for me, and lobster bisque and salmon for Chrissie. With a nice bottle of St Francis merlot, it was $117 plus tip.

We caught the shuttle bus to Nevada to look for movie theatres and discovered the Yardbirds were playing tonight in one of the casinos, but the box office did not open until 6 p.m. We got sandwiches and doughnuts from Safeway and swam a little in the pool, as the lake was too cold. We were at sixty-two hundred feet above sea level, and it was quite hard work, but altitude training is always good for you. We got our Yardbird tickets, but there was no time for dinner, so we had a beer and then vodka and OJ and found our amazing seats. The legend continued, although they only had the original drummer and a guitarist who was kicked out when Jeff Beck, Eric Clapton, and Jimmy Page came along; the rest was now made up with three twenty-five-year-olds. We remember 'Shapes of Things,' 'For Your Love,' and 'Over Under Sideways Down,' but we forgot 'Heart Full of Soul.' They really only had four hits, but we were treated to nearly two hours of great music, with lots of good blues. Then we went to the Hard Rock Cafe for an excellent Bloody Mary and a truly wonderful classic burger for $43. What a night.

On our last day, we took a three-hour cruise to Emerald Bay, which was really nice; you saw a lot of the lake. For our last dinner, we went to Tepo Villa Roma, which was voted best Italian restaurant in Lake Tahoe from 1999 to 2012. It was rubbish. You got free antipasto or soup. The Yanks were loading their plates high with disgusting-looking food, and we opted for a tepid vegetable soup. We ordered gnocchi with eggplant, which seemed to have come out of a packet, and the wine was terrible. It was an awful way to spend $60. Tahoe seemed like a culinary desert. It was 473 miles back to LA; we'll not come here again.

We went shopping, and I bought a pair of blue Ralph Lauren shorts for £36 in Bloomingdale's, and Chrissie bought underwear in Victoria's Secret, and I bought each of the girls a pair of $198 shoes in Michael Kors. And we had a great dinner in Angelino's, with a shared salad with lemon dressing and Parmesan, and linguine with clams for me, and calamari for Chrissie, which was only $50 with a glass of Chianti and Peroni. We had a long chat with Lauren about her problems; it looked like they were going for a legal separation.

It was 82 degrees, so we did a lot more swimming and played some tennis.

We went to see *Indiana Jones and Raiders of the Lost Ark*, from I think 1981, which was over two hours long but felt like two minutes; Harrison Ford just shooting the guy who wanted to fight was such a classic scene from movie history. We had a great dinner at Patty's for $28: corned beef hash with fried eggs over easy, home fries, and a Coors Lite with egg and chips and merlot.

We did more swimming and tennis in 82 degrees and then went back to Prosecco. We ate artichoke soup and pasta with a lamb ragout and started with a glass of Prosecco, followed by a bottle of merlot, which was all very good for $156 plus tip.

We went to Whole Foods and spent $163 on the ingredients for shepherd's pie (maybe some champagne and wine was included). We entertained Stephen and Jodi, which was a great success. Jodi danced with Sammy Davis Jr., Frank Sinatra, and Dean Martin and told some wonderful stories. She was going to take Lauren to Tippi Hedren's ranch for a visit.

We went again to the Getty Museum, which was great in the sunshine, and there was a really good exhibition of drawings, including an amazing Rubens; we looked in the galleries and saw Van

Gogh, Degas, Monet, Manet, and Cezanne, amongst others, which was all very uplifting.

We followed up with a drunken dinner with Bob and Jamie, at the Roosevelt Hotel in Hollywood. The food was not worth a mention, but in the cigarette break, we stepped on Errol Flynn, Natalie Wood, and Alice Cooper on Hollywood Boulevard (their stars, anyway). Before we went home, we found Angelino's closed, so we had to go to Burning Bonzai for a good $43 Chinese dinner and our last osso buco dinner at Prosecco.

I suppose we were dominated by Lauren and Eric a bit. I was sad for Lauren, but it looked like it was not going to work. I had a lot of sympathy for her downsides. I managed twenty-eight swims, eight games of tennis, and eight trips to the movies on this visit and found Carmel great as usual and Bodega Bay fun. Lake Tahoe, however, was a dump.

## November 2013

We were off to Naples for our thirty-third wedding anniversary. We arrived at the beautiful converted hotel just before dinner, and the concierge recommended a restaurant for pizza. We went and there was a long queue, so we found another local place, Pizzeria Veol. We had two margaritas, a nice bottle of E10 wine, and two limoncellos, and it was E30 all in, for a great feast.

It was sunny and around 55 degrees; we walked round the town a bit, and after a nice E13 lunch of bruschetta and Peroni, we took an open-top bus ride. There were fantastic views of Vesuvius, the Bay of Naples, and the town.

We went for dinner at the Osteria il Carum, and very nice it was too. We started with a Campari and Aperol and then shared pasta with artichoke and potato, and we both had fish with tomato, clams, and mussels, and we drank a fine bottle of E25 Amalfi, recommended by the maitre d'. It all cost E89 including service for a very nice dinner.

Then we did Pompeii. We were told the tours were too expensive; all you had to do was get on the local train and go. We went to the station and bought two tickets at E2.90 each, but it was all very complicated, and we ended up paying a man E5 to show us the right platform. The train took forty-five minutes; we had a quick OJ and entered. We decided to go without a guide and spent a wonderful two hours, wandering around. It was an amazing place, founded in around 500 BC and floored by Vesuvius in AD 79. It was a pretty good day out, and we found a fast train back.

There was a Michelin restaurant, Palazzo Petrucci, and we booked for two nights. There was no atmosphere, and the room we were in had one table with two Chinese diners, and another table with a solitary man, who all left before we finished. We were given a nice glass of pink fizz and decent amuse-bouches with marinated fish, potato, and tomato. We order the maitre d'-recommended E50 bottle of wine and both had a quite good soup to start: cuttlefish and bean for me, and chestnut for Chrissie. We shared a pasta, which was not so great and was very large, even for two, with over-al dente vegetables, tomatoes, and ricotta. I followed with rabbit, which had very little flavour, and Chrissie had fish of the day, which was again very large and undercooked. It all cost E149 for a pretty poor time. We went again but only to cancel our reservation because we needed to return to London for urgent business.

On another day, we went to the Archaeological Museum, which was fascinating. There were lots of great sculptures and things from Pompeii. Pompeii was sort of excavated between 1875 and 1910, with lots of frescos. We went to dinner at El Sol, a fish restaurant. After a strange Campari aperitif, we shared good antipasto, and I ate very good pappardelle with lobster, tomato, and chilli, and we had a nice local red; it all cost E87, but we had to pay cash.

It was Chrissie's birthday, and it rained all day; we went shopping for presents. There was no money here; it was the poor south, and all the shops looked beautiful, but everything cost E10, and we didn't buy anything. We walked to the port and found a nice trattoria for fried anchovies, king prawns, chips, prosecco, and Peroni for E32, with very nice service. For dinner, we went back to the Osteria, but it was not so good the second time; they must have had the number two chef. The artichoke and potato, which we loved before, had large potato skins, my entrecôte was on a hot plate, which kept cooking the meat, and Chrissie's fish was different and not so good. With Campari, wine, and limoncello, it all came to E85 (there was also some excitement, as a guest collapsed, with a very white face).

We were on the plane to stay one night with my sister because the following day, we were off again.

## December 2013

We went back to LA for our sixteenth visit. We got on the brand-new Airbus A380, the world's biggest plane; it all felt pristine, and we received our first glass of champagne. The captain came on the tannoy and said there was a minor technical problem; he switched off the seat belt sign. His next statement was there was a fuel leak that couldn't be fixed, and we all had to leave the plane. We all got off; we tried with difficulty to get through Connections to go out for a cigarette, but our boarding passes would not allow us back in. After three attempts, a nice BA lady got us through, but we had to give up the Moulton Brown. We eventually took off at 9.30 p.m. instead of 3 p.m., flying a 747. We had more champagne, pinot noir, smoked salmon, and mushroom risotto, and then I slept all the way to LA. We landed at 12.20 a.m. local time (8.20 a.m. UK time).

We were in Terminal 2 and tried to phone Lauren, who was picking us up. Our phone didn't work, but there was a BA lady looking after a gorgeous VIP: Rosie Huntington-Whiteley. We called Lauren, who knew where we were. We came out of the terminal, and Lauren was very excited, as Rosie just got in her black Mercedes.

Eric was gone, and this meant at long last, we can stay in our house instead of forking out on hotel bills. We were in bed at 2.40 a.m. and amazingly slept to 7 a.m. As ever, it was so nice to see Lauren again; she seemed great without Eric (and I still couldn't believe we were not allowed to stay here). We were there to think about selling the house because Lauren had decided it was time to come home. On the first night, we sat down for about three hours and just chatted with Lauren, which we had not been able to do since she got married. We felt really sorry for her with all she had to put up with.

The weather was terrible, with rain and temperatures in the mid-50s; I just about managed one game of tennis, but it was supposed to get better. We went shopping, and Chrissie (who had bought me an amazing leather jacket in our first year of marriage) bought me a Ralph Lauren leather jacket, reduced from $795 to $496. We also spent $20 at Home Depot for things needed to do the house up. We spent quite a bit of time on the DIY.

But we did go to see *Nebraska,* which was a good movie, and we ate great food at Angelino's, with penne langoustine being brilliant. Our friends from London, Stuart and Janet, came over from San Pedro, where we used to borrow her shared condo. We spent more time on the DIY and went to Prosecco for dinner, which was as good as ever, with artichoke soup and pappardelle with lamb ragu, and the Maitre D' Eric, not that he remembered us. We did discover fried chicken rice from Trader Joe's at $2.99 a pop and had that a couple of nights.

We went to the movies and saw *Dallas Buyers Club, Saving Mr Banks,* and *American Hustle,* which we liked, but the first two best, but *American Hustle* was the barnstormer and took in $600,000 in six movie houses, and it took us three days to get in. I fell asleep watching *The Victoria's Secret Show,* which all men are supposed to lust for.

We went to one of our favourites, Petit Four, on Sunset and met Winnie and Esa. I ate artichoke and calves liver, as always. Winnie and I decided to make the movie of *Butlers Crossing.*

The weather was much better; it was 80 degrees, and we played quite a lot of tennis. We went to Angelino's and Prosecco again, but it was time to go home. We were away seventy-nine nights this year.

# February 2014

It was time for the seventeenth visit to LA, to sell the house before Lauren came home, and since it was the last, we took a side trip to Hawaii, where we had never been.

I failed to upgrade to Business, but Premium Economy was only one-quarter full, and the A380 was a nice plane. There seemed no point in each paying £500 extra; you don't need the bed on the day flight. The coleslaw, chicken tikka masala, and the alcohol were fine. The house had a few open days, and it looked like we were going to sell for $682,000, which would give us a reasonable profit.

The weather was great, at around 80 degrees and sunny. We ate in the usual places: Counter Burger, Patty's, and Sushi Yuza. Then we had to wait for a table at Angelino's but it was worth it and had excellent lobster in the shell with linguine and a tomato sauce; drinking the normal Peroni and a glass of Chianti, it was still only $71. The weather was perfect, and for the first time in forty years, I smoked some grass in very good company.

I played a little tennis and went for a great hike for two hours in Runyon Canyon. It was a great walk with superb views of downtown and Catalina Island.

We had another night out with Jamie and Bob at Prosecco, who we put up in the Tangerine. We drank far too much Prosecco Superiore, St Helena Grayson cabernet, and limoncello, and ate excellent tomato soup and the pappardelle with lamb ragu; the bill was $326, and I think I paid. We went to an Irish bar, and Bob bought whisky at $80 per shot. It was very nice, but I felt a bit hungover and so had another game of tennis. And then we were off to Silver Lake with Lauren's friend, Larry, for some wine tasting. For $20, we tasted five Loire wines: one sparkling, two whites, and two reds, with some very upmarket sandwiches to wash it all down; a good way to spend Sunday afternoon. We headed off to an odd wine bar in Hollywood, but I just drank water. Larry told us a lot about financing for the film business.

It was Tuesday, and it was going to rain on Friday, which was good news for LA, which was in a drought; against a season average of 10.72 inches, there was only 4.64 inches last year. It is dry here.

For a change, we ate at home quite a lot. It was nice to be back in the house sans Eric. We then went to dinner at Girasol, courtesy of Jackie, our real estate agent; although it's been written up in *The New York Times*, the food was pretty dull and uninspiring: shredded Brussels sprouts, Jerusalem artichokes, and mussels to start, followed by steak (which was not rare as ordered), poor lamb, and an equally poor steelback fish, which is like a trout. I was glad Jackie was paying.

We saw a couple of movies: *Winter's Tale*, which we hated, and something much better, *In Secret*, and it only cost $4.50 for a Seniors Matinee. We took Lauren and a friend to Prosecco and drank a couple of bottles of St Helena Grayson cabernet, which we've become so fond of, and ate osso buco; it's not cheap, at $300, but still good.

It was Friday, and it rained so hard that all the streets were covered in huge puddles. We went shopping, and I bought a $400 Michael Kors bag for my mother's ninetieth birthday, which was coming up soon. We had dinner back at Angelino's, which was as good as ever, with large prawns with linguine and pomodoro sauce; Chrissie had two glasses of wine, so it cost $69.

The car to the airport was a Sebring convertible, which had to be one of the worst cars ever. We got on the plane, took the six-hour flight to Honolulu, which was sunny and 80 degrees, and picked up a Camaro, which was much better. We chose to stay in a place which was near where President Obama sent for Christmas; it's an okay B&B run by a lovely, nice lady called Sharon. Our bedroom was right next to the kitchen where everybody ate breakfast at the bar. The breakfast was just right for me with juice, a good selection of fruits, and nice coffee.

For our first night's dinner, we walked to a restaurant we could see from the garden: Buzz, which was a sort of steak and seafood place. We started with a pina colada, followed by artichoke and lobster for me, and calamari for Chrissie. Drinking a $36 merlot, it was $118 plus tip, for pretty good food in a nice atmosphere.

But our first day, it was raining, so we just drove around with the roof up and found the beaches, the movie house, Safeway, and a cafe recommended by Sharon. We took a rainy swim in Sharon's pretty small pool. We went to see a crap movie, *Endless Love*, which had a thirty-year-old male star who was supposed to be eighteen. And then we had a crap dinner in the Italian Addagio. I had artichoke hearts (too few), peppers (too many), flat clams with tomato sauce and linguini, and Chrissie hated her fish and roast potatoes. Mama needed to cook the food instead of the accountant. As driving, I didn't drink much, but it was still a wasted $67.

The sun was out, and Sharon told us to go the ninety-mile round trip to North Shore to see the big waves. The first stop was a wonderful two-mile stretch of beach called Haukilau. We had a swim and liked it so much, we got a picnic at the supermarket and had another swim. We got to North Shore and decided we had seen better waves at Fistral. On the way back, we stopped in the Enchanted Valley and saw nice waterfalls and rare plants and songbirds. We got completely lost going to dinner and eventually ended up in the Kaulia Pub. Good news: They had one of my favourites, shepherd's pie. Bad news: They just sold the last one. We had pretty nice burgers and very excellent chips and drank a couple of glasses of Samuel Adams and merlot, and it all cost a very reasonable $43 plus tip.

It was still sunny, so we went to Lakania Beach, which was fine, except for a bunch of Japanese girls who invaded the beach for a while. The picnic was focaccia with avocado and cheese, and we were nice and comfortable in Sharon's chairs. I had a nice swim. For dinner, we went to Uatui Island Grill, a Korean restaurant. We shared garlic chicken thighs, and I had shrimp with lemongrass and brown rice, and calamari for Chrissie. Drinking a couple of Coronado Red beers and a couple of glasses of cabernet, this was $54 plus tip. Not bad, but it will be our only visit.

I had another lovely day on the beach, with three swims in the beautiful water. Before dinner, we drove ten miles to another movie theatre to see *Pompeii*. The reviews were terrible, but we've only just been there, and it was interesting in that respect (but not a great movie). We went back to Buzz, but it was not so good the second time. The waitress was less pretty, the pina colada had too much ice, the steak only came with broccoli and cauliflower, the scampi was not cooked enough, and the bill took ages to come, but at least the artichoke was good. It cost $118 this time.

I had a great day at the beach, and we planned to go Japanese that night, but we did not, as we got lost again. We ended up in Baci Bistro, which was actually a very good Italian place. We got the last table. We both had butternut squash soup, and I had gnocchi with

# Mr. Tambourine Man

Italian sausage and tomato sauce, and Chrissie had veal Marsala. We drank two Peronis and two Chianti Classicos, and it was only $80 plus tip, for a pretty good dinner.

We now had an odd day. Sharon wanted to buy a new car, and we spent nearly the whole day with her in the Toyota garage. Ladies need men to advise them on such important matters. I had advised a Prius, which she did not like. Then we had a look at the Rav4 same again, but then we discovered the Camry. Joy, and we bought an 'S' in blue for $19,000, with a lot of backwards and forwards on the finance deal, but her credit score was 838, which I believe is quite good. And we at last find the Japanese restaurant, Tokonane. I had a nice miso soup, excellent prawn tempura, and very rare seared ali sashimi with wasabi and rice, and Chrissie had chicken. Drinking beer and merlot, it was all very good for $54 plus tip.

The next day was a big one. We went to Pearl Harbour, which was a very important part of the twentieth century. As ever in Hawaii, we found it quite difficult to find, with no obvious signposts on the freeway, and we went backwards and forwards a few times. It was sort of an early 9/11, so you sort of know and understand a lot of it and the causes. We went to the Arizona Memorial site, which was above the wreck; it was very moving. After that, we went on a tour of a submarine, which was quite fun, and we had our picture taken. It was worth a visit here because it really made you think quite deeply. We went onto Waikiki and were glad we're not staying here, as it's very large and garish; I would only give it 2 out of 10 (but it goes up to 3 because of a nice ice cream). We looked at getting a beach buggy, but it was $7.50 each, so we gave it a miss. We went home for a swim in the small pool.

To say thank you for the car, Sharon took us to the Baci Bistro, and she drove, which meant I could drink: I had a vodka martini, Chianti Classico, and limoncello, and ate pretty good bruschetta and spaghetti with shrimp.

I had a day of swimming again, and then we went to the movies for *Non-Stop*, which had a poor script but a good plane crash. We had dinner at Big City Diner for hamburgers, beer, and cabernet, and pretty cheap at $33. The next night, we saw *Frozen*, which was not a

Disney classic, despite rave reviews. We went back to the Kulia Pub for shepherd's pie (which I preordered). Drinking Samuel Adams Coldsnap with fish and chips and merlot for Chrissie, it was only $34, but sadly, the shepherd's pie was not that great; Chrissie's at home is much better.

On our last day, I did lots more swimming and saw a nice yellow fish with black stripes under the water. Our last dinner was at the Baci Bistro. We drank two Peronis and two Chianti Reserva and shared hot shrimp with garlic, wine, and lemon, and both had the $34.50 osso buco, which was excellent and as good as Prosecco's. We had a lovely waitress, and it all cost $113 plus $20 tip.

We got back to the airport after 361 miles, and because we are BA Silver, we were allowed in the American Airlines lounge. What did we think of Hawaii? Well, it's a long way from the UK: seventeen hours in the air via LA. The problem with Hawaii was that it felt just like you were in Florida. Cook Islands, in the same ocean, made you feel you were somewhere so different; here, it was just like being in the rest of the United States. We were lucky we didn't stay in the highrises of Waikiki; we were near Obama's Christmas hangout, with the great beaches. Sharon was great, and I wrote in her Visitors Book, 'I love Sharon and I love her place,' but I didn't write, 'I will not be coming back.'

But then it was back to LA for what might be my last four days here for some time. Lauren was coming home. The house sold for $675,000, and we signed all the papers, which was quite complicated, as we had to transfer the whole thing to her, as nonresidents can be caught up in withholding tax. It was also a real effort to arrange all the packing, but Jackie found someone to arrange a house sale for us for all the things Lauren didn't want to take.

The flight back was only five hours, nine minutes, and we got a grey Mustang, and it only took twenty-four minutes to the Pass ramp, which we needed, but it was closed, and we had to divert.

We had a nice last dinner with Winnie and Esa in Prosecco, with very good lobster risotto and peas. It was sunny and 90 degrees; I had enjoyed the LA weather over the years. I took a couple of swims in the pool, with the temperature showing 75 degrees, but it feels sub-70. And we had to go to Angelino's for a last dinner of their wonderful cheese ravioli pomodoro. Chrissie had Dover sole, and it cost $55. We tried to get in to see *The Grand Budapest Hotel*, but it was full, so we saw *Need for Speed*, which was only an okay road movie. I went to the Toluca Lake Tennis Club for my last hit with Christian in the fun Sunday morning group. I had a last corned beef hash at Patty's, but Lauren was driving, so I drank a Bloody Mary, and it cost $55 for three.

The next day, at 6.25 in the morning, our bed started to shake, the wardrobe doors opened, and the chest drawers came out. We were in a 4.4 earthquake. It was all quite scary, but the house stood still, and anyway, we had earthquake insurance (necessary in that part of the world). My last earthquake was in Liverpool in 1984. I was sitting at a board lunch, and the table started shaking; this was a 5.4 in North Wales, but not nearly as dramatic as LA.

The flight home was not too bad, but we had four suitcases and got searched by Customs. Alan, who was going to pick us up, had the wrong day, and we had to spend £62 on a taxi. Lauren had Estelle, the dog, on her Air New Zealand flight home in the cabin; she learnt the trick from Robbie Williams, who was on one of her earlier flights. After so long, it was nice to have her home.

# April 2004

We sometimes go away to places which are not in Cornwall or abroad. It was my mum's ninetieth birthday, and she had a lunch for all her mates in Essex; we needed to get out of there, so we took her to the Marine Hotel in Whitstable in Kent, by the sea. We were on the seafront in a nice hotel, refurbished in 2013, with nice, friendly staff. We went to the Lobster Shack for lunch, and I had a half-lobster for £9.95, which was pretty good and cheaper than Chrissie's fish and chips, which costs £13.95: weird. Due to difficulties of moving old people around, we ate in the hotel, which lacked a little atmosphere, but I ate okay beetroot risotto with butternut squash and fillet steak and drank a nice claret, and it all cost £171 for four.

We only stayed one night, and for our last lunch, we went to the Sportsman at Seasalter, an upmarket gastro pub, which was pretty good. I ate nice skate; it was sunny there and seemed quite a nice place, but one night was fine.

## July 2014

We were off on a sixty-five-minute turboprop flight from Exeter to Amsterdam, to meet our old friends Jamie and Bob, who were returning from their trip to Kilimanjaro. We searched Trip Advisor for the best Indonesian restaurant in the city and found Max. We took a long walk along the canals, found the restaurant, and booked a table for dinner. And the dinner was pretty good. We shared gravalax and duck pate to start and followed with chicken satay and sea bass with lemongrass and chilli. We drank a good bottle of Valpollicello, and it all cost E109, for a pretty good dinner. We had a nice walk back to the hotel.

The next morning, we went to a nice museum and saw four Vermeers and a load of Rembrandts, which were all pretty good. We failed to get into the Van Gogh Museum because the queues were just too long. Instead, we took a ninety-minute boat ride along the canals and saw a lot of the city. We thought Jamie and Bob were staying in our hotel, but they were not (there are two hotels with the same name), but eventually, we managed to find each other.

Off to Fifteen, where I was still a director in the UK. I booked for four under the name Paul, but they were still expecting us, and we sat down with a nice glass of Prosecco. We choose the chef's menu and had smoked salmon, fish with black potatoes and almond paste, and a rhubarb dessert. We drank a fine Sicilian wine, and it all cost E267 for four. The view was not as good as Watergate Bay, and they told us they struggled at lunch.

On our last day, we went on another boat ride with Jamie and Bob; we got off and walked round the red light district, looked at Anne Frank's house, which again had long queues, and just generally hung around. We had dinner in Flo Brasserie in our hotel and ate a half-lobster, followed by chateaubriand, with a good Loire red. Bob paid. Amsterdam was sort of fun, but it did not have the fizz of Rome or Paris.

## August 2014

We were now in Sicily for the first time; it was nice and hot, at around 90 degrees. We spent an extra E3 per day and upgraded to an Audi A1 diesel and headed to our first stop: Avola. With some luck, we found our pensione, La Terraga Sal Mare, and we had a nice room with a terrace and partial seaview.

On the first night, we just went to the beach bar next door; the food was terrible, with awful pasta, but it only cost E51.

We spent the next day on the beach, with plenty of swimming. We had dinner across the road at Paltonolta. I started with very nice grilled vegetables and followed with spaghetti with sea urchins, which the waitress tried to persuade me not to have, but it was delicious. We drink a very good house red and limoncello, and it only cost E60, and as we left, there were still people queuing to get in; they must have liked the atmosphere, which we did, a lot.

We got in the car and went to a nearby beach and paid E12 to get in, but had good Parma ham and mozzarella rolls and Peroni for lunch, and that only cost E11. We went up the road some way to Pura for dinner. It was all very good with nice linguine with clams, mussels and shrimp, and sea bass with orange and spinach, and drinking a very nice local Sicilian wine, at E12 per bottle, it all came to E62.

We took two hours and eighty kilometres to find Beach 9, which wasn't that great, and found another not-so-great. But it was all saved by *limone gellato* at E2 each. We went to a local trattoria not even in Trip Advisor. For E36, we had a very good dinner indeed of antipasto rustica, followed by tagliatelle with scampi, clams, and mussels, and an anchovy pizza for Chrissie, with a litre of local red wine.

We went back to the E12 beach and had another good day. We went back to Paltonolta for dinner again and had a very nice shrimp cocktail, followed by pasta with swordfish and lemon ice cream; with a litre of red wine and two limoncellos, it was only E59: a great value for a lovely dinner.

I had five swims on the beach, and we went off to Pura for dinner again. It was good again, with a nice fried fish starter and swordfish ravioli for me, and seafood risotto for Chrissie; with a good bottle of Avola Sicilian wine and free limoncello, it was only E50 plus tip. We met Alastair and Lizzie from our hotel and had a few more limoncello in a bar.

The next day was Montoblano day. We drove around 170 kilometres, and our first stop was Scicli: a nice town with lovely churches, but the real reason was to visit the inspector's office, which we did. It didn't really look like his office, but it was fun to be on a TV set. Our next stop was Punto Sera, for his house. We had a nice lunch of arancini and Peroni right outside and admired the view. It was time for a swim, and I had to do the crawl, just like Montoblano. It's a great TV programme, and we discovered that the Italians had to have subtitles the same as us because they cannot understand the Sicilian dialects of the original show. It was a good day out, and I celebrated my return with a marvellous Mojito made by Salvo.

We had dinner with Alastair and Lizzie in the trattoria which was not in Trip Advisor. The antipasto was not as good as the antipasto rustica we had last time, but the pappardelle with ragout, basil, pistachio, and almond was very tasty. We had plenty to drink and then onto the bar again until about 1.30; we had to rush for breakfast, which finished at 9.30.

For the next couple of days, we did more swimming and had more dinners at Paltonato and Pura. We thought this town and the area was a little dull, and although the food was nice, it could only really be described as average. We were hoping for something better from Sicily, so we'd see what the next town brought.

We went to Tamorina, up the coast from Catania, and we had a lovely room with a nice balcony with a great view overlooking a stony beach. But this was after I bumped the car in a big way. The girl from the hotel took me to our parking in an underground garage. She put me in the wrong space, so I reversed in my dark glasses and went straight into a big post. Luckily, I bought insurance for about £30 for a year for carhire, which was much cheaper than the £10 per day the companies charged. My bill was E1,000 for the damage, but I got the money back with no hassle. Everybody should buy this insurance if they are going to hire a car.

Our dinner the first night was at St Georges. We paid E3 each to take the funicular railway up to the town; it was very windy, so we had to eat inside. The food was truly wonderful. We started with a swordfish and coffee amuse-bouche and shared an aubergine cream pasta salad, which was truly world-class and scored 9.5, the highest yet on this trip by far. I followed with an excellent fillet steak with béarnaise, new potatoes, and a little spinach and fennel. For dessert, we got another amuse-bouche, chocolate mousse. With a lovely bottle of Mount Etna Rosso at E45, it all cost E131 for a really great dinner, and we booked again.

The beach and the swimming good were nice, and there were great places for lunch; I splashed out on linguine with scampi for E12, which was delicious. We bought Prosecco and sipped it on our balcony before dinner. We went up the funicular again and went to Il Contro, which should have been great but somehow failed. It went wrong from the start, when we had an English waitress and noticed all the guests were English. We ate fish and vegetable antipasto, gnocchi with shrimp and pistachio, and swordfish rolls, and drank E35 Mount Etna Rosso. Our assessment of the food was that it all felt like it came out of a Marks and Spencer packet; at E83 for the whole thing, it was a big disappointment.

To test the car out, we took a twenty-kilometre drive to a canyon, but instead of paying E13 to enter, we returned to our nice beach. We had a really good dinner at De Andrea, which was at beach level, so no funicular this time. We shared baked aubergine, and I had spaghetti with clams and *bottarga* (tuna fish roe), and Chrissie had sea bass with rosemary potatoes. We drank Etna Rosso at E25 and limoncello and smoked in the delightful garden, and it all cost E78 for something really very nice.

I went into the sea and got stung by a jellyfish. The lifeguard sprayed my arm with something, and it seemed to work. That night, we went up the funicular again, and after some time, we managed to find Osteria Rosso Divino, which turned out to be world-class. They brought our bread along with two organic olive oils and encouraged us to taste carefully and report our findings. They were both completely delicious, and it was so refreshing to have such attention to detail on something so simple as the olive oil which went with the bread. To start, we shared small red mullet, which were eaten whole, and zucchini rolls with cheese and tomato: lovely. We followed with *maupu* (a fish) baked in salt with garlic and mint, and capolta on the side, which was just superb. We ordered limoncello and were given a very cold bottle and had three each. And this great dinner only cost E111.

We returned to St Georges and had another great dinner, and this time we could go on the terrace. The amuse-bouche was a wonderful gazpacho. We then shared four quail, which were completely delicious, and I followed with spaghetti with sea urchins, and Chrissie had roast pork with applesauce, which could only be described as sublime. We had the chocolate mousse amuse-bouche again and followed with a very delicious Sicilian cake with cream, mascarpone, and ricotta. Drinking the E45 Etna Rosso and limoncello, it all cost E151 for a really great dinner: world-class.

I did more swimming; I think I covered twenty-five kilometres on this trip, enough to keep me fit. But it was time for our last dinner, which had to be at Osteria Rosso Divino. We started with three organic olive oils this time and proceed into a truly magic dish: amberjack tuna tartare with strawberries, mint, and a balsamic glaze: just brilliant. I followed with spaghetti with bottaga, tomatoes, and mint, which was a little disappointing, and Chrissie had very good gnocchi with prawns. We ended with very delicious flambe peach with lemon ice cream. Drinking Etna Rosso at E30 and free limoncello, it all came to E109. All I could say was, '*Bene, bene, bene.*'

The food in Tamarino was just so good. Apart from the jellyfish, the sea was great, and Sicily was very interesting. We would be back.

## November 2014

We did not have a very good BA Business Class flight to Hong Kong. My window seat on the A380 Super Jumbo had no window. It took ages to get the first glass of champagne, and after take-off, it took another hour to get the second. It took three hours before dinner was completed. Worst of all, they woke us all up for breakfast two hours before landing. Premium service should be so much better.

We arrived and took a £26 taxi ride to the Langham Place Hotel. It was very nice and we had a large bed on the thirtieth floor, overlooking the water. But everything was very expensive, with the dinner buffet costing £50 per head and £20 for breakfast.

We walked the streets and found a great little restaurant, Chuen Moon Kee. We ate prawns with rice and eels with rice, and two Cantonese dishes: sweet and sour pork and scrambled eggs with prawn, and had two large beers, all for HK$350 (or around £30). We were very full, the food was delicious, and the atmosphere was top-notch. In the morning, we went to a nearby Starbucks and had an okay breakfast for a third of the cost of the hotel.

We had a nice day in Hong Kong. We started with a free classics walk in the area around our hotel, but a funny Chinese girl just showed us some shops and the wholesale fruit market: not very classic. The tours were all very expensive, so we did our own thing. We got on the Metro and walked over to catch the Peak tram (got the over-65 rate on the tram). The views of HK were great. Two sandwiches and water in the Peak Restaurant was £40. We went to the Botanical and Zoological Gardens and saw birds, monkeys, and tortoises. We took about an hour's walk back along the main shopping drag: a lot of high-end designers.

For dinner, we went to Dim Dim Sum Dim Sum, which *Newsweek* called one of the best 101 restaurants in the world in 2012. There was no booze, so we had to drink tea, but we had some great food:

- steamed shrimp dumplings
- pork dumplings with crab roe
- eggwhite shrimp and vegetable dumplings
- seafood-stuffed peppers
- Mongolian lamb spring rolls
- mushroom and chicken on steamed rice

It was all excellent, world-class stuff, and our favourites were the shrimp dumpling and peppers (which were actually chillies). And it all cost £14: an amazing dinner for an amazing price.

Hong Kong felt like New York's younger, poorer brother, and our feeling was that we would not want to spend too much time there.

But our real purpose was to visit Vietnam. We travelled Business on Vietnam Airways and had a nice flight to Hanoi, with champagne before take-off and an okay lunch. We booked the whole trip with Audley Travel and were met at the airport by a nice guy who took us to our hotel. Nothing in our room seemed to work, including with wi-fi, and we had to walk the streets to buy an alarm clock for £3.

Our first dinner was in the Green Tarragon, and it cost 2.3 million (this was about £85 in real money). We drank Sancerre rouge, as you did in Vietnam, and started with a very good Hanoi soup. We followed with excellent spring rolls, deep-fried shrimp, and then beef and fish Hanoi-style, and ended up with nice ice cream. It was all very nice.

Luckily, we had our alarm clock, as we had to get up at seven in order to leave at 8.30.

First, we went to the Ho Chi Minh memorial, his house, and gardens. It was all a little thought-provoking. Next we went to the war museum, with some good planes, tanks, and so on, then to a temple and then the university. It was okay to see some sights, but it was not out of this world. Lunch at Cha Ca La Vang was an experience; they only had one dish, grilled fish, which came with noodles, chillis, spring onion, and herbs. The beer was nice, and it was all pretty good for less than £15. We went for a long walk into a park and sat down for afternoon tea, but there was no milk to go in the tea. Our last dinner here only cost 1.8 million. We took a short walk to Marlone Vien, which was supposed to be street food. It wasn't, just an okay restaurant with good quality crab and tomato soup, prawns with mayo salsa and mint chutney, prawns in a clay pot, and crab cakes with coconut milk and brown leaves; we drank a claret at 780,000.

Hanoi was ready for us to leave; it was not my favourite city. We got up at 6.30, but breakfast started early, and we headed to the airport for our flight to Hoi An (and we could smoke in the airport lounge). We stayed in the Nan, which was very exclusive and cost over £300 per night. The room was odd and a long way from the beach; the whole place was full of workers, and it became a drag constantly exchanging pleasantries: have a nice day. It was not really our sort of place.

We had an expensive lunch by the pool, at over £50 for a burger, chips, and beer for me, and a ham sandwich and sparkling Aussie for Chrissie. Dinner cost well over £100 at 3.3 million and was very average: banana flowers with smoked duck followed by steamed sea bass and roast suckling pig, which were both boring after the first couple of mouthfuls. We had Baron de Philippe Rothschild wine, but then we got poisoned. After all my years in Africa, I had a cast iron stomach, but I had to go to the bathroom three times before breakfast.

And we went on a fairly boring trip. We rode one hour in a car to Sun Valley to see dancers and blowpipers in the Cham ruins from the tenth and eleventh century. We went back to Hoi An for lemon and sugar pancake for lunch, as my stomach was still not right. And it started to rain, but I went for a swim in the pool. It was quite warm here, in the mid-80s.

But then we discovered Morning Glory, a wonderful restaurant. We went off to have dinner at Morning Glory. We got a nice table on the balcony, where you could smoke. We drank a very nice Alvor from Sicily and ate excellent prawn dumplings and crispy pancakes to start, followed by BBQ lime chicken and lime sea bass. It was a lovely dinner for less than £30, and my stomach felt much better.

We got up early again and left the hotel at 8.15. We got on a boat and took a short cruise to the market, which was filled with fresh fish, meat, and vegetables. It was all so beautiful. We spent about an hour, but then it was time to go to the Cookery School with Miss Vy, who was very famous here. We cooked four dishes, all of which were superb; we did the crispy pancakes and BBQ chicken from last night. I believe my BBQ chicken was better than the restaurant's. My favourite dish was the prawn and cabbage soup, where the flavours were just so different and difficult to describe, but simply amazing.

We finished with a superb lemongrass ice cream. Everybody should try to share this experience; it was just magical. Then we went back to the hotel for a swim in the pool.

We went back into town by taxi and wandered around; then we went to the White Table, a restaurant by the Japanese bridge. The food was not that great, although the spring rolls and fruit salad were not too bad; we drank a bottle of Australian wine, and it only cost £18.

It was a really nice, sunny day, and to avoid the hotel restaurants, we took a walk along the beach. We sat down in a nice beach bar, and the beers were 15,000 instead of 130,000 at the hotel (or 50p instead of £4); we ate fried noodles with shrimp and shrimp spring rolls. The noodles were almost to die for, and with the two beers, it was only £7 (or less than two beers in the hotel). I did a bit of swimming in the hotel pool, and we had dinner at Morning Glory again. The prawn and cabbage soup didn't taste as good as when we made it, but the rice paper with prawns, sardines, and prawn curry were all very good. We had another bottle of Alvor, and it only cost £27.

There was a 5.30 a.m. start to catch the flight to Ho Chi Minh City, where we only stayed one night before setting off early again for the Mekong Delta, on a one-night cruise. It was a very nice boat; we started off with a delicious lunch of prawns, calamari, fish, beef, vegetables, and fruit, with Saigon beers. We then found a nice chair and watched boats slowly sail past in the delta. Later in the afternoon, we all got into small boats and went ashore for a nature walk. We saw lots of fruit and went to a house for fruit and tea. I was offered my first taste of jackfruit, which was a little synthetic. The people were very nice rice farmers with TVs and mobile phones, but they lived ninety minutes from the nearest doctor. After I somehow squeezed into the mini shower in the cabin, we had a tasty dinner on the boat, with plenty of alcohol.

The engine of the boat woke us at 6 a.m., but we had an very good breakfast with lots of fruit and great bread and croissants. We got onto small boats and visited a floating market, which was fascinating. Our guide took us into the countryside for more fruit and tea, and we went for a nice cycle ride around the paddy fields. It was time to go back to Ho Chi Minh City, which was pretty dull; it took nearly four hours, but we stopped on the way for 55p tomato baguettes.

We spent two hours dodging round the city traffic trying but failing to find a restaurant. We ended up in a newish corporate place; the food and drink were okay, for £30.

We did the morning tour of Saigon, which seemed a bit drab, but maybe we were doing too much as *touristos*. The War Museum was first, which was a bit harrowing. I never fully realised the effect the Yanks had, with five hundred thousand men in this small country. They bombed the hell out of Vietnam and were also into biological warfare. It was a truly terrible story. We went to a couple of markets, a temple, a factory, and a cathedral. But the highlight was 2000, a restaurant where Bill Clinton and George Bush had been. We had a very nice cheese and tomato focaccia and lemonade, and only £8 for two.

Because it was wedding anniversary number thirty-four, we went to the Grand Hotel terrace for afternoon Earl Grey tea for Chrissie and a beer for me, which was very pleasant. But the important activity of the day is the Vespa tour, which turned out to be fucking fantastic. We were picked up at 6 p.m. by two Vespas, with a man driving me and a lady Chrissie. We went out into the rush hour traffic, with millions of motorbikes and cars, and it was like nothing you've ever experienced. First, we went to a coffee shop, to have a beer and meet the other guests and our guide. We then had a long drive over the river to the Fish Kilometre: a long road with many restaurants. We sat outside and ate crab claws, clams in soup with ginger and lemongrass, mussels with peanuts, noodles, and lastly frogs: all amazing flavours, and we downed another couple of beers. We got back on the Vespa and went to the Pancake House. It was more delicious food, with a summer roll (which was rice paper filled with prawn and vegetable), spring roll in green leaves dipped in fish sauce and chillie, and then the greatest house pancake and some beef. I had another beer. I would describe the food as millionaire's street food. We got back on the Vespa and went to the Romantic Cafe in the French Quarter. We had more beer and listened to an amazing violin and great singing from two Vietnamese ladies. It was indeed very romantic. The last stop was Woodstock, a nightclub, where a beautiful lady in a red miniskirt serves me a very large pina colada (she also had the hots for me). A band played sort of Vietnamese karaoke and finished with 'You're So Vain.' We took our sixth and last Vespa ride back to the hotel in the early hours and gave our drivers a big tip. I guess we did about twenty miles on the back, and the drink driving was great. This was such a great night, with the thrill of the traffic, millionaire's food, and terrific clubbing; we'll never be able to repeat this for future anniversaries.

It was time to move onto the island of Phu Quoc, after a thirty-minute flight, for some beach rest time. We stayed in the Javelin, which we liked a lot from the start. The room was lovely, with a super view of the beach. On the first night, we met a couple from Leicestershire, Alan and Sarah, and walked up the road in the pouring rain to a local restaurant. We had soup, spring rolls, and squid, and fish and chips for Chrissie, and with eleven beers, and it cost £24 for the four of us. And Marlboro Red cigarettes only cost 90p per packet: one-tenth of the price in England.

We got freshly squeezed orange Juice, lovely fresh mango, and brilliant pastries for breakfast; it was not like the Nan, where you had to always be polite to the staff. On the first day, we went to the beach, which was glorious; the weather was around 90 degrees and sunny. At 11 a.m., they brought us cold towels and lemongrass sorbet, and again at 3 p.m., they brought cold towels and this time orange sorbet: a lovely touch, and much appreciated. We wandered up the beach and found a lovely beach bar, and Chrissie had a ham and cheese sandwich and fried noodles, and shrimp for me; with a couple of beers, it was only $6.

For dinner, we went into town again with Alan and Sarah. We started off at the Terrace with beers and summer roll, which was not as good as Saigon. Then we went to Sim for fresh fish and had a large snapper and greyfish (weighing about one kilo each) on the BBQ, with free rice and salad. And we had more beer, and lots of it. For both places, our total bill for four was around £18. It was a real gas with great food and drink, and so cheap; we liked it there.

## Mr. Tambourine Man

It was Chrissie's birthday, and at breakfast, the hotel gave her a beautiful flower arrangement, which was so thoughtful. We had a day on the beach again, but with a great lunch of banana pancake for Chrissie, and poh fish for me, and oh, so cheap. The cold towels and sorbets arrived as before. We had a glass of sparkling wine on the terrace and went to a small theatre nearby to see a one-hour show called *The Water Puppets*. It was all pretty weird, and we didn't understand anything and were glad to leave. The hotel did the seafood dinner for £25 each, including a glass of wine, very good pumpkin soup to start, followed by BBQ scallops, crab, prawn, and red snapper. For dessert, a birthday cake for Chrissie, and the whole restaurant sang 'Happy Birthday.' We ended the evening with the local band, dancing to a long version of 'Hotel California.'

The next day was the beach again; we took a three-kilometre walk into the nice town and port, but we got a taxi back. I made a big mistake and had a £4 hamburger for lunch, which was expensive and didn't fit the ambience of the place. We returned to the first nights' restaurant and ordered a £2.50 bottle of passable Vietnam red wine, spring rolls, chicken noodle soup, and BBQ grouper and rice. The dinner was very good and cost £10 for the two of us. We went back to the hotel for more dancing.

The next day, we took the half-day £20-per-person island tour. The first stop was the pearl factory, which was pretty dull, but we did see a very small pearl in an oyster. Next was the prison, which was fascinating (if a little gruesome). The fish sauce factory followed; it was interesting to see all the ingredients. Sao Beach was very famous, but it was too rough to swim, so we just hiked along the beach. The pepper farm was next; I had never seen pepper growing, so it was interesting. The last stop was a waterfall, a very nice place.

The hotel did a Vietnamese street food night. I started with the now-famous prawn and cabbage soup, and we tasted banana flour, chicken in lotus leaf, calamari with pineapple, and fish noodle soup, which were all very good. Then we went to the BBQ for chicken and rice and lastly to the pancakes and spring rolls. We drank Vietnam wine and had a thoroughly good time, but there was no dancing that night.

We had another day on the beach, with another great Pho lunch. We ate at the hotel again and chose the 680,000-dong Asian set menu. We started with tempura prawn, squid, and vegetable, followed by seafood and seaweed soup, and then duck, scallops, and vegetable, drinking again a very nice Alvor wine.

The next day followed the previous days, and for dinner, we just went along the road to Mojito. They had free drinks until eight o'clock, and we had a passion fruit martini and a Saigon beer. We ate spring rolls and a lotus salad, followed by barramuda curry, which was very good for me, and not-so-great calamari for Chrissie, but it all came to only £12, which was just so cheap. We went back to the hotel for a long barefoot dance.

But it was time to leave this lovely country, and the Javelin was just one of the best hotels ever. I was so glad we visited here; it was just a wonderful country, and we had a lot of fun, particularly on the Vespas. The food was great. It was different from Chinese and generally very aromatic and quite delicious. The cigarettes in the duty-free were a disappointment; they cost £1.20 a packet, which was loads more than the local shops.

We were back in Hong Kong, which was not our favourite city. We rode the Metro down to the harbour and took a relaxing £7 harbour cruise, with free water and biscuits. Lunch was at Dim Dim Sum Dim Sum, where we had the shrimp dumplings and seafood stuffed pepper again, with some other delicious food, and it only cost £6.50 for one of the best restaurants in the world. We decided to keep our room until 6 p.m. (paying a lot of money to do so) and revisited Chuen Moon Kee for another nice dinner.

The flight home was a lot better.

## December 2014

We had a nice Christmas at home, with a good picnic in the sunshine on Christmas Day with the two grannies at Pendennis Point; then, we hired a Seat Leon from Hertz to drive ourselves to Heathrow (which I will explain later). We took our Business Class flight (paid for with airmiles) to one of my favourite cities: New York City.

The cab fare to the hotel, which was next to the Waldorf Astoria, was $58, and we had a horrible, small room. After a nice breakfast, we thought about going up in the Empire State Building, but it was $49 with a three-hour wait (or $59 for the thirty-minute fast track). We went to the Metropolitan Museum instead. It was all great, and we saw some fine paintings by Cezanne, Picasso, Gobi, Monet, Matisse, Pissarro, and so on; this has to be one of the great museums of the world.

But it was New Year's Eve, and we celebrated with our godson Alex and his lovely wife, Jenna (we asked Jamie and Bob from California, but they couldn't make it). We took a taxi to their $1 million one-bedroom apartment in Greenwich Village and started the night with some champagne. We went to a very noisy restaurant down in the Meat District, full of New Yorkers. I thought I was going to hate it, but after about ten minutes, it started to appeal to me. We ordered $92 wine, which did not taste like $92 wine, and had food which was best described as okayish. But then the fun began, and we got lots of silly hats, whistles, and all cheer for the New Year. And then we danced a lot; I paid the bill, which was my treat, at $940 plus tip, and eventually managed to find a taxi back at around 4 a.m.

We sort of had hangovers, but the sun was out, and it was 32 degrees (or freezing). We were on Forty-Ninth Street, and we walked into Central Park and kept walking because it was just such a beautiful day. We walked all the way up to Ninety-Sixth Street, which was important because this was where I lived when I was eighteen. We sort of saw my old house and found a Le Pain for a nice lunch of smoked salmon open sandwiches and lemonade. And then we walked all the way back, stopping in Ralph Lauren for Chrissie to buy an evening bag for $480 (reduced from $1,200), in Bloomingdale's, and to a movie house to see *Wild*. It was a wonderful day. To make it perfect, we decided to go for dinner in the Oyster Bar in Grand Central Station, but it was closed. We chose San Martin, an Italian next to our hotel. According to Trip Advisor, this was number 1,800 out of 8,800 restaurants in New York, but it seemed much better than that: prawns in wine and duck and sausage cassoulet for me, and prosciutto and ricotta spinach pancakes for Chrissie, with a nice bottle of Chianti; it was just fine and cost $110 plus tip.

The next morning, we walked to Rockefeller Centre (to watch people ice skating), Times Square (which seemed a bit rough), and Bryant Park, which we liked. Lunch was the Oyster Bar (which Trip Advisor only rated as 1,200 out of 8,800), and I indulged myself with a Long Island beer, New England clam chowder, and Maine lobster: almost the perfect lunch. Chrissie had prosecco and fish and chips, and it all cost $91 plus. Then we went to Bloomingdale's again, and we both bought a pair of jeans (they were much cheaper here): Ralph Lauren for me and NYDJ for Chrissie.

Alex and Jenna, who were having a dry January, took us to Rafele in Greenwich Village for dinner. In Trip Advisor, it was number eleven out of New York's 8,800 restaurants, and it was superb. We started with twenty-four month old Black Label prosciutto, chicken liver pate, arancini, fried artichoke, and mussels. I had a wonderful lamb ragu with pappardelle for my main course. Everything was so good, but the prosciutto was an exceptional treat. We drank a very nice Chianti Classico.

We went to the taxi rank but nobody seemed to know where the *Queen Mary* terminal was, but we eventually found a driver who got us there. We left our cases at the dock and went through security. We checked in and were given a number and went to a room where we had to wait before going on the ship. Eventually, we were allowed on; what a stupid and irritating system. The boat was not at all the glamour palace we were expecting; everything seemed a bit plastic. And the boat was full of LCDs (lowest common denominators, for those who don't know). Everybody just seemed to eat very big plates with a lot of food. We had a bowl of just okay soup for lunch in the cafeteria and waited to go. It was getting dark, but the trip out of the harbour was nice, with great views of the skyline and the Statue of Liberty.

We went to dinner. We had asked for a table of six and were most surprised to find we were seated with four other ladies, which seemed inappropriate. Our $52 bottle of Carmel Valley pinot noir did not appear until we finished our starters, and the duck terraine and rare sirloin were best described as adequate, as was the lemon meringue pie. The best part of the night was finding a nightclub where we could smoke and have a good bop.

What did we do on the boat? It was around 40 degrees, cloudy, and rainy, and the sea were pretty rough. Chrissie opted for watercolour classes, and I decided on exercise. There were very small swimming pools with swirling water from the choppy sea, so I just went to the gym. We had a light soup lunch again and go to the main theatre to see *The Best Exotic Marigold Hotel*, with a live introduction from Celia Imrie, one of the stars. Afterwards, we went to the bookshop, and we were the only ones there, so we bought her book, got it signed, and had a long chat; she was delightful.

The next day, we had some sun, and it was 68 degrees, which was great for early January. The deck tennis was cancelled without any notification, so it was down the gym again, and three times round the deck for a mile, which I did again later before afternoon tea in the Queen's Room, which was very pleasant and probably the best thing so far.

Why was it all so average, and why was there no glamour? For three nights on this trip, we wore dinner jackets and evening dress for the ladies, but it was all very flat. The staff just seemed to want to get through their nine-month stint so they could have their two-month break. Before dinner, we went to the movies again to see *Belle*, which was quite good, and then to the Champagne Bar for a martini, which was just pleasant (but no smoking). Another average dinner of asparagus and turkey roast, with a $48 New Zealand pinot noir. We went dancing (and smoking) in the nightclub.

The next day was just the same, with 61 degrees and cloudy. Afternoon tea was good, the movie was about James Brown, *Get on Up*; dinner was average serrano ham and rack of lamb, but with a nice bottle of cabernet Franc.

We were taking a southerly route and were only 280 miles north of the Azores; it was sunny and 63 degrees. But the day was just the same with the gym: seven times round the deck for 2.5 miles. Afternoon tea was the highlight, and we saw a terrible movie, *If I*

*Stay*. We had salmon cannelloni and red leg partridge and the Carmel Valley pinot noir for our average dinner. I got cabin fever; all I really wanted was dry land. We met a lady in the lift who said she hadn't been outside on the deck yet; I cannot believe it. The captain's cocktail party was also a bit of a drag. Only two more days: heaven.

But it got worse. We tried to book the Italian restaurant to get away from the ladies, but it was full, and there was a tea dance in the Queen's Room, so no afternoon tea. We had lost our highlight of the day. It was a strange food day, with kippers for breakfast, hot dogs for lunch, and weird pina colada cold soup and vegetable byriani for dinner, with Valpolicello Classico. The best bit today was Michael Jackson in the nightclub for some extended dancing.

Food the next day was corned beef hash for breakfast, hot and sour soup and tempura vegetables for lunch, and then the gala dinner. Afternoon tea was back on again, thankfully. Dinner was foie gras and artichoke terraine to start, which sounded very appetising, but it didn't taste of anything, which sort of summed up the whole experience. We had okay lobster and then a quite nice crème brûlée.

We went to the art exhibition; Chrissie had done two great pictures with a nautical theme. What did I do? Drank five martinis and the captain's champagne, six trips to the gym and a lot of deck walking, five movies, five afternoon teas, and seven trips to the nightclub. I guess the foie gras summed it up: looked good on paper, but in reality, it was just not there.

At long last, we got off the boat and caught a taxi to Europcar, who informed us that I was on the watch list, so Chrissie drove home. I should not have been on the watch list, and it was sorted out at a later date.

## March 2015

We were back in the Algarve, Portugal, after many years. We stayed in a nice apartment with two bathrooms, which was heaven. We had our first dinner in a Portuguese restaurant and ate nice fish soup and cod with a tomato sauce and drank very nice Dao wine, and it all cost E48 (or about £34 in our money).

## Mr. Tambourine Man

But the real reason we were here was to play tennis, and on the first morning, we joined the groups. We had a practice session, and I was put in the top group. We did fun things, and it was all very enjoyable. And I played tennis again in the evening with some of the guys. It was nice and sunny and around 68 degrees.

There was an Italian restaurant nearby, and I had a very nice dinner with arancini, followed by rigatoni with spicy sausage, and we drank a nice Portuguese red and limoncello, which all cost E55. It was great here, as the cigarettes were only E45 a carton, and we got the *Telegraph* every day to do the crossword. And nice lunches only seem to cost around E10 for two, with a good sandwich and beer. The tennis continued to be great.

We decided to go into Lagos to find our favourite restaurant from old times. We went to the bus stop for the 7.26, but it didn't turn up, so we got a taxi, which cost E8.75. And it cost E10.60 to get back. We failed to find our old favourite and decided on a restaurant with my favourite fish: skate. We sat down to order, but guess what? It's not on. We settled for scallops au gratin and shrimp with garlic; with a nice bottle of wine, it all cost E65. This was not the best, and we would not eat here again, and I guess we'll probably give Lagos a miss in future.

Tennis continued in its happy way. We took the car to Portimao, where they used to have fantastic sardines on the quay, but it wasn't there, as it's the wrong time of year. We found a small local restaurant and ate fish soup and sardines with boiled potatoes, and had a glass of wine and a small beer, and it only cost E33 for a pleasant evening.

For our next dinner, we returned to the Castle, for the first time in thirty-nine years. It was live music night, and some of the other tennis players were there. The music was awful. We splashed out on a E29 bottle of Alvor Reserva from the Algarve; I ate fish soup and piri piri chicken, and Chrissie had prawn cocktail and black monchique pig, and it all cost E80. There was no reason to come here again.

It was the last day of the tennis week; we practiced in the morning and had a tournament in the afternoon. I got to the final but lost 6-3, so feel a little bit low, but not for long, as we had a great last-night dinner with everybody. The food was great with prawns, octopus, and rice, followed by lamb on the bone with great potatoes and then chocolate mousse, and loads and loads of free wine. Everybody was great company, and they were all going back to work. But not me, as I was still in gap year sixteen.

The weather was great, at around 74 degrees, and I celebrated with a swim in the pool, but not the sea, which was too cold. We went to dinner at Aquarius, which was number four out of thirty-six. The downside was they didn't take credit cards, and we had to pay E85 in cash. It was not too bad, with amuse bouche of pepper, tomato, ham, and melon, followed by a very good clam starter for me, filo with prawns for Chrissie, and monkfish and roast octopus, respectively. We shared a mango crème brûlée with not a lot of mango and drank a E23 Duoro wine. This would be our only trip here.

No tennis course this week, but we had a private lesson with Louis every day. Chrissie did the basics, and I was working on my serve and volley. We went to Bagua for lunch, but our favourite restaurant on the beach was closed, so we ended up with bacon sandwiches in a cafe. We went to dinner at Chicco's, which was Trip Advisor number two. It was all very good. I had tempura shrimp and lasagne, and Chrissie had three vegetable pates and salmon, and we shared a slice of lemon meringue pie; it was all delicious and cost E71 (or around £50) for a very good dinner.

The next week went by in the same way, with private lessons with Louis, swimming in the pool, and dinners. Dinners were the Italian again, Chicco's again, the first-night Portuguese again (where we had a truly great dinner of fish soup and clam cataplana for E54), a curry at Saffron (which was quite poor), the Galley for a nice view of the moonlit sea (but average food), Pizza Red, which was very nice and cheaper than Pizza Express, and for our last night, we had a lobster (or maybe a crayfish) at the Portuguese restaurant, which costs E71, and with the most expensive E21.70 wine on the list, we spent E103 for a great dinner.

We drove 110 kilometres to see an old work friend who I had not seen for twenty years (although we always exchange Christmas cards). We had a delightful five hours together and had a really nice lunch at Capelo in Santa Luzia and then explored Tavira together. On another day, we drove to Cape St Vincent, which was the most southwesterly point in Europe. It was quite desolate, and the lighthouse was closed. We went to Sagres for lunch, but it seemed very dull.

I liked the Algarve and want to visit again. We looked in the estate agent's window, but I had no desire to buy a property there, as there were too many English; my soul was in the South of France, and I spoke the language quite well. Our apartment was very nice but only for two weeks; I think I would go stir-crazy to stay there any longer.

# July 2015

It was 93 degrees and getting hotter. We were in Sicily again, staying for the first week in Marind di Ragusa in the Hotel Miramare, a nice place on the seafront. We hired a Renault Clio, had a very nice drive through the countryside, and found our hotel without too much difficulty, but find it was difficult to park. I found a space and left the car there for a week. We had a nice terrace with a partial seaview, but the best thing was we got freshly squeezed orange juice for breakfast.

We looked around and went to Da Serefino for dinner just over the road. It was connected to a restaurant in Ragusa, which was why we came here. We started with a Campari and Aperol. I had pasta with tuna roe and tomatoes, and Chrissie had some excellent octopus. I had red prawns, and Chrissie had a seafood risotto. We drank a E25 Alvor and limoncello, and it was all very nice for E118, which was quite expensive, but we did have a very nice table, almost on the beach.

It was 97 degrees, and guess what? We spent all day on the beach and did a lot of swimming. Our second dinner was at Il Defino, which was number five out of sixty on Trip Advisor. I had good spaghetti with clams and then boring sea bass with almonds and pistachio cream, and Chrissie had a huge plate of grilled fish. We drank local wine at E15, and it all cost E74. I didn't think we'd go back.

The next night was Miramare along the seafront, after an Aperol spritz in the square. We started with arancini and caponata and then sardines and pasta with octopus. And we has desserts and Mount Etna wine (with ice, as it was so hot) and limoncello, and it was E76 all up, for a very good dinner. We booked to return.

Next was Trattoria Carmelo, which we thought was brilliant, even though Trip Advisor only had it as number eighteen. We started with a very, very good appetizer, rock bass and tomato pie with scampi and couscous croquette. And to follow was great too: red prawn ravioli and black tagliatelle with crab and ricotta. We had a nice bottle of E22 Ragusa wine, and it all cost E81. We would be back.

We returned to Miramare, but it was not so good. The boring swordfish came halfway through the starters; we gave this a miss after that.

The temperature reached 38 degrees (which is 100.4 Fahrenheit), and I had seven swims, going about three kilometres. We returned to Carmelo, and it was as brilliant as ever. We had the same starter and follow with spaghetti with sea urchins and a risotto with clams, barrota, courgette, and cream. Ragusa Classico cost E22, and our very good dinner was E82.

For our last dinner, we went to Da Serefino again and had a very nice table just off the beach. Chrissie started with octopus, and I had pasta with sardines. For a main course, we shared the famous 1953 fish soup, which was just a little disappointing. Drinking a E25 bottle, it all came to E94, which was not cheap. We went to our favourite bar for limoncello.

We found the car, which was where we left it, and set off for Taormina for the second year running. We stopped off in Syracuse for lunch and had a wander round; it was all quite nice, and we managed to buy a *Telegraph* to do the crossword later. The temperature was only 98 degrees.

We stayed in the Taormina Garden Hotel, which was inexpensive, and had a nice garden room, but the pillows were not good; the breakfast was average, and you had to buy your orange juice on the way to the beach, which was a very steep climb.

The first night, we ate a cheap E13.50 dinner at the hotel of good antipasto and pasta with a meat ragout, and with a E14 bottle of wine, it only cost E41 (or about £29 at current exchange rates).

The beach was fine, and there was a very good beach restaurant, where I had a great prawn omelette (which I think I will have every day).

We took the cable car back into town and revisited our favourite restaurant from last year, Rosso Vino, which was now number three on Trip Advisor. It was all very expensive, at E152 plus tip. We started with tuna tartare, scampi, and raw prawns, and followed with the E77 fish baked in salt. The olive oil with the bread was as good as ever, and we got limoncello on the house.

We had another day on the beach and prawn omelette. We stayed down for dinner and went to a nearby restaurant with a nice garden. We shared a yummy gnocchi with prawns and pistachio, and I had snapper Sicilienne, and Chrissie chicken, and we drank the E10 litre of house red; it all cost E71.

We were having breakfast, and our aged waiter asked if we had been to the *Godfather* village. He told us that it was only about fifteen kilometres, so we decided to go. We started our day trip by driving most of the way up Mount Etna to 1,986 metres (or sixty-six hundred feet), but it was not great, as it was covered in cloud, so we took a short stop and walked around a fairly uninteresting crater. We then drove to the village, Savoca, where they shot *The Godfather*, and by chance, we went to Bar Vitelli for lunch. There were only two other people in the bar. But as we were eating lunch, the place started to fill up, and everybody was taking photographs. We finished lunch and wandered inside and find the Godfather Museum.

The story went like this: Francis Ford Coppola wanted to shoot in the village of Corleone, but the Mafia controlled the town and wanted a lot of money, so they looked elsewhere and found Savoca. There was a only one bar, owned by Maria, which was where they decided to do a lot of the filming. They finished filming, and Coppola went to Maria and said, 'I don't know how much I owe you,' and gives her a blank cheque. She took it and just wrote, 'Grazi' [or 'thank you' in Italian].

They remain friends to this day, and every year, he tries to buy the bar, but with no success. Our total drive was 140 kilometres.

We celebrated by having a great dinner at the George, which we had enjoyed so much last year. We managed to spend E143 for a truly great dinner. We shared crispy egg with new potato and spinach, followed by pasta with tomato and ricotta, which was all sublime. To follow, I ate veal with a marsala sauce and broad bean puree. We drank a E45 bottle of Frapparo Nero D'Avola. The meal was just superb, with a great view and great service. We had a long chat with the chef, who was from Ragusa.

The next night, we returned to Rosso Vino, but we were a little sad, as seemed to have lost something. There was no tuna tartare tonight, and we decided not to get ripped off by the fish. I had mussel soup and linguini scampi, which was all just okay, and Chrissie had small fish cakes to start, which she didn't like, and the same linguini. We did get limoncello gratis, and with a E25 bottle of wine, we got out for E112, but the magic was gone.

We had another dinner at the hotel for E41, which was fine, with the antipasto followed by pasta Sicilienne (which is tomatoes, olives, capers, and onions).

For our last night, we walked down the steep path to the beach restaurant, Baracauli, for dinner and had a nice table with a great view of the beach. We ate well, with stuffed sardines on orange, red prawns in white wine, ravioli with shrimp, but best of all, eggplant Sicilienne with cheese. The cheese was Galpaninio, which was probably the nicest cheese I've ever eaten. With a E20 bottle of wine and two limoncello, it was E89 for a great dinner.

I did sixty-two swims here, for just over twenty-one kilometres, and enjoyed it so much. We were sad to leave Sicily, as the people were so nice and the food was so good. We escaped the pirates from Avis, who didn't notice the new scratches on the car.

## August 2015

Alex and Jenna, who we spent New Year's with in New York, got married at Hedsor House in Buckinghamshire.

## Mr. Tambourine Man

After a cheap night in a hotel at the Beaconsfield Services, we took the M3 down to Southampton, which is sort of on the way home, and caught a Flybe flight to La Rochelle. We got the hire car and drove over the toll bridge, meeting a lot of cars trying to leave, and arrived at the Petit Dej Hotel in St Marie de Re. The hotel was pretty downmarket. You had to smoke outside the boundaries; the town was just a lot of houses, with not much else and no sign of any restaurants. The hotel receptionist made a few phone calls, and we got a 7.15 table at the Hotel Atlantic, which was about a fifteen-minute walk. We had a couple of kirs and then got nice amuse bouche of mackerel and sardine pate, which were good, and then I had a very good tuna tartare, followed by the fish of the day, which was sea bream. Chrissie had foie gras and halibut, and we drank a bottle of Ile de Re red wine, which was a little woody. It all cost E114.

On our first day, we ate an average E8.50 breakfast and went exploring. The weather was sunny and around 74 degrees. We took a walk round the capital, St Maxime, and had lunch. The we bought some beach towels and went to a nearby beach. The tide was out, and it was not possible to swim until quite late, which was a drag. A pack of cigarettes cost E7 here, which was about half the UK price.

When we were here before, we had a very nice lunch in La Flotte, so because of the lack of local restaurants, we drove over for dinner. We walked round the quayside but found it difficult to be enthused by any of the restaurants. I had dorade tartare, and Chrissie fish soup. We both had prawns and crème brûlée but were annoyed to pay E21.50 for the Ile de Re wine, which cost E5 in the local supermarket. It costs E81.50 servis compris, and we decided it was basically not too bad but could have been better.

We spent the day exploring and got lost in Ars en Re, but then we found a nice beach cafe. We could not find anywhere to swim and returned to yesterday's beach for another late swim, after the tide came in. There was a hotel just up the road within walking distance, Ile Sous le Vent, which did dinner a couple of times a week. For E35, we were served a kir with passion fruit sorbet, a lovely tomato soup, a salad with squid, porc, and potatoes, a main fish course with vegetables, a really nice cheese in pastry, and a chocolate thing for dessert, along with lots and lots of wine. We shared a table with an English couple from Manchester and two Germans from Cologne. We had a good evening and didn't get back until after midnight.

In the morning, we went off to Loix, which was pretty drab, and returned to our usual beach and had a very nice tuna tartare with avocado and mango at La Cible. The tide was way too far out to swim, so we returned to the hotel to swim in the pool. We went back to La Cible for a pretty good dinner. No kir, as driving, just drank a couple of pressions, but the food was good. We shared melon gazpacho with serrano ham and foie gras, which were both excellent, and I had cod and Chrissie, cuttlefish. We ate outside by the beach with the tide now in, and it all cost E74.

It was time to leave. When we first came here, I thought it was wonderful, but now it just seemed filled with houses that all looked the same, and the tide always seemed to be out.

We moved on down the coast to Oleron, which we found much more to our liking. Firstly, you didn't have to pay to go over the bridge to get onto the island. We stayed in the Annex in Chateau D'Oleron. We had to wait until six o'clock to get in, so we headed off for the dunes at Sawmanaddes and found a wonderful beach where you could swim. The Annex was very French and very rustic. *Le petit dejeuner* was formidable. You got orange juice, melon, three local breads, and the most delicious homemade jams of peach, prune, or nectarine: a great start to any day.

For our first dinner, we went to La Courtini, which was highly recommended. We had kir to start, and I had tartare de poisson (fourth time this trip) and *lotte,* and Chrissie had rillettes and langoustine, prawn, and avocado assiette. We drank a local Oleron Prestige Cuvee at E14, and it all cost E70. We thought it was too touristy.

The breakfast was great again, and the weather was lovely for early September; we headed back to the dunes, where the swimming was great.

We walked into the port and had a nice kir in a cafe, lounging on sofas before our 8.30 dinner at Jardins Alienor, which was the upmarket hotel in town; it was only a hundred metres from the Annex.

We sat inside, and the dining room was lovely. We had a really good dinner; this became one of my must-go places. I started with carpaccio of croaker with marinated langoustines, which was truly good, and then had roast fillet of mousilin beef (120 grammes, or a quarter-pounder) with foie gras, herb mash, *petit oignons*, and jus (served bleu, of course, which was magnificent). This may have been the best steak I've ever eaten. Chrissie had a vegetable risotto and boned quail. This was all washed down with a E41 bottle of Sancerre rouge; the whole bill was E133: really worth it.

We went to the Saturday market and bought *pain* for E0.85, *jambom* for E3.20, and *abricots* for E3 for a picnic back in the dunes. It was all totally delicious, and the swimming was glorious again (I came across some naked people on the beach coming back from my swim).

Fifty metres from the Annex was Le Drugstore, which had a nice atmosphere and a great maitre d'. We started with two kir, and I had tuna tartare, followed by red mullet with mash and aioli, and Chrissie had foie gras and fish and chips. All the wines were E16, and we had a Chantreuse merlot. And then we had tarte au citron and armagnac, and it all cost E81, which was a very good value. This tied with Jardins for best dinner on the trip.

On the way back, we took a drive to Royan, which seemed pretty boring, and failed to get any petrol for the car, which we returned nearly empty. I didn't get charged for this, but I did get a speeding fine, which I had to pay, and a parking ticket, which I refused to pay.

Oleron was great, with two great restaurants and the lovely dunes and swimming. We would come here again, but I think we'll give Ile de Re a miss from now on.

# October 2015

We were in Luz Bay again for tennis, but this time with our daughter, Lauren, and her boyfriend, Matt.

We arrived late at 10.50 p.m., but Olna Luz, our favourite restaurant, was still open for dinner. We just had fish soup, pate and almond tart, and tarte aux pommes, and with a bottle of wine, it only cost E32.

It was quite sunny and around 70 degrees; we went to the seafront for a nice breakfast and then bought the *Telegraph* and a carton of cigarettes for £35. I managed a swim in the nice warm pool and then went back to the airport to collect Lauren. This time, they had two bathrooms, and we only had one: tough deal.

Our first night together, we went off to the beach bar for happy hour mojitos and then to Olna Luz for fish soup and clam cataplana; then we went back to the apartment for more drinks. We had a swim (with too many kids) in the adult pool and played a little friendly tennis. We had a couple of mojitos in the beach bar and then had dinner at the Italian next door, where we ate good baked aubergine and rigatoni with spicy sausage. I got a cuddle with the gorgeous waitress.

But then it was time to start the tennis clinic, which lasted for three hours each morning. They knew my skills, and I was put straight in the top group. The others were all in the lower groups. Lauren and Matt said they had a really good time.

That night, we went to the beach bar for our normal happy hour cocktails and then to the Pizza Shack, where I ate chicken jalfrezi, which was very nice; we drank wine, and it only cost E60 for four.

Tuesday was not great, as it rained one hour into the tennis clinic, and then the courts were too wet; it was not great weather for swimming, either. We went to dinner at Olna Luz, and I ate fish soup and sea bass, which was a bit dull. We drank red wine and *vino verde*, and it all cost E108 for four. We ran into some friends from Cornwall.

The next day was much better, as it was 79 degrees and sunny; we got a four-hour tennis clinic to make up for the rain yesterday. We ate lunch, had a nice swim, and then played some social tennis. We all got in taxis and went to Lagos with the tennis gang. We ate in a nice restaurant and had salad, prawns, piri piri chicken, pork, and lots of red wine for E16 each. We left and went to a bar and had beer and more beer to round off a good social night.

It was still hot and sunny, and we had three and a half hours of tennis. Lauren and Matt wanted a romantic dinner, so we went to Chico's and had very good tempura prawns and confit of duck with onion jam and ratatouille and a good bottle of wine for E64 for two. We got a free port, as they remembered us from earlier in the year.

It was the last tennis day, and after the morning clinic, we had the tournament again. But this time, I won with Marj, who was a doctor from Scotland. We were winning easily but nearly blew it before coming through. I won a bottle of white wine. And then it was party night again. We had a few beers before and then sat down to the excellent octopus and some very tender lamb with potatoes and again drank a lot of red wine. I was told I made a speech about my great victory that afternoon. I had a long talk with Louis about Madeleine McCann; he said her parents were party animals and had tried to get Marj and her husband to play, but they preferred family.

With my hangover, I drove Lauren and Matt back to the airport. We had our last dinner at, Olna Luz. It was lobster again, which was now E89 (up from E71 in March), with fish soup to start, which we always had here, and the most expensive wine at E21.80, for E118 in total.

We looked in the estate agent windows, but nothing grabbed us.

This was another excellent time of very enjoyable tennis, and it was really nice to have the kids with us.

# November 2015

Some time ago, I booked upgrade flights to Miami, with a view to going to either Belize or Costa Rica on an Audley Travel expedition, but for various reasons, we decided to spend nearly three weeks in Miami.

Because it was Miami, we had to go to Terminal 3 to board our A380. We drank champagne, and I had smoked salmon and macaroni and cheese (in Club?) with Fullers beer for lunch, followed by ice cream, and watched a couple of movies. We got through Customs and Immigration in less than an hour, and we took the $55 flat-fare cab ride to the Coral Reef in Key Biscayne. It was quite hard to find, and I felt a little disappointed. I had a sort of Grenada moment and wondered if this was a terrible mistake; we had no car, and it was so far to tennis and the movies. We found an Italian place on the strip; I drank beer and ate gnocchi, and Chrissie had Parma ham and melon and a glass of wine, and it all cost $43 plus tip. We bought a bottle of wine on the way back and got to bed by ten o'clock.

We slept until around seven, with a few wake-ups in the night, and it sort of got better. The Ritz Carlton next door had a tennis centre; there was a nice supermarket nearby, and we had a private beach just down the road, with towels, chairs, and an umbrella from the hotel. It was sunny and around 82 degrees but very windy, which meant it was too rough to swim, so we had to go in the hotel pool.

Our first proper dinner was in a Spanish restaurant, Kebo, which means 'so good' in Catalan. We sat outside, which was nice. We had five tapas and dull croquettes, good potato bravas, very good clams with garlic and white wine, good grilled artichoke, and a weird but nice tortilla espanol. We drank a good bottle of $30 Spanish wine, and it all cost $84 plus tip. It was all very nice.

The next morning, we went off to the tennis clinic and got the local rate of $22. It was good fun with some drills. Key Biscayne felt very small town. We spent a couple of hours on the beach, but the sea was still too rough to swim, so we had to go back to the pool.

We headed off to the Ritz Carlton for dinner and had a lovely outside table, overlooking the pool. It was porcini ravioli with truffle for me to start, and chicken liver pate for Chrissie. We both had lobster with pasta and a bottle of Dolcello wine for $60, and it all cost quite a lot, at $214. We booked our Thanksgiving turkey here.

There was no tennis the next morning, as it was raining, but I managed to go to the evening session. We went to Archie's Pizza for a cheaper dinner. I had an eleven-inch margarita pie, which was called a Neapolitina because it had fresh mozzarella, and Chrissie had the $15 hamburger special. There was no wine list, but we got a Chilean Grand Reserve Shiraz cabernet sauvignon, which was very nice, but at $44, it sort of ruined the bill. We won't make that mistake again.

It was sunny again, and I got to play tennis in the morning. We then went for a three-hour walk to the lighthouse, which was very pleasant. At 16.45, my Nike band said I already did 26,262 steps, with 1,538 calories. But we needed to get out of there a bit, so we booked an economy car for a week for $233, including taxes.

We went to dinner at Origins, which was Asian fusion, and it was all very nice: Malaysian roti with potatoes and curry, chicken satay, odd summer vegetable rolls, crispy duck with pancakes, and egg-fried rice. We drank a pinot noir at $28, and it all cost $77 plus tip (which was around £60), which seemed a lot for a little Chinese.

For our next night, we decided to go to the Oasis, a Cuban restaurant, but there were no customers, so we retired to an Italian place, which was not on Trip Advisor. The cheapest wine was Sicilian at $55, which was only okay. We shared a nice bruschetta, and I had a risotto with two large shrimp, artichoke, and cherry tomatoes, and Chrissie had veal in a lemon sauce. It all cost $156 including tip, which was just too much for an ordinary dinner.

I had good tennis in the morning and then went to the beach but didn't last long because was windy and cloudy, and then we had dinner at home: shrimp, macaroni and cheese, and Red Rock wine, all for $22.

I had another tennis day and another dinner at Archie's, where we managed to get a bottle of wine for $25; I ate spaghetti Bolognese, and Chrissie had fettucini Alfredo with chicken, all for $60 plus tip.

Life was now different; we upgraded to a red Hyundai. First, we drove over to Coconut Grove and visited Jaguar Ceviche for lunch; we had the best chicken and potato soup ever. We gave up on the Ritz Carlton for Thanksgiving because it was just too expensive, so we drove over to Whole Foods and bought a six-pound turkey breast, champagne, a Monterey pinot, cranberry and orange sauce, Peroni, strawberries, ANO red wine, vegetables, New England clam chowder, and beef lasagne, all for $143, which was less than the price for one at the Ritz.

The clam chowder was good, but the beef lasagne was poor. We managed to see the second half of *Planes, Trains, and Automobiles* with Steve Martin, which was such a great movie.

We went beach exploring in the Hyundai. We paid $6 to get into Victoria Park; it was all red flags and windsurfers, but we had a nice lunch in the sun. We then discovered Hobie Beach, which was very nice with a good beach and, most important, a calm sea. I went for a delightful swim in the ocean. I finished *History of Seven Killings*, which was one of the worst books I've ever read. I did not understand how it won the Man Booker and got such rave reviews. We explored North Beach and Harbour Drive, with its antiseptic houses in this antiseptic town, and decided Hobie would be our place of choice.

We celebrated Thanksgiving again in the United States with Laurent Perrier, roast turkey, mashed potatoes (which was what Americans do), broccoli, organic petit pois, a liquid cranberry and orange sauce, and the Monterey pinot. It was all very delicious.

After tennis, we went to Hobie Beach again with our turkey rolls and had three nice swims in the very calm sea. There were people waterskiing; must see if it was public so I could have a go. We went to see *Spotlight* at the movies and had a good dinner at Jaguar Ceviche. We had the six ceviche on a spoon, which were all pretty good, but the duo of squid were best. I followed with South American shrimp, which reminded me of Barbados, and Chrissie had a cheeseburger. Drinking a nice Peru beer and merlot, it was $73 plus tip.

The next day was the same, with tennis and Hobie Beach. We stayed in for dinner and had cold turkey with baked potatoes and watched some dreadful American TV.

It was now time for wedding anniversary number thirty-five. I should recount that for our first wedding anniversary, which was on a Sunday, we went down to Bray and had a lovely lunch with Michel Roux at the Waterside Inn. The second was a Monday, and we got back late from work and ended up in the Hamburger Heaven in Brompton Road (we lived in South Kensington). Would this be any better?

I started off by going to the tennis clinic, but we booked a night at the Thomson in South Beach to get away from antiseptic Key Biscayne. We headed over and found a cheap car park for $8 for twenty-four hours (compared to the hotel at $37). We dumped our cases and took a nice walk along the boardwalk to Circa 39, where we stayed last time, and had a nice lunch: a good glass of prosecco, followed by homemade tomato soup, which was as nice as I remembered, but the croutons were not quite so good. We checked in and went for a nice swim in the warm pool.

To start the evening, we went to the hotel's 1930s bar. It was too windy outside, so we sat inside, and I had a good shaken vodka martini, with Veuve Clicquot for Chrissie, which cost $16 and $30. And then we went to Cecconi's for the second time. We ordered a bottle of $89 D'Arden from Sicily (you'd never pay that much over there). We started with a $6 bruschetta and $19 tuna tartare, which was made at the table and truly excellent. I followed with spaghetti with Maine lobster, and Chrissie had pasta cervelli with lamb ragout and artichoke. It was all very good. We told them it was our anniversary, and they brought us two biscuits with 'Happy Anniversary' written in chocolate. It was a lovely meal, and it all came to $232. Back to the 1930s bar for a couple of beers, as they didn't have limoncello. A nice evening.

Breakfast was good OJ and coffee and poor waffles, and then we took another walk along the boardwalk. Then it was time to go shopping for Chrissie's birthday presents. We drove up to Bal Harbour at Ninety-Sixth Street, where it was all supposed to happen. We went to a bookshop and bought a couple of books and got our parking validated. That was lucky, as we failed to buy anything else. Emporio Armani had T shirts at $250, and Ralph Lauren had a blouse reduced to $280. It was the most overpriced shopping mall ever, with little stock in the shops and so many stores selling watches. Do not bother to come here. We went back to Hobie for hot dogs and frozen lemonade. Somehow, South Beach was not how we remembered; bizarrely, we were glad to be back in Key Biscayne.

We had dinner at home again, with a quite nice zucchini soufflé.

I had another day of tennis and then went onto Hobie Beach. We decided to go shopping at Bloomingdale's, but the rush-hour traffic was terrible. We went to a small mall by the movies and managed to buy Chrissie a jumper and socks in Banana Republic and a T shirt in Gap. We watched Tom Hanks in *Bridge of Spies*, which was quite good. We went back to Archie's and ate cheese ravioli and Alfredo and drank Peroni and a glass of merlot, and it only cost $46 plus tip.

The next day was the tennis round-robin, which was good fun. We tried but failed to find the post office to buy stamps for our cards. It was Chrissie's birthday, so we returned to Kebo (So Good). We sat outside and ordered a $35 bottle of organic Spanish wine and had a delicious dinner: anchovies in vinaigrette, small sardines with great red peppers and a green sauce, fried artichokes, and chickpeas with sausage.

The next day was the same again, with tennis and Hobie Beach. We went to see the movie *Trumbo*, which was very interesting, about the Hollywood Communist black list; we drove home in the heaviest rain, with a lot of lightning, going 20 MPH in the 40 limit, it was so bad. We ate in and had artichokes and very nice organic frozen macaroni and cheese.

The next day was a little different, as it was raining, and there was no tennis. We took a swim in the pool and then headed back to Bloomingdale's. We bought shorts, a jumper, and a shirt for my Christmas presents and a Ralph Lauren cashmere jumper and a lovely dress for Chrissie's birthday (Banana Republic and Gap don't quite do it, somehow).

It was still raining; we read in the newspaper that yesterday was Miami's wettest 4 December ever, with 3.6 inches of rain. Therefore, it was a swim in the pool and an afternoon movie: *Janis*. We had dinner at home with pork chops, applesauce, garlic, mashed potatoes, and courgettes, which was all good. Because American TV was so bad, we watched *Two Weeks Notice* on the i-Pad.

The weather got a little better, and we had our last tennis, our last visit to Hobie, and our last dinner at Archie's: tuna tartare and lasagne for me and kiddies Alfredo at $6 for Chrissie, which all cost $59 plus tip (drinking only Peroni and a glass of wine).

We had been there for nearly three weeks. Key Biscayne was pretty dull and only saved by the tennis. Hobie Beach was nice, and Kebo was probably the only worthwhile restaurant in town. Jaguar over on Coconut Beach was excellent. I did not think we would return.

## February 2016

We paid British Airways £5,800 to fly Club to St Lucia and stay for two weeks in a delightful boutique hotel, Coco Palm Resort in Rodney Bay.

We had a bad start in Gatwick again. Staying in the Premier Inn because its cheap. Last time, we got McDonald's on the way, but I thought there was a Jamie's Italian, but we ended up in Wetherspoon's in the South Terminal and had pretty poor chicken piri piri. Next, the lounge was closed for refurbishment, and the replacement was not too comfortable, and we had to buy our own newspapers.

The flight was eight hours, forty minutes, and I ate drab pear and asparagus, tomato tortelloni, and ice cream, and drank four glasses of champagne. It took ages to get through passport and we paid $70 for a ninety-minute taxi ride to the hotel. We had a nice room, with a terrace overlooking the pool. The hotel was part all-inclusive, and the people were drab. We had a just about okay pina colada and ate in the hotel. It was not great; I had very average spaghetti Bolognese, and Chrissie chicken Alfredo, and drank an Australian pinot noir, and it all cost $54. The breakfast was only okay.

The weather was not too bad: about 82 degrees and mostly sunny, with a few small showers. We walked all along the beach and settled on a place at the far end with a local beach shack, serving food and drinks and the chairs and umbrella, costing £10 for the day. For our first lunch, we went to Spinnaker's and had delicious pumpkin soup with garlic bread and a pinto beer, with a turkey and cheese baguette for Chrissie, and it all cost EC$70 (or about £18). It was nice swimming.

I reflected on the hotel and was not quite sure, as it was all very pleasant but somehow lacked the magic. I don't think I saw anybody I would want to talk to.

We returned to Spinnaker's for dinner and had a really nice beachside table. We started with pina colada, and we both had delicious smoked salmon and potato soup. We drank a very good bottle of 2013 Valpolicello, and I had lobster thermidor, and Chrissie had tagine of lamb. It was all very good, but it cost EC$416 (which was about £110), which seemed quite a lot.

I had another day on the beach. I went for my first waterski; I fell down the first time but then got up and went round the bay two times; my arms ached quite a lot. We went to Marie's beach shack for lunch and had kingfish and fried plantain and a couple of beers, all for about £10. We had a happy hour rum punch and went to the Creole Grill at the hotel. There was zero atmosphere, and we didn't have any starters; I had a whole snapper, which was nicely cooked, with rice and fried plantain, and Chrissie had the pork stew, which was fatty, and we drank a $22 cabernet sauvignon. It all cost about $68 and was not a great experience.

We discover a baguette shop and got a picnic to take the beach, buying beers from the beach shack, which made lunch about £9. We went to a local bar for our pina coladas and happily smoked but then failed to get a table at the tapas bar, which was full. Instead, we go to the Big Steak House, which had a good atmosphere. I had tuna carpaccio and chef's lobster (slightly hot), and Chrissie had clam chowder and prawns, and we drank a California pinot noir. It all cost EC$386 (or £100) again. We sat next to the man who was head of immigration, who was a good laugh.

The next day, we took a boat trip to Pigeon Island, which was quite expensive at EC$80, plus another EC$36 to enter the island. We viewed the Atlantic breakers and took a walk up to Rodney Castle, which had a good view, and then found a nice beach and sat on our towels. The best thing was lunch at Jambe de Bois, where I had a fish roti, which was just so good, and Chrissie an egg baguette, and with the beers, it all cost £11. We went back to Spinnaker's for dinner and only spent EC$260 this time. We had happy hour cocktails in the hotel first, to save, and we then had soup and rigatoni for me and coconut shrimp for Chrissie, with another good bottle of the Valpolicello.

On Sunday, the beach was wonderful, full of local kids having a great time, spending hours in the sea and then getting covered in sand. I went for another waterski and got up the first time. We booked at the tapas bar and had a big argument. We ordered the seven-course fish menu. We started with a quite nice octopus, a very nice squid, mussels with tomato (which was a bit dull), good prawns piri piri, okay sardines, and okay coconut shrimp. But where were the salt cod fritters? They gave us 10 percent off, but I complained to the manager and got 15 percent off the food and wine (which was a E$75 Naked Grape). It all cost EC$268 (or £70), which seemed a rip-off for six tapas and a bottle of wine.

We did better the next night and went to Antillia, the microbrewery. Chrissie ordered a passion fruit beer, and I had the Golden Eagle. I had mahi mahi with chips, and Chrissie had fish in batter and chips. I had a couple Moor beers, talking to some Canadians we met on Pigeon Island, and the total bill was EC$100 (or about £25): at last, something cheap to eat.

The next day was the beach again; I had a nice waterski, although the sea was a little rough. We met our new Canadian friends in Antillia for a beer and took a E$30 taxi ride to Gros Islet and the Flavour of the Grill. This was real Caribbean streetlife and not touristy, like Rodney Bay. It was all a bit slow but very nice; I had saltfish croquettes and rare lamb chops with garlic mash, and we drank a California merlot. It was only EC$188 (which is less than £50), for a very nice time.

We beat the Rodney Bay tourist trap and took the bus to Gros Islet for EC$6 return for two, instead of EC$80 on the boat, and took a beautiful twenty-five-minute walk along the sea to Pigeon Island. Unfortunately, the cruise must be in, as the beach was full of wanabees. We had another great lunch at Jambe de Bois, with a superb curried vegetable roti for me and a fish roti for Chrissie; with our normal beers, it cost less than £10.

We went with our Canadian friends to Razamataz, an Indian restaurant. We started with a couple of special mojitos at EC$15 each and then had prawn puri, which was poor and covered in spinach cream, and then prawn dhansak and fish marsala, both of which were pretty poor. We drank a glass of red wine and two local beers; they tried to charge us for Heineken, but we got it changed, and it still cost EC$300 (or around £75) for a pretty poor curry with not much to drink. We would never have put up with this at home.

I had a good waterski on the beach the next day. I got up the first time again, and it was a little calmer, so I did some good slalom. We went to dinner in a French restaurant, LaTerrasse, which cost over £100 and was just not worth it. Chrissie had tomato crème brûlée, and I had French onion soup, followed by pork medallions and chips and red snapper fillet and dauphinoise potato. The wine list was expensive, with the cheapest at EC$95; we had Baron Philippe de Rothschild pinot noir at EC$110. It was only nice and certainly not worth the money.

We revisited Pigeon Island on the EC$6 bus and had another great curried vegetable roti lunch. Dinner at Spinnaker's again. The Valpolicello was finished, so we had to drink the Chile Sunrise merlot. We shared a very, very hot prawn piri piri, and I had the rigatoni again, and Chrissie had fish au gratin. We still got the nice beachside table, and it only cost EC$232 (or less than £60), which was a reasonable price for an enjoyable dinner and not a £100 rip-off.

There were no chairs on the beach, so we had to sit on our towels; the sandwich shop was closed, so I had a very nice chicken chowder at Spinnaker's. For dinner, we went back on the EC$6 bus ride and went to another local restaurant, Golden Taste. Not too many people, but it still had a good atmosphere. We started with the local speciality, conch fritters, and I had my third lobster, and Chrissie had grilled dorado with a good sauce. We had a bottle of merlot, and it only cost EC$225 (or about £55), for a super local dinner.

Waterskiing was terrible. I failed to get up and then fell over coming back from a slalom. I used to be quite good on one ski, but now I was pretty hopeless on two. We went to Antillia for dinner again and drank some good beer and a Chilean merlot and ate jerk wings and chips for me, and mahi mahi and chips for Chrissie. It only cost EC$140 (or £35), for a nice time with nice people at a sensible price.

It was now continuous sunshine, and the temperature went up to 88 degrees. I had my last swims and counted that I had done fiftysix swims here for about twenty-two kilometres: feeling fit.

We went back to the Golden Taste for our last dinner. We shared the conch fritters again; I had garlic shrimp with rice and vegetables, and Chrissie had lambi, a new shellfish to us but quite nice. Merlot again. This time, it cost EC$205 (or around £50).

St Lucia did not really match expectations; I'm afraid to say it was our least favourite Caribbean island after four trips to Barbados, Antigua, and Grenada. Rodney Bay was much too touristy, and many of the restaurants were rip-offs. Our best food was on Pigeon Island and at Gros Islet with the local people. We didn't really like the hotel; it was certainly not boutique in the accepted sense but an all-inclusive average place with very uninteresting people. We managed to talk to nobody there.

# April 2016

Lauren returned to Los Angeles for six months, and we went to visit again. I almost lost count of how many times I've been to LA; this was actually our eighteenth trip there. We flew World Traveller Plus but returned Business with the flat beds for the overnight flight. It was not too bad, and we got a glass of cava before take-off and then a Bloody Mary and some nice potato salad with smoked salmon and smoked haddock and mash for main course. My last four flights in Business, I only ate pasta (including the now-famous macaroni and cheese).

We were only there for a couple of nights. We visit Lauren's flat, which was quite nice but a bit like a hotel. We went to Le Pain for lunch, and I had the ever good gazpacho. We went to the Arclight to see *Everybody Wants Some*, which was dreadful, and we retired for dinner at Le Petit Four on Sunset Plaza, an old favourite. Chrissie and I started with Summerland pinot noir from Santa Barbara and were joined by Lauren, Matt, and Ben, who was just picked up from the airport. We only have main courses; I just had to have the calves liver. We ended up with three bottles of the $41 wine, and it all cost $293. It was great food and a great atmosphere, and it had to be one of my favourites.

It was time to go back to Mexico, and we caught the two-hour Alaska Airlines flight to Cabo San Lucas. It would have been my dad's ninety-second birthday today, and I call my mum from the plane before we took off. We had a nice taxi ride from the airport and arrive at the Bungalows. It was near the top of the list on Trip Advisor, and it's very nice and quaint. We went for a long walk around the town and found a restaurant for dinner recommended by the taxi driver. I took a swim in the pool.

Our first dinner at Maria Jimmez is very good. We started with margaritas, which you must have here. I ate shrimp fajitas, and Chrissie had green chicken enchilada, and we drank a bottle of El Centro cabernet sauvignon from Mexico, and it was £35 all up. We got serenaded by the band playing 'Can't Help Falling in Love,' and the next table got 'Guantanamara.' We liked this place.

We had a nice breakfast and consulted the map. The main beach was about three thousand steps, or over a mile, and we found the Omega beach bar (which we discovered later was number five out of 416 on Trip Advisor). It was nice swimming but still a small chill from the Arctic current, which gets all the way down here. We had two waters, two beers, a shrimp taco, a fish taco, French fries, two beds, and an umbrella, all for £10 (or the same price as the chairs in St Lucia).

On our second night, we went to Las Mariscadas (number thirty-seven on Trip Advisor). There were only three people from our hotel when we arrived; they left, and we were the only ones, so no atmosphere. I ate a quite nice tuna tartare with avocado and a recommended sea bass, but there was too much going on. Chrissie had coconut shrimp. They managed to find us a bottle of Mexican red, and it all cost around £50.

On the second day, the cruise ship was in, so Omega had no beach chairs for us, and we had to wait for thirty minutes. We added guacamole to the lunch, and it all cost £11: bargain of the year.

We went to Neptuno's, which was quite close by; it was only number ninety on the Trip Advisor list, but we loved it. Naturally, we started with margaritas and ordered a Chilean Shiraz. To start, we shared the Cabo ceviche with mango, which was truly excellent, and

## Mr. Tambourine Man

I had a very nice shrimp curry medium, and Chrissie had chicken fajitas. We had two more glasses of red wine and an after-dinner drink on the house, and it all cost $67. A great find and so close.

It was still 82 degrees but a little cloudy, but now we had our favourite chairs reserved at Omega. We had nice swimming and walked past a good-looking restaurant with a pretty courtyard, Peacock's, which Trip Advisor has as number ninety-one, but with generally good reviews. It was simply awful, and I had a bad stomach in the morning, which I never get (except for the bad experience in Vietnam). The wine was expensive, and we ordered the cheapest El Cetto Mexican merlot, which was 650 pesos (or $38), compared to Maria's at 340 pesos. You simply should not charge that much for Mexican plonk.

All the prices were in dollars, and I had $9 tomato soup, which was boring, and a $21 roast leg of lamb, a carrot soufflé, and no sauce, which was again boring. Chrissie had a baked brie, which she quite liked, and tough shrimp ravioli. We asked to smoke and were told we had to go to the bar area; we were directed to the fire pit, but they dumped our glasses, and we didn't get the last of our wine. Although everything was priced in dollars, we then got the bill in pesos, which worked out to about $121, which was about double the norm round here. We didn't leave a tip, and the maitre d' returned with the bill, looking for a tip; no chance. We won't ever come back here again.

I finished one of the best books ever: *Alone in Berlin*, by Hans Fallada, about Nazi Berlin. He wrote in 1946 in twenty-four days; I finished it in four days. And we returned to Maria Jimmez for a great $56 dinner: margaritas to start, free cheese pies, and enchiladas with green chicken for Chrissie, and house special chicken with guacamole, black beans, and rice for me. We drank their reasonable El Cetto. It was so much better than Peacock's and half the price.

It was a beautiful, 84 degree sunny day, and we took the boat ride to Love Beach for $10 each. It was a glass-bottom boat, but you couldn't see much; we stopped and fed the fish and saw some nice angel fish, which are orange and purple. We just looked at Love

Beach from the boat (it was no good for swimming) and then carried on past the Arch into the Pacific Ocean.

We had another great dinner at Neptuno's. Starting as ever with the margaritas, this time we had sushimi (which they call *carpaccio del mare*); we had tuna, salmon, octopus, and two white fish. It was truly a dish to die for. We both had a nice sea bass with garlic and vegetables and drank a bottle of Chilean merlot. It all cost $59 for a great, great dinner.

We had a great day on the beach, with five swims, coconut shrimp tacos and guacamole and beers for lunch, and it still only cost £11 or so with the chairs included; everybody was always smiling and so kind.

We went to dinner at the local pizza place. There were a few tourists when we went in, but it soon filled up with Mexican families, giving it a really good atmosphere. We had the usual margaritas, a really nice tuna sushimi, a large margarita pizza to share, and five glasses of wine, all for £23. Why did it cost so much at Pizza Express, without the sunshine and the smiles?

Our last day on the beach was lovely as always, and Omega gave us two XL T shirts to take home with us. We had our last dinner in Maria Jimmez, which was as lovely as ever: margaritas, free cheese pastries, enchilada green chicken, and quessquillades prawn and El Cetto, all for £35. It was a great restaurant.

We thoroughly enjoyed Cabo. It was easy to get to, a nice hotel with great people and great breakfasts (cinnamon apple waffles, smoothie, juice, and coffee today). Omega Beach was fantastic; we had six great dinners, one okay, and one terrible. Every Mexican person was delightful, with that permanent smile on their faces. After she was mugged, Chrissie said she would never come here again, but her faith was restored, and she had a great time.

It was a nice two-hour Alaska flight back to LA; it took a long time to get my Mustang convertible, but I hung in there and got a nice white one. We were staying in Tangerine in Burbank again and looking forward to seeing Lauren (which after all was the point of being there).

## Mr. Tambourine Man

The first night, I achieved a first: We went to a gun club in Burbank and fired live ammo at a target. Only two people were allowed on the firing range, and Lauren joined me to load my gun. My gun jammed twice (which never happened to Dirty Harry). On the first round, I hit the target three out of five times, but on the second round, I got all five, but to the right of where I was aiming. It was very noisy, and the bullets spit out at you. It was an interesting way to spend $92 for five of us. We all looked at our targets in the car on the way back. We got to Counter Burger, and it was $207 for six; I drank a very nice North Coast pilsner. Then to an Irish bar for a 10 percent Wild Oats, Guinness, and Baileys whisky: a good first night.

My Citibank card didn't work, so I had to pay $3 to use Bank of America. We went to the local sandwich shop (where Susan Sarandon hangs out) and saw a good movie, *Hostile Border*, with only one other person in the theatre.

And it was time to get back to Angelino's. We hadn't been for two years, but we were remembered and had to eat the ravioli pomodoro and drank Chianti and Peroni. It all cost $43 and was as good as ever: a delight.

It was around 75 degrees and sunny; we played tennis in the park, I swam in the hotel pool, and I went to Toluca Lake Tennis Club for an evening session. Lauren took us to Cecconi's, which we enjoyed twice in Miami. We had to wait a long time for the table, and Chrissie was cold from the AC. They put a table of six right next to us, and it was very, very noisy. We got a dumb waitress who could hardly speak English. Chrissie and I shared creamed risotto and fried courgette, which were both boring. I had spaghetti with Maine lobster at $36, which was generous and quite good. We drank a $65 Sicilian wine, which was not much good, and followed with a $55 piedmont, which was a little better. The bill for four was $296, which seemed a lot.

But it was all about to get a whole lot worse. Jamie and Bob came to meet us, and we went to the Mexican restaurant next door and had three Pacificos and a margarita. We went to Prosecco and had red wine and limoncello and ate nice artichoke soup and lobster and pea risotto; I paid, and it cost $692 for six.

We went to the Irish bar and drank a few shots. We were pretty drunk, and it was time to walk home, but somehow, I fell over or tripped on the pavement. We got back to the hotel, and the blood was pouring. Lauren said we had to call 911, which we did, and the medics and police turned up and said I should go to the emergency room. We took an Uber, and I was still bleeding, but they gave me nine stitches and did a CT scan, and we got the Uber back after what seemed like ages.

Some time later, I got a bill for $4,000, but luckily, the insurance covered it (and a new pair of Rayban glasses). The next morning, I looked like the end of the world and missed tennis, but we took a short walk to get *The LA Times* and saw all my blood all over the pavement. I was not going to give up drinking.

We went to dinner at Patty's; I just had an orange juice with my corned beef hash and fried eggs over easy.

It was our last day, and we played a little tennis in the park and saw *Jungle Book* at the Arclight. My face still looked terrible, but we went to meet Winnie and Esa at the Magnolia on Sunset. I drank water and had an average tuna tartare and a rigatoni Bolognese.

For our last lunch, we tried to go to the Getty Villa for lunch, but it was closed on Tuesdays. We went to Frankee's on the beach at Malibu, and I had a nice lobster salad and lemonade, and it all cost $140 plus tip. We went to Santa Monica and had a nice walk along the boardwalk. It was a good flight home, with a couple of glasses of champagne and seven hours' sleep. We had a terrible drive back, as the A30 was closed for the building works so had to take the long way round through Camelford.

## June 2016

We returned to Sicily for the third year running, staying for three weeks this time because I got the booking wrong. We stayed in a small family-run hotel, Piccolo Mondo, in San Vito lo Capo. It was two hours, twenty minutes on BA Club Europe to Palermo Airport and then about an hour's drive in the taxi for E116.

## Mr. Tambourine Man

We got to San Vito around nine o'clock and were booked in for dinner next door, at Krik and Krok. We got a freebee fried chickpea flour and shared aubergine capalato, and we both has brusilia pasta with sardines and fennel, which was all very good. We drank a nice bottle of Nero D'Avola at E14 and had only one limoncello; it all cost E48 (or about £38).

We had a nice seaview from our balcony, which was just about big enough for two chairs. Breakfast was okay, and we headed to the beach. The temperature was around 80 degrees. The sand was beautiful and pure white; the chairs and umbrella were nice, and the sea was very shallow for good swimming. And everything was so close. This was a very nice town with very little traffic, as all the cars had to park outside the town.

We went to Il Gorgio for a wonderful dinner. We shared young squid with a chickpea puree; I had linguini with scampi, and Chrissie had a ricotta ravioli with a fish soup. We had a one-litre carafe of very good Etna wine and one limoncello again, and it all cost E55: excellent.

I woke up and went out onto the balcony, and it was so hot, at 104 degrees, because we have a Sirocco. We went to the beach and swam to avoid the heat. We had a nice lunch of fried aubergine and chickpea flour sandwich with a Peroni. Then we went to a bar and watched England beat Wales 2-1 in the Euros (despite Joe Hart letting in a terrible goal from Gareth Bale).

We went to a meat place for dinner: Bianconigor. We had a small glass of prosecco and a side order of prunes and bacon. We then shared a starter of Sicilian cheeses, which were very nice. I had rabbit medallions with the chef's special recipe and grilled vegetables, and Chrissie had a classic burger. We drank a bottle of E30 Nero D'Avola and two limoncellos, and it all came to E85. We decided it was a bit more expensive and not up to the standards of the first two nights.

The temperature dropped to only 75 degrees, and it was very windy; you needed a jumper at night, and the sea was too rough for swimming. We discovered that our lunch place did arancini, which were very good.

We went to dinner at Syrah but failed to get a table, so instead, we went to San Vita Tavola, which had inside tables out of the wind. This was number eleven on Trip Advisor. We shared a bruschetta with good tomatoes and mozzarella but poor bottaga, which felt like it came from a tin. Chrissie had fried fish with squid, one prawn, octopus, and whitebait, and I had fettucini with spiny lobster. We drank a bottle of E17 Nero D'Avola, and it all cost E73, which was not too bad.

It rained until 10 a.m., but then the sun came out for three hours; it got cloudy again, but it was warmer at 80 degrees, and we went swimming again. We had arancini and Peroni for lunch again.

We got a 9.30 table at Syrah, which was very nice. We shared sardine and cuttlefish done as a rillette, and I had very good pasta with one scampi and prawns, and Chrissie had ravioli with ricotta and proper bottaga. We drank a E26 bottle of Nero D'Avola, and it all cost E83. We would come here again. We had found three really good restaurants and cannot decide which was the favourite.

The weather was still good, and we had a nice day on the beach, with arancini and Peroni for lunch again. We discovered the Surf Bar for Aperol spritz and backgammon before dinner. The atmosphere was great, and the waitresses were very pretty.

We returned to Il Gorgio. I had a very delicious tartare of prawns with pistachio, and Chrissie had a tuna sauce omelette. I had a pretty good Gulf spaghetti with mussels, clams, and Sicilian bits, and Chrissie had a poor turbot, which was cold and got knocked off the bill. With the house carafe and limoncellos, it all cost E60.

I finished *War and Peace,* all fourteen hundred pages, for the first time. It was a lovely read but will choose something a little more lowbrow.

We watched England play Slovakia in a dismal draw. We returned to Krik and Krok for another good dinner. We shared chickpea cream and octopus, and I had very nice pasta with prawns, fennel, and broad beans, and Chrissie had veal tenderloin with roast potatoes. We drank our usual Nero, and it all cost a bargain E60.

We had another day on the beach, with arancini and Peroni for lunch, and back to Syrah for dinner. We had an amazing starter of sardine and orange, which was pressed together and worthy of a Michelin star. I had couscous with fish, which was lovely, and Chrissie had the pasta with scampi and prawn I had last time. With a Nero at E24, it all cost E78, for a very good dinner.

We were woken at 3 a.m. by very loud thunder, and it rained until ten o'clock and then again at lunchtime. Everybody said it would get better. I managed a couple of swims. We tried La Cambusa for dinner and were lucky to be inside. They had one-litre Nero D'Avola house wine at E10, which was a good start. We shared a nice tuna tartare, and I had spaghetti with cuttlefish and sea urchin. The spaghetti was black, and the sea urchin was hard to find. Chrissie had fried fish and chips. It all cost E63, which was quite good.

We woke up to the Brexit result, which we won by fifty-two to forty-eight. Our Italian hosts were very excited and told us that they wanted I-exit. The pound plunged, and I was glad I had a lot of US dollars in Citibank, but dinner will now cost around £3 more.

We returned to Krik and Krok for third time. I had red raw prawns with three sauces, which was very good, and Chrissie had lentil soup with cuttlefish. We shared a ragout of red mullet with lentils and tagliatelle, which was very nice too. We drank the Nero D'Avola and two limoncellos on the house, and it all cost E63.

And the next night, we returned to Syrah and had another nice dinner. We shared the ricotta and aubergine starter, which was good (but not as good as the sardine and orange). I had a very good ravioli with crab, crème pesto, and citrus, and Chrissie had the gamberi in Greek pastry starter. With a nice bottle of Nero D'Avola, it all cost E78. We watched Wales play Northern Ireland.

The next day, after the arancini lunch, we headed down to the marina and got on the E25 four-hour boat trip. Everybody except us was Italian, and we didn't understand the commentary, but the captain was very kind and came to tell us in English what was being said. We passed our beach and then the praying monk's head rock. Next was the tuna factory, which closed in 1978, and then we stopped for a snorkel. We saw some nice blue and red fish; not quite the Barrier Reef, but pretty good. Next we went to Scapello, a two-horse town, and I swam to the town beach and back. We were fed bread with tomatoes, salami, and a special tuna, and drank white wine. The music was loud; the captain danced, and the Italians laughed, and we all had great fun. It was a good boat trip.

We went to dinner at Zingaro, which according to Trip Advisor was the number one restaurant in town. We shared a very good tuna tartare and antipasto with seafood salad, tuna capatato, swordfish, and sardines. I had spaghetti with clams, which was a little dull. We drank a recommended E25 bottle of Syrah, and it all cost E75, which was not too bad.

Italy beat Spain 2-0 in the Euros. But not England; we lost to Iceland in diabolical circumstances and were so embarrassed we had to leave the bar. Dinner at Il Gorgio was much better. I started with tartare of red prawns, and Chrissie had the omelette. We then shared a nice fish from the grill with fries and fried aubergine with garlic. With our normal litre bottle of house red, it only cost E60, which was a great value.

The sea was a little choppy, and I tried to bodyboard, but the surf was not as good as Newquay. We had another great dinner at Syrah. We shared the sardine and orange again, which was still a great dish. I then had another great dish: taglioni with clams, mussels, squid, scampi, and prawns and a lot of tomatoes and dill, making a fantastic dish. Chrissie had a prawn cocktail, which was very upmarket. We drank a Cygnus Nero D'Avola at E24, and it all cost E75 for a very nice dinner.

And for our next dinner, we returned to the number one: Zingaro. We were not too impressed, as there was little atmosphere, and everything seemed to take ages. We got nice freebee melon and prawns and then shared insalata del mare, which was good. I had a pretty dull pasta with tuna, tomatoes, and pecorino, and Chrissie a gnocchi, which had slightly sweet potatoes. We drank a cheaper 2014 Nero D'Avola and a limoncello, and it all cost E65, but I didn't think we'd be coming back here, even if it was number one.

This was a lovely town without the traffic and some really nice restaurants and a great beach, but something was missing. There was no nightclub or discotheque, which seemed odd, as the place was full of young people.

## Mr. Tambourine Man

We returned to Krik and Krok. But there were downsides: They wouldn't let us have the table we wanted, the service was very slow, and worst of all, they had run out of limoncello. For the first time, we didn't leave a tip. We started by sharing a very good eggplant pie with cream of tomato and Parmesan fondue, and I had a delicious pasta with shrimp, pesto, almonds, and garlic. Chrissie had pasta with aubergine and tuna but didn't eat much. And they also ran out of our normal wine, so we had another E14 Nero. It all cost around E60 again.

The next night, we decided to have pizza. The first place we tried had no wine, so we moved on to Flash. We had Capello to start, two pizzas, and a litre of red wine, and it all cost E32 and was perfectly fine.

And the night after, we returned to Il Gorgio and had another great dinner in their lovely garden. We shared the young squid with chickpea, and I had a lovely spaghetti with sea urchin. Chrissie had fish couscous. With the normal one-litre bottle of red, it was only E55 for a lovely time.

It was my birthday number sixty-four, but nobody played me the song. We had a nice day on the beach and a E5 portion of macaroni with egg, aubergine, tomato, and pancetta for lunch. We had a nice outside table at Syrah for dinner and ordered lobster. The chef came to the table and showed us a black rock lobster from the shallows and a larger orange lobster from deeper. The chef said the deeper, the better, so we went for the orange lobster. We started with a very nice tuna tartare with spiced jams. The lovely lobster came with pasta and tomatoes and was such a great dish. We drank a E37 bottle of Ribero, and the bill was E140: a great dinner and not too much.

We then went to watch Italy versus Germany at the hotel, as the bars were too crowded. After extra time, it was 1-1; I thought Italy would win the penalty shoot-out, but they didn't; surprisingly, the Italians don't seem too upset.

For our last night, we went to Il Gorgio again. I had to have the tartare of red prawns, and Chrissie had the young squid with chickpea. We shared a Spitula fish from the grill done with oil, lemon, and oregano, which was delicious, with the French fries and grilled aubergine. With the E10 house red, it cost E70 for a nice last dinner.

At 7 p.m., I was sitting in Palermo Airport, drinking Fanta orange, as we had a long late drive home. We liked San Vito very much: traffic free, great beach, and very good restaurants. We did lots of swimming, one boat trip, and not much else. We didn't go to explore Palermo because it seemed too far. There were many food highlights, with the tartare of red prawns, and sardine and orange, which were exceptional, good spaghetti with sea urchin, and the really nice birthday lobster. Lots of nice pasta to go with it all. Three weeks didn't seem too long, somehow. Piccolo Mondo at E140 per night seemed like a good deal, with a nice room, good breakfasts, and the most lovely people. They gave us a picture to bring home, which was so kind.

## August 2016

At Lauren's request, we set off for our tenth visit to Skiathos, where we had not been for ten years. We went to bed at 9 p.m. and woke up at 2 a.m. to drive to Bristol to catch the 7 a.m. Thomas Cook flight, which was fine.

We booked a house in town, and the owners were supposed to pick us up, but there was nobody there. We didn't even know the name of our house, but we had a phone number, and after a call, we were picked up. The four of us got in a very small car (with all the luggage just fitting). The house was great, with fine views from the terrace over the harbour, two bedrooms, and three bathrooms; it would suit us very well.

A boat came in, and there was a queue at the taxis, so we took the bus to our favourite beach, Vrelimnos. We went to the beach bar, which my old Greek friend Tony Kampanaos told me was the best beach tavern in the whole of Greece. We had gavros and Tzaziki, which was not on the menu, and Mythos beers, and it was all delicious. We had a quick swim and went back to the house.

We went for a nice cocktail by the port and then returned to Stamatis. The waiter recognised me and gave me a hug, and the owner came out and warmly shook my hand. I always used to drink Grande Reserve, but they no longer carried it. I ate the classic fish soup and curried lobster. The kids ate vegetarian, and we had a nice bottle of Butari. It all cost E108 for four. The food was not that great, but it was nice to relive old memories.

We went back to Vrelimnos by taxi and had a nice swim and another good gavros lunch. We went to a nice bar on the hill for cocktails and then to Primavera, an Italian place in the square,. We had a lot of house rosé (about three litres) and tzaziki to start. The kids had pizza, Chrissie had a souvlaki, and I had devil's rigatoni, which was pretty good with tomatoes, hot pepper, and chilli. We had to pay cash, but it was only E77.70 for a nice dinner in a nice setting.

We had another day on the beach and a good dinner at First Step next door. We again drank a lot of wine, and I had chicken satay and lamb chops, which were nice and pink for me. There were good views of the harbour and pretty waitresses, and I think it cost about E100 for four.

It was Lauren's birthday; we explored the port, and she found a boat to take us out for the day for E850 (lunch included). I persuaded her that a E100 self-drive boat would be more fun. We went to the beach and got in a nice white 510. Four first stop was Tsougaris, where we went for a nice swim and snorkel and shared a bottle of Prosecco, which we managed to keep cool. We then headed to Arkos, which we were told had the best lunch. We ate nice tzaziki and sardines and drank beer. We snorkeled round the rocks and then headed off to another beach for another snorkel. We brought the boat back to the beach, and Lauren was told off for coming in the wrong way too fast, but it was still a fun and relatively cheap trip.

We went for the birthday dinner to the famous Windmill with famous prices, as it cost E173 (I didn't leave a tip). The kids had a cocktail each, and I tucked into a tomato bread bruschetta with prawns, chilli, and garlic, followed by risotto with asparagus, peas, spinach, and Parmesan, which was not bad. We all shared a Banoffi pie at the end. We drank a couple of bottles of E16 wine, but even with the stunning views, it seemed very expensive.

I got to do a waterski, which I always enjoyed, and was up first time and round the bay with no problems. We discovered the E3 boat ride back from the next beach and thought it was the only way to travel; at E6 for two, it was a lot cheaper than the E30 taxi.

We also discovered Ricchi and Poveri, which was number two on the Trip Advisor list. It was a tapas place owned by the man who also owned the tennis club. We had a lot of good food, including arancini, fried courgettes with tzaziki, samphire with walnuts, garlic bread, a smoked salmon risotto, and a vegetable risotto. We drank two bottles of a very nice organic rosé and had some very nice crème brûlée. It all cost E107, and we decided we would definitely be back.

I had another waterski and a perfect day on the beach. Lauren and Matt decided they wanted to go off on their quad bike for a romantic dinner at Kanapista. Chrissie and I returned to Stamatis and had a perfect Greek dinner. We had to have two cocktails first, as they were full. We shared fried courgettes and tzaziki; I had moussaka in a clay pot, and Chrissie had shrimp and cheese in her clay pot. We drank a half-litre of house red, and it all cost E36.90 for a great night.

For our last night, we returned to Ricchi and Poveri. We ate some of our favourites and added smoked turkey and blue cheese croquettes and prawns in batter, with a sweet chilli sauce. Nancy was our lovely waitress, and at the end, we drank Matari, which is the Greek limoncello. Our bill was E113. This was a delightful restaurant with great food.

Would I like to come here again? Maybe. We had fun with the kids, ate well, did a little waterskiing and a lot of snorkelling, and the weather was fantastic. There must be something good to have been there ten times.

## September 2016

We then returned to Lindos on Rhodes for the sixth time. It had strong romantic memories, as Chrissie and I got engaged here in 1980. It took me a long time to ask her, but once I did, she had me married within six weeks.

The journey was better, as we flew Thomson at around midday from Exeter. We were on a package holiday. We had to book two aisle seats, as they would not allow us a centre and an aisle. We had to wait ages for our luggage, and then we boarded the bus and had to wait further. We were dropped off at Eleni's and walked about a mile into town, by which time it was nearly 10 p.m. We remembered Mavrikos in the square, which used to do the best fillet steak with béarnaise, and got a nice smoking table (actually, all the tables were smoking). We had a very nice Greek dinner, sharing tzaziki and courgettes with an anchovy sauce, and both had a very good moussaka. Drinking a 2012 Pelopenese wine at E24, it all came to E61, which was great for such a nice dinner.

We were back in heaven and didn't wake up until 11.15; we got to the glorious beach by 1.15. We enjoyed the 80 degree sunshine and swimming in the warm water and had a fruit salad lunch in the beach bar.

We found Socrates Bar, which had moved, and had a nice pina colada each. We found out that Socrates died three years ago, drinking ouzo. We had to go to dinner at Hermes, which was our engagement venue, and had a nice view of the Acropolis. We shared tzaziki and prawns in garlic butter, and I had an odd fillet steak with very runny béarnaise sauce; Chrissie had spit roast chicken and chips. We drank a bottle of Chander de Rhodes, and it all cost E58; it all felt a little ordinary, but it was so nice to revisit the old romantic haunts.

We had another day on the beach and went back to Socrates; we looked at all the pictures on the wall but couldn't find ourselves. No free drinks then. We went to Maria's for dinner (which was not opened until 1982, after the engagement) and had a fine nonsmoking dinner (due to a stupid little kid at the next table): fried chickpeas and Lindian prawns (which were very small and you ate the shells) to start, followed by a 600-gram red snapper with roast potatoes and rice. We drank a E12.50 litre of the house red, and it all cost E63.

I spotted some waterskiing and thought I might have a go. In fact, I didn't and missed out for this holiday.

We went to a new restaurant, Olive Street, and had a great dinner. I had tuna tartare to start, followed by lobster pasta, and

Chrissie had a falafel of cod in batter with mashed potatoes. The baklava was a bit average, but the E27 Greek wine was very good. The service was absolutely charming, and it all cost E102, which was more than average but worth it.

And the next night, we returned to Mavrikos. I started with liver with chilli, garlic, and sweet wine, which was excellent, and Chrissie had artichokes a la Greque. I had veal ribs in a spicy sauce, which was a little dull, and Chrissie had lamb klefido. We drank a good bottle of E24 Rodos wine, and it all cost E72, for a very nice Greek dinner.

The next night was BBQ night at Eleni's. We had a good time and stayed up until after midnight, chatting to the pretty Vanessa from Leicester and her boyfriend and two gay girls from Yorkshire. We ate tzaziki, taramasalata, Greek salad, chicken, sausage, yuvi, souvlaki, and roast potatoes, and drank a lot, including raki (downed in one). The food bill was E30, and the drinks bill was E43 (even with a free glass of wine).

We had a good last dinner at Olive Street, after a margarita in Socrates. We ate chickpeas and fried cheese with courgette to start, and rack of lamb with mashed potatoes for me, and salmon for Chrissie. We drank a fine bottle of Ligari E30 wine, and it all cost about E100.

We went to the beach tavern for our last gavros lunch, and I had a nice goodbye cuddle with Alexandria. I cannot decide which I like better: Rhodes or Skiathos. They were both very good; I forgot how much I liked Greece. If we come to Lindos again, I think we'll stay in the town; we seemed to have done an awful lot of walking to the beach and to dinner every night (except BBQ night).

At the airport, we had to queue for ages and ages to check in, and the food on the plane back was not too great, but we had another wonderful holiday.

## November 2016

And then we went on our sixth holiday of the year. We flew Business to Madeira. BA were stupid and put me in row 3 and

Chrissie in row 8, but the man next to me agreed to move (which was very nice of him). As not driving, I had a couple of small bottles of champagne and an average chicken curry.

We took a E45 taxi ride and arrived at Quinta da Penha de Franca Mar in the centre of Funchal. We had a nice room with a terrace and a very good view of the sea and the swimming pool. We went for a long walk to try to find a beach but gave up and had a beer and Campari. We later saw the beach from a bus, and it was crap. In fact, if you like the beach, which we do, don't go to Madeira because there were basically no beaches.

We thought about going to the hotel restaurant for dinner, but it looked dull with no atmosphere, so we went to Casal da Penha, which was number eleven out of 509 restaurants in Funchal. Against the advice of our servers, we ordered a bottle of Madeira red, which was just about okay. I started with fish soup, and Chrissie had artichokes. I followed with Portuguese fish stew with clams, mussels, and fish, and Chrissie had a fish fillet with banana. We ended up with two glasses of house red and two free glasses of Madeira wine. It all cost E65 plus tip, which was not too bad a start.

We got in the big seven-foot bed and had a good sleep, followed by a middling breakfast. It was around 74 degrees and sunny, so we went to the pool due to the lack of a beach. I walked down some steps and into the sea, got scared by the strong currents, and retired to the pool for a longer swim. I had a nice sardine toastie and beer for lunch, and Chrissie had a ham and cheese toastie and Coke, and it all cost E14.

We had a good dinner at Dona Amelia. We shared cod rillettes and fish mousse, and I had calves liver Venetian style (with onions and pasta), and Chrissie had lobster gnocchi. We had a nice bottle of E19 Lisbon wine, and it all cost E60, for a very good dinner.

The next day, it was sunny until two o'clock; I spotted two oldish ladies going in the sea, and I felt better, even with the strong currents. I had a cheaper sardine sandwich for lunch, but the toastie was better. I finished Carly Simon's book, which did not uplift me; she even refused to say who 'You're So Vain' was about. Before this, I read Bruce Springsteen's book and had the same negative feeling.

We walked around a mile to Chris's Place, which was number one on Trip Advisor. We decided to eat the set menu. I started with a cheap but very good bean soup. Chrissie had the most expensive foie gras, of which I had a little taste, and it was delicious. I followed with another fish stew, which was very good. For dessert, we shared a panna cotta with passion fruit and a crème brûlée. We had a lot of nice red wine and a glass of white port at the end. This was all very nice, and the bill was E75.

It was a bit rainy in the morning, so we spent E15 each on the Red Bus trip, which took around ninety minutes to go round town with a commentary in your ears. We saw the market (which we visited later on foot and saw lots of good vegetables and fish), a lot of old buildings, and the village of Camara de Lobos (which was very pretty), and finally went past an awful-looking black beach with no chairs or umbrellas. After, we walked around town a bit and went to the Ritz for lunch: fish chowder and beer for me and a quiche and Coke for Chrissie; it was all a bit expensive at E25.

It was a sunny afternoon, and I had a good swim in the sea.

We went to Villa Cipriani and had a very nice dinner in beautiful surroundings. We really liked the tablecloth, and the service was great. We had nice homemade breadsticks and rosemary bread and ordered a bottle of E32 Duoro (although there was a selection at E21). The wine was very nice, and so was the food. We shared a fish starter with scallop, mussels, squid, and a white fish with tomato and a cucumber relish; it was very good. I had linguini with lobster sauce and prawns, which was excellent, and Chrissie had a starter canneloni with chicken, which suited her fine. It all cost E92, which was the most expensive but all very nice.

We had a good day swimming in the sea and a sardine toastie for lunch. We returned for dinner at Dona Amelia and shared the foie gras, salad, and marinated fish. I had calves liver Lyonnaise style, which I preferred, and Chrissie had a veal escalope. We drank another good bottle of E19 wine, and a good dinner only cost E56.

We decided to be brave and went up the cable car. It took nineteen minutes, and you got very good views. We paid extra to go in the botanical garden, which was supposed to be one of the best thirteen in the world, but in reality, it did not really impress. The orchid season was December to May, and we only saw a couple. We paid E5 to get the trolley back and saved a long uphill walk. We had lunch on a quay, watching Fred Olsen dock.

For dinner, we went into town to Armazem do Sal. We had nice food but hated the restaurant. They got our reservation wrong, and we had to sit right next to the one-man band playing 'Stairway to Heaven.' The service was patchy; we got two free glasses of wine because they took too long, and the next tables had a loud man with a stupid moustache and two people from Aurora visiting Madeira, the Canaries, Cadiz, and Lisbon; glad we were not doing that trip. I started with mackerel sushimi and lentils. Chrissie had shrimp soup. I followed with black scabbard, caught at a thousand metres deep, with Nero risotto, and Chrissie duck with a duck samosa. We ordered a bottle of 2011 Sicila but were given 2015. It was all very nice and cost E74.50; we didn't leave a tip.

After a normal pool day, we went for a margarita and kir royale in Joe's Bar and then came back to Chris's Place. The free glass of bubbly was a nice start; we had a black scabbard amuse bouche. We both had the rather good foie gras. I had a steak, nice and rare, and Chrissie had asparagus risotto with smoked sea bass. For dessert, we had a crème brûlée and a chocolate fondant. We drank a lot of red wine and the white port, and it was E75 again. We booked again for our anniversary and staggered home.

The next day, we went on the half-day Jeep excursion (with the roof down for most of the way, before it rained in the hills). We had another look at Camara da Lobos and were told that Churchill painted here. Next, we went to a three-hundred-metre cliff, which was pretty scary. Then we went off-road and smelled the eucalyptus and ended up at a nice cafe. I had the local speciality, Pancha, which was rum with lemon and orange juice and honey; it was very nice. Chrissie had a local cherry liqueur, which was also quite good. Then, we went to a thousand-metre view of a misty valley and then back. We saw everything growing: bananas, sugar cane, grapevines, cherries, and chestnuts. It was all very nice but on the whole a bit dull.

We had dinner at Villa Cipriani again. We both started with a lovely artichoke soup, and then I had the calves liver Venetian style, with pureed potatoes, served pink and very excellent. Chrissie had the starter ravioli. We drank a nice bottle of E21.50 Duoro, and this time, it only cost E91.50. We decided that we liked it so much to book for our anniversary, so we were now double-booked.

It was very sunny the next day, and we had breakfast outside again. We had another day round the pool, with only one swim in the sea, as the tide was too high, and for a change, fish soup for lunch. We went back to Dona Amelia for the third time, and this time it felt a little dull. I had crab soup and lobster taglioni, which was fine, and Chrissie had duck liver pate and seafood risotto. With our normal bottle of E19 wine, it was our most expensive here, at E67, but still a good value.

The next night, we got in a taxi and took the E6 ride to Heronca Red, which was recommended by the Jeep man; it was where all the taxi drivers went. I started with very good clams, and Chrissie had acada soup, which was vegetables and egg. We then shared a 640-gram Pargo fish, which was very excellent and served with a very nice selection of vegetables. We shared a sort of waffle dessert; with a bottle of red wine, it all came to a very reasonable E47, but with the taxi fares, we were over E60 again.

It was our thirty-sixth anniversary. That morning, we walked into town and got the *Telegraph* for the crossword on the journey home and bought some chestnuts, which were delicious. I had three more swims, which brought my total for the year to 250. On average, I swam about five hundred metres, which meant I had swum 125 kilometres (or thereabouts) this year.

We went to Joe's Bar for kir royale and then onto Villa Cipriani for our chosen dinner. We were greeted by name by the attractive lady maitre d' and shown to our usual very nice table. We were glad we were there. We shared starters and had an excellent Parmesan flan, which was simply delicious, and sweet potato gnocchi with mushrooms and cheese, which again was great. I had the pink calves liver with the lovely potato puree, and Chrissie had a starter portion of the pigeon risotto. We drank the E31.50 wine and considered dessert, but I just had a limoncello. It cost E115 plus tip for a lovely, lovely dinner. I loved Italy and really loved this restaurant.

Home for a little backgammon; I won the tournament, 15-12.

It was time to go home. The weather was pretty good, and we had some very nice dinners. Our impression of Madeira was that it was pretty dull on the whole; I did not think we will return.

# February 2017

And now for something completely different: We had done one boat trip, from New York to Southampton on the *Queen Mary 2*, but then we went on a cruise in the Caribbean.

We went on the Thomson *Dream* and started off at the Thomson check-in at Gatwick, but we didn't have to queue, as we had paid extra (about £350 each) for Premium Class. They explained that our cases would be delivered to our cabin, which was great. We got on the much-praised Dreamliner at 9.15, declining the sparkling wine. We found the Dreamliner no different from any other aircraft; the seating was just like being in BA Premium Economy. We had a tomato juice, as still too early for alcohol. We missed out on the spinach and ricotta canneloni, which was all gone, and settled for coconut chicken curry, and then it was time for a Stella Artois. During the ten-hour flight, I watched the AbFab movie, *Fawlty Towers,* and a few boring others, and we landed in Jamaica. I couldn't have a cigarette, as we got straight off the plane and into a coach and to the boat. Jamaica looked quite interesting.

We had a pina colada on the eighth deck (smoking) and went to the Orion's restaurant for waiter-service dinner. We bought a £14.95 bottle of Venetian cabernet sauvignon from a nice Serbian girl, and both ate seafood gratinee, which was quite good. I had tagliatelle Neapolitan, which was pretty dull, and Chrissie Coq au vin, which she said was not that great. We went back to Deck 8 for ciggies before 10 p.m. bedtime (three in the morning, English time). We managed to sleep until eight, which was pretty good. The breakfast was okay, with OJ, yoghurt, fruit, and coffee.

We managed to find a sunbed, which was good, as there were only about four hundred or so for the fifteen hundred people on board, and then went off to the Showhall to be bored by their expensive excursions (we decided to not buy anything, although we already bought the Hemingway tour in Havana). We returned to find our things had gone to Reception, as there was a forty-five-minute limit for the sunbeds. We had not been told; we had just gone to their stupid presentation, and so we had to sit in chairs for the rest of the day. We had nice pea and courgette soup for lunch, but why did the duty-free Becks beer cost £3.70?

We had a gin martini and pina colada and then went off to the captain's reception, where we got a glass and a half of cava. We elected to go to Kora La, a Chinese/Indian restaurant, and paid an extra £38 (plus £18 for wine). We ate chicken satay and vegetable samosas; I had a prawn vindaloo (which was not that hot), and a poor chicken kashmiri for Chrissie; we won't bother coming here again, as all too dull.

We arrived in Cuba at midday, and by 12.30, we had lunched and were off the boat. We got onto a bus for a thirty-minute ride to Hemingway's house. There was very little traffic on the road, although quite a lot of 1950s American cars, which were fun to see. Hemingway's house was on top of a hill on five-hectare estate, which he bought from a Frenchman in 1940 for £18,000. The house was gorgeous, with great light, and you could look in all the rooms from outside. The views of Havana were stunning. We went to the Terrace Bar at Coglan, which was a favourite Hemingway haunt by the sea and were given a Gregorno cocktail, which was blue and delicious. We went back to Havana and passed the Floridita restaurant, where they invented the daiquiri and which was one of Hemingway's favourites. We walked through the streets for about a mile and booked a table for dinner, and then we bought three cigars. Thinking about it, we felt the Floridita was too touristy and found the Floridan, established in 1855, and booked dinner there, instead. Havana was lovely and full of old magnificent buildings.

It was the Floridan for dinner. We started off with a daiquiri at the bar. There were not many diners, but I had a magnificent black bean soup, and Chrissie the largest shrimp cocktail ever. I followed with grilled lobster, prawns, and red snapper, and Chrissie chicken with tropical fruits, which was all delicious. We drank a bottle of Chilean merlot at $25, and it all cost $64 plus tip, which means about £64 all up, for a great dinner. We walked to a square surrounded by beautiful buildings for a pina colada and Monte Cristo cigar; I liked it there.

The ship left after lunch, so we came ashore pretty early. We had intended to take the $20 (for two) open-top bus tour, but then I thought, why not go for a ride in an old car? We got off the boat and were approached by Franklin Sosa, who showed us a picture of an old Chevy and said it cost $40 for a one-hour trip. We followed him into the back streets and met his son and saw the 1954 Chevy convertible, which was not gleaming, but off we went. We drove under the river and visited the Jesus statue, which was impressive, and looked at Che Guevera's house and went to Revolutionary Square; after ninety minutes and $40, we went back to the ship. The ride in the Chevy was truly wonderful.

Cuba was a brilliant experience; Old Havana was so wonderful, and most of all, every Cuban we met was been just lovely. What a great place.

That night we had a Bloody Mary on Deck 8 before Orion's. We both had smoked salmon and classic fish and chips and the Venetian cabernet sauvignon, which was not too bad.

Our next stop was Cozumel in Mexico. I had been to Mexico a few times and loved the place. I researched on Trip Advisor, which drew me to the Playa Azul Golf Spa (should have been put off by the 'golf '). We found a taxi; the driver said it was $12 to get us there, but it cost $20, as he had no change. We hated the place and walked up the beach to Buccannos and paid $30 for two beach chairs. The swimming wasn't very good, as the water was rough, and there were a lot of rocks. For lunch, we had to have Sol beer, as they didn't have any Pacifico, and we ate lobster tostata and chips, which are too dry even with salsa, and it cost $32: an expensive day at the beach, compared to Omega Beach in Cabo, and not nearly so nice. There were no taxis to get back, so we walked to the road and got a lift from two nice ladies from Kansas. They recommended Pepe's for dinner, and we booked a table for dinner that night. This would be the last time we had dinner off the boat.

It was nice to go into town for dinner, but Pepe's was not really that great. We started with a nice margarita and then shared three tapas. The best was the sashimi tuna carpaccio, but the tuna tartare and artichoke and spinach dip were dull. I ate softshell stone crab tempura with mash, and Chrissie had lobster pancakes, which again we found a bit dull. We drank a $23 Mexican merlot, and it all cost $75. We saw some people we knew from the boat in a bar and stopped for a beer and got back to the boat by 10.15 (against the 10.30 curfew). I loved Mexico, but Cozumel seemed like a tourist trap and lacked the smiles that you always found in the country.

And the next day, it was Grand Cayman. It only took ten minutes to get the tender, and we got a $5 ride in a minibus to Seven Mile Beach, where we paid $5 each for a bedchair. The beach and the water were fabulous, and I swam four times. We had a great lunch, with mahi mahi sandwiches and chips and Cayman beer from Caybrew. The people were all nice; this was a pretty good place, indeed.

I got my drinks bill for the first six days, which was £130: a lot better than paying £220 for the drinks package, where you only got house wine by the glass (I like my own bottle). We started having cocktails at 5 p.m. Dinner that night in Orion's was not much cop, with a really poor gazpacho and boring rigatoni with tomato and anchovy. There was a big fuss over the wine, and we eventually got a Nero D'Avola.

The next day at sea was boring, with terrible soups for lunch and a pretty poor dinner. I had the crab and prawn salad with one prawn (and I think crab sticks) and beef bourguignon, with tender meat.

Then we were back in Jamaica. We got on a $7 bus ride to the beach. Onboard was a truly obnoxious woman who spent thirty minutes trying to sell us the $25 city tour. We got off at the first beach, as we could not stand her. It was the family beach, and we paid $6 to get on. I had a swim, and we decided to stay and spent

$10 on bedchairs. Lunch was very good, with excellent jerk chicken, having a nice hint of spice, and chilli with beans and rice, and of course, Red Stripe beer.

I had five swims in all in the nice water, and even Chrissie enjoyed a swim. We had a nice taxi ride back with Raphael, who was good fun, but we didn't really like Jamaica. I talked to a couple of girls on the beach, who said they were scared and only went to the family beach; at night, they only went to the bar right next to their hotel. People on the ship who had spent their first week in Jamaica said they never left their hotel. Jamaica did not seem the Caribbean idyll.

We had had enough of Orion's, so we booked Mistral, the gourmet restaurant, which was only £17 extra each tonight. We had a good dinner: nice tomato and cheese amuse-bouche to start. I had gnocchi with cream pesto sauce, and Chrissie had the triple prawn cocktail. Next was orange sorbet. I had surf 'n' turf for the first time ever: good fillet steak with nice béarnaise sauce and very nice carrot and spinach flan. Chrissie had beef Rossini with foie gras, but her meat was tough. We had a good dessert, with the triple chocolate and crème brûlée. With a bottle of organic French cabernet sauvignon, it all cost £54.

We had a boring day at sea, but at least we got up early and bagged a bedchair. It was gala night again. We had a margarita and then went to the ballroom for two glasses of cava and the captain's speech. For dinner, we shared a table with an old (eighty-plus) farmer from Cumbria and his wife, who were not too bad. I ate Caribbean shrimp cocktail, French onion soup, and lobster tail, which was okay. Chrissie had poor lobster bisque, which reminded her of gravy, and then better roast duck. We drank a nice £20 bottle of Washington State Two Rivers merlot.

Costa Rica was our next stop; Thomson trips are so expensive. We got off the boat, and a man persuaded us that a $35 trip to a national park by the beach was much better than the local beach. He found two more people, and it went down to $30. We got in a minivan and after a while stop at a fruit stall, where for the first time, I tasted delicious water apples and lovely small bananas. After about forty-five minutes, we arrived and took a delightful walk about a mile through the rain forest by the beach; we saw sloths and monkeys and a lot of birds. We stopped at the beach, had a couple of swims, and went back for lunch at the Imperial. It was excellent; I had casados veggie with rice, beans, fried plantain, nice small pasta, tomatoes and cucumber.

Back to Limon; we took a walk around and went into a small cafe in the market; I had a nonalcoholic Tamarino, which was very nice. We went to a bar for a beer and met some nice girls (fifty-plus and seventy-plus) from Bristol. I find Solo are back to 0.51p on her phone.

We had dinner with the ladies from Bristol: moules mariniere was meagre but okay, and classic fish and chips again (which was quite good). We had a fairly good crepes Suzette and a bottle of the £14.95 Venetian cabernet sauvignon.

Then we went to Panama; the canal is eighty kilometres long and was started by the French in 1880, but they failed and turned it over to the Americans, who opened it in 1914. In 1977, President Carter signed an agreement to hand it back to Panama on 31 December 1999. In 2012, the millionth ship sailed through. It's not really a canal, as we understand it from the Canal du Midi or the Manchester Ship Canal, with only a little bit at the beginning and end and a huge manmade lake in the middle.

We paid £92 and expected a good trip. We got in a coach and went a short way to a lock. It was fascinating, and we saw two big ships go through. Two electric buggies keep each ship straight whilst it travels through the canal. We got back in the coach for ninety minutes and passed Panama City, which looked fantastic, and were taken over a causeway to an island on the Pacific, which was pretty dull. We managed to buy two muffins, as we were hungry. We got back on the bus and were given a grotty sandwich. Then we went to the train, which was old and uplifting. We took a lovely one-hour ride along the canal and back to base. Panama was full of large tenement blocks, which looked like slums, and when we got back to the boat, we didn't feel like exploring, so we retired to the ship for a beer.

## Mr. Tambourine Man

We left Panama two hours late; the sea was very rough, and it was difficult to get a cocktail on the smoking deck. We retired to dinner and got two boring people from Waltham Forest at our table. Dinner was quite nice, with Sicilian fried fish (squid, prawn, and something white) and aubergine Parmigiana and the normal bottle of Venetian cabernet sauvignon.

We next went to Cartagena, Colombia, South America. We got off the boat and met two people from Guildford to share a $20 taxi ride into town, but everybody wanted to sell tours. The town looked great, and we paid $25 each to go on the open-top bus and city walk. The drive round town was nice, and the walk was good. Cartagena was full of lovely old buildings and nice squares. We were taken to an emerald shop (60 percent of emeralds in the world come from Colombia) and saw a nice pendant for $4,800 (negotiable) and then to the Gold Museum, where we saw some fantastic pieces from the Zenu, dating from 500 BC. We got back to the dock and had a brilliant Cuba libre and took pictures of parrots and flamingos. Colombia was great; the people were very nice, and it felt safe.

We had dinner with the nice people from Guildford we shared a taxi with. I had very odd pea soup, salt cod fritters, and spag bols, which was just about okay, with the Venetian cabernet sauvignon.

We then went to Santa Marta, and I complained about the Beach Day, which cost £49 each. The brochure showed a beautiful palm-fringed beach, but we were taken to a long concrete strip to a horrid hotel, where you couldn't go on the beach except to swim because of the hawkers; it just felt like being in prison. We missed the welcome drink. The lunch was disgusting; Chrissie only ate carrots, and I had rice and beans. We demanded our money back. On the way back, we noticed that all the houses in Santa Marta had heavy fencing and barred windows; it looked pretty uninteresting, so we just went back to the boat. It was too rough.

We had a nice martini in the Explorers Lounge (but no smoking) and then went to Mistral again. I had an average gazpacho, average beef carpaccio, and average three pasta (of which the linguini with lobster was best). We also had a nice bottle of the organic French cabernet sauvignon. Then we got a glass of prosecco and went to see a show about Africa. It was so dull, I fell asleep.

We had another dull day at sea, with a Cornish pasty for lunch which was only okay. We had dinner with our friends from Bristol, but they were drunk from the wine tasting and didn't make much sense. Dinner again was only okay, with smoked salmon mousseline, duck salad with a raspberry vinaigrette, and linguine with pancetta, tomato, and basil. We drank the normal Venetian cabernet sauvignon.

We returned to Jamaica, and because we didn't like it that much last time, we sunbathed on the boat, had a hot dog for lunch, and then caught the bus to the airport, for the plane ride home.

Cruising? I'm not sure that I'm really suited to the experience. Our cabin was very nice, and the boy who looked after us was superb. I did not like many of the people on the boat. There were not enough sunbeds. The excursions were too expensive, and as we found in Santa Marta, they can be terrible. We went to some fantastic places: Cuba was the highlight, but I also really enjoyed the Cayman Islands, Costa Rica, Cartagena, and Panama. Somehow, spending just a few hours in a place was not long enough.

Food is my passion. My favourite dinners were ashore, which we were only able to do twice. We paid extra three times, and it was not too bad. We ate in Orion's nine times; I did not really like the people we were forced to share tables with, and the food was only okay. It had none of the joy of going out to a restaurant.

It may be a long time before we go on a cruise again.

# April 2017

The first book was first published in 2017 after the Caribbean Cruise but we did not stop travelling and here the story resumes.

We started our trip to Lisbon in the Hotel du Vin in Henley on Thames. A very nice dinner with Pimms, Prawns, Sea Trout and a £38 bottle of Argentine Malbec Cantena and the whole thing came to £112 which was okay as we didn't pay for parking just used the street. Nice walk around town and discovered an amazing bookshop. A first edition of Ian Fleming's Dr No is on sale for £750. We don't buy but later I am going to get it for my Birthday. Always a great read and one of my favourite films too. Much later for my 68th birthday I am going to get an autographed picture of Ursula Andress in her Dr No bikini and an autographed Fifth Draft Screenplay for the movie from my daughter.

We have an okay flight to Lisbon in Club Europe with champagne but the marvellous afternoon tea has been replaced with a 3 course meal which is stupid.

It is hot and sunny in Lisbon and around 80 degrees which is hot for this time of year. Good Portugese dinner on the first night at Casa da Comuda which is a 10 minute walk from our hotel.

For our second dinner we go to Banca da Pua which is the number 7 restaurant out of 3,600 on Trip Advisor. The food is fantastic and the raspberry vinigarette is the highlight.

The next day we decide to take the train to Estoril. It is a huge disappointment and my advice would be not to bother.

Another great dinner at Casa da Comuda with a wonderful Partridge Vignette for starters followed by the best ever Carre D'Agneau with stuffed aubergines. Euro105 for this dinner.

The next day we spend sitting around the very nice pool in the sunshine. 3 swims. We find a nice place for lunch at Leitaria and their custard tarts are brilliant.

Dinner at Casa da Praia which has the perfect tapas. Foie Gras, Black Mountain Ham, Crispy Confit of Duck and home made Chocolate Mousse. With a E14 bottle of local wine it only costs E53. Isabella is a wonderful waitress.

Another day in the sunshine around the pool followed by a great dinner at Red Fabrica in a nice old building. Great atmosphere to go with the lovely Serrana Ham and Seafood Cataplana and it only cost E54.

This has been a nice short break and the weather has been excellent. We have eaten very well indeed and it has not been too expensive. However, apart from the food and weather I do not really feel that Lisbon has a great deal to offer.

# June 2017

We are back to Sicily again. This time we are staying in a seaside town near Palermo, Mondello.

This time we are here for 18 days and it is sunny all the time with the temperature up to around 90 degrees. It is another beach holiday and I make the most of the sea with 83 swims.

The highlight of the holiday is our bus trip to Palermo. We get the 806 at about 5.30 at a cost of E1.40 each and arrive in the big city just after 6pm. Had a nice beer in a local café but its time to find the street food. We have a sort of map and make our way to the designated area but there is no sign of street food. After a while we talk to some people. 'where is the street food' answer 'it only happens at lunchtime'. We take a further stroll and end up in a lonely square Carlo V. Dinner is in a lovely restaurant and we have a good bottle of Etna Rosso at E26 and start with marinated prawns followed by Tagliari with Bottega and Lemon Zest which is wonderful. It all costs E74.

We get to the bus stop at 10.25 for the last bus at 10.30. But we wait and wait and there is no bus. Lots of agitated people including me. After an hour at about 11.30 a bus eventually arrives but takes the long way home which takes about another hour. It has been an interesting trip but I do not think I will be rushing back to Palermo despite the excellent dinner.

Now it is time to write about our other dinners.

The first night we go just down the road and have quite a good but expensive E89 dinner. Swordfish Carpacio and fried Baby Squid to start followed by a Grouper salad with a E20 bottle of Etna Rosso.

For the second night we book Badalamenti which is number 1 on Trip Advisor. We get completely lost trying to find it and had to ask three people. But we are here and have

Delicious Stuffed Courgette Flowers
Lovely Courgette Timbali with potato
Taglione with whole prawns and truffle
Nero D'Avola 2012 at E24

## Mr. Tambourine Man

And it all costs E89. About the same as first night but much better.

For the third night we have dinner at Antica Friggalerina which is where we normally have our aperitifs and play backgammon. We start with the Sicilian plate which has Caponata, Fried Chickpea and very good potato and mint croquettes followed by Linguine with Clams. It is all lovely and the food is only E34 plus E10 for a litre of red wine and E10 for cocktails. A steal.

For the next night we go to Bye Bye Blues which is around a 1 mile walk and the only Michelin restaurant in Palermo. We had to ring a bell to get in. The food is only okay and it all costs E123. I don't think we will be returning as it sort of lacks the atmosphere of the real Sicily.

Next night back to Badalamenti but did not enjoy it so much.

Then it is Palermo as above and the next night back to Antica and then back for a third time to Badalamenti which seems better this time but we do spend E104.

The next dinner is at a terrible place called Sapori where the food is not very good and we negotiate a E73 bill down to E60 but will never go there again.

But we are now going to discover Clelia, a walk up the hill run by two delightful sisters. We start with the raw fish which has to be eaten in the right order. Swordfish Carpaccio, Tuna Tartare, Squid ink salad, Marinated Red Prawns, another Tartare yellowfin tuna and prawn. I followed with Spaghetti with St Pierre and courgette. A good bottle of Montino d'Avola 2013 at E23 and it all came to a reasonable E84. Liked it so much have booked for my birthday.

Back to Antica for the third time and now winning backgammon 23-14.

We next discover Piero's down on the front. Delicious Clam Soup to start followed by a lovely pasta with prawns, clams and courgettes and house wine and it is a true bargain at E36 but we have to pay cash.

I am now 65 years old and enjoying my first edition of Dr No and a new second hand Tag Hauer watch. And we have a great dinner at Clelia. The raw fish starter , of course, followed by Spaghetti with

Sardine and courgette. We get Lemoncello on the house and it is E86.

Next night is back to Piero's for the Clam soup and Bravette with prawns, clams and breadcrumbs. All very good for E40.

For our last night we return to Clelia for more raw fish and Spaghetti this time with Bottaga and Pistachio Pesto. I have had three Spaghettis here and I simply do not know which is the best. Cost E84.

I do not think Mondello is my favourite place in Sicily but with a couple of exceptions we have eaten so well here and had a great time.

## September 2017 Sardinia

Away again. But not a good start. Chrissie is driving the car near Okehampton and we are hit by a huge stone which smashes the passenger side of the windscreen. Slow drive up the M5 and M4 to Heathrow. And for Chrissie it gets worse because her case does not arrive at the resort. It eventually turns up around midnight. The joys of travel.

We are here on our second Nielsen holiday to play tennis and maybe windsurf.

The tennis does not start off too well as it keeps raining and I just seem to have forgotten how to windsurf.

And we did not think so much of the food. I would probably give it 4.5 but I suspect Gordon Ramsay would only give it 3. We do however have quite a nice bungalow with a good terrace.

For our first night out we take 30 minute walk to Shardana and have an okay Tuna Tartare and Sardine Pasta dinner for E60.

And now we have a Mistral which means we can't go in the sea and have to swim in the pool but do manage squad and social tennis.

The food is only scoring 4 now and the sea remains closed and we think we came last in the quiz with only 20/50 but at least the tennis is good.

But we are luck as it is now a night out and we take the bus to quite a nice town San Teodoro where we start with an Americano and a Bellini and lovely nibbles for E16. Then to dinner in the garden at Da Fabio. It is all very pleasant and we share carpaccio of Swordfish and I have lovely Linguine with one-half lobster. We drink a E25 bottle of local wine and it all comes to E78. A very nice evening out and good food for a change.

We were supposed to eat in at the hotel the next night but instead we walk to Hotel Pedra Nieddaand have a very good raw fish and pasta dinner with a E9 bottle of local red all for E47. Good to go out again.

Today is the Tennis Tournament. Chrissie plays very well and loses in the final of the Blue/Green group. I also play very well and win the final of the Black/Red group. I always like to win but only got a paper certificate not the millions for a grand slam winner.

Another bus trip to Budoni this night. After Campari and Prosecco we find a really nice restaurant Mamas. We share a nice Sardinian plate and then have a delicious Crayfish Risotto with a nice E20 Sardinian wine. E86 all up.

We are staying for a second week and I go to Beginners Windsurfing. There were 70 people there so I just walked away. Looks like windsurfing is going to be off this holiday.

Poor dinner. Roast Pork but no Apple Sauce and served with a choice of rice or chips. It is just not good enough.

But not to worry as we now get to the highlight of our visit. A trip in taxi (E35 there and E50 back for 6 of us) to Agro Tourista place Muru Idda.

We sit in an old farmhose and have a 9 course dinner.
Home made bread, ham , salami and olives to start.
Courgette Croquette, yummy Liver and Ricotta
Cheese and Vegetable Lasagne
Gnocchi with tomato sauce made by Mama.
Ravioli with a different Mama Tomato sauce
Lamb with roast potatoes.
Time to a ciggie break and we watch the 25 day pork being spit roasted along with a glass of sweet wine.
Wonderful Roast Pork
Water Melon.

And all this with as much red or white wine as you can drink. To finish we have Limoncello and Grappa. The cost is only E35 each and it is completely wonderful.

Everyday I play tennis and swim a little but I don't really need to tell you that. For something different we opted for a free 20 minute Catamaran ride. We hated it and came back after 5 minutes.

Thought about going out for dinner. Wrong decision as stayed in and had another poor dinner but did a little better at quiz night.

But then next night we go to San Theodore again on the bus. Ended up having nice dinner at Disizos Sardos. Grilled Cheese with honey. Ravioli with cheese and truffles and a bottle of house wine for E68 cash. Only E3 cash left so quick visit to ATM.

An evening visit to Porto Ottioulu which is really a bit dull. We had booked a table at Il Colle but discover it is a 2 mile walk so go to La Riscacca. We eat and drink well with a litre of house wine, Potato Gnocchi, Bottaga, Crab claws and Lobster and chips all for E50.

The wind has died down and we can swim in the sea again which is a pleasure. But I miss the tennis final by 1 point.

It has been quite a nice two weeks here apart from the food in the hotel. The Agro Tourista dinner was quite special and other eating out was also enjoyable. I had 33 games of tennis (Chrissie only 21) and I had 24 swims.

## October 2017 Languedoc

We have taken a Ryanair flight to Perpignan and Europcar have given us a Hyundai i10 which I do not really like for a 120 kilometre drive to Angeles sur Mer. We have made a mistake with the hotel which seems very remote.

The first night we eat in their restaurant Bistro de la Mare. It is not that great and we pay E121 for 2 glasses champagne, foie gras and poor tornedo and duck breast and a couple of average desserts with a bottle of local D'Amour wine.

The weather is nice and the first day I go for a couple of swims in the sea which is only about 18 degrees.

We go for dinner by car in the local port. Le Petite Restaurant where we spend E58 on a Chickpea Mousseline, Fillet of Dorado and Baked apple with a bottle of house wine.

The weather turns cloudy so we decide to head off to Spain which is only 25 kilometres away.

We go to a place called Colera which is a bit of a dump. Then to Portbou where it is difficult to park. We buy loads of cheap cigarettes and look for a restaurant with Spanish Omlette. Not to be found and we end up in Brasserie Amethyste and have seafood gratin and rose for lunch.

Back to Le Petite Restaurant for dinner. Same price at E58 but I have Tete a Veau for main course which is very tasty. We are to go here once more together with an okay restaurant called L'Escole and a Vietnamese restaurant for an interesting E38 dinner when everything else seemed to be closed except the pizza places.

I think I did 9 swims on this holiday. Overall impression. Hooray going home. This is not the place for us. In France Cote D'Azur is a much better place to go and the food is much better in Italy.

## November 2017 Seychelles

It is now time for our sixth trip this year and we are flying Emirates Economy via Dubai. It takes nearly 7 hours to Dubai and we are lucky that we get three seats for two. Food is reasonable and when we get to Dubai we can smoke by Gate 7B in our 1 hour 45 minute layover for the 4 hour flight to the Seychelles.

We take a E50 taxi ride with Felix to the Beach House. There is a very nice sea view but the sea looks a little rough. But it is time for a 3 hour sleep.

We get up and explore our surroundings between the showers which are pretty heavy. Manage a swim but the sea seems very shallow.

Our first night dinner is at Pizzeria DaoDab. Need to wait 5 minutes for a table good food Spaghetti and Clams and Fish and Chips and a litre of red wine for £38.

It is a lovely sunny day for our 37th wedding anniversary and we walk about 5 minutes and find a deserted beach all to ourselves and I do 5 swims.

The Anniverary dinner is Street Food. 2 Pina Coladas sitting on the wall . Vegetable Spring Rolls) Dahl Curry in a wrap, Ruby Snapper with sauce and rice (it was all fantastic). More Pina Colada. Total cost around £20. A different way to celebrate.

Another day on the beach with lots of swims but some horrible kids took our spot so we had to go elsewhere. We have an excellent dinner just a short walk down the road at La Plage. I had a wonderful Tuna Carpaccio and Creole Octopus Curry. Chrissie Smoked Fish Mousse and Creole Tuna Balls and with a good wine it all came to around £95.

Next night its back to the Pizzeria for Spaghetti and Pizza and a litre of red wine for £35.

Its Chrissie birthday. We have a lovely lunch at La Plage with free Prosecco. Swordfish Satay with a mango salsa for me and Croque Monsieur for Chrissie. But now its time to go on our 7 day boat trip around the islands. Seem to be a lot of French but thankfully no Germans and haven't spotted any English. It is pretty rough and I am seasick. We go on deck to get an aperitif and Chrissie has her turn to be seasick. Not so great for the birthday girl.

We settle down with a Cuba Libre each and enjoy a reasonable dinner with Tuna Sashimi, Creole Soup and Job Fish (there is a beef choice). Nice desserts with good ice cream. We have a bottle of Sancerre Rouge at E56. The wine list starts at around E22. We meet some English who are good company. Bill and Sue 75 year olds from Suffolk and Tony a retired Engineer who is on his own.

After an okay breakfast we get in the small boats to go to Curieuse which is the fifth largest island with no inhabitants except the Giant Tortoises and their babies who are just lovely. We take a 1.7 kilometre walk to another beach through the mangrove swamps. It is very tranquil and has a calming feeling. Have a good BBQ lunch and three swims. First impressions - quite like the boat, nice staff, nice English people, think it will be okay.

That is until a bad dinner where we have to sit with French girls who ignored us and the Bouliabasse was quite poor.

Curiouser and coriouser. We are still at Curieuse due to force 8 winds and are going to miss the trip to Cousin to see the birds. So back to the same island for a couple of swims.

So today is the day of Grand Anse on Praslin. We do not take the E80 each tour but wait for a bus for 45 minutes and eventually get a taxi for £5 for the 5 kilometre trip. Grand Anse looks interesting on the map but actually its not with lots of seaweed and shallow water. We leave and negotiate a taxi ride back to St Anne. Nice café for a Papaya and Lime Smoothie. Supposed to go to Felicite but too rough. We go to the leeward side of La Digue for Petit Anse but its too rough here so we go to another beach and just about manage to land but sea is too rough for swimming. We have better company with the English at dinner but the food (Prawn Salad, Tomato Soup and Dorade) is a little dull. My diary says 'Still looking for the magic'.

We were supposed to go to La Digue today but instead we headed to Cousin. A few people went to the island but for us it looked too difficult so I read Daphne du Maurier on the sun deck. We are now back at Curieuse again. We had a nice snorkel on a reef in mid afternoon.

And we have paid E65 each to go on the La Digue trip which seems rather like La Dull. We waited ages for the boat to take us to the port and then went on an open sided truck for a short tour. We went to a place making Coconut oil and then looked at Platatic house which we later discover is Emmanuele's house which not at all what I remember. To the beach which was Source D'Argent which is supposed to be a very photographed beach for some snorkelling and saw 300/400 fish the largest of which about 10 inches and looked like a ray.

Packed lunch was awful.

Dinner not too bad with Smoked Marlin, Coconut and Ginger Soup and Roast Pork.

We are getting towards our last day on the boat. We go to Mayenne island which is very nice. You can see Mahe in the distance and the bay is lovely. I like this bit of the Seychelles and so glad not staying in Praslin or La Digue. Did a bit of snorkelling and saw about 300 fish.

Last night dinner okay but the entertainment is good. I did a waltz with Hilda a lovely Seychelles girl and did a poor limbo and lots of dances with Chrissie.

The boat bill is E623 including E130 for the trip so we have spent around E70 per day on booze. I am looking forward to getting off the boat and getting internet again. I do not think that I am cut out for cruising. This boat is small and much better than the larger versions but I prefer land and I like going to restaurants rather than just being served the usually dull boat menu de jour.

A E25 ride back to The Beach House. Our room is not so nice but we still have a terrace with a sea view. We thought we were going to have Street Food but only 2 stalls so we go to the Indian and have average food for unaverage £70 which is too expensive.

We are on the beach and misjudge the clouds and get soaked. But still a lovely dinner at La Plage. Seared Sesame Tuna with wasabi and pickled ginger for me and Goats Cheese Tart for Chrissie. Then £40 Rock Lobster and chips for me and cheaper Job Fish with Mussel Veloutte for Chrissie. Limoncello on the house and £110 all up.

The next day is cloudy and spend all day reading. We try Famous Retro for dinner and have an argument over the bill and get 20% off. Don't bother.

And we have now spent the best E45 ever for a great day in a Hyundai from Exoticar. The man in the General Store next door has given us a map of where to go. We take the road to Victoria and turn right just after Hertz to get on the mountain road Sans Souli and end up at Port Launey which is a beautiful bay. Nice snorkel on the reef. The bay is dominated by hotels which have expensive sandwiches so we go a little way back to Del Place and have a great lunch with Tuna Tartare and Croque Monsieur and two Seybrew. R530 and worth it. We drive along the coast and stop at a couple of beaches, then Intendence with a car park full of puddles. We end up at Anse Royal and have a calm swim. Back past the airport and then into Victoria rush hour which does not really compare with London. A nice trip out.

To celebrate we have dinner at La Plage again. Tuna Sushimi with wasabi and pickled ginger and Seafood Linguine. Cheaper than Lobster night.

After yesterday it doesn't seem so much fun and the street food is somehow lacking and we are back home by 9.

We have our last dinner at La Plage. Great dinner for £80 Fish Soup , Roast Pork with a Bell Fruit stuffed with Black Pudding for me and Seafood Chowder with a lemon air and a Fish Mousse starter for Chrissie.

The weather has been okay with 15/18 sunny days and temperatures around 86 degrees. I like the Seychelles but not in love and somehow doubt we will return. Beach House was very nice with terrace overlooking the sea, good breakfasts and nice hospitality. Boat only okay and probably not the best time of year for cruising but not sure it is my thing anyway. La Plage was an exceptional place for dinner four times and one lunch. I had some good snorkelling and ended up with 57 swims.

# February 2018 Cuba

We fell in love with Cuba when we visited on the Caribbean cruise and have decided to return.

We take the 9 plus hours flight to Havana with Virgin don't know if its better than BA.

But what is better is the ride from the airport in a 1950's Ford Hard Top - the only way to travel.

We are staying in the Floridian where we went for dinner in February last year. It is a wonderful building but a little tired around the edges and the restaurant is closed. We take a walk to O'Reillys and share a table with some Russians from New York. We have a Cuba Libra, 3 glasses of Red Wine, nice Fish Croquettes, boring Potato Bravas, and okay Grilled Shrimp and it all costs $40.

The next day is our guided tour of Havana. We have a wonderful trip in a 1952 beige Chevrolet Deluxe with a 6 litre V8 engine. Great city. We have a sandwich lunch and a couple of beers in a local restaurant for $12 and it is all very pleasant and then a Cuba Libra by 4.45 - essential.

We had the names of some restaurants and explored a little to find but they didn't appeal so we ended up in Esquina de Cuba which is easily going to get in the top 100 best places ever. It looks like a house and you go up a flight of stairs to the restaurant. We have a lovely table outside overlooking the street. The service is great and the crockery, cutlery and glassware are all lovely. It is a sort of set menu and I take the $20 Lobster option, Chrissie the $15 Chicken Frajitas. But first you get a Mojito and then Corn Soup, Fried Plantains, Black Beans, Green Salad, Dessert and Coffee. We also have 4 glasses of red wine. The food is completely wonderful and it all costs $51.

Breakfasts in the Floridian are dreadful. But its time to get exploring and we take a 3 hour 300 kilometre drive on fairly empty roads to Santa Clara. For the rest of the holiday we are staying in local houses. Our place here is lovely with a nice room and naturally nice people. We find a place for lunch with 2 Tuna sandwiches and two beers for $7.50. Then we take a $6 taxi ride in a 1950's Ford Fairline to see the Che Guevera memorial. It is a brilliant sculpture. We go back to town and sit in a park and go to Café de Revolution for a beer and coffee. The whole place is full of memorabilia and the revolution in January 1959. Che had a lot to do with it.

We have dinner at our house which is very good local fare and with a $8 bottle of Spanish wine it all costs $28.

Its now time to move onto Trinidad. This is our boutique house and it is very nice indeed.

We are recommended dinner at Ceiba which we liked a lot. We have a fruit plate and nice tomato and beetroot salad followed by a large Pork Chop with garlic infusion. With 4 glasses of red it costs $43.

We get up early to go on the 9am Bike Trip. Luckily it is a Bi

cycle Taxi and we do not have to pedal. We go to food store and learn about the rations and then to the railway station where there is a 1914 Locomotive and we go in the cab and pull the whistle. Next is a pottery where we have an excellent rum drink with honey and sugar.

Nice omlette lunch in the square for $10.90 with the necessary beers.

Tonight is a special night as we are having dinner in the house. The terrace is gorgeous and we have a beautiful table with fine English porcelain, silver cutlery and cut glasses. And the food is pretty good too. Cream of Vegetable Soup, Tomato salad with garlic and lemon dressing and then Lobster for me and Red Snapper for Chrissie. To drink we start with Cuba Libra and then 5 glasses of wine and a local beer for me. Cost a remarkable $41. This is in the top 100 too. Two so far.

We are leaving Trinidad to go to the beach. Our taxi doesn't come so we hire a local guy for $10. We are now by the sea in a nice house if perhaps a little remote.

We take a $10 taxi return to a beach about 3 kilometres away. Pay $1 for an umbrella and have 3 nice swims. Back to watch a beautiful sunset over the sea at about 6.10 pm.

Took a 15 minute walk into town and find a great cheap cheap diner La Boca. Sat at a table with some Canadians and ordered a cuba libra each. We have the $5 chicken with rice , black beans, potatoes and a tomato and cucumber salad and a bottle of Cuban wine followed by another couple of cuba libra. It is all very fine and only costs $25.

Another $10 taxi ride for a fine day at the beach with 4 swims. Dinner at the house. Cuba Libra to start , of course, very good Lobster Cocktail, Fish Fillet a la roca with shrimp and cheese but a little dull served with rice, salad and fried bananas. A $16 bottle of Chilean Cabernet Savignon and it all costs $51.

Another $10 taxi ride and today I snorkel in a natural pool which is very nice.

Good last dinner at La Boca and have a similar dinner for $23.

Pick up at 10 becomes 10.30 and after nearly 4 hours driving we are in Varadero. Nice house with a big room and only one block from the beach and close to lots of restaurants. We try unsuccessfully to get money from an ATM but its okay because we take a $7 taxi ride back in a 1956 Chevrolet Bel-Air Convertible which is the only way to travel. Check out the beach and the chairs are only $2.

First dinner is at Esquina Cuba which is all very fine. Cuba Libra, 2 glasses of Red Wine, Fried Fish, Shrimp and Lobster with the inevitable rice, black beans, potatoes and salad for $39.

Its around 82 degrees but very windy. I manage 3 swims in the morning but the afternoon sea is too rough. We then go and look at around 50 Harley Davidsons all pre 1959 and listen to a poor band.

Dinner at La Bodeguita in a nice setting. Excellent dinner with Cuban Soup, Fish Croquettes, Cajun Shrimp for me and Roast Pork for Chrissie with Cuba Libra and 2 glasses red wine all for $33 - very good value.

No umbrella today because of the wind but we put one of the chairs in the shade of the trees. I like the sun. 4 swims. Amazing dinner at Sabor Cubano. After Cuba Libra and Crystal beer we eat Pork with Yellow Rice for me and Chicken with normal rice and black beans for Chrissie. It only costs $13- a true bargain.

Normal windy day at the beach. An interesting night. We go to an Italian but it is shut Mondays. Queued a little while at a Cuban place but then decided to get 1953 pink Ford taxi to 60th Street for Varadero 60 but the driver said too expensive and no music so he took us to another closed place. We then take a 5 kilometre drive to Santa Marta and end up at La Fiesta del Carbon. As always we start with the Cuba Libra and Chrissie has a lovely Snapper and Lobster for me. Smoked a cigar to celebrate a great dinner. With 4 glasses Vino Tinto it is $73 here, our most expensive so far but worth it.

After another normal windy day we have a great dinner at La Vicaria. Cuba Libra to start, 2 glasses Vino Tinto and a brilliant Cuban Paella with Lobster for me and fried Chicken for Chrissie. And it only costs $18.85.

For breakfast we are given a Valentine's cake which is very fine. Later we have a glass of beer with our hosts to celebrate Valentines Day. Like all Cubans they are totally charming. We celebrate at one of our lunch places Vermissage. There are proper table cloths, linen napkins and a Valentines Set Menu but we need the phrase book to translate. As ever we start with Cuba Libra and eat a garlic chicken dish and spaghetti with prawns followed by a light chocolate tart. With 2 glasses Vino Tinto it is $48 for a fine evening.

Next night we take a $5 ride in a pink convertible 1950 Chevrolet to our host Illiana's favourite restaurant Varadero 60. We have to wait twenty minutes for a table drinking the obligatory Cuba Libra. The menu is a little European. I start with Shrimp Cerveche which is not as good as Sicily and have Spaghetti with Lobster and Shrimp for main. Chrissie Shrimp with Brandy. 4 glasses of Vino Tinto and smoked another cigar. $53 - not bad but not great.

It is quite difficult to get money but we take the $5 open top bus ride for 90 minutes. We go past all these large government hotels (the largest has 952 rooms). All the people look really bored and we are so glad to be staying in our lovely local house with lots of interest all around.

Dinner again at La Bodeguita. There is a signed Ernest Hemingway inscription for a Mojito so have to try it. Fantastic live music with an 8 minute version of Santana's Oya Como Va which costs me a $3 tip. For me a Chicken Casserole with Black Beans which is lovely and Seafood Paella with lobster for Chrissie. With 2 glasses of Vino Tinto each a true bargain at $35.

Second visit to Vicaro. For $22.85 we get Cuba Libra, Garlic Shrimp with Rice and Black Beans for me and another Paella for Chrissie and 3 glasses Vino Tinto. It cannot be beaten.

For our last night we return to La Bodeguita and are served by the lovely Annabella. Have to start with Mojito. We share a really nice Shrimp Cocktail and I have a rare Filet Mignon with Black Beans , Rice and Fried Bananas and Paella again for Chrissie. Forgot to record the tab but an excellent night.

Last swim before we leave to make 40 for the holiday.

Cuba has been great but I am not quite sure if I am in love - maybe. We have stayed in 4 nice casas with delightful people which is a true feature of this country. We have drunk a lot of Cuba Libra and eaten a lot of Lobster and had two dinners in the top 100. And generally it has been pretty cheap. To top it all we have had 7 rides in vintage cars. So overall, PRETTY GOOD.

## April 2018 Algarve

We are back in Prai da Luz again for tennis.

For our first night dinner we have to return to our favourite Portugese restaurant Olna Luz and have as ever the Fish Soup followed by a Lamb Stew with a bottle of Duoro and the free Port and it only costs E50.

We have a sunny 65 degree first day and get some tennis in. On the second day the weather is rainy and only around 55 degrees. We have a couple of days with showers and then the weather gets really nice with temperatures up to 72 degrees. In our 11 days here I end up playing tennis 15 times and have 7 swims in the pool. I failed in the tournament at the end of the week but feeling pretty healthy.

Talking about the food on this trip.

Second night Chitta's. Pretty good. Artesian Antipasta and Duck with a bottle of Duoro for E53.

Third night Olna Luz again. Gazpacho and shared very good Clam Cataplana with Chrissie. Duoro and free Port for E53.

Fourth night to Galios near the supermarket. Garlic Prawns followed by Piri Piri Chicken with a nice red wine for E43. And same place for fifth night with lovely soup and mackerel. Only E31.80 this time.

It is now celebration night and we eat with Lois the coach in the hotel. Octopus is very good but the Roast Pork and Potatoes is only okay. We drink a lot of wine.

Saturday night is back to Olna Luz. Fish Soup and a brilliant Monkfish Portugese style with prawns, mussels and clams and a chili rice. Nice wine and E57.

On Sunday we get in the car. BMW 1 Series Diesel which we paid extra E138 for at the airport. We are going to see my old friend John and his wife who I worked with at Vestey's. We are going to Val de Lobo and get terribly lost trying to find Julia's on the beach and arrive as they are finishing their starters. I have Avocado and Prawns and Sardines and just a beer to drink. It all feels very corporate and costs E66 which seems excessive.

On the way back we stop off at Quinta da Lago where my sister is going to buy a place. We hated it. It seems to have no soul or character and in the town centre there are 2 pubs, a Pizzeria and a Thai restaurant. Not Portugal and if you are living by the Golf Course you are going to have to drive everywhere.

We go home and walk to dinner at Booty's. Great dinner. Tuna and Couscous, Chicken Satay, Red Lentils and a Feta, Beetroot, Goats Cheese and Mint Salad with a free pizza and a bottle of Duoro all for E38.

Next night we go to A Fabrica which has no atmosphere. Shared a Crayfish and Sardine Pate and I had Piri Piri Prawns with a E15 bottle of Algarve Red. E61. And the following night its back to Booty's for some more great Tapas before Veal with a Tuna sauce. E43.

Last night dinner at Olna Luz again. Fish Soup and Chicken Piri Piri. A small beer and good bottle of Duoro for E50.

This has been another good trip with lots of tennis. As ever the food has been very good. And we got to see Quinta da Lago which we cant stop talking about. Wonder if we will ever be asked ?

# June 2018 Cardiff And Sicily

Cardiff is not a holiday hotspot but we are here to see The Rolling Stones. All the world seems to be coming to Cardiff and it takes 5 hours in the car for a journey that should only be around 3 hours. We find our hotel and ask for directions to the stadium. We are hungry and go into John Lewis but there is no food so have a Pale Ale each and then buy a £3 Hot Dog each on the way. We buy some more beer in the stadium and get to our seats by 7.45. The Stones come on at 8.20 so not too long to wait.

They played for about two hours. Keith and Mick both looked very old on the video screen but they are both 75 this year and Charlie Watts is 77. Ronnie Wood is the baby at only 70. It seems to me that they remain the best rock band in the world. My Highlights were 'Paint it Black', 'Get Off My Cloud' and 'Honky Tonk Women'. They also did a nice obscure blues number with Mick playing harmonica and a really good version of 'Like a Rolling Stone'. We got a double encore and finished with '(I Cant Get No) Satisfaction'. This has been all very very good for us oldies.

Managed to get the last seat in a Turkish restaurant for not a very good dinner and back to the Premier Inn for sleep.

We have to take a detour to Essex to see my Mum before the flight to Palermo.

At the airport we have to call to get a lift to the Car Rental place. We get a black Fiat 500 which is very nice and will take the suitcase. It could probably take 2 but mine has not arrived.

We have booked the Vittorio hotel in Porto Polo which I read about in the weekend papers. We landed at 5.15 and it is now 7.30 as we get into the car. We drive very fast on the A29 and arrive at 8.40 in time for dinner.

The dinner is very fine with Tuna Carpaccio followed by Spaghetti with John Dory Eggs and Prawns. With a nice wine and Limoncello it all costs E98.

We have a lovely new room with a terrace overlooking the beach. Breakfast is very nice but no sign of the suitcase and have 4 swims on the first day.

The suitcase finally arrives in late afternoon 48 hours late. Luckily Chrissie bought me some swimmers and a T shirt for my birthday but I haven't shaved. Bought a local toothbrush.

We are able to watch the World Cup with an Italian commentary and England beat Tunisia 2-1.

A good second dinner. Started with an Americano. 20 Marinated Shrimp followed by Spaghetti Vittorio with seafood. Nice wine and Limoncello. Did not get a bill.

Next day it rains in the afternoon but we have another good dinner. Stuffed Sardines and Pasta Vignole. No bill again.

But now the weather is fine again and have 5 swims. Dinner is as good as ever. We start with the E18 per person Seafood starter which is delicious. Tuna Carpaccio, two sorts of raw prawn, octopus in a sauce, octopus and clams, stuffed sardines from the night before and delicious fried white aubergines. All followed by a Seafood Pasta. And a similar dinner for our last night.

## Mr. Tambourine Man

We have been here 6 nights. It is certainly enough and maybe too much somehow you get a little bored with the same restaurant every night even if the food is good. The beach is okay but not spectacular and I don't think this place will be on our must go list. The best news is that the room has only cost E120 per night. I was expecting E200. The six dinners cost E615 which is not too bad with aperitifs and limoncello.

We leave at 10.05 and after 5 hours and 296 kilometres we are in our second Porto Polo of the holiday and our second Hotel Vittorio. The rooms here are only E90 per night and we have a large terrace with a view of the plaza and the sea. But the beach does not look too great here.

For our first dinner we find U Saracenu which is number 2 on Trip Advisor. No reservation and only inside tables but we get one. Shame we did as food is terrible with boring Arancini and the main courses of Grouper and Artichoke and Penne with Anchovies arrive before we have finished the antipasta. We drink a E25 bottle of Nero d'Avola and it all costs E75. We have limoncello in the bar on the way home.

It rains in the morning and the sea is too rough for swimming so we spend the afternoon walking round town. Highlight is a E3 Lemon Ice cream.

Dinner at Hotel Scala which we really like. Octopus and Potato Salad and 3 Local Cheeses to start. A Lasagne with Scampi for me and Shrimp Pasta for Chrissie with a E19 Puglia wine.

Weather is a little better and manage two swims. And then to brilliant dinner at Zibobbo. We start with Carpaccio of St. Pierre with a honey vinigarette and small mounds of Etna Avocado which is just superb. I have Linguine with Red Prawns and Chrissie small Fried Fish with red peppers. We drink a very nice Etna Rosso at E25. A heavenly meal.

We return to La Scala but somehow we do not enjoy it so much this time as Zibobbo seems to have raised the bar.

Weather is better and manage 4 swims and 2 snorkels with around 90 fish each time the largest being 5 inches with yellow stripes. We have a good lunch at Zibobbo with Invivito with tuna and potato and basil and nostra.

Dinner is at Hotel Janic which we didn't quite get. Ordered fried fish but something strange arrived and fried Riccotta. I had Spaghetti with Sardine, pine nuts and onions but lots and lots of pasta and couldn't finish. E10 Nero D'Avola and it all cost E45 but don't think we will return. Early dinner as we have to watch the football and England lose 0-1.

A good swimming day but my snorkel breaks and I have to mend with Chrissie headband. Lunch at Zibobbo lovely as ever and then back for dinner. E20 wine from Palenta, Carpaccio of Semia (Grouper) very good but not outstanding like the St. Pierre and a very rare Tuna with sweet onions and Mediterranean salsa for me which I loved. E75 for a very good dinner.

I get an attachment for snorkelling which seems to work. The weather is much better. We try La Scala again and are disappointed. The raw fish seems tired and we think we have ordered a large fish to be filleted at the table but get 2 Bream with not very good potatoes. A E20 bottle of Nero D'Avola and it all costs E70. Don't think we will be going back.

Better dinner the next night at Puglia. We share a Tuna Tartare and I have a nice Scampi dish. We drink a 14% Puglia and it costs E61.50.

And now its my birthday and I am 66 but do not feel a day older. I am pretty fit and weigh the same as I did when I was 18 and have a very good tan. We will just have to wait and see what old age brings.

Great Birthday dinner at Zibobbo. I have a Bellini in a local bar first. Then to the restaurant and free Prosecco and nice amuse bouchée. We order the E35 Etna Rosso the most expensive on the list and start with the raw fish plate - prawns, langoustines, tuna and anchovies. We have ordered Lobster with the prawn linguine which is totally delicious. Free Limoncello and the bill is a very reasonable E125. Nice way to celebrate.

We decide to buy an umbrella for E10 and buy a bread, ham, cheese and tomato picnic for E4 and another E10 for the boat ride to the nearby island. Its quite nice but the sea is a little shallow and no beer for lunch. We leave at 4pm and go straight to the bar for a beer. The umbrella pays for itself in the following days.

England beat Columbia in a penalty shootout.

We go to a Pizza place for dinner and have a very pleasant cheap night after all the excitement.

A perfect sunny day nearly 90 degrees and the umbrella has now paid for itself. Dinner at U Palanguru which we did not particularly like. For Starters you get 7 antipasta and not sure about three of them and far too much. Pasta with two large prawns for main course and the E8 lire of red wine for E59. Do not think will be going back. We have a long discussion about where we have been in Sicily and here comes close to our favourite. Nice hotel, two good restaurants and okay beach.

Better dinner next night at Zibibbo. Free prosecco and amuse bouche as ever and then we share Aubergine dish which is very good. I have lovely Tagliane with Mussels, Tuna and Courgette Flowers and Chrissie a very good Yellowtail fish which seems to come from the southern oceans. E25 Etna Rosso and free limoncello and it is great value for E65.

Another dinner at Puglia which is very good. Raw Shrimp with an egg souffle and I have the Scampi again. Nice bottle of wine and E62.

Last day at the beach and I get the swims up to 81.

Last dinner at Zibibbo - it had to be. 9 Langoustines baked with parsley and a Yellowtail Tartare with mulberry are superb. I have the Tuna with sweet onions again and Chrissie the small fried fish with red peppers. We drink a bottle of Nota at E25 and it all costs E90.

It is 400 kilometres to the airport so we get up early and leave at 8.30 just getting breakfast. We have a local lunch and still get to the airport one hour early as there is not a lot of traffic.

Another great trip to Sicily.

## August 2018 Los Angeles, Mexico

Less than a month and we are off again to LA to celebrate our daughter Lauren's 29th birthday and take a little side trip to Cabo. The tan from Sicily is still looking good.

The flight is 10 hours 23 minutes but then it takes nearly two hours to get through Immigration. A long long time without a cigarette. But its great to see Lauren again. We no longer own a house and Lauren's apartment has no room so we are staying at The Grafton on Sunset.

To bed at 10.30 or 6.30am home time and manage to sleep to 7am and head off to the very famous Matts Diner established in 1947 OJ, Waffles and Coffee. It all costs $34 plus tip which seems quite a lot. After a swim in the pool back to Matts for lunch. Corned Beef on Rye and a beer and $38 plus tip for two. Its nice to be back in LA.

First night dinner we meet with Lauren and Winnie and Isa and go off to one of our favourites Petit Four on Sunset. I have Gazpacho and a taste of somebody's Artichoke and then my normal Calves Liver which is good as always. We drink quite a lot including a good Napa at $49 per bottle. It is my turn to pay and it is $495 for 5 which seems very expensive.

Next day we go shopping for my Ralph Lauren jeans and end up going to three places until I buy a pair which are not quite right for $89 plus tax.

We have to return to Angelino's which is as lovely as ever but the Cheese Ravioli is off. We drink Prosecco, Peroni and eat Ravioli and Gnocchi and Sorbet and it is all $149 plus tip.

It is time to meet our old friends Jamie and Bob and we get together at Obaci's Mozarella Bar. I give them a copy of the first edition of Mr Tambourine Man. We order some Etna Rosso at $58 per bottle and go straight into the mozarella collection which is very good. We then have the starters with lots of interesting things including an exceptional caponata. I have Papadelle with Duck Ragout for main course. Some more Etna Rosso, ice creams and limoncello make it a memorable night with our old friends.

## Mr. Tambourine Man

Its Lauren's birthday and it's a beautiful day and we have lunch in a Mexican Vegan called Gracias Madre sitting in a very nice garden. Its all very vegan and the tacos are quite nice. $78. She wants to go to Catch for dinner with a girlfriend. It seems like a dump to me. Security tell us to move on while we are taking a photograph to celebrate the occasion, the table is not ready and we have to wait in the bar. We order a Bourdin White at $55 and a Paso Dobles Petit Syrah at $45. The food is not that great and we complain. Offered free dessert and get a cake with candle. Also get a reduction in the bill to $192 so ends up quite cheap. Follow it up with trip to Cecconi's for limoncello and prosecco and spend $63 on drinks.

Glad to be getting out of the Grafton and back to Cabo San Lucas. A nice 2 hour American Airlines flight in Business with Champagne and Chicken Salad. We are staying in a lovely small hotel Casa Bella which is nearer the centre than our last trip. We are upgraded to a nice Kingsize room with a great bathroom.

The next thing we do is go next door for the best Margaritta in town - $7 for two. And for our first night we return to Maria Jimmez which seems as nice as ever. We have another Margaritta and a bottle of Mexican Cabernet Sauvignon at about $20. We eat Shrimp Frajitas and Enchiladas and it all costs around £30.

There is a huge rainstorm in the night which may have come from a hurricane and the streets are all flooded and it is going to be difficult to get around. After a very nice breakfast with good pastries we go off walking and after a lot of difficulty get to the beach. The sea does not look inviting. Omega our previous favourite has no chairs and no food so we go to a restaurant for an okay lunch with Pacifico beer and Fish Tacos for about $30. We find a nice hotel Casa Dorado and pay $30 to sit around the pool but with free drinks. Leave after a time and go to the cinema and pay $3 each to see Mission Impossible in English with Spanish subtitles.

Dinner is at Peregrino's which is the number 1 restaurant in town on Trip Advisor. It is all very fine with Asian Tuna Tartare and New York Strip with a bottle of Mexican Reserva and Margarittas to start. Not bad for $48.

The beach is still not great so back to Casa Dorado. For dinner we return to another favourite Neptuno's but we are the only customers. Sashimi to start with very good Octopus and then Shrimp Curry. With the Margarittas and an Argentine Cabernet Sauvignon it is $69 but I hate having no atmosphere.

We can now go to the beach and choose Cachet for our custom. It is quite cheap and the Ceveche for lunch is very good.

We return to Peregrino but it is not so good the second time. And the next night we go to Invita Bistro next door which we don't like too much as it feels more like LA than Mexico. And the night after we go to La Taquiza which is proper Mexico and we drink Margarittas and Pacifico beer and eat Stuffed Peppers and it only costs $26.

Time for the movies again and we see Estaba about a Columbian drug lord and starring Penelope Cruz who is as good as ever. Then we go to the local pizza place Jo's where we have been before. We didn't like the California Roll with Tuna or the Pizzas and with poor margaritas and 2 glasses of red wine it cost S22.

Our charming hostess is taking us and her family on a 45 minute road trip in two cars to Cerritos. A soulless hotel but with a good pool and a great Pacific beach. I take a walk on the beach and meet a lovely USA surfer girl who seems to fancy me because of my accent. We have a nice lunch and swim a lot in the pool and it is fun playing with the kids. I always liked being a Dad. Something different and a lovely day out with such nice people.

The day is spoilt by dinner at Lorenzilla an up market place. We spend 3,000 pesos or 3X normal or 6X cheapo for Margarittas, not the best Tuna Tartare, Lobster Taco and a Lobster Shrimp starter pancake for Chrissie. It is just not worth it.

Better night at Maria Corona with a nice setting and dancing. As ever we start with Margaritta, then very interesting bone marrow and good Pork Leg with garlic, orange and cinnamon for me and Chicken with Chocolate for Chrissie. We drink 3 Pacificos and it all costs $70.

We have a great last night at Crazy Lobster and wish that we had found it earlier. 2 Margarittas, free and very good Tortilla Soup,

2 Lobster Tails at $14 each and 6 glasses of Cabernet all for $48. Then we do some dancing with the Mexicans - Mum, Dad and three girls aged 10,7 and 3 all tremendous. Had to carry Chrissie home as we are all a little drunk.

Cabo apart from the initial flood has been fun. Casa Bella is wonderful, with some exceptions we have eaten well and reasonably, I have managed 50 swims and downed 19 Margarittas. Liked our second visit and will probably come back here again.

Good flight back and we are through Immigration 40 minutes after the plane has landed. We are taking Lauren to Santa Barbara for her birthday but end up waiting 45 minutes for her. 3 hours later after a lovely drive along Pacific Coast Highway we arrive. The hotel is very nice, one block from the beach and we have a nice terrace for smoking. Given a free very good local Pale Ale.

We want to have dinner on the Pier but can't find anywhere we fancy so end up at Due Lune. The Limoncello Martini is terrible, but the Linguini with Clams is very nice. With a good bottle of Red it all costs $158.

Next day after poor free breakfast we go to the beach and I have 2 swims in the Pacific which doubles my score in the Ocean. Previously only been in at Coronado because I had to relive ' Some Like it Hot ' and after playing beach volleyball. In the afternoon Lauren and I get on the free cycles and I get my glasses fixed. To celebrate we go and have a 3 Rose wine flight which is marvellous. We cycle round the harbour but don't find any suitable places for dinner just run into some drunk girls.

We go back to Santa Barbara Collection for a Rose and then take a UBER about 2 miles to a local restaurant Jane's. We all eat well and drink well and it costs $154.

I go swimming in the Pacific again so it is now six. For second day we have lunch at the Goat Tree which has very good Avocado tart. I have enjoyed Santa Barbara but the drive back is slow in the traffic.

We are now returning to the London hotel. The room is as nice as ever but something seems to be missing in the vibe. No doormen, no turndown at night and the pool area seems all wrong and it does not seem worth $500 per night and even the breakfast is only okay and Gordon Ramsay has left. We meet Lauren at Mozarella Bar Obaci and I have the best Americano ever made with Vermouth Professoro. We go to Petit Fours and are joined by her friend Megan. I have a Draft Beer, Artichoke and naturally the Calves Liver and share a $49 bottle of Napa Red. Only $280 this time.

Its time to go home again and leave my lovely daughter.

# September 2018 Calabria

Six weeks and we are off again on another Nielsen tennis holiday.

We fly BA into Lamezia Terme which is not crowded and take a 100 minute boring transfer in the dark to our hotel.

Nice room with terrace overlooking the tennis courts. They have saved dinner for us and it is quite nice and better than Sardinia.

Although it is the last day of September it is quite warm and sunny at 72 degrees. But the sea is a little rough so I have a swim in the pool and then tennis in late afternoon. The next day manage to get in the sea and it has got warmer. Playing tennis 3 times a day.

Although the food is quite good here it is good to get out and we go to a restaurant just down the beach. Brilliant Tuna Carpaccio and Lobster with a claw and pasta (at E19.50) and a good bottle of local wine. Chrissie had Fried Fish with Brocolli. E69.

Next time out we take a taxi to Rossano. There were supposed to be 8 sharing but only 4 of us turned up so cost E40. Bought some cheap Marlboro Red and found a restaurant called Byzantini. Ordered the Rossano platter - 7 dishes with lovely Potatoes and Peppers, 2 nice Arancini, good Meat balls and some nice vegetables. We both had a reasonable Veal Stew and a litre of local wine For E48. A nice refreshing change.

The food here is quite good. An example for dinner. Tuna and Swordfish Carpaccio, Spaghetti with Scampi.

We do have another night out at the beach restaurant which is equally as good as the first time.

The tennis tournament is called off because of rain and we play ping pong indoors. In total I have managed 19 games of tennis here and 11 swims.

Like Calabria. Seems like a cool place. Like the hotel Airone with much better food than Sardinia and a nice location. Bar bill E312 including E32 for a racket restring. Spent E170 on three dinners out so not too expensive overall.

## November 2018 Marrakesh

And now its time for our sixth holiday this year and we are off to Marrakesh.

We fly BA Business and get a £25 taxi ride to the hotel which seems very nice but also seems a long way from anywhere.

First night dinner is in hotel. Its quite pleasant. We share some Moroccan starters and I have Lamb Cous Cous and Chrissie Chicken Tagine. We have a bottle of Maroc Cab Sauvignon at £30 which is the cheapest on the list and with our cocktails it all costs £90. Quite a lot.

The next day we take a £12 taxi ride to the Yves St. Laurent museum which costs us £30 to get in and the museum and the garden are all very nice. We walk around and find a local place in the sun around 70 degrees for lunch. Spanish Omlette which failed to get in Spain and lemonade as no beer. It all cost about £10.

For the evening we take the free shuttle into Newtown. Have a Casablanca beer at Café de la Poste and walk around. Nothing much appeals and we return to the Café for dinner. Courgette Soup and Spring Rolls and Fish Tagines are all very good and with another beer to start and a bottle of wine it is £75.

A day sitting around the pool and swimming. At night we take the free shuttle again and meet an old friend Lucinda who lives here. Not sure I would have recognised her but she spotted us. We have a drink in Kosy Bar watching the sunset. We take a walk to the main Square and the street food looks interesting but we go to El Bahia restaurant. We order the D200 menu. 8 salads which are all very nice and I have a very authentic Chicken and Lamb Tagine. We drink 2 bottles of Cabernet and it all costs about £80 for three. But not really in love with Marrakesh and do miss Italian food.

The next two nights we eat at the hotel and it is a little dull. The next night we do better at Café de la Poste with Monkfish Carpaccio and an upside down Shepherds Pie.

We go to see Lucinda again and find our way to her Riad. A lot of building work and a bit of a mess but with a great terrace overlooking the roofs. We go to a local place and eat lamb cooked in a hole with cumin and bread which we eat with our fingers.

Nice last dinner but not sure will come here again. Lucinda seems to love it but somehow for me it just does not add up. Looking forward to next year.

# January 2019 Langkawi

We fly to Kuala Lumpur Premium Economy and we will stay here one night. A 12 hour flight and onto the Majestic Hotel which seems rather nice.

For dinner we take a taxi to Central Market, Chinatown. None of the foodstalls have any beer but we eventually find a place with beer and plastic red tables and chairs. We eat well - Penang Noodles, Fried Noodles with Chicken, Fried Rice with Vegetables and Spring Rolls and with 3 Asahi beers it all costs about £18. Back to the hotel and find the Smoking Room and have a glass of Prosecco and a glass of French Bordeaux which costs more than dinner.

We take the hotel shuttle to the railway station and spend £2 on supplies for our journey. Water, Sausage Rolls, Vanilla Cake and Bananas. It takes around 5 hours to get to Alor Setar but it does not seem that long. Nice to travel this way.

We take a taxi to 38PC, a boutique hotel but not really. Lisa the receptionist takes us on a walk around town. Then we go to dinner. It is all very fine with 2 660cl Tiger beers, Rice, Fried Chicken and Squid. £4 for the beer and £4.40 for the food. To the bar next door which will later keep us awake until 4am for more beer and a free dark rum chaser from the owner. We dance to our honeymoon song

## Mr. Tambourine Man

' Hungry Heart , by Bruce Springstein and ' The Last Time ' by the Stones. All good fun and pretty cheap.

Breakfast very odd with rice dishes so glad only staying one night. But now its time for Chrissie's nightmare.

We take a Grab (the local UBER) for £3 to the ferry. Grab a couple of waters for 20p each and we are away on the shortish crossing to Langkawi.

To Chrissie's surprise our house where we are going to be staying for 29 nights is delightful. We booked it through Airnb for a remarkable price of £24 per night and it is called Tropical Chalet at The Botok near to the town of Cenang. It is divine and Chrissie is very happy. A lovely terrace, huge room with large bed, 2 air conditioners, fan, settee and low table and seating and a brilliant open bathroom. All you could need. Shahan is our host and he takes us into town to look around. It is a 10 minute walk to town and the beach.

Shahan recommends Orkid Ria for dinner and we go there the first night. It is very popular and we have to queue for about 15 minutes for a table. But it is worth it. For £18 we have Chicken Satay, Dim Sum, Deep Fried Prawns with garlic, Fried Noodles and 3 Tiger beers. Seems like stupid prices. We go to the Duty Free Shop and without a passport manage to buy 2 bottles of Australian wine for around £6 per bottle. In bed by 12 but get woken up by religious chanting at 6.30 but then sleep until 10.00. Okay breakfast with fresh OJ, fruit and Nescafe.

Off to the beach and we only manage to get chairs at the third place. 2 Chairs and Umbrella for £4 but we manage to do a deal for the rest of our stay for £2.80 per day. I have some nice swims and Malay Chicken Noodle Soup for lunch with more OJ (no beer here) for about £11 for 2. There is a bar on the beach for a 4pm beer which keeps me in the right mood.

Its Saturday night so we go to Kasbah just down the road for the BBQ. We have the Seafood Platter which is very good with well cooked fish, large prawns, calamari, mash and red cabbage. I glass of not great red wine and 2 beers for £19, our most expensive dinner so far. We go back the next morning for the £15 breakfast which is very good with fresh OJ, Pancakes with the trimmings, good local Coffee and Earl Grey for Chrissie.

During the night we have watched a huge electric storm out at sea but it is dry here and a very warm 90 degrees. We are in the dry season so hopefully no rain.

Nice day at the beach but then make a big mistake and go to La Sal at Casa Del Mar for dinner. A 5* resort with 5* prices. We start with Asian Seafood which is quite good. I have the Malayan plate with 4 large portions and 4 smaller portions and soggy pappodoms. The waiter half explains the dishes but they all taste the same. Chrissie has Snapper of the day which looks tired. We drink a Chilean Merlot at £27 and it all comes to £68 which is UK prices and 4X what we have been paying and just not worth it.

My flipflops are hurting me and a buy a new pair of Puma slip-ons which are much more comfortable and spend £7 on a new snorkel. We find a great place for lunch on the main street Bella where we will return again and again to eat good Malay food and drink soft drinks. 6 swims and then the beer at 5 pm.

Dinner at Kasbah again. Very good with Chicken Satay to start, Malay dinner with excellent aubergine and pineapple curry for me and Vegetable Korma for Chrissie. With 5 Tiger beers only £19.

Next day only 5 swims as a little windy and excellent Bella lunch - Laska, which is a lovely Fish Soup with Noodles, Vegetables and Egg all for £1.25.

Look up somewhere for dinner and take quite a long walk to Cliff. Looked at the menu outside and it seems to be La Sal prices so we go along the beach to Yellow Beach Café which has a nice atmosphere. We have a beer and then both Penne with Seafood and two glasses of French Rose for £26.

And today I do my first water ski in a long time. Various prices from 200 down to 100 for 15 minutes but I manage to negotiate 5 minutes for 50 or around £10. Up first time and round the bay. No glasses but still exhilarating.

We try unsuccessfully to find a restaurant called Nam in a taxi and end up at Orkid Ria again and have to queue for 20 minutes but it is worth it. We start with very good Spring Rolls then have a whole

## Mr. Tambourine Man

Snapper which costs £12 at £2.25 per 100 grams steamed in a ginger sauce with Fried noodles. With 2 Tiger beers it all costs £17.30 and you can pay by credit card.

Tonight is Street Food just across the road. It is all lovely. First we have gorgeous potato in pastry, a large piece of nice chicken good and average chicken satay washed down with Tiger beer. We return for Crème Caramel and Banana Panckes and it all costs 17.50 or about £3.50 for dinner. To celebrate we go to Kasbah and spend 33 on a Mojito and Pina Colada double the price of dinner.

We have now been here a week and having a fine time. Only 3 more weeks to go.

Next night we take a taxi to Sun Café. It is all very pleasant. Vegetable Tempura to start followed by Chicken Cordon Bleu for Chrissie and Prawns and Malay Noodles for me. 4 Tiger beers and it all costs £25. We walk home and buy cigarettes for £2.10 per pack.

And the night after it is back to Kasbah for their very good Saturday Night BBQ. It is closed for Sunday breakfast and we walk up the road and have a different breakfast of OJ, Pancakes and Egg on toast with coffee and it all costs less than £6.

And now it is all starting to make sense. I have got a bit fed up looking in Trip Advisor and we want to eat Malay. Shahah tells us a good local place but it seems closed. We go to the supermarket and buy beers and water. There is a restaurant next door which looks all right with people drinking beer. They do not serve beer but give us 2 glasses to drink our own. We both eat Mamas Noodles which are brilliant with Chicken, squid, vegetables and chili and it costs £1 each. Drinking 3 beers at 60p each our dinner comes to £3.80. This is the way to go and now it makes sense.

Its time to do something different and we have booked Island Happy. We are picked up in town at 1.45 and drive about 3 miles to the jetty. 30 minute wait and a bumpy rough crossing to a nice island beach. Don't swim as not many fish to be seen but walk to a jetty and find girls feeding 2 inch striped yellow fish and see what looks like a swarm of anchovies. Back on boat. They throw chicken into the sea and eagles swoop down and pick it up. Quite impressive. Then to another island with an inland lake but we do not really get it. An okay trip for £6 each but wouldn't do it again.

On Shahah's recommendation we go to Asam Petros just down the road having a beer first. It opens at 8pm and we are the first at 8.10. Great dinner. I have Mackerel with a hot and sour sauce (chili, turmeric and lemongrass) and Spinach with a Prawn Paste and Chicken for Chrissie and rice and 2 very nice lime drinks and it all costs £6 which is 1/11 of La Sal. This is the way to go.

We return to the supermarket restaurant and have another brilliant dinner. Mamas Noodles again for Chrissie and I have Fried Rice with Shrimp. We are given free Watermelon and the bill is £2.60. It is difficult to believe that we can eat so well for so little.

It is the end of Chinese New Year and the queue at Orkid Ria is shorter. Brilliant dinner with Chicken Satay, Sea Bass with ginger and Fried Rice and 4 Tiger beers all for £18. It seems stupid for such great food in a lovely atmosphere.

Another night of Street Food. We spend £2.40 and it is all very nice.

Now there are jellyfish in the sea. Somebody got stung but the beach man sorted it out.

Been here for 2 weeks now. Having discovered good cheap Malay food much more into it.

And tonight it feels like we have had a Michelin Star dinner. Back to the restaurant by the supermarket which we find is called Santai. The Friday special is Nasi Lemak. It is a magnificent dish. Coconut Rice, Cucumber, Peanuts, Anchovies, Deep Fried Egg, Chicken, Chili Paste and a tomato sauce. Followed by Watermelon. It only costs £2.40 for 2 and our 4 Tigers cost the same. How can you have a Michelin dinner for £4.80 - come here.

More jellyfish in the sea but still swimming and not yet stung.

We try to go out for breakfast to eat Roti Bananas but the place has run out and we end up buying Watermelon and taking it home. Thinking that maybe we need to explore a little. Another good £6 dinner at Asam Petros.

We try a new place Islandish Seafood. We need to spend £20 to use the credit card. Easy I have the Lobster. Some Spring Rolls to start and 4 Anchor beers all for £27. A fab meal for a fab price.

Back to Orkid Ria for a fourth time. It is all very good with Satay, Duck Indonesian style, Noodles and Garlic Bean Sprouts and 4 beers for £16.

Think about going to the Mangrove Swamps but reject.

Santai is closed so we end up in Café Keladi after a quick beer at home. A shortish walk towards the beach. Chrissie has Pattaya - fried rice with chicken in an omlette envelope and I have Fried Noodles with Soy, Chicken, vegetables and chili. With 2 Limes it costs £6. Santai is open the next night and we have another Michelin dinner and I have a very good Spicy Prawns and Chrissie Sweet and Sour Chicken. Food is £2.70 and our 3 beers cost £1.80.

Most afternoons after our 4pm beer we have an ice cream and today they give us a free lemon tart which we have after the Street Food. Tonight it is brilliant. 3 Red Bean Patties, 2 Sweet Corn and Sugar Rotis, 2 Chicken and Potato pastries and 5 Chicken Satay. The cost is unreal at £1.50. such a nice night.

We invite Shahah to dinner at Santai. He tells us his life story. At aged 47 he married the widow of a pilot who had died of a heart attack aged 36 and left her with her 5 children. We eat Nasi Lemak again although not quite as good as first time. The freebie tonight is bananas in coconut milk and dinner for the 3 of us is £4.

Shahah very kindly offers to drive us to Kok Beach but he drops us off at the cable car. We walk along the road to a private hotel and then another 1 mile to a nice beach for some swimming. At the other end of the beach we find some Street Food - not sure what we had but it was not that great. Back to the cable car the wrong way which seems to take forever. We have an ice cream and pay R110 for a ticket. The trip takes about 25 minutes and there are some very good views. A £7 taxi ride back to the house and the first beer of the day. I guess it was good to see a little more of the island. But in reality I like where we are. You get beach chairs and we have found places to eat that we love.

A fifth trip to Orkid Ria for another great dinner. Spring Rolls, Deep Fried Garlic Prawns, Fried Rice, Bean Sprouts with garlic and 4 Tiger all for £16. And the next night is Santai again with very good Mackerel Curry for me which was very hot and the fish lovely. Chrissie Sweet and Sour Chicken and all for £3 plus 4 Tigers from the supermarket.

Shahah has bought us each a Malay smock which we wear for breakfast - getting native. Back to Café Keladi for dinner and I have very good Spicy Vegetable with Oyster Sauce and Chrissie Chinese Chicken Fried Rice. A beer before we go and 2 Limes there and £5.40 all up.

Now it is time to do something different. We go to the Tiger bar on the beach to watch the sunset. My man tries to give us 2 Tigers but we have a Pina Colada and Aperol Spritzer. The beach is full of people and it is all very nice. A good dinner at Orkid Ria with Chicken Satay, Snapper with Ginger, Rice and Garlic Beansprouts and 4 Tigers all for less than £20.

Back to Santai for another close to Michelin. I had Prawn Petra spicy with chili and Chrissie Sweet and Sour Chicken again. With 2 Rice only £3.

Get attacked in the sea by a 9 inch Blackfish - very scary. Another fun night at the Street Food and spend £2.60 on Orange and Green balls, Chicken Roti, Potato Pastries and Chicken Satay.

For our last night we go back to Santai but the Nasi Lemak is finished so I return to the Mackerel Curry and again Chrissie has Sweet and Sour Chicken. We get a freebie of Fried Ice Cream which is very good and it costs us £3 again.

Our 31 nights here have been a real pleasure. We have had 3 hours of cloud and 30 minutes of rain at night and the rest of the time it is just sunshine. We have eaten very well. Lunches at Bella are a joy, 16 nights we have eaten for less than £6 and another 10 for less than £20. Santai is close to Michelin. Shahah has been a great host and all the people are generally charming. And I have done 170 swims in the sea. How could anything be more perfect.

But you do have to get home and we catch a Malaysian Airlines plane to Kuala Lumpur and then it is 13 hours 35 minutes on BA back to Heathrow with maybe 7 hours sleep. The worst bit.

# June 2019 Sicily

After an extended period of over 3 months we are off again. We stay in the normal hotel near the airport and have to get up at 4.30 for an early flight. After breakfast in the Lounge and on the plane in 2 hours 45 minutes we are in Catania. We get a Nissan Micra Diesel (not a 500 this time which we had requested and drive around 120 kilometres back to Porto Polo. Hotel Vittorio give us the same room as last year and a bottle of Prosecco. It is nice to be back.

We have nice Panini and Peroni at the Plaza del Sol and head to the beach but no chairs so have to make do with our towels. Only I swim as the water sees cold but it is 18 June.

The reason we have returned is because of Zibibbo. A free glass of Prosecco and cheese amuse bouche and we share a sublime Tuna Tartare. I have the rare Tuna with Sweet Onions which is as good as ever and Chrissie the fried Fish with Red Peppers. We drink a E35 bottle of Etna Rosso and 2 glasses of not so good Lemon Liquer as Limoncello off. A lovely dinner for E85. Not used to these prices.

Get chairs at the beach and have 5 swims and 1 snorkel and see a large school of over 100 small fish and 12 larger 3 inch striped fish.

Return to Liguria for a very good dinner. Tuna Tartare again but not as good as Zibibbo. I have Pasta Paceni with Red Prawn and Tomatoes which is lovely and Chrissie Prawn Risotto. A bottle of house Red at E10 and 2 Limoncello and it is not too bad at E64.

And the next night it is back to Zibibbo again for another brilliant dinner. Free Prosecco and Cheese on Toast to start and then Carpaccio of Dorado with honey vinigarette and cherries which is divine. I follow with outstanding Linguine with Cozze (Mussels), Black Garlic, Orange and Red Peppers. Chrissie has Tagliatelle with Red Prawns. We drink a less expensive E22 Nero d' Avola and get 2 free lemon liquers and it is a more reasonable E68 for such a great dinner.

We get in the car and revisit Avola. I remember it is not my favourite place in Sicily and this proves to be true again. Have 4 swims and an average lunch. The restaurant opposite the beach which used to be our place does not appear to be even open yet. For dinner tonight we return to Hotel Jonic. We share Fish Crudite which is quite good. Chrissie has a Fish Cernia Ravioli and I have Linguine with Clams and Burrata. A E10 bottle of Nero d' Avola all for E68. We return to the bar where we watched the World Cup for limoncello.

Cheap lunch with Arancini. Stupid dinner went back to U Palanguru where we went last year. Did not have 7 antipasta - did not fancy anything so just had a cheap pizza.

The next day we drive to a nice nearby beach and I have a Hotdog for lunch. Dinner at Zibibbo again. We have the Carpaccio of Dorado again which remains good. I have Linguine with Sea Urchins which you sort of have to have, and Chrissie Red Fish with potatoes and a surprising stuffing. A local Nero d'Avola and it all costs E78.

The lady at the hotel gives us a lovely Orange Cake, some papaya and OJ which is all very nice. We return to Puglia and have another very good dinner.

Buy postcards, stamps and a book for the hotel lady. Dinner again at Zibibbo with an excellent Carpaccio of St. Pierre and Grilled Octopus with Lemon Potatoes for me and Red Snapper for Chrissie. Local Nero d'Avola at E22 and E70 all up.

Time to try somewhere different and we go to Butchers Cutelli and order the E17 spread and a litre of E7 Red Wine. We start with a nice tomato and garlic brochetta and then a vegetable course with nice peppers, mushrooms, grilled courgette and aubergine, onions and olives. They show us the meat and we choose. The portions are very large and it is mostly pork but a little disappointing. We have to pay E34 cash - interesting and different.

Last night here and naturally we go to Zibibbo. Carpaccio of St. Pierre again and rare Tuna with Sweet Onions for me and Yellowtail for Chrissie which she loved. Marimba Nero d'Avola and it is only E65.

We are now off to Marsala. It takes over 6 hours to do the 400 kilometres and I have to do 4 sharp brakes for crazy Italian drivers but we arrive safely. Phoned the man at the B&B and he is waiting outside to show us in. Nice room but no outside seating. We are paying E1,000 for 14 nights which is not too bad.

We need to drive from the town or maybe city to the beaches but there are trips to the islands.

For our aperitifs we find a nice bar with a chatty girl.

Our first dinner is at Bodega del Curmine. Liked the food but not the décor or atmosphere, too corporate. We share a very nice flan with anchovy, orange and fennel. I have the local special pasta, Basiata with Mussels, Prawns, Squid and tomatoes and Chrissie a Potato Ravioli with seafood. We drink a local Perrigrine Nero d'Avola and the bill is E60. We go to a bar and drink Dry Marsala Superiore E10 for 2. Prefer Limoncello.

We go to the square for breakfast and have nice fresh OJ, good coffee and chocolate croissants and get very dirty hands.

Time to find a beach. Our man recommends a place about 5 kilometres away which we find and pay E10 for the chairs and umbrella. Sea a little rough but still do 5 swims.

For second night we go to Trattoria Da Pino and get the last table. We reject the E8 Buffet and I have Basiata again with Swordfish, Aubergine and Tomatoes. Chrissie Risotto with Prawns and Clams. A small plate of delicious cherries - a nice E16 bottle of Red and it only costs E41.

Another day at the beach and then a brilliant night. It did not start so well as walked to Taverna 48 and found it is closed on Tuesdays. Walking back we stop at La Vecchia and get an outside table. We order a litre of House Red and start with Sicilian Stuffed Bread. Tomato, Basil, Garlic and Pesto and very good indeed. I have Basiata again and Chrissie Stuffed Pepper. A larger bowl of delicious cherries and then we are given a bottle of chilled Dry marsala Superiore and I have 2 and Chrissie 1. It all costs E44 - we will be back.

Next night we do get to Taverna 48. We share Tuna Meatballs which are very nice and Chrissie has Potato Gnocchi with Speck and Pistachio and I have Potato Gnocchi with Red Prawns after getting a wrong order. With a E15 bottle of wine they reduce the bill from E52 to E42 because of the mix up. Limoncello at La Vecchia. Given the bottle and no charge - such nice people.

Today we are up with the larks before 8am as we are due on the quay by 9.10 for the 9.30 boat to Levanza. We arrive at 10.30 and walk for about 20 minutes to some pretty rocks and do some swimming. Back to town for only a reasonable lunch. A walk to another beach which is not quite so nice. Boat back is 90 minutes late. An expensive day out and don't think we will be doing it again.

Terrible dinner at Garibaldi. Nice setting in a small square but atmosphere, staff and food are all deplorable. We order wine and get a bottle of white and then a dodgy red. Smoked Tuna, Salmon and Swordfish for starters has no taste. Cous Cous Fish could not finish as such a boring dish. E52 and will never return.

We take the car to see the island of Mozic but Chrissie too hungover for boat ride. The sea seems very shallow so we return to our beach. And we return to La Vecchia for another great dinner. Start with Sicilian plate - Salamis, Cheese, Caponata and olives which is all very nice. I have Basaiti again and Chrissie Stuffed Sardines. With 1 litre of house red, cherries and Marsala it is all very good for E50.

Disaster. Its Sunday and all the tobacco shops are closed. We only have 37 left which is nowhere near enough for the day. You need ID to use the machines but I find a man who helps us and I give his son E1 for the trouble. Off to a great dinner at La Caserie Locanda di Charme. We start with a Tuna Carpaccio which is excellent. I have an equally good Fettucine with Lobster ragout and Chrissie Ravioli with Scampi and Pistachio. Parmengino Nero d'Avola and it would have been E67 but we added cherries and limoncello to bring it up to E80. The quiet street with the outside tables is delightful.

The next night we take quite a long walk to Le Isole. We arrive by 8.15 to watch the sunset and are given free prosecco. We share excellent Sea Bass Carpaccio and I have the best Tortelloni ever with Stone Bass. Chrissie Pork Roll with Mashed Potato. A local Nero d'Avola and free limoncello for E63. An even longer walk back as the park is closed.

And the next night is yet another good dinner at Osteria Socilianda. We start with Caponata with Grouper and Aubergine and I have Spaghetti with Raw Red Prawns which may be the best pasta dish ever. Chrissie has Gnocchi. A lovely E22 wine from Fogata and it is E60 with a free Marsala.

Its now my 67th birthday and I do not feel a day older. 3 nice presents from Jack Wills and we drive again to Mozic and take the boat. The boat is E5 but then another E9 to get on. Nice 90 minute walk around. We then find a good beach and I have panelle for lunch.
5 swims and all very lovely. We have dinner at La Caserie but it is a complete disaster. Poor service, awful chefs Antipasta and a Secondi Tuna which is in season but no good. Retire to my favourite bar Alagna for limoncello and watermelon.

Alagna persuade us to have dinner. We start with Aperol. Tomato and garlic Broschetta, Lasagne Ragu for me and Veal Cutlet and chips for Chrissie. Good Nero d'Avola and limoncello and we leave after over 3 hours for E61.

We return to Osteria Socilianda but the Lobster is off and we order for Saturday. But still a great dinner with shared Red Tuna Tartare, Basiata with Red Shrimp, Clams and Almonds for me and Ravioli with Grouper and Shrimp for Chrissie. Nice bottle of E22 Fugato and free Marsala and it all costs E64.

But now it is a special night. A quick dinner at Alagna and then to the open air cinema. It is the most beautiful setting in a courtyard with a starlit night. There are 220 seats and maybe 140 taken. The movie is 'Il Professore e il Pazzo' all in Italian which makes it a little hard to follow. The stars are Mel Gibson, Sean Penn and Lawrence Fox who all have a good Italian accent. Sean Penn deserves an Oscar. There is a break half way through and we have a cigarette. A wonderful evening and a great experience.

For our last night we have a great dinner at Osteria Socilianda. Fugato vino, Caponata with Grouper and Aubergine and one-half Lobster each with big claws and Tagliatelle. Free Marsala and E65 - a true bargain.

A long drive back to Catania via Palermo another 400 kilometres. Its is hot and the maximum temperature is 104 degrees. We return to Mondello for lunch. The girls place is closed but we have a nice lunch but I worry about somebody breaking into car and losing car keys and i pad. We stop off at Enna in the middle. A no horse town but then to Pateno where we find 'The View' of Etna which is very pleasing and have 2 Moretti.

So our sixth year in a row to Sicily and I still love it. Cant wait to come back. A great 24 night stay. Many highlights, the lady in Hotel Vittorio in Porto Polo, Zibibbo dinners, Marsala which is a wonderful place, the 125 swims and the movie under the stars.

## August 2019 Scilly Isles

My friend Davina took a flying lesson last year from Bodmin Airport over the north Cornish coast and posted some great pictures on Facebook. I decided that we should buy each other flying lessons for Christmas which is what we do.

One Friday at the fourth attempt because of weather we finally have our flying lesson. After a short lesson on how to fly, we take off from the very long runway at Newquay Airport in our 4 seater 1 engine Piper and head towards the Scilly Isles. There are great views of the coast and I steer towards St Ives so I can look at one of my favourite restaurants, Porthminster Beach Café. The pilot decides to fly over the islands and we get good views of Tresco, St Agnes and a few others. We land at the airport on St. Marys and walk around the airfield to a café for lemonade and lemon drizzle cake. I have to go in the back as its Chrissie's turn to fly. She loves it just as much as me. Just a superb day out and a great Christmas present to each other.

## September 2019 Calabria

We return to Nielsen in Calabria for the second year running. It is as nice as ever but I am not going to write too much as it will seem more of the same.

We eat out 3 times. Aurora on the beach twice and we have two very good dinners for around E60 both times with their excellent raw fish. The third night we try Snoopy's a little further along the beach and I have Linguine Vognole which is very very good and maybe the best ever.

The worst experience was the Tournament which is a real lottery. I am going well and winning but then I get a Red Girl who plays worse than Chrissie who is a blue in the lower tournament. Of course, we lose badly and I am out. Chrissie does better and gets to the semis but same problem poor partner. So we are not winners this time.

I play tennis 15 times and have 16 swims mostly in the sea which can be a little rough.

The food here has been as good as ever and apart from my tennis partner the other guests have been very nice. A good Active Holiday.

# November 2019 Venice

Our fourth holiday this year and third time to Italy.

We take Easyjet from Bristol. We have to sit in the plane for an hour due to Italian ATC strike but then have a nice 1 hour 45 minute flight with a marvellous crew from Rome. We buy a E15 Boat Ticket to San Marco but it is a rather boring 1 hour 28 minutes in the dark.

Immediate problem. No cigarettes again, this is the second time this year. Find a waiter in a restaurant who lets me wander off with his ID. Find a machine and are saved. Find our hotel which is near San Marco with lots of activity all around. We find a Trattoria and order the E12.50 menu. I have a good Spaghetti Pomodoro and Liver Venetian style with polenta - very good. Chrissie has Vegetable Soup and Chicken Breast. We drink a E24 bottle of local Valpolicello and it all costs E54.88 service included.

We have an all right breakfast and venture out but the streets are flooded. We have to spend E20 on feet protection. Wander around in the 50 degree sunshine and have a panini lunch outside and then take a Vaporetto ride around the city.

We have booked dinner at Osteria Alle Testiere which we have seen on television. It is only a short walk. It is going to be one of the best 10 dinners ever. Table is booked at 7pm so we start with an Aperol and Campari Soda. Great starters. 7 Scampi Crudo for me which is delicious and Artichoke Soup with King Prwan for Chrissie and I have a little taste and it too is delicious. We order a E52 Valpolicello and I have Sweet and Sour Prawns with onions which is lovely and Chrissie small Monkfish which has to be the greatest fish I have ever tasted. We have nice Tartes for dessert. The tables are close together and there is a great atmosphere of eveyrbody enjoying everything. The cost is E192 but worth it.

Next day we take a vaparetto to Academia and wade through the water. Chrissie's protection breaks and we have to spend another E15 on Wellingtons which do work better. We are here for the Guggenheim Museum. We saw 2 Magritte (my favourite is a picture of a house with 2 lights) 7 Picasso, 6/7 Jackson Pollock and lots of other uplifting pictures. Lunch in the café is very pleasant. On the way back we have a capaccino and tea just off San Marco for E13 which is very expensive.

We return to Noemi where the waiter lent me his ID. It turns out to be one of the best 50 ever dinners. A free Prosecco. Shared Tuna Tartare which is the best ever with a lovely citrus sauce. We manage to get a E52 Valpolicello for E39 because our choice is not available. I eat Liver Venetian style again with onions and polenta and Chrissie has gorgeous Mushroom Ravioli with Black Truffle. One Limoncello each and the bill is E118 but really worth it.

Time to see if we can get to Torcello (with the wonderful Locanda Cipriano recommended by Michael Winner where we had a wonderful lunch in September 2012 - see earlier) . To San Marco - high tides no boats. Take a long walk and eventually get a boat to Burano. Stopped at Torcello but did not get off but not sure the way back and so onto Burano. Lots of pretty houses and a leaning tower and flooded streets. We have a lovely lunch at Trattoria Da Primo. Fried Baby Calamari and Soft Shell Crabs which have perfect seasoning and are very enjoyable - one of the best 100 lunches ever and with Moretti costs E45. We manage afternoon tea for E5.

We return to Madonna for dinner where we first went 37 years ago with Trish and Chris (we did have lunch here in September 2012 - see earlier). We share some small shrimps which are okay but not as good as Falmouth Bay and I have the Scampi and Chrissie Monkfish. With 1 litre of Valpolicello at E12 it all costs E71 - they have no limoncello which is a drag.

Next day we walk to Leonardo de Vinci Museum. Mona Lisa was painted in 1502 and he invented the bicycle, aeroplanes and lots of other interesting machines - a good tour. Then to Saint Rocco a very fine building with many Tintoretto's on the walls and ceiling - highly rated by David Bowie and us.

Its our 39th Wedding Anniversary and we return to Testiere. Nowhere near the top 100 tonight. Not such a good table with non-talking Italians next to us so lacking the fun atmosphere. I ordered Seabass Carpaccio which had no flavour, I think they forgot the dressing. Chrissie had nice Scallops. My main course is Spaghetti with carpet baby Clams which is not too bad and Chrissie an excellent Turbot. We have to pay for Limoncello and it all costs E172 which seems too much. This is the second time this year that a celebration night has been spoilt revisiting a restaurant which has not lived up to the first time. And at 3.20 in the morning I was sick which is highly unusual for me. But the evening was not a disaster as we had started in Harry's Bar. A marvellous and memorable place. A Bellini for Chrissie and an Americano for me. Drinks cost E42 and seem a little small but you do get nice nibbles.

Next day, still feeling sick we take the Vaparetto to the Lido. We think it is very dull and return after 25 minutes. We return to the Academia Museum. Very good with lots of Tintoretto's and 3 Titian's. Lunch in a nice cafeteria and then off to the Doges Palace. Its all very okay with a Rubens exhibition, the prison cells and the Bridge of Sighs.

For our last night in Venice we just have a pizza as we are getting up very early at 5am to get back to the airport. We take the ferry from Rialto and it only takes 35 minutes which is much better. I was worried about being mugged so early in the morning so everything hidden. Chrissie sick on ferry. Nice Easyjet flight with a Venice crew this time.

I think we stayed too long this time. The flooding was a drag but we did have 2 great dinners and 1 great lunch so it can't be too bad.

## January 2020 Singapore And Indonesia

We have used our Avios to upgrade to Club for the outward 12 hour flight. Worst thing is that there is no duty free allowance for cigarettes in Singapore and we have to pay £110 duty which makes our duty free cigarettes over £10 per packet or almost as expensive as home. The hotel fails to send a taxi and we have to pay but get it back later.

We have booked the Amoy where we stayed before and liked a lot but it is not the hotel we stayed in before. No pool and our bedroom windows boarded up but at least it is quite a vibrant area.

We wander around and up for dinner in a Vietnamese restaurant. Nice Spring Rolls, poor Fish Cakes and below average Noodles with Prawn and Pork and 3 beers for £30.

Next day with some difficulty we take a cable car to Sonasta which is pretty boring. We come back and visit some Gardens and have a cheap Chicken Satay lunch - 20 plus beers for £15. Back to the hotel and have to go and sit in another garden as no light in our room.

We walk to Chinatown for dinner in less than 10 minutes but we cannot find the marvellous place we went before how ever hard we try. We end up in a Mancurian restaurant. We have good Steamed Dumplings, boring Prawn Wantons, good Fried Rice with Smoked Duck and not great Sweet and Sour Pork. With 2 large beers it costs £44. Not a great end to our time here and to be honest I have found Singapore a little disappointing on this trip.

But now we are taking the I hour ferry trip to Bintan, Indonesia. Get transfer to the resort and I think I have got it all wrong. We are staying in a very nice lodge with views of a small lake and the sea but it is all part of a much larger organisation called Nirwana Gardens with hotels, villas and restaurants. Thinking we need to escape. And the sea is rough and there is a Red Flag for no swimming. We are going to have to stay here for 23 nights - oh dear !

We have not a great lunch for £30 with the beers costing £5 each and I have a swim in the pool.

For our first night we go to the Saturday Night BBQ. The BBQ is quite nice but the drinks are expensive with cocktails costing £9 each and the Cheapest wine is a 2016 Australian Cabernet Sauvignon at £36. Best thing was the dessert - Sarane Sernut with coffee ice cream. But it is very expensive and ends up costing £133 which feels like a RIPOFF.

Sleep very well for 11 hours and nearly miss breakfast. We have to walk a long way to get it. In the day a couple of pool swims and lunch in Dino Italian which still costs £26.

Its time to escape and we take the free bus to Plaza Lagoi. To be honest it is not really Indonesia but just a shopping mall that you could find anywhere in the world. There are 3 empty restaurants and we try one Idola which turns out to be quite good. We have okay dumplings followed by Hong Kong Noodles with fish and vegetables which are excellent and then good Chicken and Pak Choi with garlic. We have Bintan beers and it only costs £33 or less than the price of 1 BBQ. We buy 8 cans of beer for £1.80 each a good saving on the hotel.

Next day I have a couple of swims in the pool, another lunch at Dino's and try to go bowling with our free gift. Not possible as have no socks. This is what it is like here. Find another beach but Red Flag despite no waves. At least the weather is good and it is sunny and around 86 degrees. It is dead here with only 11 people taking towels at the pool.

Back on the shuttle to the Plaza and dinner again at Idola. We have the same dinner with a variation on the Chicken and it costs £29.

14 towels today and I do another couple of swims in the pool. Different from Langkawi or Sicily where I would do 5/6 swims per day in the sea. Somehow the pool does not have the pull of the ocean.

We eat at the resort at Spice. There are 5 tables so a little atmosphere. Food is quite good with Samosas, Prawn Marsala,

Lentils and Spinach, Basmati rice, Papodoms and Garlic Naan. With 2 Gin and Tonic and 2 beers it costs £55.

Only 6 towels today and 2 pool swims. Finished one of the greatest books ever The Grapes of Wrath by Steinbeck. 476 pages in 4 days - there is not a lot to amuse you here.

We do however have a great dinner. We venture 400 yards from the Plaza to the beach and find Warung Yeah. This feels like proper Indonesia. The Chicken Satay is great as is Nasi Goreng Kambing which is Mutton Fried Rice and then we have Ikan Buker Sagai and Nasi Putih which is a delicious grilled fish. The food only costs about £11 but we pay £15 for drinks - Gin and Tonic, Cuba Libra and 2 beers. A great find.The food is almost Michelin. Bought some more beers for lower price.

Strange day as we have pizza for lunch which with 2 beers costs more than last night's dinner. Did not really come here for this. I read the BBC news about Coronavirus and there is a quarantined ship off Yokahama with 3700 people. Back for Indonesian food at Warung Yeah. Great Chicken Satay and nearly great Nasi Goreng Michut (fried rice with egg and sausage) and Garlic Fried Chicken. Food costs about £7.50 but we spend £16 on 2 Gin and Tonics and 2 Beers.

Next day gets cloudy in the afternoon which is a drag. Go by bus to Kelong Seafood Restaurant. We both have Crayfish to start which you need to eat with a knife and fork but it is good and then share a small (good advice from waitress) Malaysian Noodles which we still cannot finish. With 2 beers around £56.

It rains from 1pm but we do get to try Spice for lunch and discover a very delicious soup - Sota Akam which is Indonesian Chicken Noodle soup with eggs and chili. All very good and its slightly cheaper. Back to the Plaza and visit long name place Waroeng Cek Bakars Masakan Khas Melayu. Chicken Satay, Fried Duck with rice and Seafood Noodles which are all okay but not great. We have 5 Beers. The food costs £10 and the drinks the same so seems like a bargain.

Stay at home due to weather but Neydles is closed so go to Dino's for dinner. I have Lasagne and Chrissie Fish and Chips which costs £39 with 2 beers - not really Indonesia but redress by returning to Spice for lunch. Next night have to return to the Plaza and Warung Yeah for some good Indonesian food.

The next night we do go to Neydles but it is empty except for us so no atmosphere. Start with Gin and Tonic and then Merlot. The food is all very nice with Dim Sum, Rice with Scallops and Prawns and Indonesian Noodles with lamb. £60.

It is time to be adventurous and we take a £6 taxi to Treasure Bay in great expectations of something different. We have to pay £14 to get in. told not allowed to pay cash for anything and offered prepaid vouchers which we decline. A big 1 kilometre pool with a few chairs. We wander around for about an hour and leave. What an awful place. We walk to the port. No restaurants but a taxi driver tells us there is a village just opposite Treasure Bay. We find a busy food market and we buy beers for just over £1 each and I eat 2 sorts of Noodles which are very good for 60p and Chrissie splashes out on a 90p Omlette. Taxi back costs £9.

Dinner again at Warung Yeah which is as good as ever.

Its sunny again and Valentine's Day. The maids put flowers on our bed. We return to Kelong Seafood and have good Crayfish and Seafood Rice with pineapple. We pay for 2 Gin and Tonics and do not get charged for 2 Merlot. £48.

Soto Ayam for lunch at Spice which seems quite special and back for another good dinner at Warung Yeah and meet some nice Italians - the first other people we have yet to talk to. We think we are going to meet them at Warung Yeah again the next night, but we are stood up. Still a good dinner.

In our complex there are 38 cabins and only 4 seem to be occupied. There is nobody at breakfast so the hotel must be empty too and most of the villas seem to be empty. We discover that normally there are a lot of Chinese here, but Coronavirus is keeping them away. We are told that we are in some ways lucky they are not here because they bring their own food and probably take all the pool chairs. Maybe a godsend but it is all so dull. And they insist on keeping the red flag up even though there is hardly any swell. My enquiries fall on deaf ears.

Quite a nice dinner at Spice for £40. 2 Gin and Tonics, 2 Merlots, Seafood Noodles and Prawns Indonesian with rice.

Spice for lunch again and back to Warung Yeah. I make an error and read a terrible book by Robert Galbraith who I discover is J K Rowling. Only 3 of our cottages now occupied.

Spice for lunch and Neydles for dinner. Very similar to last time and again we are the only customers.

Feeling a little down as had pizza for lunch again but dinner at Warung Yeah lifts my spirits. The only problem is the bus ride takes 30 minutes there and back and the driver is not very friendly. It would be so nice to just wander into town for dinner but you cannot do that here.

Not a great dinner at Kelong Seafood. Noisy kids and then our main course is brought to us while we are still eating our Crayfish - sent it back. £66 for dinner tonight - they charged us for the wine and the price has gone up from its already very high level.

Now in our 22nd day but it is so boring it feels like the 122nd day. The only respite is getting out to dinner at Warung Yeah again.

We have our last dinner at Neydles all alone as ever.

This has not been a great success. Red Flag has persisted and I have had 40 swims in the pool or less than 2 per day. The hotel is expensive and it has cost us around £1200 for 10 dinners and 22 lunches. The only upside has been our many dinners at Warung Yeah but then we still had to get the bus. Looking back at Cuba and Langkawi they were so much better.

On our return trip we are temperature tested on leaving Indonesia and again on entering Singapore.

This is a sign of things to come. In the UK we have had lockdown or partial lockdown for over 4 months to the end of July 2020. It has not been a great year. And now we have to wear masks when we go shopping and my glasses steam up and I cannot see. Instead of eating out on Saturday night we get takeaways from restaurants that are now open. I have had pizza from my favourite Italian, Pieros and prawn tempura and duck noodles from my favourite Asian, Xen but I have no desire to eat in the restaurants which have little atmosphere and PPE servers. And I guess this goes for travel too. We have nothing booked and my desire to leave home and sit amongst possible infection on an aeroplane is nil. WILL WE EVER TRAVEL AGAIN - WHO KNOWS!!!

# March 2020 Cyprus

It is over two years since we have been away and here, we are at Heathrow Airport waiting to board our Club Europe flight to Cyprus. Here's hoping we do not crash. Why ? My mother has just died and there is a clause in her will that I have to live for 30 days after her death to inherit and it is only 28 days. We get there safely and take a euro 100 taxi ride to Colombia Beach Hotel in Pissouri. We have had dinner on the plane and arrive just before midnight. The room is very nice and discover a nice terrace with a sea view in the morning. Maybe an upgrade as not very busy. Nice breakfast . The outdoor pool is nice but cold and so is the indoor pool and also full of kids. Do not fancy. The weather is also a little cool. We take a wander around and discover the beach which is pebbles. Go to Kastros just up the road and have some nice Greek food for E22. In the afternoon we try out the tennis courts and play for about 45 minutes. In fact we play everyday but I will not bother to write about it again. Pre dinner we go for a cocktail but they are E12 each which seems a bit much. We stay in the hotel for dinner. It feels a little corporate but we have tzatziki and a very good taramasalata and both have Chicken Souvlaki and with a E24 bottle of 2017 Pathos wine it is E68 which is not too bad. Thought would be more somehow. Next day a nice lunch at Bay Tree for E13.60, the beers were only E2. Dinner at Saffron a local Indian for E59 with two large beers. The weather has got better and it may be 70 degrees but resist the cold water. Dinner at Bacchus in the hotel. Started with Sea Bass Creveche which is not the best ever. I had a Loin of Lamb which was done rare which they said they could not do with aubergine purée and gnocchi and onion which was quite nice. Chrissie had Mushroom Risotto which also quite nice. With another bottle of Pathos it cost E95 which is rather expensive.

The weather is nice so we spend the day around the pool and have a nice Greek lunch at Kastro. And return for dinner. It is all great and we have garlic prawns and Moussaka with a E14 carafe of red wine all for E56 plus tip. Next night we go to another local restaurant and have a beetroot stater and Grouper and a local wine at E19 all for E68.

It is still sunny and I go for my one and only swim in the sea with a wet suit. A good feeling but I feel a little tired. We have a good dinner again at Kastro with free beetroot, the prawns and garlic and Kleftiko which is very good. E59 for that dinner with the carafe of wine. The next day we go on a taxi ride to see a bit of the island. We start off at Aphrodites Rock which is a bit boring. Next up is the Sanctuary of Aphrodite which is a bit more interesting, it goes back to 1400BC. We finish in Pathos old town which is again boring. We head back. It is supposed to cost E25 per hour and we have only been just over two hours. It is supposed to last four. We negotiate E80 which seems a rip off. Another good dinner at Kastro for less than E60. The weather has got a little cooler but we manage the pool almost alone. For the next two nights we have good dinners at Harmony and Artemis eating Greek food and paying between E50 and E60. The weather is still not great. We have our last game of tennis and give the balls to reception. Good last dinner at Kastro with Garlic Prawns and Moussaka with carafe of red E59 again. We have had a very nice hotel and 7 really good dinners out of 10 nights in local places. Kastro is the star. I am not in love with Cyprus as it does not have the joy of Sicily and early March is probably not a great time for the weather. It has been over 60 but only briefly nudged 70. Not sure will return.

# June 2022 Los Angeles

We are on our way back to Los Angeles. Lauren was in a UBER crash and is having an operation to fix her back. We have an early flight so stay in Sofitel for convenience. I would not go here for choice as expensive and food not that great.

## Mr. Tambourine Man

A very short flight only 10 hours 8 minutes and we meet Lauren. We have hired a house in Marina del Rey so that we can all be together for her recovery. The house costs £6400 for the month we are going to be here. Not that great and seems dirty. A scruffy back yard for smoking and no stair rails, looks dangerous. And the pool was full of kids. The weather seems nice at around 80 degrees. Off to Wholefoods to buy dinner. Ravioli with Bolognese and Vodka sauce which quite nice and a Californian Syrah. In bed by 9pm and managed to sleep to 6.45 not too bad. Took the 45 minute walk along the canal to Marina Del Rey, good lunch and same walk back in the sunshine.

Wine warehouse next door and stocked up with some Tuscany wines. Lauren took us to Shutters in Santa Monica for dinner which you will know from previous times is one of my favourites. The cheapest wine was $92 so we drank beer. We all shared Guacamole and chips. I had a Wagu burger and the girls fish and chips and pizza and it all cost $218 plus tip which seems a lot. We had to get up at 6.30 to drive Lauren to hospital. Tried to find local tennis but failed. Did not swim as pool full of kids. Dinner at Sapori, a short drive away. Almost like being in Italy. We ate Roman Artichoke with garlic and I had Spaghetti with tomato and garlic which was all very nice. With a Peroni and a glass of Chianti it was $82 plus tip which again is not cheap. Lauren has had her operation so we take the 58 minute drive to see her. She looks very well but is going to stay a second night. Again fail to find tennis. Finding it difficult to find a restaurant which is not full. End up at Tony P's Grill where we do not have to wait. I eat Louisiana Fish Creole which is quite good. A local beer and glass of Merlot costs $68 plus tip. Lauren stays another night in hospital. She manages to get upstairs to her bedroom which is good. We have Dungeness Crab Cakes at home. We find the tennis courts which are only a 10 minute walk. We will play nearly everyday for the rest of our stay. Most days I swim in the pool so staying fit. As this is not a holiday and we are looking after Lauren and eat in quite a lot.

So I will just highlight some of our dinners out. Marina del Rey - Killer Shrimp. Not bad, hot Peel Shrimps and Lobster MacnCheese $62 but I think they forgot to charge for wine. Sapori again with a lift from a friend of Lauren. Celebrated with a bottle of Nero d'Avola at $50 ( it costs $4.99 in Trader Joes ). A great starter with Mussels, Clams, Beans and Sun Dried Tomato. A disappointing Lasagne. $130. Samosa - just up the road. An Indian. There are many choices but you get three things in a box plus rice. I had Dhal, Potato Curry and Potato and Aubergine and a Mango Lassi. It all cost $32 with no need to tip. Sapori again. Repeat of Mussels and Clams and Gnocchi with Tomato and Mozerella all very good. With a beer and glass of wine only $80 plus tip. Sapori for the fourth time. No starters but I had Spaghetti Seafood and Chrissie Chicken. With a beer and a glass of wine still $83 plus tip. Ritz Carlton. We are meeting Jamie and Bob our friends from Mexico who I have written about before. We start with a Veuve Cliquot rose and then to dinner. We drank a very nice Russian River Pinot Noir. I had Tuna Crudo which was quite nice and Beef Spare Ribs only okay.

No idea of the cost as they kindly treated us. Back to our place for more red wine, tequila and a puff of the joint. Very hungover the next day. Samosa again. Still very nice and only $26 this time. Sapori for the fifth time. With Lauren this time as she is almost fully recovered. I had the Mussels and Clams as a main course. With two glasses of wine and a beer for me $99 plus tip. Our last dinner here. I have not mentioned that on this trip I turned 70 and had a wonderful day with my family. The girls hired me a Ferrari California soft top for the day. I have had two Porsche 911 which I loved but this was something different. You drive along and feel like you are glued to the road . I drove it 27 miles to Sunset in Malibu. Nice lunch. I had a Virgin Mary as driving and a very good Tuna Tartare. $116 plus tip for three. Nice 27 miles back. We dropped Chrissie off and went back on the freeway. I got to 87mph, totally exhilarating and then let Lauren have a go which she loved.

Dinner was back to Santa Monica to Elephanta a flash local. We were on the third floor with a good ocean view but very noisy. Joined by Winnie, Esa and her brother Otto. I started with a Margarita, well you have to and we drank a lot of good $80 wine. Nice starters but can't read my writing, I had Lobster Pasta which was what it said on the tin. The bill was $760 but I shared it with Winnie. Back home with Esa for more champagne and a couple of nice drags on her cigarette. I still feel young and am pretty active and cannot really believe that I am this old. When I was younger old people always seemed ancient but I do not feel that in the least. Before I left I did something that may surprise you. I got a tattoo, first one at 70 you say. Lauren has a tattoo 8/11 in Roman numerals which is the date Chrissie and I met and the date we first heard about her . We photographed it and now it is on the inside of my left arm just above the elbow. Quite subtle. A strange time away. We did the job and Lauren is now fully recovered. Did she really need us, who knows ? But it was good to be there because you need to look after your kids.

## AUGUST 2022 Sicily

We are going back to Sicily again after what seems like ages but is actually three years. We are getting a 7.10 in the morning flight to Catania so have to get up at 4.30. Takes ages to get to Gatwick due to a crash on M5 and have to stay in Premier Inn which is not my favourite. Poor £42 dinner in Sofitel. Do not sleep that well because worried about waking up and WH Smith has no papers as too early. Nice bacon bap in the lounge as flying Club Europe. After 2 hours 25 minutes we are back in Sicily. We do not get a Fiat 500 which I love but a slightly larger Lancia which I hate and will find in the trip is not very good at going uphill. Stopped for lunch at a little cafe and with water only cost E5.60. We find our Agriturismo, Antico Borge Etneo in Calatbiano. It does have a view of Etna and it looks very nice but there is a problem that they do not do dinner. Told the village is only a 15 minute walk but I have a bad leg.

Drive around a little looking for somewhere for dinner but draw a blank and only manage to buy cigarettes which luckily are cheap here. We drive into the village and have quite a nice dinner in La Tata. We order Patina because we think we remember them as chickpea pancakes but are brought chips which we send back and do not get charged for. We both have Polpette which are supposed to be meatballs but seem more like hamburgers and as driving share a half litre of house red. E34 all up but I give them E40. We drink our free bottle of Prosecco on our return. The breakfast is niceish but the peach is not ripe. Off to beach Lido Sole which costs E16 and have a couple of swims and then hard panini and Peroni for lunch which costs E14. It starts to rain which is not supposed to happen in August so we head home. Tonight we are going to do something different. The train station is only a short walk away and we catch the 18.38 to Tamorina . The last train back is at 21.27. Do not have to pay so a free ride but there is a problem. The station is miles from the town which we know and love so we walk backwards to the neighbouring town for about 30 minutes and get a table at Opera Prima which seems very nice. We have an Aperol Spritz and then raw shellfish. Red prawn, white prawn, scampi and king prawn which are all delicious. Then we share Linguine with Scampi which is very good. We drink a E38 bottle of Etna Rosso and the bill is E103.90. We don't leave a tip and have to get a taxi as have missed the last train. E30 to get back. Another day at the beach at Aurora although there is light rain at lunchtime. Panini are better and the beer is only E2 so it only costs E12. We return to our place and I decide do not want to stay here so I book another Agriturismo near Marsala. It is not confirmed but tomorrow we will go anyway. We have last dinner in La Tata which is very good. For E40 we get Parmangiana Siciliana, Spaghetti Vignole and Macaroni Ragout with the half litre of house red . We get home and drink a bottle of limoncello which we have bought.

We say goodbye and they seem sad to see us go but only charge us for our three nights. E351. We head off to Marsala which will be about a three hour drive.

## Mr. Tambourine Man

Stop for lunch near Palermo at Rotonda which is very nice and have panini with olive paste, ementhal and salami with freshly squeezed OJ all for E14. We are soon at Sanacore our second chance Agriturismo. Our booking was not confirmed because they are full but the restaurant is open. The nice proprietor offers us a room nearby but we do not fancy so head into Marsala. It is now getting on for 5pm and we have nowhere to stay. Will we be sleeping in the car. We try a place called Roma but there is no reply. We see a sign for Best Western and think if needs must but cannot find it. We ask a young man for directions. He says get in my car. He was from Hungary originally and we end up at the Hotel Carmine which looks wonderful, has a room for 4 nights at E130 per night, has parking so we are all set. The room is wonderful with high ceilings and a small balcony and it is close to our favourite bar and restaurants. We try to book a table at Siciliano but they are full until 10.30 so we book the next night. We go to our favourite bar but it is now a restaurant so we go next door and have one G&T and two Americans for E18. Drinks only used to be E5 each but still a lot cheaper than Cyprus - see earlier. We take a short walk to La Vecchia and have a very good dinner. Caponata followed by great Lasagne for me and the best Chicken ever for Chrissie. We drink a E20 bottle of Sicilian Syrah and are given the whole bottle of limoncello to indulge. It all costs E64 for a great evening. The girls at the next table are singing and it is all so much fun. The next day we go off to find our favourite beach. Some difficulty as part of the route has become one way. At last we are there and have to pay E2 to park and E25 for chairs and umbrella. We manage to get Panelle for lunch which is the chick pea dish. I manage 5 swims and feels a little like heaven. And it is heaven to be back in Siciliano. We share a very nice Tuna Tartare and I have the Spaghetti with raw red shrimp which is as delicious as ever and Chrissie lamb chops. We drink a 2018 Nero d'Avola and it all costs E71. Back to the bar for Marsala wine and limoncello. Back to the favourite beach for good lunch and four swims. A swim is about 15 minutes and 500 strokes - yes I do count.

On way back we check out the cinema but nothing showing and I have one of my favourites , lemon granita. We make a mistake and take the advice of our receptionist and go to dinner at Bottega Carmine. I check my book later and find did not like the time we went before. It is just a very corporate place.

We share a vegetarian antipasti which is not the greatest with hard crostini. I had boring Gnocetti with Tuna and aubergine and Chrissie some fish and with a bottle of 2019 Nero d'Avola it was E70. Normal day at beach with five swims. Good last dinner here at our favourite La Vecchia. Caponata again, and I had Burata Matarocco which is garlic, tomatoes, olive oil and pine nuts. Chrissie repeated her chicken. Same wine and bottle of limoncello again but this time cost E73. We are now off to a favourite place, San Vito lo Capo. On the way we try to find a nice beach we know near Tripani airport but fail. Go to Plage Rio which is quite nice and have a couple of swims and for E11 two hot dogs and two Moretti. Takes a little while to find Il Piccado Giardino but we have a nice room with a sunny balcony. Have to pay the bill in cash. For 8 nights it is E741 which I pay. Go for a walk round town and buy our beach chairs and umbrella for E119 for 7 days and book one of our favourites for dinner I Giorgini. First of all we have to revisit our favourite bar for backgammon and drinks. Dinner is excellent. An amuse bouchée followed by a trio of tartare. Tuna, red shrimp and sea bream. Chrissie had an amazing Ravioli with raw red shrimp and I had Red Tuna with onions. A good bottle of Nero d'Avola at E24 and free Marsala and not too bad at E93. Our table is laid outside for breakfast on our terrace. Only okay but we are promised freshly squeezed OJ and water melon the next day. The coffee is very good. A great day. First we visited our old hotel and said hello to son and mother. Beach is nice and I have five 500 swims and lunch at the local cafe. Arancini, panini cotto and two beers for E13. And a lemon granita on the way home. Really like it here. Only an okayish dinner at Jaziri. Tuna Tartare, Burata with mussels, scampi and sea urchin for me and sea bream with caponata for Chrissie. An Italian red and two limoncello for E78.

## Mr. Tambourine Man

Do not think will return. Breakfast is a delight with freshly squeezed OJ and water melon which we now get everyday. Nice day on beach but then in evening it rains and get wet going for cocktails. I Giorgini is still open with a large umbrella to cover us, but the dinner is spoilt by noisy kids. The parents should have taken them home but they stayed for desserts and coffee whilst their kids ran riot. We started with a very nice trio of sardines and I had Tortinelli ( which is like spaghetti ) with scampi, yellow tomatoes and broad beans which was not that great and Chrissie Stuffed Squid which she liked. A nice bottle of Etna Rosso at E25 and two limoncello for E88. Nice breakfast again and at the beach by 9.40. Six swims, normal lunch but had to have an almond granita which is not so good.

We are going to have a great dinner at Divino recommended by our hostess. We order a Nero d'Avola at E24 and it is put in a decanter. We start with Lobster Arancini which is very nice but cannot really taste the lobster. We both have Risotto with Oysters, Black Garlic, Lemon and Butter which is absolutely delicious. With two limoncello the bill is E94 and worth it. Only five swims today and normal lunch and try a new place for lemon granita and have largest size for E4. Back to I Giorgini . No kids today but very busy. I start with the totally delicious raw red prawns and Chrissie has Caponata. Chrissie has a Seafood Salad with Octopus And Squid and I have the Burata with garlic and tomatoes and almonds. A good bottle of Etna Rosso but it seems expensive at E96. Normal day and back to Divino's for dinner and the lovely waiter Giuseppe. We have Nero D'Avola in the decanter again. We started with Smoked Aubergine that was absolutely divine and seemed to sing in your mouth. I had a pretty good Fish Cous Cous and Chrissie nice pork with a red pepper sauce. I had two limoncellos and Chrissie one and we started to talk with two people at the next table who spoke no English but bought us more limoncello. Lovely couple and our bill was E90 or E75 excluding limoncello and well worth it. Beach again and went to beach bar so I could have my first pizza of trip.

Nice dinner at Laccialoro which is opposite our bar. Nice appetiser of Panelle, Arancini and Croquttes. I had Ravioli with goats Ricotta and fish sauce which was nice and Chrissie fresh fish with gavros. Nero D'Avola to drink. E77 plus E10 for two limoncello. Our last dinner is at Dal Cozzaro. Nice location but had to talk to a Scottish man which did not like. I started with Crudo Red Prawns which were not the best. I then had Burata with lobster which was minimal and Chrissie Gnocchi with Bottega. With a bottle of Nero d'Avola it was E94 which is too much. Back to our bar for the last limoncello. Before we leave, I give our place an excellent review on booking.com. This has been a very interesting holiday for a number of reasons. We have had some great food and some food that has been disappointing and sometimes it has been too expensive. It at the end of the day I love Sicily and hope to be back here soon.

## Mr. Tambourine Man

# Conclusion

*Mr Tambourine Man* is supposed to mean something out of the ordinary. I started life with no money. I went to the United States the day after my twenty third birthday for three months and have never looked back. Against my will, I became a chartered accountant at a pretty young age and then worked very hard for over twenty years; I took my first gap year at age forty-six and am now in my eighteenth gap year (because I am too young to retire).

What have I achieved in my twenty three gap years?

I travelled a lot, and my journeys are detailed in the text. I am not a true gap year person, because I spent £350,000 on my travels, which is a little unusual.

What else have I done?

I was a mentor for the Prince's Trust for a while, until they became too politically correct. They introduced rules that you could not meet one-on-one in a nonpublic place. You had to meet in a public place, which was their place of work. I mentored one girl who was a healer with stones; I considered her totally weird. I only met her in a café, except for two times at her place, when I took someone else. But I did do a tax return on a girl's bed (because that was the only place there was any space). I helped ten young people who had been given loans to start businesses. I am still in touch with three who have become good friends, and I still do the annual tax return for two of them (the third is clever enough to do it herself).

I was treasurer of the tennis club for four years, and then I was chairman for nine years, with Chrissie as the treasurer. I moved the tennis club from near-insolvency to having loads of money and being the best club in Cornwall, with a thriving membership. I supported the juniors because I like young people; I'm very proud that we managed to get three youngsters to go to school in London and train full time. I was a counsel member of Tennis Cornwall but found it hard to contribute. I played tennis in the teams in summer and winter and a lot of social tennis, and my records show that during my gap years, I played tennis around thirty-eight hundred times. I am quite good and a better player than in 1999. The most I played was 2005, when I played 317, times and the lowest was 2008, when I only managed 189 times. A side effect of my activity is weight. When I left school at eighteen, I weighed ten stone. In a nonsmoking period in the late 1980s, my weight increased to twelve stone two pounds, but now, despite my love of food and drink, I am back to around ten stone.

I was a non-executive director of Jamie Oliver's Fifteen Cornwall for four years, up to 2015. It is a wonderful organisation and fits in with my love of food and young people. I think I was able to contribute there, but I left following disagreements with my fellow directors about the restaurant's direction.

Cornwall Council is responsible for the Cornwall Area of Outstanding Natural Beauty (AONB), and they set up the Friends of Cornwall AONB to promote awareness and look for fundraising. I was appointed to the board as a non-executive and then named chairman. We started to look at a membership scheme and a restaurant discount scheme to raise funds. It was all going quite well, but then the council changed their mind, and it was dissolved.

I also applied to become a non-executive director of Channel 4 and the Met Office but never even got an interview. Against this background, I am currently seeking non-executive director opportunities in something that will interest me.

When I was not doing all of this, I spent a lot of time in our first house's three-acre garden. I developed an amazing kitchen garden to provide food for our table. I was quite successful; I guess the best bits were the asparagus, artichokes, and raspberries. In our current town garden, we don't have too many flowers, but we look more like an allotment, with many vegetables happily growing in the walled garden.

We played around by investing in property a little. First, we bought a nice two-bedroom flat and got a tenant. Picking up the local paper one Thursday, I discovered that my flat had been raided by the police because my tenant had stolen furniture from his previous digs. He was let out on bail and absconded to Gibraltar. He came back, stole a boat, and was murdered by Senegalese pirates.

We sold out at a tidy profit and bought two three-bedroom holiday properties in Hayle for about £37,000 each. They were fully managed and produced a good income for a number of years, but we sold them for £72,000 and £59,000.

And we also have the time to go to the movies. In this period, I think I have seen over six hundred movies on the big screen. When you see so many movies, they are not all great. I informally score every movie that I see and keep a record. I have included my review of the best and worst movies for every year. I also had time to read a lot of books. I have included a similar list for the books.

I love food, and I love to cook. I have included a few of my favourite recipes. I can guarantee that if you follow these recipes, you will have just the greatest food.

I have also spent a reasonable amount of time writing this book. I think there is a book in all of us, and it is so good to have the time to indulge. After this book, I am going to write some fiction.

I have done a lot, but somehow, I think I could have done more. Maybe that is what gap years are all about.

In essence, I have not earned one penny in the whole time but I am still solvent with enough money to travel and enjoy life. We have our beautiful Georgian townhouse mortgage free which is now worth over £1 million, a lovely nearly new Audi A5 Cabriolet to drive, a healthy pension fund which I leave alone and some money in the bank. I still play the lottery but even if I won a large fortune, I am not sure it would change my life as it is quite good as it is.

# Mr. Tambourine Man

# Restaurants

### The Best Restaurant in the World

### Raymond Blanc's Manoir aux Quatre Saisons

I have stayed here twice and eaten dinner the day after my fortieth birthday and again when I had made a lot of money; I also had lunch here seven or eight times. The food is always ridiculously good, and I'll always remember taking my eight-year-old daughter here for an anniversary lunch. The kids' menu was terrific, with prawn cocktail, roast chicken, and chocolate mousse, and Lauren was happy to sit for three hours. There were two things that made it special: the kitchen garden, which you can walk around, and it just seems like a magic place where they grow all their vegetables for the very fine food, and Raymond: On our second stay, we had a quick chat with him before dinner and thought that was it nice to meet the man. After dinner, we were sitting by the fire with our coffee and armagnac, and he came and joined us for about thirty minutes. He was a delight and in love with food.

### The Place with the Best Restaurants in the World

### Cornwall

After all my travelling, this seems like a strange choice. When we arrived in 1999, there was only one restaurant: Rick Stein's Seafood Restaurant. Today, the whole county is full of brilliant restaurants, producing world-class food. I have not been to every restaurant in

Cornwall, including some notable restaurants, but here is a list of my favourites:

### Rick Stein's Seafood Restaurant

The original and still maybe the best. I have eaten lunch and dinner here many times, and the fish is always superb in brilliant surroundings. Rick Stein's Cafe in Padstow is also great for less-expensive fare.

### Rick Stein's Fish and Chips, Falmouth

There is also one in Padstow, but the ambience here is better. The fish and chips is simply the best in England; you cannot get better.

### Rick Stein's Porthleven and Fistral

With great harbour and seaviews more fine seafood dining.

### Fifteen

I was a non-executive director here for four years. The first thing to say is that it has the most stunning view of Watergate Bay, with its Atlantic rollers. The food is Italian and always very good. I had a brilliant dinner here for my sixtieth birthday. It has many standout dishes, but I would pick out their stuffed courgette flowers, which are truly world-class; I always have to order a second helping. The arancini also beats anything you can get in Italy. Nearly every dish is still a delight.

### Outlaw's Fish Kitchen, Port Isaac

This is a lovely inexpensive restaurant, with lunch normally costing less than £40 for two, including drinks. They have a tapasstyle menu, and on a typical day you may get the following:

- smoked cod roe dips
- beetroot-cured salmon
- blood orange-cured gurnard
- cuttlefish fritters
- pan-fried mackerel (which is the best you will ever have)
- monkfish with curried cauliflower, chickpeas, and spinach
- lemon pousset
- rhubarb jelly
- The food is just so good.

### Portminster Beach Cafe, St Ives

This is set right on the beach in St Ives, and the view is just brilliant, particularly from the outside terrace. They always have lovely fish, and they do a citrus vinaigrette dressing, which is all you would ever want on your salad (but the recipe is a secret, and they won't tell you the ingredients). The atmosphere is always great, even if it is full of tourists.

### Gurnard's Head, Zennor

This is a great pub a few miles outside St Ives, which serves award-winning food in a great atmosphere.

### Victoria Inn, Perranuthnoe

This is another award-winning pub. I ate a really good lunch here with courgette, mint and lemon soup, followed by gnocchi with peas, spinach, and chilli.

### Star and Garter, Falmouth

This is a pub that should win many awards, with the greatest food and the finest views over Falmouth Harbour. The menu changes daily, and if you are lucky, you will get their cod roe with cucumber and crostini, marmalade ham, and ricotta and chard dumplings, with a tomato soup. If you book a table before 6.45, you even get a free bottle of wine.

**Tresanton, St Mawes**

This is a special, expensive hotel with a fine restaurant. One February, we had Sunday lunch here outside on the terrace, overlooking Falmouth and the sea. The Doom Bar and the crab salad were excellent for me, and a crab sandwich and prosecco for Chrissie, all for £48 plus tip.

**Hooked on the Beach, Swanpool**

This is another great place for fine views of the sea and really good seafood.

**Cove, Maenporth**

Great seaviews and very nice dining on the terrace in the summer and cosy inside in the winter.

**Truro**

This is our hometown, and we live about a quarter of a mile from the restaurants, so we don't have to worry about driving and can drink to our heart's content. There are a lot of good neighbourhood restaurants, and our favourites are Hooked (seafood), Thomas Daniel and Rising Sun (good pub grub), Zen (Asian), Truro Tandoori (curry), Katmandu (award-winning curry), Pierro's (Italian, run by Italians), Hub Box (burgers), and Falmouth Oyster Bar (seafood).

I have to give a special mention to Saffron. One Saturday before Christmas, as we were going out the front door, we showed up at Saffron for dinner.

'Have you booked?'
'No.'

We got the last table right at the back. There was a bench against the back wall and a chair facing the back wall. We decided to share the bench and look out on the many couples (who didn't seem to have much to say to each other). We ordered a bottle of wine, which we mostly drink before the food and so had to order another. We had some fine food and did a lot of giggling, and then I asked for the bill. The waitress came with the bill and said, 'It's lucky you were at the back, so that your other halves could not see you.' She was convinced we were having so much fun that we must have been playing away.

There are a lot of other great restaurants in Cornwall which I have not yet visited, but I think my list shows the possibilities for a lot of very fine dining and so many gorgeous views

There are other good places to eat in the world.

**Los Angeles**

Having been here eighteen times, I have several favourites:

Starting in Toluca Lake, where Lauren lived, I have to begin with Angelino's. This is just a simple trattoria, but the ravioli pomodoro with cheese has to be one of the best dishes ever, and their tomato sauce is also a secret. The other pasta dishes are always so good; this is a neighbourhood restaurant not to miss. Prosecco for finer dining is also a delightful place, and their osso buco is top notch. Patty's is the finest diner in the United States; I always enjoy the corned beef hash with fried eggs over easy and the waffles, which are the best. My favourite hotel, if I am feeling rich, is the London; they have a Gordon Ramsay restaurant which is fine dining at its best, for both lunch and dinner. Petit Four just down the road on Sunset is the nicest French restaurant outside France.

**New York**

I have been here many times and having spent six weeks here when I was just eighteen it is very close to my heart. I have two favourites. The Oyster Bar on Grand Central Station is a magic place with great seafood and a fantastic atmosphere. Down to Greenwich village where we find Rafele which is in Trip Advisors top ten restaurants in New York. The food is just amazingly good and the stand out has to be such a simple dish the twenty-four month old Black Label Prosciutto.

## Other US Restaurants

We have eaten so much over the years, but I would pick out the following.

**Carmel.** This is a delightful place that is in our hearts from our honeymoon days. Andre's Bouchee is our favourite restaurant, with great food and a very fine wine list. Everybody should come to Carmel and eat there.

**New Orleans.** This is another great city to visit. Our favourite dinner is Coop's, where you have to queue in a line to get in. The fried crayfish and jambalaya are great, they only serve wine in magnums, and it's all dirt cheap at $68 (including the magnum).

**Tulsa.** The Ambassador Hotel is lovely, and dinner at the Palace is great fun. Somehow, this is a town worth visiting.

**Miami.** I just have to mention Cecconi's, which is Italian at its best.

## Mexico

The joy of dinner in Mexico is the margarita aperitif. We have had some nice food in Mexico, but Cabo San Lucas on our last visit was the highlight. Neptuno's gives you some of the best sashimi ever. Maria Jimmez is great for authentic Mexican food and a wonderful atmosphere. The local pizza place is pretty good. Best of all, Omega on the beach is just delightful; you can stay all day on the chairs under the umbrella, eat lovely shrimp taco and guacamole, and drink Pacifico and a bottle of water, and it all costs around £10.

## Italy

A food lover's heaven. I have to start in Venice, which is such a brilliant city. You just have to take the one-hour boat ride to Torcello and go to Locando Cipriano. The garden on a sunny summer's day is one of the best places ever for lunch, and the food is delicious too. In Venice, we also love Trattoria Maradonna by the Rialto Bridge, which is great for fried scampi and other seafood and has not changed for thirty years.

Sicily is also wonderful for food. We have been three times to St Georges in Taormina, and the setting, service, and the food are truly world-class. On our third visit, we went to San Vito Lo Capo, which is a delightful, traffic-free town with many good restaurants. Our favourites were Il Gorgio, with its delightful garden, shrimp tartare, and E10 litres of Etna house wine, and Syrah (which spelt backwards is Harys), where you even get to choose your lobster from the rocks or deeper.

We had a great holiday in Marina del Cantone near Naples, staying in the hotel La Certosa. Every morning, as we were having a lovely breakfast, we could see them making pasta in the kitchen. The town had two Michelin restaurants, where we had expensive dinners that were disappointing, but all our meals in the hotel were fantastic, with very good Italian food at its best. We had a later winter holiday in Naples and enjoyed Osteria Il Carum again, for simple Italian food at its best. We also had great pizza in a simple local place.

Rome is a fantastic city and full of many lovely places to eat. Our favourite was Trattoria Cabonara, which again was simple Italian food at its best.

Simple Italian food at its best is not so hard to find in Italy. As just mentioned, we were disappointed by the Michelin restaurants in Marina del Cantone (you may remember the restaurant in Naples that we hated so much we cancelled our second reservation on the pretext that work called us back to London).

I should recount an experience in Florence in the early 1990s. It was our last day and Chrissie's birthday. I asked if she would like to go somewhere smart for lunch, to which she of course replied yes.

Instead, I took her to the market, and we sat down at a communal table with a load of chatty Italians (who we could not understand) and ate a cheap lunch of Parma ham, tagliatelle with cream and truffles, and a jug of red wine. It was one of the best lunches ever, and she was so glad we resisted the smart. This is maybe the way to eat in Italy.

## France

Over the years, we have eaten many memorable meals in France. My favourite place at the moment is the island of Oleron, just south of La Rochelle. There are two reasons: the fantastic sand dune beaches with great swimming, and two great restaurants. Jardins Alienor served one of the best steaks ever. Le Drugstore is a brilliant bistro with great food and a great atmosphere. This all makes for a perfect holiday destination.

Another favourite place in France is the Cafe de Paris in Monte Carlo: again, a brilliant bistro in a pretty boring town.

## Far East

We had only two trips to the Far East.

On the first trip, we discovered Food Street in Singapore, which is full of amazing restaurants with amazing food. We then went on to Kuala Lumpur, where we discovered the Food Market, where you just sit at a table and choose food from many different cooks and pay cash as it arrives to your table. Kungs in Kho Lak was a lovely, reasonable restaurant with great food. We also found a great beach bar (whose name I do not recall) for some more great lunchtime food.

The second trip was Vietnam. Our first culinary experience was at Dim Dim Sum Dim Sum in Hong Kong, which *Newsweek* named one of the best 101 restaurants in the world. It was a magical place with great dishes and wonderful, even with only tea to drink. Onto Vietnam. We really enjoyed Morning Glory in Hoi An and ate great food and drank wine from Sicily. The food highlight of our trip to Ho Chi Minh City was the Vespa tour, where we had such a great time and ate so well. We loved Phu Quoc and thought the Javelin was one of the best hotels ever, and we enjoyed their food. But what we liked best was to go out to the local restaurants; we ate very well and very cheaply, with wonderful fresh fish and other local delicacies.

We enjoy food, and our two trips to the Far East have provided many memorable meals and an awful lot of great food.

## Caribbean

Maybe you do not come here for the food. However, on our trip to Antigua, we were very lucky to stay at Chez Pascal. Pascal cooks classic Lyons food at its best, and it was such a pleasure to stay with him. Giorgio Armani has a house just opposite, and I am sure he is always there, as the food is so good.

We were also lucky to eat very well in Grenada. The Beach House restaurant on Grooms Beach is one of the nicest beach restaurants anywhere in the world. LaLuna next door is a great Italian. It was great to be staying right next door to two such great restaurants.

St Lucia was a little disappointing for food, probably because we were in a tourist area. However, Jambe de Bois on Pigeon island is truly worth a visit for their superb roti.

## Not on the List

Greece is not on the memorable list. This is a shame, as I would recommend the gavros for lunch at Vrelimnos Beach. We had many delightful dinners in Greece, but a good plate of fried courgettes, tzaziki, and moussaka are maybe not intended for the list.

The Cook Islands were a wonderful experience, and again, we had great lunchtime sandwiches, but the food generally is not world beating.

We also failed to find anywhere for the list in Australia or Hawaii. For different reasons, both of these trips did not live up to our expectations; perhaps part of the problem is that I am not able to record any memorable meals.

# Recipes

I wrote about food a lot in this book, and I also like to cook at home. Here are some of my favourite recipes:

**Crab Tart with Chilli Pastry**

This is a great dish; living in Cornwall, we are very fortunate to have the greatest crab on our doorstep (serves four).

**Pastry**

> 200g plain flour, sifted
> 1 level teaspoon mild chilli powder
> 50g freshly grated Parmesan
> 150g unsalted butter, diced
> 1 medium egg, beaten
> Olive oil

**Filling**

> 450g white crabmeat
> 4 medium eggs
> Juice of 1 lemon
> A pinch of mild chilli powder
> 200ml crème fraiche

For the pastry, place the first four ingredients with a pinch of salt in a food processor and process briefly. With the machine running, add the egg and ½ tbsp oil. Process briefly until combined, adding a little extra oil if necessary. Clingwrap and chill for 1-2 hours. Roll out to fit a 28cm loose-based tart tin, prick all over, and chill for 2-3 hours or overnight. Fill with foil and baking beans, then bake blind at 190C for 15 minutes. Remove and cool.

Beat together the filling ingredients with salt and pepper, pour into the pastry case, and bake for 40-45 minutes until set and tinged with golden brown. Serve warm or cold.

This makes the most wonderful dish.

## Sole Florentine

Another wonderful dish which benefits from our great fish caught in Cornwall (serves four):

1kg fresh spinach
125g butter
Nutmeg
8 fillets of lemon sole
1 glass white wine
50g flour
500ml milk
Freshly grated Parmesan

Wash the spinach, place in a pan, cover, and cook for a few minutes with a little salt and only the water that clings to the leaves, turning them over until they crumple. Drain well, return to the pan with 25g of butter, and sauté briefly; season with salt, pepper, and a pinch of nutmeg and set aside.

Heat the wine with 25g butter and salt and pepper in a frying pan. Poach the sole fillets for five minutes, then remove the fish and let the sauce reduce to about three tablespoons.

Meanwhile, make the white sauce: melt 50g butter, add the flour, and stir well. Add the reduced sauce and milk gradually, stirring all the time until the sauce thickens. Season with salt and pepper and as much nutmeg as you like.

Grease an ovenproof dish with the remaining butter, line the bottom of the dish with the spinach, lay the sole on top, and coat with the sauce. Sprinkle liberally with Parmesan and bake at 200C for 20 minutes, until a crust has formed on top.

It is completely delicious.

## Spaghetti with Clams, Tomato, and a Dash of Cream

We are very lucky to get our clams from Hayle; this makes a great dish (serves two):

500g small clams
2 garlic cloves, peeled, 1 left whole and 1 chopped
3 tablespoons olive oil
200g chopped fresh tomatoes
Good pinch of ground chilli
2 tablespoons whipping cream
Clump of parsley with stalks
60ml white wine
2 tablespoons chopped parsley
160g thick spaghetti (preferably homemade)

Soak the clams in a large bowl of cold salted water for a couple of hours to get rid of any sand or grit. Give them a good swishing round in the soaking water a few times, and change the water if there is any sand or grit. Discard any clams that are well opened.

In a large frying pan that will hold the pasta later, stir in the chopped garlic in 2 tablespoons of olive oil until it smells good. Add the tomatoes and season with salt and pepper and chilli. Simmer for about 10 minutes, squashing any tomato lumps with a wooden spoon. Add the cream and heat through, then remove from the heat.

In another pan that has a lid, heat the last tablespoon of olive oil with the whole clove of garlic. When the garlic has perfumed the oil, add the drained clams, parsley, and a grind of black pepper. Pour in the wine. Put the lid on and turn the heat right up to steam the clams open (this should only take around 5 minutes). Remove from the heat and cool a little. Discard any clams that haven't opened. When they are cool enough to handle, pluck out around one half of the clam meat, putting it back in the pan and discarding the shells. Leave the rest of the clams in their shells in the pan. Remove the whole garlic clove and parsley. Add the clams to the tomato pan.

Bring a pot of salted water to the boil and cook the spaghetti to al dente. Add the spaghetti to the tomato and clam sauce and turn through well. Let it heat through for a minute and then scatter the chopped parsley and serve at once with a good grind of black pepper.

Enjoy you will.

**Grilled Langoustine with Pernod**

In Cornwall, the langoustines normally come from Scotland, but this is still a wonderful dish (serves four):

16 large (or 24 smaller) langoustines
2 small shallots, finely chopped
½ tablespoon roughly chopped fresh tarragon
½ tablespoon roughly chopped fresh flat-leaf parsley
1 teaspoon Dijon mustard
1 teaspoon dark soy sauce
85ml extra virgin olive oil
2 tablespoons fresh lemon juice
1 teaspoon Pernod
50g melted butter

Pre-heat the grill to high. Cut the langoustines open lengthways and scoop out the creamy contents of the heads and any red roe with a teaspoon. Put this into a small bowl and stir in the shallots, tarragon, parsley, mustard, soy sauce, oil, lemon juice, Pernod, and a little salt and pepper to taste. Place the halved langoustines cut side up on a baking tray and brush with the melted butter. Season lightly and grill for 2-3 minutes, until the shells as well as the meat are heated through. Put the langoustines on 4 serving plates and spoon over a little of the dressing. Divide the rest of the dressing between 4 dipping sauces and serve.

## Brandade and Haricot Bean Soup with Truffle Oil

A different take on fish soup (serves four):

175g dried haricot beans
450g unskinned thick cod fillet
1 pint milk
6 garlic cloves, sliced
100ml extra virgin olive oil
300ml double cream
1 tablespoon truffle oil
Chopped fresh flat-leaf parsley to garnish

Cover the haricot beans with plenty of cold water and leave to soak overnight. Sprinkle a ½-inch layer of salt over the base of a plastic container, put the cod on top, and completely cover it with another layer of salt. Cover and refrigerate overnight.

Next day, drain the beans and put them in a saucepan with 900ml of water. Bring to the boil, then cover and simmer for up to two hours, until they are soft and just starting to break apart. Remove the cod from the brine and rinse it under cold water. Cover with fresh water and leave to soak for 1 hour. Drain the beans, reserving the cooking liquor.

Put the prepared salted cod into a large saucepan with the milk. Bring to a simmer and cook for 4-5 minutes, or until just done. Lift the cod out onto a plate, and when it is cool enough to handle, break it into flakes, discarding the skin and any bones. Reserve the milk.

Put the flaked fish and garlic into a liquidiser.

Heat the oil and the cream together in a small pan until boiling, then add the fish with the beans and blend together until smooth. With the machine still running, add the reserved milk. Return the soup to the pan and reheat gently, but do not let it boil. Add a little of the bean cooking liquor if necessary to obtain a good consistency. Ladle the soup into 4 warmed bowls. Drizzle over the truffle oil and garnish with a little chopped parsley.

## Malaysian Fried Lemon Sole with Roasted Tomato and Chilli Sambal

Another spicy dish for a lovely Cornish fish (serves four):

3 lemon sole weighing about 450g each, filleted and skinned
175g cornflour
Sunflower oil for deep-frying
Sea salt and freshly ground black pepper

**For the roasted tomato and chilli sambal**

2 dried pasilla chillies
350g tomatoes, cut in half
6 red finger chillies
3 shallots
2 tablespoons lime juice
2 tablespoons Thai fish sauce

**For the chilli sauce**

6 red finger chillies, roughly chopped
4 garlic cloves, roughly chopped
1 teaspoon turmeric powder
5cm piece fresh root ginger, roughly chopped
4 tablespoons sunflower oil
1 teaspoon salt
2 tablespoons vinegar
4-6 tablespoons cold water

First, make the sambal. Cover the dried chillies with boiling water and leave to soak for 15 minutes, or until soft. Put the tomatoes, whole red chillies, and shallots on a grilling tray and grill for 5-10 minutes, turning now and then, until well blackened. Drain the soaked chillies and chop them finely and mix with the roasted vegetables, lime juice, and fish sauce.

Put all the ingredients for the chilli sauce into a liquidiser and blend until smooth. Pour into a pan and simmer gently for 10 minutes or until the mixture begins to separate.

Put the sunflower oil into a large pan and heat the oil to 190C. Put the chilli sauce in a shallow dish and the cornflour in another. Season the fish fillets and dip them first into the chilli sauce and then into the cornflour, making sure that the fish is coated evenly. Cook the fillets for about 2 minutes or until crisp and golden. Serve with the sambal.

## Tagliatelle with Chicken from the Venetian Ghetto

A change from fish and a dish that will beat roast chicken any day (serves four):

3lb chicken
2 tablespoons olive oil
Needles from 2 or 3 sprigs rosemary, chopped very finely
50g sultanas, soaked in warm water for 30 minutes
100g pine nuts, lightly toasted
500g freshly made tagliatelle
Preheat the oven to 180C

Rub the chicken with oil and sprinkle with sea salt and freshly ground black pepper; place breast down in a baking dish and cook for around 90 minutes until well browned, turning over towards the end to brown the breast.

By hand, take the meat off the bone, leaving all the glorious burnished skin on, and cut into small pieces. Put all the juices from the roasting pan into a saucepan. Add the rosemary, the drained sultanas, and the pine nuts. Begin to simmer while you cook the pasta.

Cook the pasta al dente and put in a large warmed bowl with the chicken and the sauce, and at the last minute, sprinkle some chopped flat-leaf parsley over it. This is just delicious and needs no cheese.

# Movies

I love to go to the movies, and the book has recorded quite a few trips to the movies, mostly in America because they speak English, which helps. I am setting out below the number of movies I have seen each year, with my favourite movie, my worst movie, and who won the Oscar, from 2001, when I first started listing and scoring movies.

## 2001. Ten Movies

I hadn't started scoring yet, but my favourites were *The Dish*, *Bridget Jones's Diary*, and *Amelie*. I didn't enjoy *Harry Potter*. *A Beautiful Mind* wins the Oscar, which we saw in 2002, and it gets in our top five.

## 2002. Fourteen Movies

We have now started scoring, and my favourite is *About a Boy*, which scores 9.0. Not far behind is *My Big Fat Greek Wedding* and *The Bourne Identity*. *Bend It Like Beckham* and *Beautiful Mind* also scored well, with over 8.0. Scoring over 7.0 are *Oceans Eleven*, *Gosford Park*, *Minority Report*, and *Die Another Day*. Bottom with 2.0 is *Lord of the Rings*. Five out of fourteen good movies. *Chicago* wins the Oscar; it was okay.

## 2003. Eighteen Movies

The favourite with 9.5 is *The Italian Job*, with *Two Weeks Notice* and *Love Actually* both scoring 9.25. Scoring over 8.0 are *Blue Crush*, *The Pianist*, and *Calendar Girls*. As I take Lauren to the movies, *Lord of the Rings* is bottom again by a long way, and it wins the Oscar.

Six out of eighteen good movies. I give 7.0 or more to *City of God*, *Matrix Reloaded*, *Bruce Almighty*, *Finding Nemo*, and *Seabiscuit*. This means eleven out of eighteen have made the grade. I still watch *Love Actually*, and it's just so good, even after a few times.

## 2004. Twenty-Nine Movies

And the winner this year is *The Passion of the Christ*, with 8.8. This has been a good year for movies, with the following all scoring over 8.0:

*Cold Mountain*, *School of Rock*, *Along Came Molly*, *Mean Girls*, *The Bourne Supremacy*, *Billabong Odyssey*, *Finding Neverland*, *Ladies in Lavender*, *Bridget Jones: The Edge of Reason*, and *The Incredibles*. This means eleven out of twenty-nine scored well. Two sequels get another high rating, but *Lord of the Rings* is bottom again. Scoring over 7.0 are *Lost in Translation*, *Girl with a Pearl Earring*, *Starsky and Hutch*, *50 First Dates*, *Troy*, *Day after Tomorrow*, *Spiderman 2*, *The Village*, *Dodgeball*, and *Riding Giants*. This gives us twenty-one movies getting a good score. *Million Dollar Baby* wins the Oscar, which I saw later on the TV; again, it's only okay.

## 2005. Thirty-Six Movies

We have joint winners this year at 9.1, with *Pride and Prejudice* and *Broken Flowers*. The following scored over 8.0:

*The Aviator*, *The Closer*, *Meet the Fockers*, *The Island*, *Crash*, *Nanny Macphee*, and *Keeping Mum*. *Harry Potter* came last. Only eight out of thirty-six good movies.

Scoring over 7.0 are *Ray*, *Sideways*, *Hitch*, *Be Cool*, *Sahara*, *The Interpreter*, *Kingdom of Heaven*, *Sin City*, *Batman Begins*, *War of the Worlds*, *The Descent*, *Wedding Crashers*, *Herbie Falls Down*, *The Play That I Wrote*, *Mrs Henderson Presents*, and *King Kong*. Twenty-four movies (or two-thirds) scored quite well.

*Crash*, which I gave 8.6, wins the Oscar. *Harry Potter* is the dog.

## 2006. Fifty-Two Movies

*Borat* wins with 9.0, and *The Holiday* is a close second with 8.9. *The Holiday* is a movie which I still like to watch at Christmas; I love it every time. Scoring over 8.0 are:

*March of the Penguins, Munich, Brokeback Mountain, Match Point, Walk the Line, Poseidon* (for the wrong reasons: we laughed so much at the tense moments that the three of us were nearly ejected from the cinema), *Prime, The Lake House, Wah-Wah, Snakes on a Plane, The Wind that Shook the Barley, The Queen, Children of Men, Volver, An Inconvenient Truth, Little Miss Sunshine, Little Box of Sweets,* and *Casino Royale.* It was a pretty good year for the movies, with twenty scoring more than 8.0.

These are the movies scoring over 7.0: *Fun with Dick and Jane, Jarhead, Syriana, Good Night and Good Luck, American Dreamz, The Da Vinci Code, Enron: Smartest Guys in the Room, The Break Up, Miami Vice, You, Me & Dupree, Severance, My Super Ex-Girlfriend, The Sentinel, Adrift, Driving Lessons, The Black Dahlia, The Departed* (at 7.3, which wins the Oscar), *Click, History Boys, Marie Antoinette,* and *Red Road.* This gives us forty-one movies I liked a lot, which is pretty good.

The dud is *When a Stranger Calls,* which only gets 3.9.

## 2007. Fifty Movies

*The Bourne Ultimatum* (the third in the series) is the winner with 8.8; the Bourne movies are just so good. Scoring over 8.0 are:

*Last King of Scotland, Music and Lyrics, Blood Diamonds, Babel, The Black Book, The Lives of Others, Die Hard 4, Michael Clayton, Hallam Foe, Breach,* and *Rendition.* Not such a good year, with only twelve making it over the 8.0 line.

The movies scoring over 7.0 are:

*The Pursuit of Happyness*, *Stranger than Fiction*, *Miss Potter*, *Hollywoodland*, *London to Brighton*, *Notes on a Scandal*, *Sunshine*, *Amazing Grace*, *After the Wedding*, *The Painted Veil*, *Away from Her*, *Hairspray*, *Tell No One*, *Knocked Up*, *Atonement*, *The Hoax*, *Goldfinger* (original), *The Kingdom*, *Ratatouille*, *The Heartbreak Kid*, *2 Days in Paris*, *Born and Bred*, *Elizabeth*, and *The Singer*. Thirty-seven out of fifty movies getting across the line is pretty good.

Our least favourite was *1408*, with 4.5.

*No Country for Old Men* wins the Oscar, but I only give 6.9.

## 2008. Fifty-Eight Movies

Not such a good year, with *The Changeling* winning at 8.5. There are only five other films scoring over 8.0: *Diving Bell and Butterfly*, *21*, *In Bruges*, *W*, and *Man on the Wire*.

Scoring over 7.0 are:

*The Kite Runner*, *Charlie Wilson's War*, *The Savages*, *Juno*, *Before the Devil Knows You're Dead*, *In the Valley of Elah*, *The Ruins*, *Iron Man*, *What Happens in Vegas*, *Sex and the City*, *Indiana Jones*, *Mama Mia*, *Angus, Thongs, and Perfect Snogging*, *Mutiny on the Bounty* (1935 version), *Pineapple Express*, *Brideshead Revisited*, *Elegy*, *Vicky Christina Barcelona*, *Traitor*, *Summer Hours*, *The Duchess*, *Married Life*, *The Boy in the Striped Pajamas*, *Burn after Reading*, *Ghost Town*, *Quantum of Solace*, *Easy Virtue*, *Four Christmases*, and *Cadillac Records*. Thirty-four good movies for the year, just below 60 percent.

We hated *Australia*, which only scored 3.0. *Slumdog Millionaire* wins the Oscar, but I found it a little trite and dull and only gave it 7.0 when I saw it in 2009.

## 2009. Sixty-Seven Movies

A better year, with *An Education* winning at 8.6. The others over 8.0 are:

*Up in the Air*, *Frost/Nixon*, *The Reader*, *The Bicycle Thief*, *Revolutionary Road*, *Gran Torino*, *Young Victoria*, *The Damned United*, *State of Play*, *Julie and Julia*, and *Broken Embraces*. Twelve again, but it's less than one-fifth of the movies we saw.

Scoring over 7.0 are:

*Rivals*, *Slumdog Millionaire*, *La Zona*, *Valkyrie*, *Benjamin Button*, *The Wrestler*, *Milk*, *Che* (part 1 and 2), *The Boat that Rocks*, *Il Divo*, *Star Trek*, *Last Chance Harvey*, *The Hangover*, *Looking for Eric*, *Public Enemies*, *Paris 1936*, *My Sister's Keeper*, *The Hurt Locker*, *Coco before Chanel*, *End of the Line*, *Final Destination 3*, *Inglorious Basterds*, *Everlasting Moments*, *Frozen River*, *Up*, *500 Summers*, *Men Who Stare at Goats*, *Taking Woodstock*, *Precious*, and *Avatar*. This gives forty-three movies over 7.0: not a bad year, with two-thirds scoring well.

The least liked was *The Road*, with 4.9. *The Hurt Locker*, which I give 7.8, wins the Oscar.

## 2010. Seventy-Four Movies

We have joint winners again with 8.2. We saw *Shutter Island* in LA with Lauren and Eric and spent the whole of dinner afterwards discussing the reality. It was spoilt on TV with a different script explaining all. It is rumoured that the release of the movie was delayed because Martin Scorsese couldn't decide the end. Our movie house version was brilliant. Joint winner was *Social Network*. Also scoring above 8.0 were *Inside Job*, *The Girl with the Dragon Tattoo* (Swedish version with subtitles), *The Blind Side*, *Harry Brown*, and *Whatever Works*. The dog with only 1.0 was *The Lightning Thief*. But only seven highly rated movies, which is less than 10 percent. We have quite a lot of films over 7.0:

*Nine, The Informant, It's Complicated, Sex and Drugs and Rock 'n' Roll, Nowhere Boy, Crazy Heart,* Invictus, *A Single Man, Valentine's Day, Brothers, Green Zone, Last Station, I Love You Phillip Morris, Cemetery Junction, Date Night, Robin Hood, The Bad Lieutenant, Toy Story 3, Salt, The Kids Are All Right, I Am Love, The Girl Who Played with Fire, Going the Distance, Eat Pray Love, Made in Dagenham, Wall Street 2, The Town, Wild Grass, Red, Africa United, Another Year, Due Date, Conviction, Hereafter, The Next 3 Days, Fair Game, 127 Hours, Unstoppable,* and *The Way Back.* This makes forty-six movies over 7.0, which is not too bad.

*The King's Speech* is the Oscar winner, which I saw in 2011 and scored 7.9.

## 2011. Sixty-Seven Movies

The winner this year, which we saw in the Sydney Opera House, was *Jack Johnson* (with 9.6), probably because the live music and setting were so good. Otherwise, *Senna, The Fighter, The Ides of March, My Week with Marilyn,* and *We Need to Talk about Kevin* all got over the 8.0. *The Help* only scores 3.0 and is bottom. Only six good movies out of sixty-seven is pretty poor. The films scoring over 7.0 are:

*The King's Speech, Black Swan, Winters Bone, True Grit, No Strings Attached, Wasted on the Young, The Lincoln Lawyer, Barney's Version, Jane Eyre, Win Win, Of God and Men, Limitless, Arthur, West Is West, Blue Valentine, Water for Elephants, Hangover 2, Hanna, Bad Teacher, Bridesmaids, Meek's Cutoff, The Inbetweeners, Final Destination 5, Midnight in Paris, Crazy Stupid Love, The Debt, Drive, Straw Dogs, Killer Elite, Moneyball, Tinker Tailor,* and *The Guard,* which gives us thirty-seven movies over the 7.0, which is more than one-half.

I saw *The Artist* in 2012; it wins the Oscar, and I scored 7.5 for an interesting older-style movie.

## 2012. Sixty-Seven Movies

The winner this year is *Argo*, with 8.5, and it also wins the Oscar for best movie, which is the only year where my favourite movie also wins Best Picture.

Another disappointing year, with only five films scoring 8.0: *The Sweeney*, *Trade of Innocents*, *Hitchcock*, *The Girl with the Dragon Tattoo* (in English with Daniel Craig), and *The Iron* Lady. There are, however, a lot of films over 7.0: *War Horse*, *J. Edgar*, *The Artist*, *The Descendants*, *Man on a Ledge*, *This Means War*, *Carnage*, *A Separation*, *Martha Marcy May Marlene*, *Salmon Fishing in the Yemen*, *Le Havre*, *This Must Be the Place*, *Weekend Retreat*, *The Angels Share*, *The Amazing Spiderman*, *Chariots of Fire* (the original), *Ted*, *Bourne Legacy*, *Hope Springs*, *Untouchable*, *Skyfall*, *The Sessions*, *Hello I Must Be Going*, *Flight*, *Hyde Park on Hudson*, and *Great Expectations*. This gives twenty-six movies over 7.0. *Lincoln* comes bottom at 2.9; we all hated it.

## 2013. Seventy Movies

*Zero Dark Thirty* wins with 8.5.

Scoring over 8.0 are *The Impossible* (about the Thailand tsunami and featuring the hotel we stayed in, Koh Lak), *Django Unchained*, *Captain Phillips*, and *Philomena*. And the loser (I must have gone with Lauren) with only 4.2 is *Hunger Games*. Only five good movies again.

Scoring over 7.0 are *Gangster Squad*, *Les Miserables*, *No*, *Olympus Has Fallen*, *Place Beyond the Pines*, *The Look of Love*, *Dans La Maison*, *Behind the Candelabra*, *Renoir*, *Lone Ranger*, *Blue Jasmine*, *The Butler*, *Indiana Jones*, *Prisoners*, *Rush*, *Out of the Foundry*, *Nebraska*, *Saving Mr Banks*, and *Dallas Buyers Club*. This makes only twenty-four films to make the grade. *Oblivion* and *Worlds End* at 4.8 tie for the worst movie of the year.

The Oscar winner is *12 Years a Slave*, which I saw in 2014; it's pretty good and scores 7.9.

## 2014. Seventy-Four Movies

This is a pretty poor year, with only two films scoring 8.0. Kate Winslett again in *Labour Day* and a second viewing of *Love Actually*, just before Christmas. There are, however, quite a lot of films scoring over 7.0:

*All Is Lost, 12 Years a Slave, Jeune et Joli, Jack Ryan, Wolf of Wall Street, Lone Survivor, Her, Sorcerer, Calvary, Two Faces of January, Devils Knot, The Past, Jersey Boys, Omar, The Hundred-Foot Journey, Two Days, One Night, Northern Soul,* and *Imitation Game*, making twenty films out of seventy-four making the higher grade.

The lowest with 4.1 is *Winter's Tale*.

The Oscar winner is *Birdman*, which I see in 2015 and only score 6.5, as the subject matter seems pretty dull.

## 2015. Eighty-Five Movies

We did start the year on the *Queen Mary*, going to the movies every late afternoon. But with so many movies, it was not a great year, with nothing scoring over 8.0. Southpaw is the winner with 7.9. Here are the movies that scored more than 7.0: *Best Exotic Marigold Hotel* (on the *Queen Mary* with an introduction from Celia Imrie), *Whiplash, Selma, Woman in Gold, My Hero, Ted 2, Trainwreck, The Walk, Brief Encounter* (from way back), *Spotlight*, and *Bridge of Spies*. Only twelve over 7.0 The lowest scorer with 4.1 was *Sisters*. *Spotlight* wins the Oscar; it was pretty good, but we only scored it 7.0 because the plot seemed a little obvious.

## 2016. Sixty-Nine Movies

Not another great year, with only the delightful and poignant *Julieta* scoring 8.2 and *Eye in the Sky* scoring 8.0.

There are a lot over 7.0, with the most memorable being the world premiere of *Eight Days a Week*, screened to Truro from London. Others were *Joy, Danish Girl, Big Short, Eddie the Eagle, Jungle Book, Our Kind of Traitor, Jason Bourne* (again), *Shallows,*

*War Dogs, Bridget Jones's Baby, I, Daniel Blake, Light between Oceans, Starfish, American Pastoral, Nocturnal Animals, A Street Cat Named Bob, Sully,* and *United Kingdom.* Twenty movies scored over the 7.0. The lowest seems to be *Bad Neighbours,* 2.

It seems that 2004 and 2006 were the best years; the last five years have not been so good. I have to admit that I cannot remember some of the movies listed here, even though I marked them quite high at the time. At the same time, even if I don't enjoy a movie, it can still be a great night out.

My impression of movies is that the acting is normally top notch; I have some favourites, of which I will mention George Clooney and Kate Winslet, both of whom I could watch forever. I think the real problem comes with the scriptwriting. There seem to be so many movies with great actors talking rubbish or with a plot that is just too confusing.

### 2017. Fifty -Nine Movies

This has been a pretty poor year with the highest score Jackie about JFK's wife scoring 8.0. Manchester by the Sea scored 7.9 and a rerun of The Shining got 7.8 and The Graduate 7.5. Only 6 other films score 7.0 or more. Pretty bad when the old movies are the best. Worst films of the year are follow-ons from Blade Runner and Star Wars.

### 2018. Fifty Movies

It does not improve this year. The highlight is Three Billboards which scores 7.9 and First Man which scores 7.8. The Post, Mama Mia and Bohemian Rhapsody also score quite high. Only 6 other movies score above 7.0. Seems like you need music to make me happy.

## 2019. Thirty-Two Movies Plus Three Netflix

Seeing less. Our local cinema, The PLAZA has missed some big films. My favourite film of the year is Netflix The Irishman which scores 7.9. On Netflix also watched Roma at 7.2 and the third was Marriage Story which I didn't get. Best cinema was Once Upon a Time in Hollywood also 7.9 and also really enjoyed Green Book and Blinded by the Light. Clint Eastwood did well in The Mule and Official Secrets was very good as was Le Mans 66. Including Netflix 11 movies scored over 7.0.

## 2020. Eleven Movies to end of July plus lots of TV during Lockdown.

The highlight at the cinema was 1917 which was brilliant and scored 8.3. nothing else above 7.0. But on TV I loved yet again Dr. No which scored 9.0. first saw on release in 1962 when I was only 10 years old and still love it today. I am a great fan of Ian Fleming and have a first edition of Dr. No - see earlier and this year for my birthday got an autographed copy of the fifth Draft Script of the film and a signed picture of Ursula Andress in her Dr. No bikini. Watched all 3 Godfathers with Godfather possibly the greatest movie ever scoring 9.5 and Godfather 2 only 9.4. Thoroughly enjoyed As Good as it Gets with Jack Nicholson and Helen Hunt at 7.8 and Notting Hill with Julia Roberts at 8.0. and watched Grease one dull Sunday afternoon. Summer nights has a great two lines. Boys singing 'did you get far ' Girls singing ' did he have a car '. Worth it just for that. Rolling Stones gave us another 9.0 with Live Hyde Park 2013 and there Stripped movie was very good.

Due to lockdown, there were no more movies this year.

**2021. 13 Movies Due to lockdown another poor year for visiting the cinema.**

But 11 of the movie scored 7.0 or more. My favourites were Stillwater, No Time To Die ( Bond of course ) and King Richard all about the Williams sisters. The Courier and Last Night in Soho were also very good and a special mention to the remake of West Side Story such a great tale and fantastic music.

**2022. 19 Movies to end of September**

Not a great year for the cinema with a lot of duds including the Oscar nominated ' Licorice pizza '. My favourite film so far has been Top Gun but I really enjoyed The Railway Children Return , great nostalgia, Elvis and strangely Death on the Nile.

All this means is that I have got to sea over 1,000 movies at the cinema over the last twenty-two years - a true fan.

# Books

It is great to have time to read books; here are the books I have read over the years, with my favourites (and not-so-favourites):

## 2001. Seventeen Books

I am not scoring yet but my favourite book, which is also my all-time favourite, must have been *The Grapes of Wrath* by John Steinbeck. Chapter 1, which describes the devastating conditions in the dust bowl of Oklahoma, is simply brilliant:

To the red country and part of the grey country of Oklahoma the last rains came gently, and they did not crust the scarred earth.
---- In the water-cut gullies the earth dusted down in the dry little streams. ---- In the roads where the teams moved, where the wheels milled the ground and the hooves of the horses bear the ground, the dirt crust broke and the dust formed. ---- Men and women huddled in their houses, and they tied handkerchiefs over their noses when they went out, and wore goggles to protect their eyes. ----The people came out of their houses and smelled the hot stinging air and covered their noses from it. ----The men sat still - thinking - figuring.

And so begins an amazing story of poverty, and you can only reflect that I am so glad I have not been driven from my home by the elements and have to suffer such a great deal.

I liked *The Olive Farm* by Carol Drinkwater very much, a great story of living a nice different life. I thought *Deep Water* by Tim Jeal was rubbish.

## 2002. Seventeen Books

And now we are scoring:

My favourite book this year is *The Constant Gardener* by John le Carre, one of our great modern authors. Nearly as good are an old classic, *Rebecca* by Daphne du Maurier, and *A Parrot in the Pepper Tree* by Chris Stewart, reliving his different style of living in Spain. There may be a theme here, but although I travel a lot, I have no desire to have an overseas dream. Above 8.0, we also have *Atonement* by Ian McEwan, *Dark Room* by Rachel Seiffert, and Alan Clark's *Last Diaries*. In one of Clark's diaries, he recounts Margaret Thatcher drinking a whole bottle of Cointreau all to herself; I was amazed that the press have never made more of this. The dud of the year is *Sea Room* by Adam Nicholson. Surprisingly, I did not enjoy *The Veteran* by Frederick Forsythe, who has been one of my favourite authors. Six books (or over one-third) score 8.0 or more.

## 2003. Twenty-Two Books

The favourite this year is *The Stars Tennis Balls* by Stephen Fry, which scores a resounding 9.5.

We have three books at 9.25: the classic *Catcher in the Rye* by J. D. Salinger, *Astonishing Splashes of Colour* by Clare Marshall, and *Life of Pi*. And there are two more scoring over 8.0 with *Lovely Bones* by Alice Sebold and *Winston's War* by Michael Dobbs. *Berlin* by Anthony Beevor is a hard read, and the least favourite is Alex Smith with the *No 1 Ladies Detective Agency*, which is simply pointless. Six books over 8.0 again. I also managed for cultural and historic reasons *Living History* by Hillary Clinton, which only scored 6.0 but was remarkable in that it stated that she picked Bill because she saw in him the potential for him to be president and for her to be the first lady. And of course if it hadn't been for the Russians and Donald Trump, she would have been the first lady president of the United States.

## 2004. Twenty-Seven Books

This is not such a great year, with only four books scoring over 8.0: *Vernon God Little* by DBC Pierre, *Long Way Round* by Ewan McGregor and Charley Borman, *Starter for Ten* by David Nicholls, and *A Sweet Obscurity* by Cornish author Patrick Gale. Of the old favourites, John le Carre only scored 7.0 with *Absolute Friends*, and Daphne du Maurier only scored 6.9 with *Jamaica Inn*. The least liked is *Olivia Joules* by Helen Fielding, which is a little surprising, as I loved *Bridget Jones*.

## 2005. Twenty-Two Books

Not quite so many books, but I very much enjoyed a lot of what I read; the lowest scorer with 4.0 is a favourite novelist, Nick Hornby, with *A Long Way Down*, which I just don't get. We have two this year with 9.5. When I was on the Greyhound in September 1970, travelling from Seattle to New York and then again before we reached Spokane, I was quietly reading Philip Roth's *Portnoy's Complaint*, and a gorgeous blonde girl came and sat beside me and suggested it may not be appropriate. As an aside, we swapped addresses, and I lost hers, but she sent me a Christmas card for the next six years. This year, I read *The Plot against America*, which is a great, great book. Also scoring highly is *Insider* by Piers Morgan, which is a fascinating insight into the big world.

We have three books scoring 8.0 with *The Traveller's Wife* by Audrey Niffeneger, *The American Boy* by Andrew Taylor, and *The Pact* by Jodi Picoult. But there are twelve books scoring 7.0 or better, which makes it a good reading year. This includes Ian McEwan with *Saturday*, *Adrian Mole* (as good as ever), Carole Drinkwater again with the *Olive Harvest*, and *The Godfather: The Lost Years*, by Mark Winegardner.

## 2006. Twenty-One Books

This is another good year, with seventeen of the books scoring 7.0 or more. The favourite again is *Grapes of Wrath*, which you just have to read every few years to remind you just how good it is. We also read *The Constant Gardener* again, but it only scores 8.0 this time. Scoring above 8.0 are *Everyman* by Philip Roth, *The Highest Tide* by Jim Lynch, *The Island* by Victoria Hislop, *Blinding Light* by Paul Theroux (one of my all-time favourites, starting with *The Old Patagonia Express*, which I read again for 7.0), *Restless* by another favourite, William Boyd, and *Grandmother Wolf* by Patricia Tyrell. Among the interesting 7.0 or above are Pink Floyd's Nick Mason's autobiography, the Mary Bryant story, *To Brave Every Danger* by Judith Cook, *Almond Blossom Appreciation Society* with Chris Stewart (in Spain again), and *Freakanomics* by Steven Levitt, as I still enjoy a good business read. The loser this year despite being one of my favourite authors is *The Great American Novel* by Philip Roth which simply fails to inspire.

## 2007. Twenty-Four Books

This is another great reading year, with nineteen of the books scoring 7.0 or more. The lowest-ranked, *Marie Antoinette* by Antonia Fraser, scores a healthy 6.0.

There are four equal best at 9.0: all classics, two by John Steinbeck (*The Winter of Our Discontent* and *East of Eden*) and two by George Orwell (*1984* and *Animal Farm*). Somehow, there is a lot to be said for the classics. Scoring over 8.0 are *Electricity* by Victoria Glendenning, *Chesil Beach* by Ian McEwan, *The Importance of Being Kennedy* by Laurie Graham, *The Afghan* by a back-to-form Frederick Forsythe, and another classic, *Treasure Island* by Robert Louis Stevenson.

Scoring over 7.0, we have George Orwell again with *Down and Out in Paris and London* and Joseph Conrad with *The Secret Agent*, making it a classic year.

## 2008. Twenty-Four Books

Not such a great year, with only eleven books scoring 7.0 or above.

The winners with 9.0 are *Any Human Heart* by William Boyd, *The Outcast* by Sadie Jones, and back to the classics with *Of Mice and Men* by John Steinbeck.

Scoring over 8.0 we have *Cannery Row* by John Steinbeck and *America Wife* by Curtis Sittenfield. John Steinbeck features at 7.5 with *Tortilla Flat*.

Most interesting is possibly *The Blair Years* by Alistair Campbell, which scores 7.6. John le Carre features with *A Most Wanted Man* at 7.0. We were disappointed by Jools Holland's *Barefaced Lies*, *Devil May Care* by Sebastian Foulkes, and *Cranford* by Elizabeth Gaskell.

## 2009. Twenty-Five Books

Not too bad a year, with fourteen books scoring 7.0 or better. And the winner again is *The Grapes of Wrath*.

We have four books in second place, with 8.8 score. There are two by Khaled Hosseni: *The Kite Runner* and *A Thousand Splendid Suns*, *Revolutionary Road* by Richard Yates (which was also a favourite movie), and William Boyd again with *Ordinary Thunderstorms*. Scoring over 8.0 I have *The Great Crash of 1929* by JK Galbraith, *The Reader* by Bernhard Schlinkand, and *Red Riding 1980* by David Peace, which is somehow better than *Red Riding 1977* and *Red Riding 1983*. Among the books over 7.0 there is *The Red Pony* by John Steinbeck and *All in the Mind* by Alastair Campbell. The lowest score this year is *Wolf Hall* by Hilary Mantel, which wins the Booker, but I don't really get; interestingly, I enjoyed it when it was adapted for TV by the BBC.

## 2010. Nineteen Books

A small number, but they all score 6.0 or more.

There are four winners with 8.8: *Open* by Andre Agassi, a brilliant biography by the man who hated tennis, and with such a good ghost writer. What I remember most was how his dad made him hit one million balls a year to become a champion and how he went into a livid fit if Andre failed to hit the ball over the net. *Travels with Charley* and *The Grapes of Wrath,* again by John Steinbeck, for two great classics. *The Girl who Played with Fire* from the Dragon Tattoo series. They were all very good reads.

For my business reading, I had *The Snowball* by Alice Schroeder, a book about Warren Buffett. I enjoyed *The Girl Who Kicked the Hornet's Nest* again from the *Dragon Tattoo* series and *Catcher in the Rye* again. The least favourite was *The Snowman* by Jo Nesbo, which seemed to lack the glamour of *Dragon Tattoo*.

## 2011. Twenty-Five Books

This was quite good year, with eleven books scoring 7.0 or above.

The favourite is *The Long Walk* by Slavomir Rawicz. Scoring over 8.0 are three James Bond books by Ian Fleming: *Casino Royale*, *Live and Let Die* and *Moonraker,* as I have always loved James Bond; *Great Expectations* by Charles Dickens, which is a wonderful classic; my business book of the year, *The Big Short* by Michael Lewis; and last but not least, *Our Kind of Traitor* by John le Carre. Scoring well are *What's It All About,* Michael Caine's autobiography, and *The Great Gatsby* by F Scott Fitzgerald. The lowest scorer with only 4.8 is *The Finkler Question* by Howard Jacobson.

## 2012. Thirty-One Books

This is not such a great year, with only eleven books scoring over 7.0.

Topping the list is the classic *Robinson Crusoe* by Daniel Defoe. We find another three James Bond books scoring over 8.0, with *From Russia with Love*, *Dr No,* and *Goldfinger*. Also scoring well are *Beyond the Bounty* by Tony Parsons and *Waiting for Sunrise* by William Boyd. The business book is Michael Lewis again with *Boomerang*, which is a fun read. For the classics, we have *Madame Bovary* by Gustave Flaubert, which I used to read in French when I was sixteen years old, and *Our Man in Havana* by Graham Greene, both of which are enjoyed a lot.

Coming in at the bottom is the rubbish of *Fifty Shades Freed* and *Antwerp* by Robert Bolano.

## 2013. Thirty Books

I have two favourites this year, both scoring 8.0: *Last Train to Zona Verde* by Paul Theroux and *Solo* by William Boyd.

Scoring over 7.0 are *The Paris Wife* by Paula Maclain, *Ambition* by Stephen Maitland-Lewis (who I became friends with in LA and shared many memorable dinners), *Mission to Paris* by Alan Furst, *The Lower River* by Paul Theroux again, *Anna Karenina* by Tolstoy, *Live by Night* by Dennis Lehane, *The Racketeer* by John Grisham, *Stoner* by John Williams, *Butchers Crossing* by John Williams again, and *The Wolf of Wall Street* by Jordan Belfort.

Only twelve books scored over 7.0. My least favourite was *A Small Circus* by Hans Fallada. The classics didn't do too well; I did not enjoy *David Copperfield* by Dickens or *Northanger Abbey* by Jane Austen.

## 2014. Thirty-Five Books

Yet again, the favourite is *Grapes of Wrath* by Steinbeck. There are three scoring over 8.0: *Labour Day* by Joyce Maynard, the classic

*Jamaica Inn* by Daphne du Maurier, and *Half of a Yellow Sun* by Chimanda Adichie. Scoring over 7.0 are *The Old Man and the Sea* by Hemingway, *Lincoln Lawyer* by Michael Connely, *Emeralds Never Fade* by Stephen Maitland-Lewis again, *Two Faces of January* by Patricia Highsmith, *Kill List* by Frederick Forsythe, *Sycamore Road* by John Grisham, *The Mountains Echoed* by Khaled Hosseni, *Rogue Male* by Geoffrey Household, *Gone Girl* by Gillian Flynn, *Narrow Road to the Deep North* by Richard Flannagan, *Dark Places* by Gillian Flynn, and *Goldfinch* by Donna Tartt.

That makes sixteen books scoring over the magic 7.0. I have two equal least-favourite books: Dickens again with *A Christmas Carol* and *Life and Fate* by Vasily Grossman.

## 2015. Thirty-Four Books

This is not a good reading year, with only four books scoring over 7.0. The winner is *The Martian* by Andy Weir. Ian Fleming reads well with *Thunderball* and *Diamonds Are Forever*, and Paula Hawkins makes up the list with *Girl on a Train*.

There are a lot of average books, but the worst are *Catastrophe* by Max Hastings (a very difficult war read), the classic *Far from the Madding Crowd* by Hardy, *Deep South* by Paul Theroux (usually one of my favourite writers), and *Cornish House* by Liz Fenwick, which does not reflect Cornwall at all.

## 2016. Forty-Four Books

A better scoring year, with the clear winner being *Alone in Berlin* by Hans Fallada, a simply brilliant read. We have two other books scoring over 8.0: *The Graduate* by Charles Webb and *Where My Heart Used to Beat* by Sebastian Faulks. Scoring well at over 7.0 are *Taming of the Queen* by Phillipa Gregory, *Thunderball* and *Diamonds Are Forever* by Ian Fleming again, *The Cartel* by Don Winslow, *Our Kind of Traitor* by John le Carre, *Coffin Road* by Peter May, *Little Man, What Now?* by Hans Fallada, *Washington Square* by Henry James, and *Portrait of a Lady*, also by Henry James. Bottom is *A Small Circus* by Hans Fallada, which I read again after his two great books listed above, but I still do not like it.

Only twelve books score well, with a lot of average reading.

## 2017. Forty-Six Books

Another good year with lots of good books. My favourite is my first edition of Dr. No which has to score 10.0. A close second at 9.5 is Jane Eyre by Charlotte Bronte, truly a great book. William Boyd also scores 9.0 with his excellent The New Confessions - he deserves to be one of my best. There are some old favourites all scoring above 8.0 - Old Man and the Sea by Hemingway which I read close to Cuba, My Cousin Rachel by Daphne du Maurier and Rebecca by the same author and an old favourite The Old Patagonia Express by Paul Theroux. Scoring well are The Life of Ian Fleming by John Pearson and as we know the 007 creator fascinates me, Legacy by John le Carre and two Steig Larsson books. Daphne du Maurier scores well with two lesser known books - Mary Anne and Ill Never Be Young Again. Continue to enjoy Hemingway because of my love of Cuba with Islands in the Stream, For Whom the Bell Tolls, and To Have and Have Not. Philip Roth's Plot Against America also intrigues.

There is one major disappointment. I like Henry James but hate Wings of the Dove.

## 2018. Thirty-Seven Books

Not quite such a good year but Dr. No wins again. My favourite other book is Sons and Lovers by DH Lawrence. Next best are Burmese Days by George Orwell and On Chesil Beach by Ian McEwan. I also like a Maigret book by George Simenon and The Rainbow by DH Lawrence. The House on the Strand by Daphne du Maurier is also quite good.

Interesting reads have been Great Crash of 1929 by JK Galbraith and the actor Tom Hanks Uncommon Type.

## 2019. Thirty-Six Books

For the third year running I have read Dr. No and it wins closely followed by my new first edition Octopussy by the great Ian Fleming. Casino Royale is also a very good read and I reread The Life of Ian Fleming. For my next favourite we have to go back to John Steinbeck and East of Eden and I also enjoy Winter of our Discontent and The Pearl . I thoroughly enjoy Vietnam by Max Hastings and in contrast Middlemarch by George Elliot. Les Miserables by Victor Hugo is a long read but worth it. William Boyd scores well with his Bond novel Solo and Any Human Heart. Also enjoy 1984 by George Orwell.

Some other good reads including A Little Life by Hanya Yanagihara and surprisingly The Reckoning by John Grisham.

## 2020. Fifty Books to end of July

Lockdown has got me reading more. The highlight is my birthday present from my daughter Dr. No - autographed (including Ian Fleming, Sean Connery, Ursula Andress and Jack Lord) Fifth Draft Screenplay. I read it and then watched the movie a brilliant experience. In Indonesia I read The Grapes of Wrath again having bought a new copy as the original was falling to bits. I also read a lesser Known Steinbeck The Pastures of Heaven. I read the three Dragon Tattoo books by Steig Larsson and the three follow ups by David Lagercrantz. The original is best. I read The Godfather by Mario Puzo which is not as good as the film and one of his follow-ups The Sicilian about Michael in Sicily. I also enjoy Pappilon and the follow-up Banco by Henri Charrier. This is real lockdown reading and comes from my library and Amazon as for most of the time the bookshops are closed.

A surprising favourite this year is a new author to me Far from the Madding Crowd by Thomas Hardy. I also enjoy The Goldfinch by Donna Tarrt and Munich by Robert Harris. I also really enjoyed Jane Eyre by Charlotte Bronte

In this time, it seems that I have read 650 books, a little less than the movies seen. My favourite writer has to be John Steinbeck. It seems that it is always a good idea to go back to the classics, but you can still miss out, with *A Christmas Carol*. Ian Fleming is always a great read. Of the modern writers, I feel that from the UK, John le Carre and William Boyd are the best, and from the United States, I would pick Philip Roth.

Only 8 more books to the end of the year. My favourite wave East of Eden by John Steinbeck who remains my favourite writer. I enjoyed rereading my books The Telltale and My Back Pages both again by Nicholson which have not really sol but are great reads. I also read Ian Fleming's War of whom I am a great fan.

## 2021. Sixty-Four Books

A good reading year. I started with a first edition Christmas present of ' The Man with the Golden Gun ' by Ian Fleming which I really enjoyed. The highlights were Restless by William Boyd, Deepwater by Patricia Highsmith, Rebecca by Daphne du Maurier, Once Upon a Time in Hollywood by Quentin Tarantino, The Grapes of Wrath by Steinbeck yet again, The Godfather by Mario Puzo, Revolutionary Road by Richard Yates, The Graduate by Charles Webb and the Constant Gardener by John Le Carre. I also read more Fleming with Dr No and Casino Royale and read my Nicholson books again The Telltale and My Back Pages.

## 2022. Thirty-Six Books to end of September

Another good years reading although I have gone over some old ground. For my birthday I got a first edition of Ian Fleming's The Spy Who Loved Me which was great. For Christmas I got a first edition of You Only Live Twice which is not the greatest. I reread some Steinbeck and du Maurier which were as good as ever. I read some Dickens and thought Great Expectations and David Copperfield were tremendous. For the first time I read Patricia Highsmith's The Talented Mr. Ripley which is another great read. My most unsatisfactory read was The Thursday Murder Club by Richard Osman. I am a great fan of his and watch Pointless nearly every day but I thought the book was dreadful and cannot understand how it has sold millions. I think I am a much better writer and sell only a few.

# About the Author

Paul Taylor had a successful career in international finance, and at the age of forty-six, he started on a gap year which has now extended to twenty-four years.

# About the Book

The book is a short history of how to make enough money to have twenty-four gap years from the age of forty-six. It details the author's travels all over the world and finishes with his favourite recipes and lists of films and books that he has enjoyed.

www.ingramcontent.com/pod-product-compliance
Lightning Source LLC
LaVergne TN
LVHW021757060526
838201LV00058B/3126